International Review of
Industrial
and Organizational
Psychology
2009   Volume 24

International Review of Industrial and Organizational Psychology
2009 Volume 24

Edited by

Gerard P. Hodgkinson
The University of Leeds, UK

and

J. Kevin Ford
Michigan State University, USA

A John Wiley & Sons, Ltd, Publication

This volume first published 2009
© 2009 John Wiley & Sons Ltd.

Wiley-Blackwell is an imprint of John Wiley & Sons, formed by the merger of Wiley's global Scientific, Technical, and Medical business with Blackwell Publishing.

Registered Office
John Wiley & Sons Ltd, The Atrium, Southern Gate, Chichester, West Sussex, PO19 8SQ, UK

Editorial Offices
The Atrium, Southern Gate, Chichester, West Sussex, PO19 8SQ, UK
9600 Garsington Road, Oxford, OX4 2DQ, UK
350 Main Street, Malden, MA 02148-5020, USA

For details of our global editorial offices, for customer services, and for information about how to apply for permission to reuse the copyright material in this book please see our website at www.wiley.com/wiley-blackwell.

The right of the editors to be identified as the authors of the editorial material in this work has been asserted in accordance with the Copyright, Designs and Patents Act 1988.

Library of Congress Cataloging-in-Publication Data has been applied for.

ISBN 978-0-470-68000-1

A catalogue record for this book is available from the British Library.

Typeset in 10/12pt Plantin by Aptara Inc., New Delhi, India
Printed in the United Kingdom by TJ International Ltd, Padstow, Cornwall

CONTENTS

ABOUT THE EDITORS

Gerard P. Hodgkinson *Leeds University Business School, The University of Leeds, Leeds, LS2 9JT, UK*

J. Kevin Ford *Department of Psychology, 315 Psychology Research Building, Michigan State University, E. Lansing, MI 48824 USA*

Gerard P. Hodgkinson is Professor of Organizational Behaviour and Strategic Management and Director of the Centre for Organizational Strategy, Learning and Change (COSLAC) at the University of Leeds, UK. He earned his BA, MSc and PhD degrees at Wolverhampton Polytechnic and the Universities of Hull and Sheffield, respectively. He has (co-) authored three books and over 60 scholarly journal articles and chapters on topics of relevance to the field of industrial and organizational psychology. A Fellow of both the British Psychological Society and the British Academy of Management, and an Academician of the Academy of Social Sciences, his work centres on the analysis of cognitive processes in organizations and the psychology of strategic management. In recent years, his work on these topics has been taken forward through the award of a Fellowship of the Advanced Institute of Management (AIM) Research, the UK's research initiative on management funded by the Economic and Social Research Council (ESRC) and Engineering and Physical Sciences Research Council (EPSRC). From 1999–2006, he was the Editor-in-Chief of the *British Journal of Management* and currently serves on the Editorial Boards of the *Academy of Management Review, Journal of Management, Journal of Organizational Behavior* and *Organization Science*. A practising chartered occupational psychologist, he has conducted numerous consultancy assignments for leading private and public sector organizations. Further information about Gerard and his work can be found at http://www.leeds.ac.uk/lubs/coslac/ and http://www.aimresearch.org.

J. Kevin Ford is a Professor of Psychology at Michigan State University. His major research interests involve improving training effectiveness through efforts to advance our understanding of training needs assessment, design, evaluation and transfer. Dr Ford also concentrates on understanding change dynamics in organizational development efforts and building continuous learning and improvement orientations within organizations. He has published over 50 articles and chapters and 4 books relevant to industrial and organizational psychology. Currently, he serves on the editorial boards of the *Journal of Applied Psychology* and *Human Performance*. He is an active consultant with private industry and the public sector on training, leadership, and organizational change issues.

Kevin is a Fellow of the American Psychological Association and the Society of Industrial and Organizational Psychology. He received his BS in psychology from the University of Maryland and his MA and PhD in psychology from The Ohio State University. Further information about Kevin and his research and consulting activities can be found at http://www.io.psy.msu.edu/jkf.

CONTRIBUTORS

Timothy T. Baldwin   *Kelley School of Business, Indiana University, Blooming-*
ton, IN 47405, USA

Edward G. Bitzer, III   *Department of Psychology, Colorado State University, Fort*
Collins, CO, USA

Brian D. Blume   *School of Management, University of Michigan, Flint, MI*
48502-1950, USA

Rob B. Briner   *School of Management & Organizational Psychology,*
Birkbeck, University of London, London, WC1E 7HX,
UK

Peter Y. Chen   *Department of Psychology, Colorado State University, Fort*
Collins, CO 80525, USA

Arik Cheshin   *William Davidson Faculty of Industrial Engineering and*
Management, Technion, Israel Institute of Technology,
Haifa, 32000, Israel

Neil Conway   *School of Management & Organizational Psychology,*
Birkbeck, University of London, London, WC1E 7HX,
UK

Erik Dane   *Jesse H. Jones Graduate School of Management, Rice Uni-*
versity, Houston, TX 77005, USA

Richard P. DeShon   *Department of Psychology, Michigan State University, E.*
Lansing, MI 48824-1116, USA

J. Kevin Ford   *Department of Psychology, Michigan State University, E.*
Lansing, MI 48824, USA

Verlin B. Hinsz   *Department of Psychology, North Dakota State University,*
Fargo, ND 58108-6050, USA

Roger G. Johnston   *Argonne National Laboratory, Argonne, IL 60439, USA*

Jared L. Ladbury   *Department of Psychology, North Dakota State University,*
Fargo, ND 58108-6050, USA

Susan Mohammed   *Department of Psychology, The Pennsylvania State Uni-*
versity, University Park, PA 16802, USA

Michael G. Pratt

Carroll School of Management, Boston College, Chestnut Hill, MA 02465, USA

Anat Rafaeli

William Davidson Faculty of Industrial Engineering and Management, Technion, Israel Institute of Technology, Haifa, 32000, Israel

Shy Ravid

William Davidson Faculty of Industrial Engineering and Management, Technion, Israel Institute of Technology, Haifa, 32000, Israel

Tara A. Rench

Department of Psychology, Michigan State University, E. Lansing, MI 48824-1116, USA

Alexander Schwall

Development Dimensions International, Inc., Bridgeville, PA 15017, USA

Dana M. Wallace

Department of Psychology, North Dakota State University, Fargo, ND 58108-6050, USA

EDITORIAL FOREWORD

This is the twenty-fourth volume of the *International Review of Industrial and Organizational Psychology*. As in previous volumes, the chapters we have commissioned survey major developments across a range of established and emerging topics.

New topics covered in the present volume include Conceptualizing and Measuring Intuition (Erik Dane and Michael Pratt) and Sensemaking in Virtual Teams (Anat Rafaeli, Shy Ravid, and Arik Cheshin). The chapters by Edward Bitzer, Peter Chen, and Roger Johnston (Security in Organizations: Expanding the Frontier of Industrial–Organizational Psychology) and Richard DeShon and Tara Rench (Clarifying the Notion of Self-Regulation in Organizational Behavior) also address emerging themes of growing importance in the field.

The remaining chapters in the present volume revisit topics surveyed previously in this series. Covering a 20-year period, from 1988–2008, Timothy Baldwin, Kevin Ford, and Brian Blume provide 'An Updated Review and Agenda for Future Research' on the 'Transfer of Training', while Neil Conway and Rob Briner similarly consider advances in 'Psychological Contract Research,' spanning the past five decades. Verlin Hinsz, Dana Wallace, and Jared Ladbury review developments in 'Team Performance in Dynamic Environments,' while Susan Mohammed and Alexander Schwall address 'Individual Differences and Decision Making: What We Know and Where We Go from Here'.

Once again, the contents of the present volume as a whole reflect the dynamism and diversity of I/O psychology more widely. It is precisely for this reason that the series has become established as the primary source of choice for professional psychologists, managers and scholars alike, seeking authoritative, state-of-the-art overviews of developments at the forefront of the field.

GPH
JKF
October 2008

Chapter 1

CONCEPTUALIZING AND MEASURING INTUITION: A REVIEW OF RECENT TRENDS

Erik Dane

Jesse H. Jones Graduate School of Management,
Rice University, Houston, TX, USA

Michael G. Pratt

Carroll School of Management, Boston College, Boston, MA, USA

Discussion surrounding intuition has burgeoned in a variety of arenas in recent years. In popular writings, for example, a number of authors have pointed to the role that intuition may play in organizational and managerial decision making (e.g. Gigerenzer, 2007; Gladwell, 2005; Klein, 2003; Myers, 2002). Concurrently, there has been an outpouring of academic research directed toward understanding intuition, mirroring interest in psychology in automaticity (Bargh and Chartrand, 1999) and dual-process theories (e.g. Epstein, 2002; Kahneman, 2003; Sloman, 1996). Emerging research has centered on (1) what intuition is (e.g. Dane and Pratt, 2007; Hodgkinson, Langan-Fox and Sadler-Smith, 2008; Kahneman, 2003; Lieberman, 2000; Sadler-Smith and Shefy, 2007; Shirley and Langan-Fox, 1996; Sinclair, Sadler-Smith and Hodgkinson, 2009); (2) the factors that prompt individuals to trust and use it (e.g. Denes-Raj and Epstein, 1994; Epstein, 2002; Hodgkinson, Langan-Fox and Sadler-Smith, 2008; Hodgkinson and Sadler-Smith, 2003); and (3) the factors that account for when intuition should be used, especially in terms of when it is as or more effective than analytical decision making (e.g. Dane and Pratt, 2007; Hogarth, 2001; Khatri and Ng, 2000). In addition to growth in these conceptual areas, there has also been a wide range of methods proposed to examine intuition and intuitive processes.

Fortunately, this proliferation of ideas has not entirely fragmented the field. As we discuss below, there is emergent agreement on some crucial facets of

International Review of Industrial and Organizational Psychology, 2009, Volume 24.
Edited by G. P. Hodgkinson and J. K. Ford. Copyright © 2009 John Wiley & Sons, Ltd

intuition. This growing conceptual convergence marks a critical juncture in the study of intuition; it demonstrates that a phenomenon that historically has been slippery to formal conceptualization and measurement may indeed be amenable to systematic interpretation and exploration. The main goal of our review is to explore these conceptual and methodological advances. We begin by looking at how intuition is defined. In this vein, we review in detail the critical functions of intuition and the possibility that there may be different 'types' of intuitions based on variations in these underlying functions. Thus, we strive to point out key areas of convergence and divergence regarding the nature of intuition. Building on this discussion, we provide a brief review of literature focused on the other lines of intuition research noted above concerning when people trust and use their intuition and as well as when it should be used. We then examine how researchers have attempted to capture intuition methodologically. Here, we do not focus on convergence, as there appears to be little of it. Rather, we seek to detail the breadth of techniques that researchers have used to prime, identify, and evaluate intuition, both in the laboratory and in the field. We conclude this chapter by discussing critical issues raised in our review that have implications for the future of intuition research.

THE STUDY OF INTUITION: CONCEPTUAL CONVERGENCE AND DIVERGENCE

As noted above, there has been an outpouring of research concerning three conceptual questions: (1) What is intuition? (2) When do people trust and use their intuition? (3) When should intuition be used? Although we address all three questions to some degree, we spend most of our efforts on the first question as it has garnered much attention in existing work, and because new perspectives on what intuition is continue to emerge. We also feel that it is only through achieving a comprehensive understanding of what intuition is that scholars may systematically investigate issues concerning the use and effectiveness of intuition.

What Is Intuition?

Because writers have discussed intuition across a range of academic and nonacademic domains, the intuition concept has had a wide range of terms associated with it. We devoted a significant portion of a previous article (Dane and Pratt, 2007) to the question of what intuition is. We identified the features of intuition that are 'common and central' across many definitions of intuition and across a variety of disciplinary domains (e.g. Barnard, 1938; Bruner, 1962; Hogarth, 2001; Jung, 1933; Kahneman, 2003; Lieberman, 2000; Rorty, 1967;

Shapiro and Spence, 1997; Shirley and Langan-Fox, 1996; Simon, 1996; Wild, 1938). On the basis of our review, we noted that the 'outcome' of intuiting is an intuitive judgment. With regard to the process of intuition, we found that most conceptualizations include the following features: (1) nonconscious information processing, (2) holistic associations, (3) affect, and (4) speed. Below, we briefly describe each of these process features (for a more detailed explanation, see Dane and Pratt, 2007).

First, a central feature of intuitions is that they arise from operations that occur in the nonconscious system of information processing. The concept of nonconscious processing links intuition to a growing consensus among scholars that humans process information through two distinct cognitive systems: nonconscious and conscious. This nonconscious system, which is believed by some to be the evolutionarily older of the two systems (Epstein, 1994; Reber, 1992), has been referred to as 'experiential' (Epstein, 1994), 'automatic' (Bargh and Chartrand, 1999), 'associative' (Sloman, 1996), 'impulsive' (Strack and Deutsch, 2004), and 'system 1' (Kahneman, 2003; Stanovich and West, 2000). Nonconscious processing is contrasted with conscious processing, which has also been referred to as 'rational' (Epstein, 2002), 'intentional' (Bargh and Chartrand, 1999), 'rule based' (Sloman, 1996), 'reflective' (Strack and Deutsch, 2004), and 'system 2' (Kahneman, 2003; Stanovich and West, 2000). While the conscious system of processing permits individuals to analyze problems in a deliberate, sequential, and attentive manner, the nonconscious system allows individuals to learn from experience and develop feelings of knowing in the absence of conscious attention (Dane and Pratt, 2007; Hogarth, 2001). Intuition falls squarely within the nonconscious system of information processing (Dane and Pratt, 2007; Epstein, 2008; Hodgkinson, Langan-Fox and Sadler-Smith, 2008).

Second, intuition involves drawing holistic associations (Epstein, 1994; Shapiro and Spence, 1997). These associations may stem from relatively simple cognitive heuristics (Tversky and Kahneman, 1974), or more complex pattern 'chunks' developed through years of training and experience (Simon, 1997; Simon and Chase, 1973). As nonconsciously held patterns are linked to environmental stimuli through a holistic and associative cognitive process, intuitive judgments arise.

Third, intuitions are viewed as being 'affectively charged'. We have argued that affect may accompany both the intuition process as well as the outcomes of this process – intuitive judgments (Dane and Pratt, 2007). At the process level, intuitions arise via the nonconscious system of processing, a system often viewed as being imbued with emotionally based content and operations (see Epstein, 2002). This contention is complemented by neuroscience research pointing to a link between intuition and affect via activation of basal ganglia and related structures (see Lieberman, 2000, 2007). At the judgment level, intuitive judgments may be accompanied by affect. This is reflected in the expressions 'gut feelings' and 'gut instincts' – terms that reflect the affective tenor of the intuitive judgments themselves.

Fourth, intuition is notable for its speed (Bastick, 1982; Dane and Pratt, 2007; Kahneman, 2003). Unlike analytical evaluations, intuitions arise rapidly through 'immediate apprehension' (Rorty, 1967, p. 74). This feature of intuition is tied to intuition's relationship to the nonconscious system of processing – a system that operates relatively automatically and rapidly (Bargh, 1996; Epstein, 1994; Reber, 1992).

On the basis of evidence supporting the integration of the above features, we argued that intuitions are 'affectively charged judgments that arise through rapid, nonconscious, and holistic associations' (Dane and Pratt, 2007, p. 40). In advancing this definition, we contended that the defining features of intuition account not just for what intuition is, but also for how it differs from other decision-making processes. For instance, we noted that analytical decision making is highly dissimilar to intuition in that analytical approaches involve the use of systematic procedures designed to thoroughly assess all pertinent information, evaluate costs and benefits, and invoke conscious deliberation. Our definition of intuition also helped to differentiate the concept of intuition from related constructs such as 'insight'. Although both concepts involve some degree of nonconscious thought, we observed that insight involves an ultimate recognition of the logical connections supporting a particular solution, whereas intuition does not.

While scholars appear to be converging on what intuition is[1] (i.e. what features constitute intuition), a review of the literature reveals that scholars continue to look at intuitions in different ways. In particular, intuition has been posited to play a role toward multiple and distinct ends. Researchers have viewed intuitions as serving at least three different functions: as a vehicle for problem-solving, as an input to making moral decisions, and as an instrument facilitating creativity. As a shorthand description, we refer to these functions of intuition as different 'types' of intuition. We suggest that besides their different functions (e.g. moral intuitions are used to make decisions about what is right or wrong in a given situation), these intuition types may also differ in certain ways with regard to the nature of their holistic associations, affect, and speed (three of the four definitional features of intuition noted above). All types of intuitions are posed to arise through nonconscious processes. Table 1.1 summarizes our observations regarding how these types of intuition may differ. Below, we explore these potential distinctions in detail.

---

[1] We should note that some perspectives on intuition take a more spiritual or psychic explanation regarding the sources of intuition (Vaughan, 1979; Wild, 1938). Rogers and Wiseman (2006) recently found that individuals who consider themselves highly intuitive will sometimes give spiritual or psychic explanations for their intuitive abilities. Acknowledgment of the spiritual side of intuition can be found in research on nurses (e.g. Smith, Thurkettle and dela Cruz, 2004) and midwives (e.g. Davis-Floyd and Davis, 1996). While we acknowledge that there may be spiritual aspects to intuition, this area of intuition is beyond the scope of this review.

Table 1.1 Intuition types

Intuition Type	Description	Nature of Associations	Affect	Level of Incubation
Problem-Solving	Automatic acts of recognition due to pattern matching (e.g. Hogarth, 2001; Simon, 1996)	Largely convergent/tight Based on highly specific domain knowledge	Relatively low intensity	Low to none
Moral	Affective, automatic reactions to issues that are viewed as having moral/ethical content (e.g. Haidt, 2001; Sonenshein, 2007)	Largely convergent/tight Based on moral prototypes	Relatively high intensity	Low to none
Creative	Feelings that arise when knowledge is combined in novel ways (e.g. Miller and Ireland, 2005; Policastro, 1995)	Largely divergent/broad Based on integration of knowledge across different domains	Relatively high intensity	Often high

Problem-Solving Intuition

The most common conceptualization of intuition in the literature is what we refer to here as 'problem-solving' intuition. Problem-solving intuitions, as the name implies, are intuitions used when individuals are faced with a problem-solving or decision-making dilemma. These problems may range from a chess player selecting a move during a chess game (Simon and Chase, 1973), to a fire chief determining how to deploy his or her firefighters to combat a house fire (Klein, 1998), to a brand manager predicting how consumers will respond to a marketing initiative (Blattberg and Hoch, 1990).

The process underlying these intuitions is 'pattern matching', which is often honed through repeated training and practice (e.g. Hogarth, 2001; Simon, 1996). As such, problem-solving intuition has been connected to domain knowledge, or expertise (e.g. Dreyfus and Dreyfus, 1986; Hogarth, 2001; Simon, 1987, 1997; Simon and Chase, 1973). Indeed, this type of intuition has even been referred to as 'intuition-as-expertise' (Sadler-Smith and Shefy, 2004). However, we decided not to label this type of intuition with an 'expertise' modifier for three reasons.

First, we view expertise as an antecedent to intuitive judgments, rather than as a characteristic feature of such judgments. Thus, we sought to avoid conflating this type of intuition with one of its causes. Second, we recognized that each of the types of intuition we discuss, particularly creative intuition, may be related to expertise. Third, not all problem-solving intuitions arise as a result of expertise. Some problem-solving intuitions are fostered through relatively simple heuristics (Tversky and Kahneman, 1974). Consequently, viewing expertise as unique to problem-solving intuition may be misguided. Keeping these provisos in mind, we reassert our contention, consistent with the view of many scholars, that problem-solving intuition involves pattern matching. That is, we argue that no matter what the complexity of one's cognitive structures, problem-solving intuition involves a process whereby current situations are viewed in terms of their similarity or differences with past experiences.

The various characteristics of problem-solving intuitions can be found in Table 1.1. As noted in this table, the associations made when employing problem-solving intuition are largely 'tight' – that is, convergent. The tightness of associations is evident when considering that this type of intuition involves 'recognition' – does something belong to a certain category or not? For example, experts have accrued complex cognitive schemas that permit them to partially circumvent limits on attention and working memory through the internalization and automation of cognitive processes that formerly may have proved effortful and challenging (Prietula and Simon, 1989; Schneider and Shiffrin, 1977; Simon and Chase, 1973). The result is that experts, when exposed to particular scenarios they have encountered numerous times before, may match patterns between their environment and deeply held knowledge structures. In support of this claim, Miller and Ireland (2005, p. 21) argue that intuition via 'automated expertise' involves 'recognition of a familiar situation' as well as 'previous learning related to that situation'. This notion complements Simon's (1996) contention that an intuitive act of recognition includes (nonconscious) recognition of the situation itself, and also the most appropriate action for dealing with it. However, one need not have extensive experience for such pattern matching to transpire. Matching on simple stereotypes and other uses of heuristics may also occur.

With regard to the other characteristics of problem-solving intuition, relatively less theorizing has occurred. Concerning affect, it has been suggested that the strength of the 'affective tag' associated with intuition may vary depending on the type of judgments made (Sadler-Smith, Hodgkinson and Sinclair, 2008). Along these lines, research on intuition-as-expertise, a form of problem-solving intuition, suggests that these intuitions often involve relatively low levels of affective intensity (Sadler-Smith and Shefy, 2004), at least compared to other intuition types.

In terms of speed, problem-solving intuitions are typically viewed as occurring very fast. Simon (1987) noted that chess grandmasters can play speed chess against as many as 50 opponents concurrently without a significant decrease in performance because of their ability to intuitively assess what move to make next by a quick glance at the position of pieces on each chessboard. A focus on the rapid nature of intuition is common to many conceptualizations of intuition rooted in the problem-solving framework (e.g. Kahneman, 2003; Lieberman, 2000).

The nature of problem-solving intuitions described above (i.e. that they arise through rapid, convergent pattern matching and tend to involve low levels of affect) will serve as the baseline for which we compare other intuition types. Toward this end, we turn to the concept of moral intuition.

Moral Intuition

In recent years, there has been increasing interest in the role that intuition may play with respect to moral judgments. Perhaps the most well known is the 'social intuitionist' perspective (see Haidt, 2001, 2007). This perspective calls into question 'rationalist' approaches that suggest moral reasoning is a deliberative, conscious process (e.g. Jones, 1991; Kohlberg, 1981; Rest, 1986). The social intuitionist view, which has had support from studies in neurophysiology (Greene and Haidt, 2002; Greene *et al.*, 2004), suggests that many if not most moral judgments stem from nonconscious, affective processes (e.g. Greene and Haidt, 2002; Haidt, 2007; Haidt and Kesebir, 2008; Sonenshein, 2007). A similar conclusion is also drawn from recent work on the 'universal moral grammar' (UMG) perspective on moral intuiting (Hauser *et al.*, 2007; Mikhail, 2007). One critical difference between UMG and the social intuitionist approach, however, is that the former draws heavily on linguistic theories (especially Chomsky's), likening moral development to language acquisition (see Hauser *et al.*, 2007 for a broader discussion of the differences between the UMG and social intuitionist perspectives).

Moral intuition, as the name implies, focuses specifically on ethical dilemmas. Haidt (2001) starts his foundational paper asking readers to think about the morality of consensual, adult, and safe sex between a brother and sister. Hauser and colleagues (Hauser *et al.*, 2007) discuss various 'trolley' or 'train' scenarios whereby one has a choice of whether and how to stop a trolley that is heading toward five people on the same track. And Sonenshein (2007) raises issues involving plant closures and cheating suppliers. While these may be seen as problem-solving scenarios, they differ from the types of judgments discussed in the preceding section, which are often assessed through a criterion of 'effectiveness' (Dane and Pratt, 2007). Moral decisions are not typically viewed as being effective or not, but rather as being right or wrong. Moreover, moral decisions are often appraised 'anthropocentrically' through culturally based customs, interactions, and interpretations (see Haidt and Kesebir, 2008).

Nonetheless, as reflected in Table 1.1, there are a number of similarities between problem-solving and moral intuitions. First, as with all types of intuitions, moral intuitions are said to occur nonconsciously. Support for this assertion – in both social intuitionist and UMG perspectives – comes from the observation that people are often not able to explain why they think something is right or wrong (Haidt, 2001, 2007; Haidt and Hersh, 2001; Haidt, Koller and Dias, 1993; Hauser *et al.*, 2007). That is, while individuals may sometimes be able to identify and delineate available ethical principles that justify their intuition (such as certain 'principles of harm' – see Cushman, Young and Hauser, 2006), the rationalization process may prove difficult in many cases.

Second, like problem-solving intuitions, moral intuitions may involve a pattern matching process whereby features of a given scenario are rapidly and automatically compared to prototypes of ethical situations that have been stored in the 'X-system' of the human brain – a nonconscious, automatic system of processing often linked to intuition (see Lieberman, 2000; see also the 'experiential system' of dual-processing theories noted above). Reynolds provides a case in point:

> When a supervisor ... secretly offers a promotion in exchange for sexual favors, the elements of this experience are immediately processed, organized, and matched to an existing prototype of quid pro quo sexual harassment. The situation can then be presented reflexively to consciousness as an ethical (and legal) issue. In this way, ethical prototypes allow decision makers to recognize ethical situations automatically (Reynolds, 2006, p. 739).

Because moral intuitions involve a matching categorization process between a situation and a prototype, moral intuitions are often conceptualized as involving relatively tight or convergent cognitive associations.

Whereas the development of the cognitive structures underlying problem-solving intuition have been shown to be largely a by-product of learning under appropriate conditions (Dane and Pratt, 2007; Ericsson and Charness, 1994; Hogarth, 2001), the source of morality-based structures – or 'prototypes' – remains a somewhat open question. Evidence suggests that the foundations of the ethical 'prototypes' underlying moral intuitions are part innate and part social. Haidt (2001) discusses research that has indicated a biological basis of behavior among primates in line with prescriptive rules. Despite this innate basis for moral intuitions, culture undoubtedly shapes and influences the acceptable ethical codes of its members (Haidt, 2001; Haidt, Koller and Dias, 1993). Most or all cultures appear to emphasize some combination of five types of moral issues: harm/care, fairness/reciprocity, ingroup/loyalty, authority/respect, and purity/sanctity (Haidt and Graham, 2007; Haidt and Joseph, 2004). Cultures differ in that they influence which of these issues get the most attention. By culture, we mean not only national or ethnic cultures, but also 'smaller' cultures such as organizational and professional ones. For example, as noted by Sonenshein (2007), individuals may internalize the moral values of their organizations as they undergo socialization. UMG also takes an interactionist perspective, noting that the development of an intuitive 'grammar' is based on cognitive systems that are 'largely pre-determined by the inherent structure of the mind, but whose ontogenetic development must be triggered and shaped by appropriate experience and can be impeded by hostile learning environments' (Mikhail, 2007, p. 144).

Finally, like problem-solving intuitions, moral intuitions are believed to occur rapidly. According to Reynolds (2006), ethical situations are likely to have prototypical characteristics that are recognized and responded to almost immediately through a pattern matching process. As Haidt (2001, p. 818) notes, 'One sees or hears about a social event and one instantly feels approval or disapproval.' This suggests a relatively straightforward stimulus–response type of association in which an external pattern is rapidly equated with one that has been previously encoded internally.

The biggest difference between problem-solving and moral intuition is that the latter is often conceptualized as involving more intense emotions – that is, emotions that are higher on the arousal continuum. As Haidt, Koller and Dias (1993) observe, judgments of immorality are often grounded in feelings of disgust – feelings that involve a considerable degree of affective arousal. Haidt and colleagues note further that intuitive responses to moral issues often involve 'strong and clear' convictions (1993, p. 626) and that moral arguments often consist of 'bitterness' and 'self-righteousness' (Haidt, 2001, p. 823). Perhaps for this reason, Haidt (2007) stresses that moral intuitions are heavily 'affectively laden'. On this characteristic, moral intuition is closer to creative intuition.

Creative Intuition

While problem-solving and moral intuition are similar in that they ultimately involve a type of convergent categorization (e.g. is this right or wrong, good or evil?), some research has argued for the existence of a potentially different type of intuition – one linked to a creative act of synthesis in which disparate elements are fused together in novel combinations (e.g. Crossan, Lane and White, 1999; Duggan, 2007; Policastro, 1995; Raidl and Lubart, 2000/2001).

Following Policastro (1995, p. 99), who views such intuition as 'a vague anticipatory perception that orients creative work in a promising direction', we refer to this type of intuition as 'creative' intuition. This is not to say that intuition is the same as creativity, or that all intuitions lead to creative outcomes. Rather, this label accords with the view shared by some that intuition may be a key *input* in the creative process. To illustrate, Langer (1989, p. 117) makes the claim that creativity arises through an 'intuitive experience of the world'. Supporting this contention, Garfield *et al.* (2001) found a positive relationship between the use of an intuitive creativity technique and the generation of novel ideas in a laboratory study.

Occupational applications of creative intuition may include identifying and developing a radically different type of automobile to bring to market (Hayashi, 2001), devising entrepreneurial ideas (Crossan, Lane and White, 1999; Mitchell, Friga and Mitchell, 2005), and generating scientific discoveries (Marton, Fensham and Chaiklin, 1994). Creative intuitions may also be particularly relevant in strategic decision making (Khatri and Ng, 2000) and in situations where few precedents for a particular course of action exist (Agor, 1986).

A number of scholars have drawn distinctions between intuitions that serve creative ends (i.e. creative intuition) from those that do not. For example, Isenberg (1984) contrasts intuitions that allow managers 'to perform well-learned behavior patterns rapidly', involving an effortless, automatic performance of 'learned behavioral sequences' (1984, p. 85), from intuitions that involve synthesizing 'isolated bits of data and experience into an integrated picture' that is more than the sum of its parts (1984, p. 85). Similarly, Crossan, Lane and White (1999) differentiated between 'a process of (past) pattern recognition' that permits experts to 'no longer have to think consciously about action' (1999, p. 526) – and an 'entrepreneurial' view of intuition, concerned with making novel connections and discerning new possibilities. Crossan, Lane and White (1999) suggested further that some intuitions support 'exploitation', while other intuitions support 'exploration'.

One hallmark of creative intuition, setting it apart from problem-solving and moral intuition, is that the cognitive associations fostering creative intuitions tend to be more divergent than convergent. In discussions of the role of intuition in creativity, intuition has been described as a process of 'linking disparate elements of information' (Raidl and Lubart, 2000/2001, p. 219), and as a method for 'bringing past elements together in a new and useful way' (Duggan, 2007, p. 152). Likewise, Miller and Ireland discuss 'holistic hunch' intuition as involving a 'subconscious synthesis of information drawn from diverse experiences' in which information is 'combined in complex ways' (2005, p. 21). Similarly, Crossan, Lane and White (1999) note that entrepreneurial intuition (akin to what we are calling creative intuition) is relevant to innovation and involves making novel connections, perceiving new relationships, and discerning possibilities. They point to a role of this type of intuition in 'exploration', much as Bowers et al. (1990) point to a role of intuition in 'discovery'. In sum, because creative intuitions tend to involve blending or integrating fairly diverse aspects of information in novel ways, they are often associated with discovery or the generation of something 'truly new', rather than simply 'old wine in a new bottle' (George, 2007, p. 449). The other types of intuition reviewed here are less relevant to creativity because they rely on convergent associations – operations less conducive to creativity than divergent thinking (Amabile, 1996; Barron and Harrington, 1981; George, 2007).

Creative intuitions also differ from problem-solving intuitions in terms of their affective intensity. For example, Miller and Ireland (2005) equate holistic hunches (a creative form of intuition) with 'strong feelings', and Sadler-Smith and Shefy (2004) label a concept similar to what we refer to as creative intuition as 'intuition-as-feeling' to accentuate its connection to relatively high levels of affect. Along like lines, the experience of a creative-type intuition has been described as a 'subconscious, visceral feeling' that 'just felt right' (see Hayashi, 2001, p. 60) – characteristics associated with a highly affective experience.

Finally, as noted in Table 1.1, creative intuition appears to take longer than either problem-solving or moral intuition from the point at which an issue is presented to the point at which the intuitive judgment arises. Viewing intuition as anything but immediate is rare, although Hogarth (2001) raises this possibility. More recently, work suggests that that some sort of extended processing time, akin to incubation, may precede some forms of intuition, such as creative intuition (see Dijksterhuis and Nordgren, 2006; Smith and Dodds, 1999). Before proceeding along this line of reasoning, it is important to acknowledge that in so doing our intent is not to reentangle concepts that have recently been disentangled (see Dane and Pratt, 2007; Hodgkinson, Langan-Fox and Sadler-Smith, 2008). First, we should be careful not to mistake insight (Sternberg and Davidson, 1995) with creative intuition, even though both may involve an incubation period. Unlike insight, in which one 'suddenly becomes aware of the logical relations between a problem and the answer' (Lieberman, 2000, p. 110), creative intuitions – like all intuitions – involve a feeling that cannot be accounted for consciously or logically. Second, although creative intuitions appear to be preceded by an incubation period, it is critical to note that the ultimate emergence of the intuitive judgment (as with all types of intuition) occurs via a rapid associative process. To be clear, the timing difference between creative intuitions and problem-solving and moral intuitions lies in the period between the point at which the decision scenario is presented to the decision-maker and the point at which the intuitive response emerges. With creative intuition, some degree of incubation appears to be an antecedent to the rapid, holistic, and associative operations that produce the intuition; with the other two types of intuition, problems are presented and intuition nearly instantly follows.

To illustrate the concept of creative intuition, consider an anecdote offered by Hayashi (2001). After pondering what products might help save then-struggling Chrysler in 1988, company president Bob Lutz experienced an intuition while taking a weekend drive. This intuition was that it would behoove Chrysler to produce a high-end sports car. The result was the development of the Dodge Viper, which became a runaway success. This intuition appears to be of the creative type in the sense that it appeared following an incubation period. Further, unlike insight, there was no accompanied recognition of how the logical relations of the problem fit together.

Unconscious Thought Theory (UTT; Dijksterhuis, 2004; Dijksterhuis et al., 2006; Dijksterhuis and Nordgren, 2006) provides a theoretical basis for the role of incubation in producing creative intuitions. The theory posits there are two modes of thought – a conscious mode and an unconscious mode. As stated by Dijksterhuis and Nordgren (2006, p. 96), 'Conscious thought is thought with attention; unconscious thought is thought without attention (or with attention directed elsewhere).' According to UTT, the unconscious mode of thinking is capable of drawing divergent associations; as such, it may produce judgments akin to those described here as creative intuitions.

In support of their theory, Dijksterhuis and colleagues have documented a number of instances in which focusing one's attention to matters besides a given (complex) task can induce a period of unconscious thought that may precipitate intuitions of the creative variety. Dijksterhuis's findings and underlying theoretical framework support proverbial wisdom that, at least in some instances, individuals may benefit from 'sleeping on it' rather than either engaging in conscious thinking or acting immediately upon 'snap judgments'. While this line of work and others point to the existence of a creative type of intuition, proposing a creative type of intuition does raise some conceptual concerns. We address such concerns later in this chapter, in our future research section.

We now turn away from conceptual issues surrounding intuition. However, this departure is only temporary. We will return to issues concerning what intuition is and whether it may fairly be said that there are different types of intuition in the final section. Next, we turn to related lines of inquiry by reviewing research on when individuals rely on their intuitions to make decisions and when it is in their interest to do so. We note up front that the bulk of research examining these issues tends to view intuition from a problem-solving framework. Hence, there may be important boundary conditions concerning the findings noted below with regard to different types of intuition.

When Do People Trust and Use Their Intuition?

A number of researchers have investigated the conditions under which people take stock of and employ their intuitions. This research has revealed factors predicting whether individuals will use their intuitive judgments to make decisions. Most work has tended to focus on two factors in particular, mood states and individual differences.

First, several studies (Bless et al., 1990; Elsbach and Barr, 1999; Isen et al., 1982; King et al., 2007; Ruder and Bless, 2003) indicate that individuals tend to rely on their intuitions when they are in positive mood states. In a review of the relationship between mood and decision making, Isen (2000, pp. 426–427) suggests that positive mood may facilitate complex decision making by increasing an individual's openness to information, thus leading to a 'greater integration of cognitive material'. In these situations, individuals may be more open to data gleaned from the nonconscious system of processing. An additional explanation is offered via the affect-as-information perspective (Schwarz and Clore, 1983). This view contends that negative moods signal that the environment is problematic; as such, individuals may attempt to ameliorate their situation by engaging in analytical, systematic approaches to processing information and making decisions. In contrast, positive moods signal a more benign environment; hence, individuals have less motivation to expend cognitive effort and are content to rely on their intuitions (Bless et al., 1996; Schwarz, 1990). In reviewing these findings, it is worth noting that while mood is a factor associated with whether individuals will trust and use their intuitions, it also is a feature associated with the experience of intuition itself (to varying levels of intensity – see previous discussion). Scholars may benefit from keeping these distinctions in mind as they further consider the role of affect as both a determinant and a characteristic of intuitive decision making.

Second, research has explored whether there are individual differences in individuals' propensities to use intuition. For example, drawing on Jung's (1933) conception of intuition as a personality characteristic, the Myers–Briggs Type Indicator (MBTI; Briggs and Myers, 1976) includes a measure of 'intuition' (i.e. 'intuiting' vs. 'sensing') as an individual's propensity to perceive and rely on implicit patterns, meanings, and possibilities (Quenk, 2000). Although intuition, as conceptualized within the MBTI, is not synonymous with intuition as we defined it above, the MBTI provides evidence that individuals perceive reality in different ways, and suggests that those individuals with a preference for intuitive perception may rely on intuition in making judgments. In a related vein, Epstein and colleagues (Epstein *et al.*, 1996; Pacini and Epstein, 1999) argue that individuals differ in their reliance on each of two independent modes of thinking: analytical–rational and intuitive–experiential. Accordingly, Pacini and Epstein (1999) constructed a Rational–Experiential Inventory (REI) that assessed individual personality differences in the use of rational versus experiential (intuitive) thinking. This research suggests that individuals have distinct preferences for using their intuitions and/or their analytic capabilities to make decisions. Recent work by Hodgkinson and colleagues (Hodgkinson and Sadler-Smith, 2003; Hodgkinson, Langan-Fox and Sadler-Smith, 2008) provides strong support for Epstein's independent modes perspective (as compared to a uni-dimensional perspective – see Allinson and Hayes, 1996) on both theoretical and empirical grounds.

While there is evidence that mood states and individual differences play a role in determining whether an individual will use intuition to make decisions, other factors have been proposed as well. For example, some have posited that organizational culture (or even climate-like) factors will influence the degree to which organizational members trust their intuitions. Along these lines, Burke and Miller (1999) suggest that intuition will flourish in an organization to the extent that it is valued and cultivated through leadership, political climate, and socialization processes. Agor (1986), in contrast, notes that many executives operate in cultures that emphasize the use of analytical skills and logic, thus making the open use of intuition 'taboo'.

Dane and Pratt (2007) further suggest that more macro-cultural forces may impact upon individuals' use of intuition. They note that individuals living or working in cultures characterized by a low emphasis on 'uncertainty avoidance' (Cyert and March, 1963; Hofstede, 2001) are willing to 'take unknown risks' and are 'comfortable with ambiguity and chaos' (Hofstede, 2001, p. 161). Because intuitions are difficult to justify rationally and often involve unknown risk levels, members of cultures low in uncertainty avoidance may be more inclined than others to rely on their intuitions to make decisions.

Finally, Keltner, Gruenfeld and Anderson (2003) have drawn upon research on social cognition (e.g. Fiske, 1993; Neuberg and Fiske, 1987) to propose that high levels of power may lead individuals to make judgments through relatively automatic, as opposed to conscious and deliberative, channels of information processing. For example, it has been demonstrated in an experimental setting that individuals assigned to a high-power condition tend to unconsciously ignore information that would challenge stereotypes concerning internship applicants they are instructed to evaluate (Goodwin et al., 2000). This suggests that power holders may be inclined to rely on stereotypes rather than to engage in more analytical forms of thinking that may help overcome stereotype biases. Considerable scholarship has found that stereotypes may be automatically activated via the nonconscious system of information processing (e.g. Banaji, Hardin and Rothman, 1993; Devine, 1989; Macrae, Milne and Bodenhausen, 1994) – the same system responsible for the production of intuitive judgments. Insofar as individuals in positions of elevated power rely on the products of their nonconscious system, and avoid thinking analytically, such individuals may be more inclined to trust their intuitions than low-power individuals, who may tend to employ a more controlled, conscious approach to decision making (Keltner, Gruenfeld and Anderson, 2003).

When Should Intuition Be Used?

A third long-standing issue concerns if and when intuition should be used to make decisions. This issue is typically framed in terms of comparing the effectiveness of judgments stemming from problem-solving intuitions versus those stemming from rational or analytical procedures. For decades, a number of scholars largely dismissed the usefulness of intuition for making decisions in organizations due to its potential to lead to erroneous, biased, or inaccurate decisions, and instead argued for the superiority of analytical decision-making methods (e.g. Dawes, Faust and Meehl, 1989; Kahneman, Slovic and Tversky, 1982; Meehl, 1954). Thus, the prescription among many decision-making researchers was – and often continues to be – that managers should avoid making intuitive decisions, and instead be analytical whenever possible (e.g. Bonabeau, 2003; Schoemaker and Russo, 1993). In recent years, such prescriptions have been challenged. As organizational decision-making environments become increasingly fast paced and dynamic, a rising focus on how to achieve decision making that is both rapid and effective among today's managers has led some scholars to reconsider the potential merits of intuition (e.g. Gigerenzer, 2007; Sadler-Smith, Hodgkinson and Sinclair, 2008; Sadler-Smith and Shefy, 2004, 2007). In this vein, a number of researchers now contend that, in certain cases, intuition may prove more effective than previously believed. And, while some researchers continue to present arguments for the limitations of intuitive decision making, for example in the area of clinical decision making in health care (e.g. Croskerry, 2006; Groopman, 2007), there is a growing recognition that the question of whether intuition is superior or inferior to analysis is a complex one – a question not necessarily susceptible to a simple yes/no answer. Indeed, several recent articles (Dane and Pratt, 2007; Hodgkinson, Langan-Fox and Sadler-Smith, 2008; Sadler-Smith and Sparrow, 2008; Sinclair, Sadler-Smith and Hodgkinson, 2009) have suggested that the effectiveness of intuitive decision making may be contingent on a range of factors. Along these lines, evidence suggests that intuitions tend to be relatively more accurate when decision-makers have accrued significant levels of expertise such that their cognitive schemas are 'complex and domain relevant' (Dane and Pratt, 2007). Such schemas arise as individuals accrue domain experiences while receiving feedback that is 'relevant and exacting' (Hogarth, 2001). The investment it takes for individuals to attain high levels of expertise is far from trivial. Khatri and Ng (2000, p. 58) argue that for managerial intuition to be effective, it 'requires years of experience in problem solving and is founded upon a solid and complete grasp of the details of the business'. This perspective fits with research suggesting that the acquisition of expertise in many domains requires a number of years of 'deliberate practice' and training (Ericsson and Charness, 1994).

While expertise is a critical factor accounting for intuition effectiveness, research also suggests that intuitive judgments may be relatively more accurate in relation to certain types of tasks than on others. In particular, the effectiveness of intuition has been shown to vary to the extent a task is intellective versus judgmental. Intellective tasks, which involve a 'definite objective criterion of success within the definitions, rules, operations, and relationships of a particular conceptual system' (Laughlin, 1980, p. 128), may be ill suited to intuitive decision making. Such tasks tend to be highly structured and have a definite, objective criterion of success. These properties make such tasks conducive to the use of an analytical decision-making approach. Analysis permits individuals to decompose a structured problem into constituent parts and reason toward a solution (Dane, Rockmann and Pratt, 2005; Shapiro and Spence, 1997). In contrast, judgmental tasks, which involve 'political, ethical, aesthetic, or behavioral judgments for which there is no objective criterion or demonstrable solution' (Laughlin, 1980, p. 128), may be well suited to intuitive as opposed to analytical decision making. These tasks involve unstructured problem situations. Intuition, as an associative process, may help to integrate the disparate elements of such problems into a coherent perception of how to proceed (Dane, Rockmann and Pratt, 2005; Dane and Pratt, 2007).

In addition to the structure of a given task, the effectiveness of intuition may also vary with regard to the time pressure associated with that task. It is perhaps not surprising that intuition has been examined with regard to the decisions made by firefighters (Klein, 1998), military commanders (Kaempf *et al.*, 1996), emergency room surgeons (Abernathy and Hamm, 1995), and corporate executives operating in time-sensitive conditions (Agor, 1986; Burke and Miller, 1999; Hayashi, 2001). Within these occupations, poor outcomes often result from a failure to take action. In some cases, lack of action is a result of excessive decision analysis, or so-called 'paralysis by analysis' (Langley, 1995; Mintzberg, 1994, p. 325). For this reason, the effectiveness of intuitive decision making compared to analytical decision making may increase positively as a function of time pressure.

Despite growing convergence on the conditions that favor intuitive judgments over analytical, scholars continue to suggest that optimal decisions may involve the use of both types of decisions. For example, in an oft-cited work in the intuition literature, Simon (1987) argued that effective managers will approach problems using both intuition and analysis, switching decision styles as conditions warrant. This view accords with empirical evidence that managers frequently draw on intuition and analysis as separate 'inputs' when making decisions (Burke and Miller, 1999). Even the UMG perspective on moral intuition views the process of moral decision making as incorporating both intuitive and rational modes of decision making (Hauser *et al.*, 2007).

While agreeing that combining analytical and intuitive approaches may bear considerable returns, researchers have rarely considered the best method by which to employ or integrate them, and the work that does exist is somewhat contradictory. For instance, Shapiro and Spence (1997) suggest that there is merit in recording one's intuition first and then assessing a problem analytically. In contrast, Agor (1986) recommends intuition as a means of synthesizing information that has been previously gathered and analyzed. This and other conceptual points of disagreement will be taken up again in the final section of this chapter. We now turn to a topic that has engendered far more divergence than convergence among scholars: the methodological assessment of intuition.

CAPTURING INTUITION EMPIRICALLY

Despite a growing interest among researchers in the various types and potential merits of intuition, empirical research on intuition remains limited. In part, this is because intuition is a nonconscious process that is difficult to pin down methodologically. Intuition researchers face the challenge of determining how best to access, view, or demonstrate intuition processes and outcomes as they occur or have occurred. Despite a lack of agreement on which methodological approaches are most efficacious toward this end, a number of approaches have emerged. The purpose of this section is to summarize and critique extant research methods for capturing intuition. In this pursuit, we review a range of research methods directed toward fostering and assessing intuition in laboratory and field settings.[2] Moreover, in line with our conceptual review, we note which of the existing measures have been used to assess which types of intuition. Our review of existing methods is summarized in Table 1.2.

Direct Instruction

One method, which we will refer to as *direct instruction*, is premised on the assumption that decision making can be manipulated by instructing individuals to adopt an intuitive approach to decision making for a given set of tasks. This method has been employed almost exclusively through experimental research on utilizing problem-solving intuition (and analysis). A foundational study that relied on this approach was conducted by Wilson and Schooler (1991), who placed participants into either an analytical or control condition and asked them to perform a judgment task. Similar methods have also been employed by Hammond *et al.* (1987) and McMackin and Slovic (2000). However, in these studies researchers did not directly instruct participants to make decisions either analytically or intuitively. Instead, one condition involved instructions to induce analytical reasoning, but the other condition served as a control condition – one in which no decision-making instruction (e.g. to make decisions intuitively) was given.

In the effort to create a more balanced and direct experimental inducement of decision-making approaches, Dane, Rockmann and Pratt (2005) instructed participants in their lab studies to perform tasks either analytically or intuitively. Consistent with previous research (e.g. Wilson and Schooler, 1991), participants in the analytical condition were first asked to write down a list of factors they thought would be important to making their decisions and were instructed to think about each task in depth before making a decision. Participants in the intuitive condition did not write down a list of decision factors and were instructed to avoid thinking very hard about the tasks and to make decisions on the basis of their gut instinct reactions. Manipulation checks revealed that participants made decisions in line with the condition to which they had been assigned. Moreover, task performance varied as a function of condition on several tasks, providing additional support for the effectiveness of these manipulations.

Jordan, Whitfield and Zeigler-Hill (2007, p. 1073) employed a similar method to inducing analytical (or, in their words, 'rational') and intuitive

---

[2] In reviewing a range of intuition measurement techniques in this section, we refrain from discussing measurement scales concerned with individual differences in decision-making styles (see Allinson and Hayes, 1996; Hodgkinson and Sadler-Smith, 2003; Pacini and Epstein, 1999). Intuitive decision-making is conceptually distinct from an individual's inclination to think intuitively (an intuition 'use' factor – see the section below, entitled 'When Do People Trust and Use their Intuition?'). The focus of the present section is on identifying and measuring intuition when it actually occurs, as opposed to assessing an individual's natural tendency to employ intuitive (or analytical) decision-making approaches.

Table 1.2   Intuition measurement methods

Method	Primary Strength	Primary Weakness	Intuition Type(s) Most Commonly Associated	Representative Research
Direct Instruction	High level of researcher control	Difficult to assess whether intuition is being employed	Problem-solving	McMackin and Slovic (2000); Wilson and Schooler (1991); Jordan, Whitfield and Zeigler-Hill, (2007)
Retrospective Reports	Can be employed in field research	Involves post-hoc interpretation	Problem-solving	Hoffman, Crandall and Shadbolt (1998); Klein (1998)
Incubational Method	Limited likelihood of demand artifacts	May be difficult to ascertain relative contribution of intuition versus analysis	Creative	Dijksterhuis (2004); Dijksterhuis et al. (2006)
Scenario Based	Separates personal attachments from moral judgments; allows assessment of relatively subtle differences in moral intuiting	May not be generalizable to 'real world' moral intuiting	Moral	Greene et al. (2004); Hauser et al. (2007)
Neurological and Physiological	Potentially provides direct, observable evidence of intuitive processing; can be used in conjunction with other measures (e.g. scenarios)	Costly, time intensive, and complex; moral reasoning likely involves multiple systems; measurement often done under artificial settings	Problem-solving, Moral	Casebeer and Churchland (2003); Greene and Haidt (2002); Lieberman (2000); Moll et al. (2002)
Affective Priming	Limited likelihood of demand artifacts	Affective processing may not be synonymous with intuition	Moral	Hsee and Rottenstreich (2004); Small, Loewenstein and Slovic (2007)

decision making; in a laboratory decision-making task, these researchers instructed participants in the intuitive condition to 'use gut feelings to decide', and instructed those in the analytical condition to 'decide carefully, to write down each consideration and why they felt it was important'. These experimental instructions were complemented with a further manipulation designed to enhance participants' compliance with their assigned decision-making condition. Prior to receiving the direct instruction to make decisions intuitively (or analytically), participants were told that intuitive (or analytical) decision making was supported with evidence as being an effective way to make decisions. Those in the intuitive condition were told, 'There is clear evidence that people who adopt an intuitive approach to decision making are more successful in many areas of their lives.' Those in the analytical condition were told, 'People who adopt a rational approach to decision making are more successful.' Manipulation checks revealed that participants assigned to the intuition condition reported greater 'faith in intuition' than those in the analytical condition, providing at least indirect support that they relied on intuition as they made their decisions.

We contend that there are certain advantages to using direct instruction to assess intuition empirically. The use of direct instruction permits researchers a relatively high degree of control over the way in which research participants make decisions. This allows researchers to perform comparative tests of the effectiveness of different decision-making approaches on a variety of tasks. Additionally, direct instruction is relatively straightforward to employ. Participants may be instructed to 'rely on their gut feelings', or, in contrast, to 'be as analytical as possible'. The analytical decision-making approach may also be induced or enhanced by instructing participants to develop and rely on decision factors, criteria, or weightings.

Directly instructing participants to make decisions intuitively or analytically also carries limitations including but not restricted to those common to any form of making direct requests in a laboratory setting (e.g. demand characteristics). For example, although studies have found differences in task performance between analytical and intuitive (or nonanalytical) conditions, there is no way of knowing with certainty whether participants are truly thinking analytically or intuitively. This lack of an independent criterion renders the overall approach especially difficult as a basis for assessing the use of intuition.[3] To illustrate, instructing an individual to think intuitively may result in an individual making a 'guess' rather than formulating and relying upon an intuition. To help differentiate guessing from intuition, researchers could ask

---

[3] To help assess whether analytical methods were employed by participants in our own laboratory studies we examined participants' self-generated decision criteria for analytical decision-making. We found that nearly all participants listed a number of decision factors, which indicated that participants had complied with the analytical condition task instructions (for further details, see Dane, Rockmann and Pratt, 2005).

participants to report their confidence in their decisions. Confidence is often associated with intuitions, but not guesses (Dane and Pratt, 2007).

Furthermore, instructing individuals to rely on their intuition to make decisions may be difficult outside of laboratory conditions. Professional decision-makers would undoubtedly require a great degree of trust in the process and goals of the research program before they would be willing to perform occupational tasks (many of which may involve critical outcomes, such as making investments) according to directions issued by a researcher. Finally, because direct instruction typically involves instructing participants to 'go with their gut' on a task that they perform soon after instruction, the use of this method may be limited to capturing problem-solving or moral intuitions – intuition types that do not involve an incubation period.

Retrospective Reports

Another type of intuition measurement technique that is also associated with problem-solving intuition involves the use of *retrospective reports*. Through retrospective reports, research participants indicate to a researcher how they approached a decision-making problem after the problem has been solved. This process may be guided by research interviews, written descriptions of the decision-making process, or survey questionnaires and may occur immediately after task completion or take place at a later point in time. For example, in researching intuitive decision making among firefighters, Klein (1998) asked firefighters to talk about specific fires they had fought during the course of their careers. In a related vein, scholars have developed and employed a detailed, retrospective approach, the Critical Decision Method (CDM – see Hoffman, Crandall and Shadbolt, 1998), designed to enable decision-makers to recall the details of how they made decisions with regard to particular situations they encountered. Others have probed decision making retrospectively via the use of survey questionnaires to determine whether participants employed intuitive decision making as directed in experimental research (Dane, Rockmann and Pratt, 2005). Direct instruction and retrospective reports may thus be used in tandem within a single study to prompt intuitive decision making and detect the extent to which participants behave in accordance with experimental directions.

From a methodological perspective, retrospective reports are strong where priming is weak. Retrospective reports allow research participants the opportunity to indicate their perceptions about how they actually made their decisions; direct instruction, in contrast, rests on the assumption that participants will follow decision-making instructions. If participants deviated from following their prescribed decision-making approach (and were aware of doing so – an assumption we recognize as problematic), they can report this to researchers. In contrast, participants are not typically permitted the opportunity to notify researchers of this deviation in a laboratory research design that relies exclusively on direct instruction. Retrospective reports may also be more practical to use than priming when conducting field research with organizational and professional participants. Such participants are likely to be more comfortable discussing or indicating how they made decisions rather than being compelled to make decisions through researcher-mandated approaches. Finally, retrospective reports may conceivably be used to capture all three intuition types reviewed above. That is, research participants could describe having used intuition during a particular episode, and researchers could identify which type of intuition was most likely at play on the basis of such factors as whether the research participant described an incubation period, or the degree of affect discussed by the research participant.

Like priming, retrospective reports also carry limitations. For instance, individual recall of past events may be incomplete or inaccurate (see Hoffman, Crandall and Shadbolt, 1998, for discussion). Thus, an individual may falsely report that a decision was made intuitively (or analytically) when, in fact, the decision was made in a different way. Furthermore, individuals may have different understandings of the concept of 'intuition'. As such, researchers must be very clear about what they mean by intuitive decision making when asking participants to indicate how closely their decision-making process drew upon intuition as it is scientifically defined.

Incubational Method

Dijksterhuis and colleagues (Dijksterhuis, 2004; Dijksterhuis *et al.*, 2006) have developed a novel approach that could be used to capture the nonconscious incubational aspect of what we have referred to in this chapter as creative intuition. Specifically, Dijksterhuis and colleagues have demonstrated that when participants are first presented with a task and then given a second task designed to occupy their conscious system of processing, their nonconscious system continues to operate upon the original task. To carry this out, researchers assign participants to a range of conditions, one of which is a nonconscious thought condition in which participants are exposed to a scenario and then distracted for several minutes by a task that consumes their conscious attention (e.g. an anagram task). Following the distraction task, participants are then directed back to the original scenario and asked to make a judgment (e.g. a creative judgment). One advantage of this method is that it is not highly subject to the demand characteristics that may arise with regard to the direct instruction technique.

The incubational method has successfully identified conditions under which the use of intuition (via incubation) performs particularly well when compared with other, more analytic, approaches.[4] As such, Dijksterhuis's research is

---

[4] It is important to note that Dijksterhuis also uses the incubational approach to assess what might be referred to here as problem-solving intuitions – intuitions which can be evaluated by their 'effectiveness'. We see additional merit to the incubational approach as a means of capturing creative intuitions given the incubation facet of this approach. We briefly return to the issue of which intuition type(s) Dijksterhuis and colleagues are concerned with in the final section of this chapter.

noteworthy not only for its methods but its contribution to theory as well. Nonetheless, the effectiveness of this experimental approach appears limited to cases in which researchers are interested mainly in intuitions that follow from incubation. The period of nonconscious thought (incubation) upon which this method hinges may limit the extent to which this method can accurately assess or document intuitions of the other varieties explored here. Additionally, because this method may lead research participants to think both consciously and nonconsciously about a problem, it could be difficult to pinpoint the relative contribution of intuitive versus analytical thought in guiding decision making under this approach.

Scenario Based

One means of priming moral intuitions is through the use of ethical scenarios. A popular set of scenarios are the 'trolley' or 'train' scenarios (Greene *et al.*, 2001, 2004). An example of such a scenario can be found in Hauser *et al.* (2007, p. 18):

> Denise is a passenger on a train whose driver has just shouted that the train's breaks have failed, and who then fainted of the shock. On the track ahead are five people; the banks are so steep that they will not be able to get off the track in time. The track has a side track leading off to the right, and Denise can turn the train onto it. Unfortunately there is one person on the right hand track. Denise can turn the train, killing the one; or she can refrain from turning the train, letting the five die.

Once administered, participants may be asked whether a particular action (e.g. Denise pulling a switch to turn the train) is moral or not. The use of intuition is deduced as individuals are often at a loss when attempting to explain the justifications for their particular choices (Hauser *et al.*, 2007). Alternatively, as we discuss below, participants may be assessed in terms of their neurological or physiological reactions. Moral intuition is assumed to occur here by differentiating how the body processes ethical scenarios differently from other scenarios (e.g. examining how different parts of the brain are activated by ethical scenarios vs. rational or nonethical scenarios). Thus, one advantage of such scenarios is that they can be used to examine the outcomes of moral intuiting – moral judgments – as well as to assess which heretofore hidden processes are occurring as moral intuiting is engaged. In addition, because these scenarios are artificial, individuals are less likely to have preexisting emotional entanglements with the issues raised, thus helping to make the results cleaner (see Hauser *et al.*, 2007).

Another advantage is that scenarios can be modified to gain nuanced understandings of how moral intuitions work. Recently, researchers have attempted to vary the scenarios in an attempt to show how UMG may add explanatory power over existing perspectives (e.g. rational or emotional). For example, Hauser and colleagues (2007) use ethical scenarios to explore how individuals differentially evaluate impersonal (e.g. pulling a switch a switch to turn the train) versus personal (e.g. throwing a person in front of the train to block it) moral choices. They find evidence that these types of scenarios are processed differently, bolstering the work by Greene and colleagues (see Greene et al., 2001, 2004) that has been used to support the social intuitionist approach. However, they go beyond the personal versus impersonal dimension by altering scenarios to get at another critical dimension of moral intuiting: intentionality. Specifically, they examine whether there are differences when harming another is viewed as a means to an end versus as a foreseen side effect (see the 'principle of double effect'). By showing that various demographic subsamples of individuals make similar distinctions, even if they cannot justify why, Hauser and colleagues support their notion that there may be a UMG.

The main shortcomings of scenario-based methods for capturing intuition are similar to the others we have discussed. First, as with the other approaches (e.g. direct instruction), the presence of intuition must be inferred; that said, assessing lack of justifications does help assuage this shortcoming. Second, and perhaps more problematically, the artificial nature of the scenarios limits their potential applicability in understanding 'real world' moral decision making. For example, individuals faced with moral decisions, such as whether to recall a defective product, are not emotionally detached from these events.

Neurological and Physiological Approaches

There has also been an increasing interest in exploring the physiological and neurological processes involved in intuition. Some of this research has focused on intuition of the type we have referred to as problem-solving intuition. For example, Lieberman (2000, 2007) offers a 'social cognitive neuroscience approach' to intuition which, as noted earlier, highlights the importance of the basil ganglia and related structures in both intuition and implicit learning. Other approaches have examined the area of 'moral cognitions' (see Casebeer and Churchland, 2003, for review). While some of this research specifically mentions 'moral intuitions' (e.g. Greene and Haidt, 2002), other writers do not refer to intuitions directly – rather they use terms such as 'moral emotions' (Moll et al., 2002), 'moral cognitions' (Moll et al., 2005), or 'moral judgments' (Greene et al., 2001). Thus, researchers should be cautious about lumping together all physiological and neurological research on intuition, moral intuitions, and moral cognitions because it is not yet clear whether these researchers are examining the same or similar phenomena even though they use apparently similar terms. Further, it is unclear how these terms relate to each other. For example, while all moral intuitions are likely to involve moral emotions, the reverse is not necessarily true. Researchers, therefore, should clearly state whether they are examining intuition or some facet of intuition. Along these lines, it would be interesting to examine whether different types of intuition, such as problem-solving and moral, may have different physiological and neurological substrates.

Regarding intuition, broadly defined, a fair amount of recent work, including that cited above, involves brain imaging. Drawing on the pioneering work of Damasio and colleagues on brain injuries and social judgments (e.g. Anderson *et al.*, 1999; Eslinger and Damasio, 1985) researchers have used neural imaging techniques (such as functional magnetic resonance imaging – fMRI), to map out those areas of the brain most associated with moral cognition. As Moll and colleagues (2005, p. 800) note in their review:

Overall, there is remarkable agreement between functional imaging and clinic-anatomical evidence about the brain areas involved in moral cognition. Activated regions include the anterior PFC (encompassing the frontopolar cortex, Brodmann's area (BA) 9/10), orbitofrontal cortex (OFC, especially its medial section, BA 10/11/25), possibly STS (BA 21/39), anterior temporal lobes (BA 20/21/38), insula, precuneus (BA 7/31), anterior cingulate cortex (ACC, BA 24/32) and limbic regions.

Extract reprinted by permission from MacMillan Publishers Ltd: *Nature Reviews Neuroscience*, Moll, J., Zahn R., de Olivera-Souza, R. *et al.*, The neural basis of human moral cognition, **6**, 800, Copyright 2005.

To map these areas and differentiate them from those involved in making other types of judgments and decisions, researchers often provide participants with contrasts, either through scenarios (e.g. trolley scenarios) or visual images (e.g. abandoned children). These contrasts include: moral versus non-moral dilemmas (Greene *et al.*, 2001), easy versus difficult personal moral judgments, utilitarian versus nonutilitarian personal moral judgments (Greene *et al.*, 2004), and moral pictures versus unpleasant, pleasant, visually arousing, neutral, and scrambled pictures (Moll *et al.*, 2002).

Results from this brain mapping research suggest that intuitions, particularly moral intuitions, are closely related to affect (Greene *et al.*, 2001; Greene and Haidt, 2002; Moll *et al.*, 2002, 2005) and the areas of the brain associated with social cognition (Greene *et al.*, 2001; Greene and Haidt, 2002). Greene and Haidt (2002) have drawn upon this research as support for their social intuitionist model and Reynolds (2006) has synthesized this research to develop a neurocognitive model of moral decision making. While these lines of research are promising, Casebeer and Churchland (2003) caution researchers to remember that moral representations are likely to be highly distributed throughout the brain, and not centered on a specific region. Some research has taken this line of reasoning further to suggest that intuition may involve other areas of the body. For example, McCraty, Atkinson and Bradley (2004a, 2004b) suggest that the heart plays a role intuition. Specifically, using measures of heart rate variability, they demonstrate that the heart recognizes and responds to intuitive information, and may receive this information before the brain does. Similarly, Bechara *et al.* (1997) link intuitive knowledge and galvanic skin responses by demonstrating that when engaging in a gambling game, individuals exhibit 'micro-sweating', or changes in skin conductance, prior to attaining a conscious understanding of the game's risks.

By seemingly providing visible evidence that intuitive processes are indeed occurring, neurological and physiological measures have a distinct advantage over the previously noted measures where the use of intuition has to be assumed. Moreover, given that such testing also involves the prompting of intuitive processing, neurological and physiological measures may be used in conjunction with other methods (e.g. scenario based). However, there are also some distinct disadvantages of these types of measures. To begin, neurological and physiological measures are highly costly (e.g. equipment, training) and intensive in terms of time, as participants cannot be run in groups. In addition, as noted by Casebeer and Churchland (2003), such tests cannot yet be done in the 'field', thus intuitive reasoning is often being induced under very artificial conditions. Finally, if intuitive processing is indeed a system-wide phenomenon, researchers must be careful about where they seek to measure intuition, especially if they are focusing on only one part of the body (e.g. the brain).

Affect Priming

Recent research has shown that an affective mode of processing – a processing mode that may be closely aligned with intuitive, nonconscious operations – can be 'primed' via tasks that engage affective processing (Hsee and Rottenstreich, 2004; Small, Loewenstein and Slovic, 2007). For example, to induce an 'affective' method of judgment, experimenters may pose the following question to participants, 'When you hear the word "baby", what do you feel?' When given a decision-making task immediately following the 'affect' task, participants tend to make judgments based more on affect than on conscious, analytical processes. This method mitigates one of the key limitations associated with direct instruction. Specifically, this approach – which we refer to as *affect priming* – is less susceptible than direct instruction to hypothesis guessing. The link between asking participants about how they feel with regard to a particular topic and assessing their feelings on an ostensibly unrelated judgment task is not an explicit or obvious one; rather, the effect involves subtle and nonconscious priming (for a review of studies that employ priming techniques, see Bargh and Chartrand, 1999).

One limitation of the affect priming approach is that, as noted above, it is not a method that was designed to capture intuition per se. Instead, Hsee and Rottenstreich (2004) developed and employed this method so as to induce 'valuation by feeling', whereby individuals assess or express their preferences toward a stimulus or target on the basis of their feelings. Although this approach is potentially useful from an intuition research standpoint in that it hones in on affect – a critical element of intuition (particularly in the moral and creative types of intuition) – it is not yet clear that the experimental procedures associated with affective priming induce intuitive processes and intuitive judgments. Also, because affect priming is generally followed by an instruction to participants to make an immediate decision, this approach may not provide an opportunity for incubation (which, we have argued, is a core element to creative intuitions). Thus, this approach may not be well suited to the study of creative intuition. It could, however, be very useful to capturing intuitions that involve a high degree of affect and no incubation period – i.e. moral intuition.

LOOKING AHEAD: INTUITION RESEARCH AVENUES

We have argued that research on intuition has centered on what intuition is, which factors prompt individuals to trust and use it, and when intuition should be used. We have also reviewed a myriad of ways that researchers have attempted to measure intuitive processes and/or outcomes. To conclude, we turn to relatively unexplored research avenues in each of these areas. Our suggestions for future research are meant to be illustrative of the types of work that might be undertaken in each of these areas, rather than being comprehensive.

What Is Intuition? Issues with Differentiating Intuition Types

We argued for the possibility that there may be different types of intuition. Drawing on a number of lines of extant research, we suggested that there is some degree of evidence for the existence of problem-solving, moral, and creative intuitions. While we posited that each of these intuition types fits the definition of intuition we advanced previously (Dane and Pratt, 2007) we view these types of intuition as varying in some respects with regard to their underlying features. Because scholars have only recently begun to converge on a set of properties that characterize the concept of intuition and distinguish intuition from related phenomena (e.g. intuition vs. insight), the delineation of intuition into different types raises at least two conceptual questions that may require further research to sufficiently resolve.

First, we contended that a feature differentiating creative intuition from problem-solving and moral intuition is the degree to which incubation plays a role in the formation of the intuitive judgment. Although we argued that creative intuitions arise via an incubation period, we have maintained that creative intuitions are conceptually distinct from insights – a potentially similar outcome of cognitive incubation that is also of relevance to problem-solving and decision making (see Sternberg and Davidson, 1995). Because literature speaking to the concept of creative intuition is both relatively limited and primarily theoretical, further research is necessary to confirm that creative intuitions do indeed differ from insight. In a related vein, if these phenomena are in fact different, as maintained here, it remains an open question whether any process that requires a significant incubation period merits the descriptor 'intuition' given that numerous scholars have identified 'speed' as a hallmark characteristic of intuition (see Dane and Pratt, 2007; see also Hogarth, 2001, for a dissenting view). In evaluating this issue, scholars may wish to focus in particular on the work of Dijksterhuis and colleagues (Dijksterhuis, 2004; Dijksterhuis et al., 2006; Dijksterhuis and Meurs, 2006; Dijksterhuis and Nordgren, 2006), whose research not only provides a theoretical rationale for the role of incubation in creativity, but also posits that a type of problem-solving intuition may also be contingent on an incubation period.[5] Specifically, Dijksterhuis and Nordgren (2006) discuss the notion of 'summary judgment' intuitions, which are purported to arise via incubation in response to decision tasks that are largely noncreative (e.g. making a decision concerning which apartment to rent). For arguments against posing a creative intuition type, researchers may look at Hodgkinson and colleagues (2008) who see incubation as intimately tied to insight only.

To avoid a proliferation of intuition 'type' taxonomies, we suggest that researchers may need to avoid lumping many if not all nonconsciously based forms of judgment under the rubric of intuition. At the same time, until more empirical work has been done in the area, researchers must also be cautious to avoid dismissing certain forms of cognition (e.g. processes that involve incubation) as definitely nonintuitive, as doing so might minimize the power and richness of the intuition construct.

Second, in drawing distinctions among different intuition types, we argued that the nature of the affect associated with the intuitive experience may in part differentiate some intuitions from others. In particular, we posited that moral and creative intuitions may be imbued with a higher level of affective arousal than problem-solving intuition. Not only is further research necessary to substantiate this claim, but there is also another meaningful distinction concerning affect not discussed thus far. Although we have explored intuitions with regard to the arousal dimension of affect, it is worth noting that affective experiences can also be categorized by their degree of pleasantness (see Russell, 2003). Extant literature is relatively limited with regard to assessing the degree to which different types of intuition may vary along the pleasantness dimension. However, it bears mentioning that researchers have identified some intuitions as being of a pleasant variety and others of a more unpleasant nature. For example, when executives make certain intuitive decisions, they often experience positive feelings of excitement and harmony (Agor, 1986). As Michael Eisner, CEO of Walt Disney, has stated, the sensation associated with certain intuitive judgments is often like, 'looking at a great piece of art for the first time' (as reported in Hayashi, 2001, p. 62). Other notable examples of intuition involve negative emotions. For example, Klein (1998) reports an incident in which, when fighting a fire, a fire lieutenant immediately ordered his men to leave a burning residential house when he started to feel as if something was 'not right'. As soon as his men left the building, the floor on which they had been standing collapsed. Our own field research (in progress) on firefighters similarly suggests that these intuitions are often associated with negative affect. Likewise, other empirical research has shown that prior to airline disasters, pilots often have an unpleasant feeling that something is amiss (Bangs, 2004).

---

[5] Astute readers will notice that the notion of problem-solving intuitions being grounded in incubation goes against the claim, advanced here, that problem-solving intuitions tend to involve little to no incubation. Clearly further work is necessary to conclude whether incubation can be a precursor to at least some instances of non-creative intuition.

While the intuitions in the examples above may fit the problem-solving or creative types, scholars have suggested that moral intuitions may also be either positive or negative in their valence. Indeed, in conceptualizing moral judgments (and positing that these judgments arise intuitively), Haidt (2001, p. 817) defines them as 'evaluations *(good vs. bad)* of the actions or character of a person that are made with respect to a set of virtues held to be obligatory by a culture or subculture' (italics added for emphasis). From both a philosophical and psychological perspective, the valence issue lies at the core of moral intuition; it is because a potential course of action feels 'right' (a pleasant feeling) or 'wrong' (an unpleasant feeling) that one develops a sense of how to behave ethically in a given situation. That said, as we have noted earlier, most research in this area has focused on negative emotions, such as disgust.

In sum, pleasant versus unpleasant affect would seem to be a relevant dimension to consider in evaluating the emotional underpinnings of moral intuitions, as well as the other types of intuition reviewed above. However, because current understanding concerning the nature of and variations along the various dimensions of affect in relation to intuitions is limited, further research is necessary, especially regarding the role of the pleasantness dimension, with regard to the different types of intuition enumerated above.

When Do People Trust and Use their Intuitions?

The Case of Moral Intuition

As noted earlier, at present most of the research on the factors leading people to trust their intuitions has focused on problem-solving intuitions. However, research on moral intuition has expanded in recent years (e.g. Greene and Haidt, 2002; Haidt, 2007; Haidt and Graham, 2007). While this research has suggested that moral intuitions should generally be followed, further research is needed to identify the conditions under which individuals actually do (or do not) – or even when they should (or should not) – follow their moral intuitions.

In addition, it would be helpful to stand back and investigate the factors that facilitate or impede the formation of moral intuitions. For example, Moore and Loewenstein (2004) argue that self-interest exerts an influence on decision making primarily via nonconscious channels, whereas consideration of ethical and professional obligations tends to be activated through more conscious cognitive avenues. As such, in situations in which self-interest and ethics are in clear tension, individuals often focus on self-interest concerns through a largely nonconscious, automatic process, and hence, fail to notice or devote significant thought to considerations of ethics. This phenomenon aligns with the position put forth by Tenbrunsel and Messick (2004) that individuals have a tendency to engage in self-deception so as to disguise or distort violations of ethical principles. In essence, individuals often do not 'see' the ethical elements of a given scenario because they 'fade' the ethics from the dilemma, leaving only an 'ethically colorless' view of the issue. This tendency not to recognize that an ethical issue exists until it is perhaps too late has been used to partially account for recent corporate scandals (see Bazerman, 2006; Moore and Loewenstein, 2004).

Integrating the observations noted above with our earlier discussion of the features of moral intuition, it appears that the relationship between the nonconscious system of processing and ethical judgments is complex and potentially contradictory: nonconscious processes often work against the identification of problems as being ethical, but when a problem is categorized as an ethical issue (see Sonenshein, 2007), the nonconscious system produces moral intuitions that provide decision-makers with a sense of right and wrong. Given this conundrum, researchers might fruitfully explore how to overcome the nonconscious barriers of moral problem recognition in order to better facilitate the generation of moral intuitions.

As an aside, the issue of ethical fading in more mundane, 'real life' situations may also serve as evidence that assessing moral intuitions via scenarios – where the ethical components of the decisions are quite obvious (e.g. someone will die) – may be overly artificial (Hauser et al., 2007). This suggests that in the future researchers should employ scenarios that vary in the starkness of their ethical overtones.

The Potential Role of Mindfulness

The above discussion suggests that individuals can only use intuitions when they are aware of them. While various scholars have commented on whether and how conscious and nonconscious systems of processing may be engaged concurrently (e.g. Epstein, 2002; Ferreira et al., 2006; Hodgkinson and Sadler-Smith, 2003; Hodgkinson, Langan-Fox and Sadler-Smith, 2008), and debated the extent to which they are linked to particular neurological pathways and related mechanisms (e.g. Hodgkinson, Langan-Fox and Sadler-Smith, 2008; Lieberman, 2000, 2007; Lieberman, Jarcho and Satpute, 2004), relatively little attention has focused on the extent to which and in what ways individuals can consciously adopt particular frames of mind that make them more or less aware of or attentive to the products that emerge from their nonconscious system of processing, such as their intuitive judgments.

Recent work has raised the possibility that the degree to which individuals are in touch with nonconscious operations (and the 'products' of the nonconscious system – e.g. intuitive judgments) may be related to the concept of *mindfulness* (Brown and Ryan, 2003; Brown, Ryan and Creswell, 2007; Weick and Sutcliffe, 2006). Following the lead of Brown and Ryan (2003: p. 822), we conceptualize mindfulness in a manner consistent with its historical meaning among Buddhist and other contemplative traditions: 'the state of being attentive to and aware of what is taking place in the present'. From this perspective, mindfulness is a type of consciousness that occurs when one's attention to the present situation becomes highly open and receptive (Brown and Ryan, 2003). It should be noted that the heightened sense of awareness and attention to the present moment that marks mindfulness applies not only to events surrounding the individual, but also to the mental and emotional processes that occur *within* the individual. These two distinct loci of attention for an individual experiencing mindfulness are reflected in the claim that mindfulness involves the 'clear and single-minded awareness of what actually happens *to* us and *in* us, at the successive moments of perception' (Thera, 1972, p. 5, emphasis as per original).

When individuals are in a state of mindfulness, they may have greater awareness or access to internal processes or the products thereof to which they might otherwise not be attuned. In this vein, Brown and Ryan (2003) have demonstrated that mindfulness is positively related to the degree of congruity individuals experience between their explicit and implicit emotions. This suggests that individuals are more consciously aware of or in touch with their underlying emotions to the extent that they are in mindful states of consciousness.

Drawing on the notion that mindfulness may perhaps attune individuals to nonconsciously based phenomena, Sadler-Smith and Shefy (2007) included a mindfulness task in the catalog of techniques they employed with the aim of training sample managers who were enrolled in an MBA program to become more 'intuitively aware'. Following a period of instruction designed to inculcate awareness of mindfulness and related states of consciousness, the participants of this study reported that they were better able to identify the contexts in which they were most in tune with their intuitions and became more confident in their ability to draw on their intuitions in decision-making situations. These observations suggest that scholars might benefit from further exploring the role of mindfulness in permitting individuals to become more aware of certain intuitive judgments that might otherwise be difficult to access (e.g. moral intuitions). Taking this further, such a perspective shifts attention from a focus on conscious *versus* nonconscious decision making toward a focus on how we can use one information system (conscious, analytical) to help us become more aware of the other system (nonconscious, intuitive). Building on the notion derived from dual-process theories of cognition that both processing systems may play complementary roles in decision making, we next examine how intuitions (of different types) can be used in tandem with analysis to produce effective decisions.

When Should Intuition Be Used?

Earlier, we provided a brief overview of research concerned with when individuals should use their intuition to make decisions. We noted the role of expertise and task characteristics toward this end. Additionally, we argued that effective decision making may, in some instances, involve the combined use of intuition and analysis. Unfortunately, despite arguments that individuals may benefit from switching between intuitive and analytical approaches to problem-solving (e.g. Hodgkinson and Sadler-Smith, 2003; Louis and Sutton, 1991; Simon, 1987), little research agreement has emerged concerning the preferred sequence by which individuals should employ these approaches (e.g. Should one take stock of one's intuition first and then engage in analysis? Or, should one expect intuition to play a key role after engaging in an analytical decision-making process?).

Drawing on the framework advanced here, we suggest that part of the reason for the existence of different prescriptions is that scholars have not considered or specified how different types of intuition may be relevant to consider during different stages of the decision-making process. In particular, individuals are likely to experience problem-solving and moral intuitions prior to assessing a problem analytically. Such intuitions, as argued above, tend to appear with little to no incubation, in direct response to a problem scenario. Taking note of these intuitions as they occur may be critical in light of evidence that individuals may be led inappropriately astray from highly accurate intuitive judgments when they are instructed to adopt an analytical approach to making decisions (e.g. Fallshore and Schooler, 1995; McMackin and Slovic, 2000; Wilson and Schooler, 1991). Indeed, as discussed above, the emergence of moral intuitions early in the decision-making process should be given particular weight, given that the nonconscious system often filters out the ethical features of a problem. Hence, when individuals are fortunate to experience these intuitions, they should take careful note of them. At the same time, we suggest that individuals should be wary of immediately acting upon their intuitions – particularly problem-solving intuitions. The roots of this admonishment lie in the vast body of research on intuitive and heuristic biases (e.g. Ariely, 2008; Bazerman, 2006; Tversky and Kahneman, 1974). Accordingly, for a decision-making problem in which a decision does not need to be made immediately, a reasonable course of action may be for individuals to take note of their problem-solving and/or moral intuitions at the outset, and then perhaps put these intuitions on hold. By recording initial intuitions and then temporarily placing them on the backburner, decision-makers may be less prone to make confirmation biases (see Nickerson, 1998, for review) as they enter into a more conscious phase of problem analysis.

Following an analytical assessment of the problem, we contend that individuals should not only return to their initial intuitions, and assess them vis-à-vis the products of their analysis, but they should also remain attuned to the emergence of creative intuitions. In contrast to problem-solving and moral intuitions, individuals are likely to experience creative intuitions after a problem has been given a period of consideration and incubation. Creative intuitions may serve as integrating mechanisms – gut feelings that tie together and perhaps build upon a variety of aspects associated with a complex problem. Thus, in recommending that intuition be applied as a way to 'synthesize' information that has already been gathered and analyzed, Agor (1986) appears to be addressing the type of intuition referred to here as 'creative'. Dijksterhuis and Nordgren (2006) advocate a similar role for intuition (i.e. as a synthesizing form of cognition) and suggest that the effectiveness of such intuitions is likely to vary with the amount of analytical information gathering as well as the length of the incubation period that occurred preceding the emergence of the intuition.

Taken together, we speculate that individuals may benefit from intuition both before and after engaging in analysis. The key to making sense of the multitude of prescriptions on this issue is to understand which type of intuition one is considering. Future research should seek to validate and extend upon these conjectures to better orient our understanding of when, in the course of the decision-making process, individuals should use their intuitions.

To close this subsection, we recognize that we have for the sake of parsimony limited our discussion of future research thus far to the three questions we used to organize the conceptual portion of our chapter. However, researchers also need to ask new questions, and therefore explore even more unchartered territory. For example, research on intuitions has largely been at the individual level. Much less attention has been paid to how individuals within problem-solving groups may come to combine their intuitions to make decisions. Similarly, given that moral intuitions are culturally bound (Haidt and Kesebir, 2008), it would be interesting to see how multicultural groups process moral issues. These new questions may entail developing new methods – such as observational and other qualitative methods. It is to such methodological issues that we now turn.

Measuring Intuition

As we have discussed, there is little consensus regarding how intuitions are captured methodologically. At some level, this is not surprising. Some methods are aimed at assessing specific types of intuitions (e.g. problem-solving or moral). Some are concerned with how intuitions are processed (e.g. neurological approaches), while others are more concerned with outcomes in the form of intuitive judgments (e.g. direct instruction). Hence, one might expect that different methods will reflect the different aims of researchers. However, a common issue to most of the measurement methods we have reviewed is the question of whether intuition is really occurring at all. With the possible exception of neurological and physiological methods, our measures are, at best, indirect. Of course, this criticism can be leveled against many psychological measures.

Given the paucity of research addressing the methodological issues involved in capturing intuition, several avenues of inquiry remain open. For example, work needs to be undertaken to assess the validity and reliability of the various measures currently in use. Moreover, it would be interesting to use multiple measurements within single studies or across sequences of studies in order to assess the degree to which they result in similar sets of findings. In so doing, it would be especially interesting to compare intuition measurements aimed at specific types of intuition to see if there is an empirical basis for the tripartite distinction we have enumerated in this chapter.

Another potentially fruitful avenue for research would entail considering new combinations of the approaches summarized in Table 1.2. For example, would using direct instruction rather than visual images (e.g. abandoned children living on the streets) trigger activation of the neural mechanisms implicated in the operation of intuitive systems? Might it be possible to verify retrospective accounts of intuition using neurological and physiological tests? Ideally, findings obtained through advances in physiological and neurological measures of intuition will converge with those obtained by means of conventional self-report, interview, and observational measures.

Finally, we encourage researchers to continue to craft new measures and methods for capturing intuition. In particular, an examination of Table 1.1 reveals a need for additional measures of creative intuition. Moreover, moral intuition researchers might borrow from research on affect priming, or research in neurophysiology that uses visual images, as opposed to relying exclusively on scenarios to trigger moral intuitions.

CONCLUSION

We are heartened that scholars operating in fields within or related to industrial and organizational psychology have increasingly taken up the 'nonconscious' torch and used it to illuminate understanding of a variety of work-related phenomena. The recent rise in research concerning the role of intuition in effective problem-solving, moral judgments, and creativity illustrate the diversity of these efforts. Our review suggests that although intuition research has converged on some key definitional issues, further conceptual development is certainly needed for the field to maintain its momentum. While we focused here on whether there are different types of intuition, it should be noted that scholars have only recently begun to agree on a scientific conceptualization of the construct. There is perhaps room for additional work on what intuition is at a general level, as well as whether there are various types of intuition in the more specific senses explored herein. Equally critical, our review suggests that empirical research on intuition remains largely fragmented in terms of how intuition is measured. Further work is thus necessary to better understand the most effective approaches for capturing intuition empirically. We thus appeal for more research that clarifies and assesses intuitive processes and outcomes.

REFERENCES

Abernathy, C. M. & Hamm, R. M. (1995). *Surgical Intuition: What It Is and Where to Get It*, Philadelphia: Hanley & Belfus.

Agor, W. A. (1986). The logic of intuition: how top executives make important decisions. *Organizational Dynamics*, **14**, 5–18.

Allinson, C. W. & Hayes, J. (1996). The cognitive style index: a measure of intuition-analysis for organizational research. *Journal of Management Studies*, **33**, 119–35.

Amabile, T. M. (1996). *Creativity in Context*, Boulder, CO: Westview.

Anderson, S., Bechara, A., Damasio, H., Tranel, D. and Damasio, A. (1999) Impairment of social and moral behavior related to early damage in human prefrontal cortex. *Nature Neuroscience*, **2**, 1032–1037.

Ariely, D. (2008). *Predictably Irrational*, New York: HarperCollins.

Banaji, M. R., Hardin, C. & Rothman, A. J. (1993). Implicit stereotyping in person judgment. *Journal of Personality and Social Psychology*, **65**, 272–81.

Bangs, K. (2004). Hearing voices: intuition and accident avoidance. *Business and Commercial Aviation*, **95** (3), 44–49.

Bargh, J. A. (1996). Principles of automaticity. In E. T. Higgins & A. Kruglanski (Eds), *Social Psychology: Handbook of Basic Principles* (pp. 169–83). New York: Guilford Press.

Bargh, J. A. & Chartrand, T. L. (1999). The unbearable automaticity of being. *American Psychologist*, **54**, 462–79.

Barnard, C. I. (1938). *The Functions of the Executive*, Cambridge, MA: Harvard University Press.

Barron, F. B. & Harrington, D. M. (1981). Creativity, intelligence, and personality. *Annual Review of Psychology*, **32**, 439–76.

Bastick, T. (1982). *Intuition: How We Think and Act*, New York: John Wiley & Sons, Ltd.

Bazerman, M. H. (2006). *Judgment in Managerial Decision Making*, 6th edn, Hoboken, NJ: John Wiley & Sons, Ltd.

Bechara, A., Damasio, H., Tranel, D. *et al.* (1997). Deciding advantageously before knowing the advantageous strategy. *Science*, **275**, 1293–95.

Blattberg, R. C. & Hoch, S. J. (1990). Database models and managerial intuition: 50% model + 50% manager. *Management Science*, **36**, 887–99.

Bless, H., Bohner, G., Schwarz, N. *et al.* (1990). Mood and persuasion: a cognitive response analysis. *Personality and Social Psychology Bulletin*, **16**, 331–45.

Bless, H., Clore, G. L., Schwarz, N. *et al.* (1996). Mood and the use of scripts: does being in a happy mood really lead to mindlessness? *Journal of Personality and Social Psychology*, **71**, 665–79.

Bonabeau, E. (2003). Don't trust your gut. *Harvard Business Review*, **81** (5), 116–23.

Bowers, K. S., Regehr, G., Balthazard, C. *et al.* (1990). Intuition in the context of discovery. *Cognitive Psychology*, **22**, 72–110.

Briggs, K. C. & Myers, I. B. (1976). *Myers–Briggs Type Indicator*, Palo Alto, CA: Consulting Psychologists Press.

Brown, K. W. & Ryan, R. M. (2003). The benefits of being present: mindfulness and its role in psychological well-being. *Journal of Personality and Social Psychology*, **84**, 822–48.

Brown, K. W., Ryan, R. M. & Creswell, J. D. (2007). Mindfulness: theoretical foundations and evidence for its salutary effects. *Psychological Inquiry*, **18**, 211–37.

Bruner, J. S. (1962). *On Knowing*, Cambridge, MA: Harvard University Press.

Burke, L. A. & Miller, M. K. (1999). Taking the mystery out of intuitive decision making. *Academy of Management Executive*, **13** (4), 91–99.

Casebeer, W. & Churchland, P. (2003). The neural mechanisms of moral cognition: a multiple-aspect approach to moral judgment and decision-making. *Biology and Philosophy*, **18**, 169–94.

Croskerry, P. (2006). Critical thinking and decisionmaking: avoiding the perils of thin-slicing. *Annals of Emergency Medicine*, **48**, 720–22.

Crossan, M. M., Lane, H. W. & White, R. E. (1999). An organizational learning framework: from intuition to institution. *Academy of Management Review*, **24**, 522–37.

Cushman, F., Young, L. & Hauser, M. (2006). The role of conscious reasoning and intuition in moral judgment. *Psychological Science*, **17**, 1082–89.

Cyert, R. M. & March, J. G. (1963). *A Behavioral Theory of the Firm*, Englewood Cliffs, NJ: Prentice-Hall.

Dane, E. & Pratt, M. G. (2007). Exploring intuition and its role in managerial decision making. *Academy of Management Review*, **32**, 33–54.

Dane, E., Rockmann, K. & Pratt, M. G. (2005). *Should I trust my gut? The role of task characteristics in intuitive and analytical decision-making*. Paper presented at the 2005 meeting of the Academy of Management. Honolulu, HI.

Davis-Floyd, R. & Davis, E. (1996). Intuition as authoritative knowledge in midwifery and homebirth. *Medical Anthropology Quarterly*, **10** (2), 237–69.

Dawes, R. M., Faust, D. & Meehl, P. E. (1989). Clinical versus actuarial judgment. *Science*, **31**, 1668–74.

Denes-Raj, V. & Epstein, S. (1994). Conflict between intuitive and rational processing: when people behave against their better judgment. *Journal of Personality and Social Psychology*, **66**, 819–29.

Devine, P. G. (1989). Stereotypes and prejudice: their automatic and controlled components. *Journal of Personality and Social Psychology*, **56**, 5–18.

Dijksterhuis, A. (2004). Think different: the merits of unconscious thought in preference development and decision making. *Journal of Personality and Social Psychology*, **87**, 586–98.

Dijksterhuis, A., Bos, M. W., Nordgren, L. F. *et al.* (2006). On making the right choice: the deliberation-without-attention effect. *Science*, **311**, 1005–7.

Dijksterhuis, A. and Meurs, T. (2006) Where creativity resides: the generative power of unconscious thought. *Consciousness and Cognition*, **15**, 135–146.

Dijksterhuis, A & Nordgren, L. F. (2006). A theory of unconscious thought. *Perspectives on Psychological Science*, **1** (2), 95–109.

Dreyfus, H. L. & Dreyfus, S. E. (1986). *Mind Over Machine: The Power of Human Intuition and Expertise in the Era of the Computer*, New York: The Free Press.

Duggan, W. (2007). *Strategic Intuition*, New York: Columbia University Press.

Elsbach, K. D. & Barr, P. S. (1999). The effects of mood on individuals' use of structured decision protocols. *Organization Science*, **10**, 181–98.

Epstein, S. (1994). Integration of the cognitive and psychodynamic unconscious. *American Psychologist*, **49**, 709–24.

Epstein, S. (2002). Cognitive-experiential self-theory of personality. In T. Millon & M. J. Lerner (Eds), *Comprehensive Handbook of Psychology, Vol. 5. Personality and Social Psychology* (pp. 159–84). Hoboken, NJ: John Wiley & Sons, Ltd.

Epstein, S. (2008). Intuition from the perspective of cognitive-experiential self-theory. In H. Plessner, C. Betsch & T. Betsch (Eds), *Intuition in Judgment and Decision Making* (pp. 23–37). New York: Lawrence Erlbaum Associates.

Epstein, S., Pacini, R., Denes-Raj, V. and Heier, H. (1996) Individual differences in intuitive-experiential and analytical-rational thinking styles. *Journal of Personality and Social Psychology*, **71**, 390–405.

Ericsson, K. A. & Charness, N. (1994). Expert performance: its structure and acquisition. *American Psychologist*, **49**, 725–47.

Eslinger, P. and Damasio, A. (1985). Severe disturbance of higher cognition after bilateral frontal lobe ablation: Patient EVR. *Neurobiology*, **35**, 1731–1741.

Fallshore, M. & Schooler, J. W. (1995). Verbal vulnerability of perceptual expertise. *Journal of Experimental Psychology: Learning, Memory, and Cognition*, **21**, 1608–23.

Ferreira, M. B., Garcia-Marques, L., Sherman, S. J. *et al.* (2006). Automatic and controlled components of judgment and decision making. *Journal of Personality and Social Psychology*, **91**, 797–813.

Fiske, S. T. (1993). Controlling other people: the impact of power on stereotyping. *American Psychologist*, **48**, 621–28.

Garfield, M. J., Taylor, N. J., Dennis, A. R. *et al.* (2001). Research report: modifying paradigms—individual differences, creativity techniques, and exposure to ideas in group idea generation. *Information Systems Research*, **12**, 322–33.

George, J. M. (2007). Creativity in organizations. *Academy of Management Annals*, **1**, 439–77.

Gigerenzer (2007). *Gut Feelings: The Intelligence of the Unconscious*, New York: Viking.

Gladwell, M. (2005). *Blink: The Power of Thinking without Thinking*, New York: Little, Brown & Co.

Goodwin, S. A., Gubin, A., Fiske, S. T. *et al.* (2000). Power can bias impression processes: stereotyping subordinates by default and design. *Group Processes and Intergroup Relations*, **3**, 227–56.

Greene, J. & Haidt, J. (2002). How (and where) does moral judgment work? *Trends in Cognitive Sciences*, **6** (12), 517–23.

Greene, J., Nystrom, L., Engell, A. *et al.* (2004). The neural bases of cognitive conflict and control in moral judgment. *Neuron*, **44**, 389–400.

Greene, J., Sommerville, R., Nystrom, L. *et al.* (2001). An fMRI investigation of emotional engagement in moral judgment. *Science*, **293**, 2105–8.

Groopman, J. (2007). *How Doctors Think*, Boston, MA: Houghton Mifflin.

Haidt, J. (2001). The emotional dog and its rational tail: a social intuitionist approach to moral judgment. *Psychological Review*, **108**, 814–34.

Haidt, J. (2007). The new synthesis in moral philosophy. *Science*, **316**, 998–1002.

Haidt, J. & Graham, J. (2007). When morality opposes justice: conservatives have moral intuitions that liberals may not recognize. *Social Justice Research*, **20**, 98–116.

Haidt, J. & Hersh, M. A. (2001). Sexual morality: the cultures and emotions of conservatives and liberals. *Journal of Applied Social Psychology*, **31**, 191–221.

Haidt, J. & Joseph, C. (2004). Intuitive ethics: how innately prepared intuitions generate culturally variable virtues. *Daedalus*, **133** (4), 55–66.

Haidt, J. & Kesebir, S. (2008). In the forest of values: why moral intuitions are different from other kinds. In H. Plessner, C. Betsch & T. Betsch (Eds), *Intuition in Judgment and Decision Making* (pp. 209–29). New York: Lawrence Erlbaum Associates.

Haidt, J., Koller, S. H. & Dias, M. G. (1993). Affect, culture, and morality, or is it wrong to eat your dog? *Journal of Personality and Social Psychology*, **65**, 613–28.

Hammond, K. R., Hamm, R. M., Grassia, J. *et al.* (1987). Direct comparison of the efficacy of intuitive and analytical cognition in expert judgment. *IEEE Transactions on Systems, Man, and Cybernetics*, **17**, 753–70.

Hauser, M., Cushman, F., Young, L. *et al.* (2007). A dissociation between moral judgments and justifications. *Mind and Language*, **22** (1), 1–21.

Hayashi, A. M. (2001). When to trust your gut. *Harvard Business Review*, **79** (2), 59–65.

Hodgkinson, G. P., Langan-Fox, J. & Sadler-Smith, E. (2008). Intuition: a fundamental bridging construct in the behavioural sciences. *British Journal of Psychology*, **99**, 1–27.

Hodgkinson, G. P. & Sadler-Smith, E. (2003). Complex or unitary? A critique and empirical re-assessment of the Allinson-Hayes Cognitive Style Index. *Journal of Occupational and Organizational Psychology*, **76**, 243–68.

Hoffman, R. R., Crandall, B. & Shadbolt, N. (1998). Use of the critical decision method to elicit expert knowledge: a case study in the methodology of cognitive task analysis. *Human Factors*, 40, 254–76.

Hofstede, G. (2001). *Culture's Consequences*, 2nd edn, Thousand Oaks, CA: Sage.

Hogarth, R. M. (2001). *Educating Intuition*, Chicago: The University of Chicago Press.

Hsee, C. K. & Rottenstreich, Y. (2004). Music, pandas, and muggers: on the affective psychology of value. *Journal of Experimental Psychology: General*, 133, 23–30.

Isen, A. M. (2000). Positive affect decision making. In M. Lewis & J. M. Haviland-Jones (Eds), *Handbook of Emotions*, 2nd edn (pp. 417–35). New York: Guilford Press.

Isen, A. M., Means, B., Patrick, R. & Nowicki, G. (1982). Some factors influencing decision-making strategy and risk taking. In M. S. Clarke & S. T. Fiske (Eds), *Affect and Cognition*, (pp. 243–61). Hillsdale, NJ: Lawrence Erlbaum Associates.

Isenberg, D. J. (1984). How senior managers think. *Harvard Business Review*, 62 (6), 81–90.

Jones, T. M. (1991). Ethical decision making by individuals in organizations: an issue-contingent model. *Academy of Management Review*, 16, 366–95.

Jordan, C. H., Whitfield, M. & Zeigler-Hill, V. (2007). Intuition and the correspondence between implicit and explicit self-esteem. *Journal of Personality and Social Psychology*, 93, 1067–79.

Jung, C. G. (1933). *Psychological Types*, New York: Harcourt, Brace, and Company (first published in 1921).

Kaempf, G. L., Klein, G., Thordsen, M. L. *et al.* (1996). Decision making in complex naval command-and-control environments. *Human Factors*, 38, 220–31.

Kahneman, D. (2003). A perspective on judgment and choice. *American Psychologist*, 58, 697–720.

Kahneman, D., Slovic, P. & Tversky, A. (1982). *Judgment under Uncertainty: Heuristics and Biases*, Cambridge: Cambridge University Press.

Keltner, D., Gruenfeld, D. H. & Anderson, C. (2003). Power, approach, and inhibition. *Psychological Review*, 110, 265–84.

Khatri, N. & Ng, H. A. (2000). The role of intuition in strategic decision making. *Human Relations*, 53, 57–86.

King, L. A., Burton, C. M., Hicks, J. A. *et al.* (2007). Ghosts, UFOs, and magic: positive affect and the experiential system. *Journal of Personality and Social Psychology*, 92, 905–19.

Klein, G. (1998). *Sources of Power: How People Make Decisions*, Cambridge, MA: MIT Press.

Klein, G. (2003). *Intuition at Work*, New York: Doubleday.

Kohlberg, L. (1981). *Essays on Moral Development, Volume 1. The Philosophy of Moral Development: Moral Stages and the Idea of Justice*, San Francisco: Harper & Row.

Langer, E. (1989). *Mindfulness*, Reading, MA: Addison-Wesley.

Langley, A. (1995). Between 'paralysis by analysis' and 'extinction by instinct'. *Sloan Management Review*, 36 (3), 63–76.

Laughlin, P. (1980). Social combination processes of cooperative problem-solving groups on verbal intellective tasks. In M. Fishbein (Ed.), *Progress in Social Psychology*, Vol. 1 (pp. 127–55). Hillsdale, NJ: Lawrence Erlbaum Associates.

Lieberman, M. D. (2000). Intuition: a social cognitive neuroscience approach. *Psychological Bulletin*, 126, 109–37.

Lieberman, M. D. (2007). Social cognitive neuroscience: a review of core processes. *Annual Review of Psychology*, 58, 259–89.

Lieberman, M. D., Jarcho, J. M. & Satpute, A. B. (2004). Evidence-based and intuition-based self-knowledge: an fMRI study. *Journal of Personality and Social Psychology*, 87, 421–35.

Louis, M. R. & Sutton, R. I. (1991). Switching cognitive gears: from habits of mind to active thinking. *Human Relations*, **44**, 55–76.

Macrae, C. N., Milne, A. B. & Bodenhausen, G. V. (1994). Stereotypes as energy-saving devices: a peek inside the cognitive toolbox. *Journal of Personality and Social Psychology*, **66**, 37–47.

Marton, F., Fensham, P. & Chaiklin, S. (1994). A Nobel's eye view of scientific intuition: discussions with the Nobel prize-winners in physics, chemistry and medicine (1970–86). *International Journal of Science Education*, **16**, 457–73.

McCraty, R., Atkinson, M. & Bradley, R. (2004a). Electrophysiological evidence of intuition: Part 1. The surprising role of the heart. *The Journal of Alternative and Complementary Medicine*, **10**, 133–43.

McCraty, R., Atkinson, M. & Bradley, R. (2004b). Electrophysiological evidence of intuition: Part 2. A system-wide process? *The Journal of Alternative and Complementary Medicine*, **10**, 325–36.

McMackin, J. & Slovic, P. (2000). When does explicit justification impair decision making? *Applied Cognitive Psychology*, **14**, 527–41.

Meehl, P. E. (1954). *Clinical versus Statistical Prediction*, Minneapolis, MN: University of Minnesota Press.

Mikhail, J. (2007). Universal moral grammar: theory, evidence and the future. *Trends in Cognitive Science*, **11** (4), 143–52.

Miller, C. C. & Ireland, R. D. (2005). Intuition in strategic decision making: friend or foe in the fast-paced 21st century? *Academy of Management Executive*, **19** (1), 19–30.

Mintzberg, H. (1994). *The Rise and Fall of Strategic Planning*, New York: The Free Press.

Mitchell, J. R., Friga, P. N. & Mitchell, R. K. (2005). Untangling the intuition mess: intuition as a construct in entrepreneurship research. *Entrepreneurship Theory and Practice*, **29**, 653–79.

Moll, J., de Olivera-Souza, R., Eslinger, P. *et al.* (2002). The neural correlates of moral sensitivity: a functional magnetic resonance imaging investigation of basic moral emotions. *The Journal of Neuroscience*, **22**, 2730–36.

Moll, J., Zahn, R., de Olivera-Souza, R. *et al.* (2005). The neural basis of human moral cognition. *Nature Reviews Neuroscience*, **6**, 799–809.

Moore, D. A. & Loewenstein, G. (2004). Self-interest, automaticity, and the psychology of conflict of interest. *Social Justice Research*, **17**, 189–202.

Myers, D. G. (2002). *Intuition: Its Powers and Perils*, New Haven: Yale University Press.

Neuberg, S. L. & Fiske, S. T. (1987). Motivational influences on impression formation: outcome dependency, accuracy-driven attention, and individuating processes. *Journal of Personality and Social Psychology*, **53**, 431–44.

Nickerson, R. S. (1998). Confirmation bias: a ubiquitous phenomenon in many guises. *Review of General Psychology*, **2**, 175–220.

Pacini, R. & Epstein, S. (1999). The relation of rational and experiential information processing styles to personality, basic beliefs, and the ratio-bias problem. *Journal of Personality and Social Psychology*, **76**, 972–87.

Policastro, E. (1995). Creative intuition: an integrative review. *Creativity Research Journal*, **8**, 99–113.

Prietula, M. J. & Simon, H. A. (1989). The experts in your midst. *Harvard Business Review*, **67** (1), 120–24.

Quenk, N. L. (2000). *Essentials of Myers–Briggs Type Indicator Assessment*, New York: John Wiley & Sons, Ltd.

Raidl, M. H. & Lubart, T. I. (2000/2001). An empirical study of intuition and creativity. *Imagination, Cognition and Personality*, **20**, 217–30.

Reber, A. S. (1992). An evolutionary context for the cognitive unconscious. *Philosophical Psychology*, **5**, 33–51.

Rest, J. R. (1986). *Moral Development: Advances in Research and Theory*, Minneapolis: University of Minnesota Press.

Reynolds, S. J. (2006). A neurocognitive model of the ethical decision-making process: implications for study and practice. *Journal of Applied Psychology*, **91**, 737–48.

Rogers, P. & Wiseman, R. (2006). Self-perceived high intuitiveness: an initial exploration. *Imagination, Cognition and Personality*, **25** (2), 161–77.

Rorty, R. (1967). Intuition. In P. Edwards (Ed.), *Encyclopedia of Philosophy*. New York: MacMillan.

Ruder, M. & Bless, H. (2003). Mood and the reliance on the ease of retrieval heuristic. *Journal of Personality and Social Psychology*, **85**, 20–32.

Russell, J. A. (2003). Core affect and the psychological construction of emotion. *Psychological Review*, **110**, 145–72.

Sadler-Smith, E., Hodgkinson, G. P. & Sinclair, M. (2008). A matter of feeling? The role of intuition in entrepreneurial decision-making and behavior. In W. Zerbe, N. Ashkanasy & C. Hartel (Eds), *Research on Emotions in Organizations (Vol. 4), Emotions, Ethics, and Decision-Making* (pp. 35–55). Bingley: Emerald.

Sadler-Smith, E. & Shefy, E. (2004). The intuitive executive: understanding and applying 'gut feel' in decision making. *Academy of Management Executive*, **18** (4), 76–91.

Sadler-Smith, E. & Shefy, E. (2007). Developing intuitive awareness in management education. *Academy of Management Learning & Education*, **6**, 186–205.

Sadler-Smith, E. & Sparrow, P. R. (2008). Intuition in organizational decision-making. In G. P. Hodgkinson & W. H. Starbuck (Eds), *The Oxford Handbook of Organizational Decision Making* (pp. 305–24). Oxford: Oxford University Press.

Schneider, W. & Shiffrin, R. M. (1977). Controlled and automatic human information processing: detection, search, and attention. *Psychological Review*, **84**, 1–66.

Schoemaker, J. H. & Russo, J. E. (1993). A pyramid of decision approaches. *California Management Review*, **36** (1), 9–31.

Schwarz, N. (1990). Feelings as information: informational and motivational functions of affective states. In E. T. Higgins & R. Sorrentino (Eds), *Handbook of Motivation and Cognition: Foundations of Social Behavior*, Vol. 2 (pp. 527–61). New York: Guilford.

Schwarz, N. & Clore, G. L. (1983). Mood, misattribution, and judgments of well-being: informative and directive functions of affective states. *Journal of Personality and Social Psychology*, **45**, 513–23.

Shapiro, S. & Spence, M. T. (1997). Managerial intuition: a conceptual and operational framework. *Business Horizons*, **40** (1), 63–68.

Shirley, D. A. & Langan-Fox, J. (1996). Intuition: a review of the literature. *Psychological Reports*, **79**, 563–84.

Simon, H. A. (1987). Making management decisions: the role of intuition and emotion. *Academy of Management Executive*, **1** (1), 57–64.

Simon, H. A. (1996). *The Sciences of the Artificial*, 3rd edn, Cambridge, MA: MIT Press.

Simon, H. A. (1997). *Administrative Behavior*, 4th edn, New York: Free Press.

Simon, H. A. & Chase, W. G. (1973). Skill in chess. *American Scientist*, **61**, 394–403.

Sinclair, M., Sadler-Smith, E. & Hodgkinson, G. P. (2009). The role of intuition in strategic decision making. In L. A. Costanzo & R. B. McKay (Eds), *The Handbook of Research on Strategy and Foresight* (pp. 393–417). Cheltenham: Edward Elgar.

Sloman, S. A. (1996). The empirical case for two systems of reasoning. *Psychological Bulletin*, **119**, 3–22.

Small, D. A., Loewenstein, G. & Slovic, P. (2007). Sympathy and callousness: the impact of deliberative thought on donations to identifiable and statistical victims. *Organizational Behavior and Human Decision Processes*, **102**, 143–53.

Smith, S. M. & Dodds, R. A. (1999). Incubation. In M. A. Runco & S. R. Pritzker (Eds), *Encyclopedia of Creativity*, Vol. 2 (pp. 39–43). San Diego: Academic.

Smith, A., Thurkettle, M. A. & dela Cruz, F. (2004). Use of intuition by nursing students: instrument development and testing. *Journal of Advanced Nursing*, **47**, 614–22.

Sonenshein, S. (2007). The role of construction, intuition, and justification in responding to ethical issues at work: the sensemaking-intuition model. *Academy of Management Review*, **32**, 1022–40.

Stanovich, K. E. & West, R. F. (2000). Individual differences in reasoning: implications for the rationality debate? *Behavioral and Brain Sciences*, **23**, 645–65.

Sternberg, R. J. & Davidson, J. E. (1995). *The Nature of Insight*, Cambridge, MA: MIT Press.

Strack, F. & Deutsch, R. (2004). Reflective and impulsive determinants of social behavior. *Personality and Social Psychology Review*, **8**, 220–47.

Tenbrunsel, A. E. & Messick, D. M. (2004). Ethical fading: the role of self-deception in unethical behavior. *Social Justice Research*, **17**, 223–36.

Thera, N. (1972). *The Power of Mindfulness*, San Francisco: Unity Press.

Tversky, A. & Kahneman, D. (1974). Judgment under uncertainty: heuristics and biases. *Science*, **185**, 1124–31.

Vaughan, F. E. (1979). *Awakening Intuition*, New York: Doubleday.

Weick, K. E. & Sutcliffe, K. M. (2006). Mindfulness and the quality of organizational attention. *Organization Science*, **17**, 514–24.

Wild, K. W. (1938). *Intuition*, Cambridge: Cambridge University Press.

Wilson, T. D. & Schooler, J. W. (1991). Thinking too much: introspection can reduce the quality of preferences and decisions. *Journal of Personality and Social Psychology*, **60**, 181–92.

Chapter 2

TRANSFER OF TRAINING 1988–2008: AN UPDATED REVIEW AND AGENDA FOR FUTURE RESEARCH

Timothy T. Baldwin
Kelley School of Business, Indiana University, Bloomington, IN, USA

J. Kevin Ford
Department of Psychology, Michigan State University, E. Lansing, MI, USA

Brian D. Blume
School of Management, University of Michigan, Flint, MI, USA

In organizational contexts, positive transfer of training – the extent to which the learning that results from a training experience transfers to the job and leads to meaningful changes in work performance – is generally regarded as the *paramount* concern of training efforts (Goldstein and Ford, 2002). The critical point is that positive transfer is more than a function of original learning in a training experience. For transfer to have occurred, learned behavior must be generalized to the job context and maintained over a period of time.

Twenty years ago, the first two authors (Baldwin and Ford, 1988) reviewed and critically analyzed the research literature devoted to transfer of training. They observed a growing recognition of a transfer 'problem' in organizational contexts whereby there was concern that too little of the training conducted in organizations was positively transferring to the job. Existing reviews of the more general training literature of the time were mixed in their assessment of the utility of the extant research for understanding and improving transfer. Some had concluded that the existing literature offered little of value to trainers and researchers concerned with transfer (Campbell, 1971). Others, however, were suggesting that practitioners too often failed to apply the scientific knowledge that did exist (Goldstein, 1980; Wexley, 1984).

International Review of Industrial and Organizational Psychology, 2009, Volume 24.
Edited by G. P. Hodgkinson and J. K. Ford. Copyright © 2009 John Wiley & Sons, Ltd

Rather than argue for one viewpoint or the other, the goal of the 1988 review was to 'provide a critique of the existing transfer research and to suggest directions for future research' (Baldwin and Ford, 1988, p. 64). Toward that end, the authors presented a specific definition of the conditions of transfer which included the knowledge and skills acquired as a function of training and the retention of the training content. Transfer was defined as the generalization of knowledge and skills acquired in training to the job and the maintenance and enhancement of that initial learning over time. The researchers further presented an organizing framework consisting of three categories of training input factors: training design characteristics, trainee characteristics and work environment characteristics. The review uncovered 63 empirical studies spanning the period of 1907–1987 and served as something of a 'call to arms' for a more concerted research effort to address the key issues associated with transfer of training (Kraiger, 2001).

It has now been two decades since the publication of that original review and it has been gratifying to see the explosion of interest in training transfer since that time. The 1988 review has been extensively cited in research papers from many different disciplines and these citations have continued unabated throughout the full 20 years. It is clear that transfer of training is widely recognized as an important arena for research and practice.

With that in mind, the time seemed right to again take stock of the state of transfer research, and to offer an updated agenda for moving forward. More specifically, the purpose of this chapter is threefold. First, we identify the significant advances in empirical research since 1988. Toward that end, we systematically analyzed 140 journal articles that cited our prior review in the intervening 20 years. In the course of our analysis, we highlight several well-designed studies which have explored important transfer relationships. Our intent was to assess the progress made with respect to several significant limitations in the research literature circa 1988, and to spotlight the type and form of empirical investigations that are providing the best yield in new transfer knowledge.

Second, we briefly discuss two *conceptual* advances that help clarify and expand our understanding of transfer. In 1988, we proposed two dimensions of transfer, generalization and maintenance, and presented a set of factors that might influence those two dimensions. Since then, other researchers have made a compelling case for a multidimensional perspective of transfer and we review and comment on that work. We also discuss other intriguing new work that reconceptualizes and categorizes different types of training content and linking different content types to correspondingly different transfer objectives.

Third, we use our review of the existing body of transfer research as a springboard for presenting what we believe are some timely and important directions for the future of transfer research. These directions include exploring the 'personalization' of transfer by trainees, examining transfer experiences as *episodes* in organizational life, and applying different models of change to understand transfer phenomena.

ADVANCES IN EMPIRICAL TRANSFER RESEARCH

As a starting point for our review, we systematically searched for all journal articles that had cited the Baldwin and Ford (1988) review since the time of its publication. We then categorized each study in terms of task/training content, variables studied, research design, transfer criteria, and key results. A first observation was that many of these studies were from disciplines *outside* the fields of management or industrial psychology. Indeed, interest in transfer issues extends to disciplines such as education, health care, industrial engineering, ergonomics, advertising, and several others.

In all, we found nearly 300 articles with at least one Baldwin and Ford (1988) citation, but a significant number of those articles were only tangentially concerned with transfer, *per se*. We therefore narrowed our domain to 140 articles that were primarily focused on training transfer. Most of these articles were published in psychology and human resource management journals, such as *Personnel Psychology*, *Journal of Applied Psychology*, *International Journal of Training and Development*, and *Human Resource Development Quarterly*. Included in our set were 7 qualitative reviews of transfer, 2 meta-analyses relevant to transfer (i.e. Alliger *et al.*, 1997; Taylor, Russ-Eft and Chan, 2005) and 17 nonempirical reviews or commentaries. The remaining 114 articles were empirical studies.

For the empirical papers, we further delineated whether a study described an *intervention* to enhance transfer or was a study of one or more factors thought to predict transfer outcomes. Studies were also classified in terms of being lab or field based and cross-sectional or longitudinal in research design.[1]

Taken as a whole, the studies in our sample reveal at least four encouraging research trends that represent significant advances since 1988: (1) researchers now increasingly get beyond simple motor tasks and study the transfer of complex and authentic training content, (2) there is a notable increase in the use and investigation of actual *interventions* expressly designed to enhance transfer outcomes, (3) there has been a significant movement to look outside of the training design itself to explore pre- and posttraining influences on transfer, and (4) there has been a far greater variety of measures and time intervals used to evaluate transfer. We elaborate and comment on each of these advances below.

Studying Complex and Authentic Learning Content

The dramatic increase in training transfer research has led to a much wider range of samples and skills included in studies over the last 20 years. Baldwin and Ford (1988) found many of the studies had used simple motor and memory tasks completed in laboratory settings with college students. A major limitation

---

[1] A summary table of all 140 studies is available from the authors. Requests should be submitted electronically to Brian D. Blume of the University of Michigan, Flint at: blume@umflint.edu

of such tasks is that they do not mirror the more complex, organizationally relevant tasks that typically make up employee training programs. In addition, the predominate use of student samples invariably limits the generalizability of the results found in such studies.

Fortunately, research samples in training transfer studies now commonly include business employees and managers, health professionals (e.g. nurses and doctors), public safety workers and technical or computer specialists. Studies now also cover a much wider range of training content as well.

For example, Kirwan and Birchall (2006) studied nurse managers who participated in a 12-day management development program. Tracey, Tannenbaum and Kavanagh (1995) investigated new supermarket managers participating in supervisory skills training. Burke et al. (2002) researched hazardous waste workers in a study of safety training, while Kirkman et al. (2006) examined transfer results from a computer skills training program using data collected from 40 geographically dispersed *teams* in a high-technology company.

The increase in diverse samples and authentic skills is a positive trend that has the potential to increase the generalizability of training transfer findings. At the same time, this is an area that remains sorely in need of further systematic work. As noted by Goldstein and Ford (2002), once transfer validity has been established, the next steps are to consider issues of intraorganizational and interorganizational validity. Questions rightfully arise regarding the extent to which findings from a single sample of learners, or particular training content, can be compared to another sample in the same or different organizational settings. For example, if a specific training approach has proven effective in enabling pharmaceutical sales managers to transfer interpersonal skills back to their workplace, does this mean that a similar approach will be effective with doctors who are being trained in interpersonal skills to work more cooperatively with their hospital nursing staff?

So, while the movement away from artificially simple and contrived learning tasks is encouraging, there is still a need to develop categories or taxonomies of skills and contexts that can lead to cumulating results of transfer studies across different types of knowledge and skill training. One grossly understudied factor impacting transfer remains the objectives of the training in question. Indeed, we find it curious that such information is still conspicuously absent in the reporting of most transfer studies. It is difficult to contemplate a cumulative body of evidence that would provide practical guidance to learning professionals without further classification and taxonomic work on just *what* is being trained, and what objectives are desired. As Campbell (1989) noted, the question of whether training can work (transfer) has now been affirmatively answered. The more pertinent questions regard what learning content and which learning events can best promote mastery of key knowledge and skills. This orientation leads to different types of research questions such as what should be the content of a training program in leadership and how should it be structured differently across different learner populations and organizational contexts? It is the investigation of theory-driven substantive issues like those that will most advance the field in the next 20 years.

One good example of such work is a study by Heslin, Vandewalle and Latham (2006) in which the researchers found that the implicit person theories held by trainees in an employee coaching program had significant effects on their subsequent coaching behavior. The researchers further explored ways in which implicit person assumptions could be induced and strengthened in a population of coaching trainees. The movement toward the study of authentic training content in naturally occurring contexts (not contrived for research studies) has been one of the most positive shifts in transfer research of the last two decades. It is a trend that must continue if the field is to advance and inform future training design and implementation.

Increased Focus on Transfer Interventions

One of the predominant limitations of the research literature reviewed in 1988 was that it was, for the most part, not action oriented. That is, most existing studies at that time stopped at the point of identifying, describing or measuring factors that may influence transfer without investigating how those factors might be effectively *changed or managed.* More specifically, of all the studies described in the Baldwin and Ford (1988) review, only those dealing with training design dealt much with change or intervention.

Twenty years later, there has been a notable increase in the introduction and study of different interventions before, during and after training experiences. In the pretraining period, for example, Karl and Ungsrithong (1992) examined the impact of realistic training previews. They found that when quantity of information was held constant across training preview conditions, the optimistic training preview had a more positive impact on outcome expectations, motivation, learning, reactions to training, and training transfer than the realistic training preview.

Other researchers have looked at the effects of how training can be framed prior to a training event. Martocchio (1992) framed a computer training program as either an opportunity or a neutral experience. He found that, even after controlling for pretraining expectations about computer usage, trainees in the opportunity condition had higher efficacy and learning and lower computer anxiety than trainees in the neutral condition. Similarly, Quinones (1995) examined the impact of labeling upcoming training as remedial or advanced. He found that the training assignment (as moderated by attributions and expectations) impacted fairness perceptions and motivation to learn. Motivation, in turn, had a positive effect on learning. While these findings are intriguing, it must also be noted that the framing effects have yet to be linked directly to training transfer.

Intervention in the design of the training includes some intriguing applications of error training/management. For example, Heimbeck *et al.* (2003)

allowed trainees to make errors in the belief that such mistakes might lead to the richest and most lasting (transferred) learning outcomes. Results indicated that training transfer (near and far) was greater for trainees given error training with error management instructions compared to an error training condition and to a group that was prevented from making errors during the skill acquisition phase. In addition, Gully et al. (2002) examined the effectiveness of error training for trainees in a decision-making simulation with different levels of cognitive ability, openness to experience, and conscientiousness. Findings suggested that the effectiveness of error training is dependent on the cognitive ability and the dispositional traits of trainees.

Baldwin (1992) examined the use of negative and positive model displays on outcomes of a behavior modeling training program. Trainees in a program on assertive communication who observed a combination of positive and negative model displays had both greater retention and a higher level of generalization of the trained skills. Holladay and Quinones (2003) examined the relationship of practice variability, self-efficacy and near and far transfer. They found that variable practice was superior to constant practice in promoting high levels of self-efficacy. In addition, self-efficacy served as a mediator between practice variability and far transfer.

There has also been a significant amount of research in the area of behavior modeling. Taylor, Russ-Eft and Chan (2005) performed a meta-analysis on 66 (i.e. 9 published and 57 unpublished) studies that evaluated the effects of behavior modeling training on job behavior. They found that for training that incorporated behavior modeling, transfer was greatest when mixed (negative and positive) models were presented, when practice included trainee-generated scenarios, when trainees were instructed to set goals, when trainees' superiors were also trained, and when rewards and sanctions were instituted in the work environment (Taylor, Russ-Eft and Chan, 2005).

Investigation of *posttraining* interventions has also increased and among those studied are relapse prevention (e.g. Gaudine and Saks, 2004; Noe, Sears and Fullenkamp, 1990), self-management, goal setting, training in self-talk, and posttraining instructor follow-ups (May and Kahnweiler, 2000; Russ-Eft, 2002). Although not unequivocal, the findings generally show positive effects and suggest that transfer is quite susceptible to intervention (Burke and Baldwin, 1999). A study by Gist, Bavetta and Stevens (1990) explored the use of two popular posttraining interventions: goal setting only versus goal setting and self-management (the latter included identifying obstacles and a plan to overcome them, self-monitoring progress in the implementation of plans, and using self-reinforcement methods to motivate interim accomplishments). After training MBA students on negotiation skills, Gist, Bavetta and Stevens (1990) found that skill generalization was more limited among the goal setting only trainees as compared to the trainees that also received the self-management intervention. While trainees in the goal setting only condition generalized fewer skills to the novel tasks, these skills tended to be used more repeatedly. In contrast, trainees who also received the self-management intervention showed higher rates of skill generalization and higher overall performance levels on the transfer task, even after the effects of outcome goal level were controlled. In a study of 38 managers participating in an interpersonal skills training program, May and Kahnweiler (2000) investigated the effects of a posttraining mastery skill practice protocol drawn from research in cognitive psychology. Dependent measures included knowledge retention, behavioral skill demonstration, and far transfer to the workplace based on multirater 360-degree survey instrument. Results indicated improvements in retention and behavioral demonstration measures but failed to document any effects on transfer. A key constituency of transfer research is the community of learning professionals who design and implement training initiatives. Such professionals are rightfully interested in evidence-based interventions that have been shown to positively influence transfer. Therefore, studies that explore intentional interventions have the potential for the greatest yield in new and practical transfer knowledge and researchers should be mindful of that reality.

Pre- and Posttraining Transfer Influences

Transfer of training, by definition, can occur only *after* a learning experience. Not surprisingly, then, the majority of transfer studies in 1988 focused on the nature of the training event itself. Research in the interim, however, has reflected the reality that who enters training experiences and what happens once they are back on the job are also important predictors of transfer outcomes.

The notion that performance, in any setting, is a function of ability, motivation and opportunity is one of the most enduring conceptualizations in industrial/organizational psychology. Facteau *et al.* (1995) noted succinctly that for transfer to occur trainees have to believe: (1) they are capable of learning, (2) the expended effort to learn will change performance, and (3) that changed performance will lead to valued outcomes. Drawing on the seminal work of Bandura (1986) and his social cognitive theory, a number of studies have demonstrated the effects on learning and transfer of self-efficacy and its variants (e.g. Gist, Stevens and Bavetta, 1991; Kozlowski *et al.*, 2001) as well as a variety of outcome expectations related to the organizational context, such as job identification and organizational commitment (Carlson *et al.*, 2000; Cheng and Ho, 2001; Tannenbaum *et al.*, 1991). Other studies have found that the choice to participate can influence training and transfer outcomes – though not always in intuitively obvious ways (Baldwin, Magjuka and Loher, 1991). For instance, in a study of pharmaceutical company managers, Baldwin and Magjuka (1991) found that mandated training signaled a higher level of importance than did voluntary training participation and resulted in higher intentions to transfer.

While research linking ability (e.g. cognitive aptitude) to learning outcomes has a long and robust history (Ree and Earles, 1991), researchers have also turned their attention to training motivation. In a meta-analytic review, Colquitt, LePine and Noe (2000) concluded that dispositional and situational factors do explain significant incremental variance in learning outcomes (including transfer) over and above cognitive ability. Several studies have shown that individuals who are motivated when they approach a learning situation have a higher likelihood of achieving positive outcomes than those with lower motivation (Mathieu and Martineau, 1997; Mathieu, Tannenbaum and Salas, 1992).

Naquin and Holton (2002) argued that, in organizational contexts, conceptions of motivation have to expand beyond a generic motivation to learn and move toward motivation to *transfer*. They incorporated both the motivation to learn and motivation to transfer into a construct they labeled motivation to improve work through learning (MTIWL). Using structural equation modeling to better understand the antecedents of MTIWL, Naquin and Holton found that extraversion, positive affectivity and work commitment attitudes directly affected MTIWL. The authors also found that MTIWL predicted transfer at a significantly greater level than measures of training proficiency and more general assessments of motivation to learn.

Similarly, Warr and Bunce (1995) extended existing conceptions of motivation to learn and introduced the notions of distal and proximal motivation. In distal terms, individuals vary in the favorability of their attitudes to training as a whole. More proximally, those general attitudes are reflected in specific motivation about a particular set of training activities. The authors studied 106 junior managers over a 7-month period and found significant relationships between their learning scores and both distal and proximal motivation.

For anyone with organizational experience, it is self-evident that the work environment can be a powerful facilitator or *inhibitor* of training transfer – and the emerging empirical evidence increasingly supports this intuitive notion. Ford et al. (1992) found that the opportunity to use skills can vary significantly among learners and predicts ultimate transfer. Others have found that the quality of the worker/supervisor relationship (Bates, 2003), feedback and performance coaching (Mathieu, Tannenbaum and Salas, 1992; Smith-Jentsch et al., 1996; Xiao, 1996) and a group norm of openness to change (Tracey, Tannenbaum and Kavanagh, 1995) are all significant predictors of training transfer.

One study explored the extent to which supervisors actively opposed the use of new knowledge and expertise (Tziner, Haccoun and Kadish, 1991) and the deleterious effects of that on transfer. In this vein, harking back to the work of the great sociologist Kurt Lewin, Eddy and Tannenbaum (2003) suggest that a first step and expeditious path to transfer is to focus less on carefully orchestrated interventions and more on removing the *obstacles* that are so commonly present in organizational contexts. It is now widely accepted that elements that enhance transfer extend beyond the actual training intervention and can be found in both the pre- and posttraining context. Continued research interest that takes a broad and multidimensional perspective will be the most fruitful in advancing our transfer knowledge.

Measurement of Transfer

Baldwin and Ford (1988) closed their review by noting, 'Conclusions from the existing research are problematic, given the relatively short-term, single source, perceptual database that has been created (p. 100).' These issues pertain primarily to how training transfer is measured. Two advances in training transfer research include a broadening of the measurement of outcomes and the collection of multiple measurements of training transfer over time.

Measures of training transfer now include supervisory or observer ratings. For example, Richman-Hirsch (2001) obtained supervisor and even peer evaluations of trainee transfer 4–6 weeks after customer service training for university employees. More studies are also including objective measures of training transfer such as faster performance (Swezey, Perez and Allen, 1991) and the increased accuracy of performance (Lintern et al., 1989). Studies like these indicate that researchers have given more careful attention to effectively measuring training transfer rather than simply relying on trainees' perceptions of their transfer (Ford and Weissbein, 1997).

In addition, following the suggestion by Kraiger, Ford and Salas (1993), recent studies now commonly examine the role of self-efficacy in transfer of training research (e.g. Brown, 2005; Gaudine and Saks, 2004; Kozlowski et al., 2001; Schwoerer et al., 2005). Studies show that individuals high in self-efficacy are more likely to be active in trying out trained tasks and attempting more difficult and complex tasks on the job. For example, Ford et al. (1992) found that trainee self-efficacy was related to the opportunities they had to perform the trained tasks on the job. Results indicated that airmen high in self-efficacy performed more tasks than airmen low in self-efficacy, as well as performing more complex and difficult tasks. Gist, Stevens and Bavetta (1991) also found that trainee self-efficacy was related to the acquisition and maintenance of negotiation skills. Therefore, we now know that self-efficacy is an important variable that is relevant to training transfer outcomes and is a good example of how both theoretical and empirical research has increased our understanding of training transfer outcomes.

The second advance is that researchers are conducting more longitudinal studies of training transfer. Many of these studies include measures at multiple times and/or multiple types of measures. More specifically, common times to obtain longitudinal measures in the studies we reviewed were 1 week (oftentimes shorter time frames were seen in lab studies using undergraduate students), 4 weeks, 2–3 months, and 6–12 months. Nearly all measures were taken within 1 year, although the longest time frame in the articles we reviewed was 2 years (i.e. Hazucha, Hezlett and Schneider, 1993). We found nearly a dozen studies obtained longitudinal measures (i.e. not including measures taken immediately after the training) at more than one time after the training session, with several of these obtaining measures 6 months to 1 year after the training.

One good example of this is a study by Axtell, Maitlis and Yearta (1997). They examined factors affecting the initial and sustained transfer of interpersonal skills training to the workplace. They measured transfer using both self and managerial ratings at 1 month and 1 year after training. One limitation to this study and others that attempt to obtain manager ratings after a significant time lapse (e.g. Cromwell and Kolb, 2004) is that the sample size of managerial ratings is not large enough to use in the analyses. This is often due to low response rates as well as the fact that some employees and managers change positions. Although this was the case in Axtell, Maitlis and Yearta (1997) and Cromwell and Kolb (2004), they were still able to compare managerial ratings to self-ratings to give more credibility to the self-ratings.

These types of longitudinal studies are encouraging, given that such work is needed to examine the transfer maintenance curve. In fact, a recent meta-analysis of the effectiveness of behavioral modeling training illustrates how close we are getting in at least one area to being able to aggregate primary research studies to examine the maintenance curve. When Taylor, Russ-Eft and Chan (2005) regressed meta-analytic effect sizes on the number of months between training and posttest, they found a positive relationship for measures of procedural knowledge skills. They also found a positive relationship for on-the-job behavior, although it was nonsignificant. Taylor, Russ-Eft and Chan (2005) interpret this to mean that the skills represented in their meta-analysis are actually greater with the passage of time after training, which would indicate that the maintenance curve would have a positive slope. Taylor, Russ-Eft and Chan (2005) point out that the majority of the studies included in their meta-analysis measure transfer behavior within 6 months of training. Despite this limitation, it is exciting to begin to see attempts to examine posttraining maintenance curves.

CONCEPTUAL ADVANCES IN UNDERSTANDING TRANSFER

The scope and length constraints of this chapter prohibit discussion of all the different themes and commentaries that have been offered on transfer. However, there are two conceptual advances that we believe warrant particular mention and discussion. Those are: (1) expansion of the dimensions of transfer and (2) more precise specification of what is being transferred.

One conceptual advance in transfer research has been the expansion in the dimensions of its definition. The conventional definition of transfer suggests that trainees' need to effectively apply the knowledge, skills, and attitudes gained in a training context to the job context. Expected outcomes of the transfer process have traditionally included both the generalization of trained skills to the job and the maintenance or long-term retention of trained knowledge and skills (Baldwin and Ford, 1988; Ford and Kraiger, 1995).

Smith, Ford and Kozlowski (1997) contend that in addition to these outcomes, the capacity to adapt what has been trained in the face of novel or changing situations is also a key indicator of learning (see also Schmidt and Bjork, 1992). Smith, Ford and Kozlowski (1997) reviewed the applied cognitive literature that distinguishes between routine and adaptive expertise. Routine experts apply solutions or strategies to well learned and familiar contexts but have more difficulty with novel problems (Holyoak, 1991). In contrast, adaptive experts can invent new procedures based on their knowledge and skills attained (through training and experience) to make new predictions and recognize when current strategies must be changed to respond to novel circumstances (Cox, 1997). The importance of building adaptive expertise as a goal of training has started to become a focus of transfer research – at least in laboratory settings (e.g. Kozlowski et al., 2001).

A second conceptual advance toward greater understanding of transfer has focused on the context surrounding the process of transfer. Yelon and Ford (1999) present a conceptualization of potential training content that consists of two dimensions. One dimension deals with the types of skills being trained. Many jobs have moved from an emphasis on 'closed skills' to a necessity to train for more 'open skills'. Closed skills are those where workers must respond in one particular way according to a set of rules – implemented in a precise fashion. For example, an auto mechanic changing turn lights on a car has a prescribed process and time to complete this task. On the other end of the scale are highly variable open skills – where there is not one single correct way to act but rather freedom to perform. With open skills the objective is generally to learn *principles* and not solely discrete steps. For example, a manager who is trying to motivate staff members cannot look up a 'cookbook' of steps to take. A manager could, however, use motivational principles to accomplish the objective. A similar argument is made by Salas, Milham and Bowers (2003) with respect to the evolution of many military jobs from what were once primarily physical roles to now more cognitive demands. Salas, Milham and Bowers argue that not only are the skills more difficult to train but also that tasks requiring high-level cognitive components are subject to greater and more rapid decay then are simpler motor skills.

Yelon and Ford's (1999) second dimension focuses on the extent of supervision. With increased emphasis on downsizing (or rightsizing) and empowerment, many jobs have moved from situations where individuals are heavily supervised to situations in which workers have more autonomous jobs (and thus less direct supervision). Autonomous workers can decide what they will do and how they will do it as a supervisor may rarely directly see the person actually performing the job.

The training field has typically been concerned with jobs that could be considered as having closed skills and being heavily supervised (Kraiger and Ford, 2007). Today's reality, however, is that more jobs require open skills and are not heavily supervised. This makes it more difficult to determine what to look for in the job setting after training. It is also more difficult to evaluate job impact given the limited supervision. Yelon and Ford (1999) conclude that the intersection of these two dimensions – the quadrant where skills are open and the individual is autonomous – poses the greatest challenges for training transfer research. Indeed, the framework supports the need for transfer research to consider measuring both how well individuals can generalize from the training to the job context and how well trainees can adapt their strategies gained in training to the changing conditions of the job context. In addition, research on how individual, design, and environmental factors may impact training transfer should consider the potential for the transfer situation (closed or open skills, heavily supervised or autonomous) to moderate the impact of those factors on job performance.

Along the same lines as Yelon and Ford (1999), Barnett and Ceci (2002) have developed a taxonomy of near and far transfer. They contend that two key characteristics of transfer are: (1) content – what is transferred; and (2) context – when and where it is transferred. The content factor is divided in turn into three dimensions: (1) the specificity/generalizability of the learned skill, (2) the nature of the performance change to be assessed, and (3) the memory demands of the transfer task. For example, a learned skill could be a procedure to follow or a principle to apply. This dimension is quite consistent with the Yelon and Ford (1999) discussion of closed versus open skills. Performance change desired could be about improving speed or improving accuracy or changing one's approach or strategy. Memory demands can be minimal (execute what you already know – application is obvious) to more extensive (recall, recognize and then execute an action). The transfer context includes issues of knowledge domain, physical context, temporal context, functional context, social context and modality which are aligned in terms of what it means in a near transfer versus far transfer setting. For example, the functional context concerns whether the activities in training are presented in a way that is similar to how they would be viewed in the 'real world' (e.g. academic exercises versus problem-oriented training on real-world issues). The social context concerns whether the task is learned alone or in a group and is then performed alone or in collaboration with others. The taxonomy provides a potentially useful way to classify and bring order to a vast literature on workplace training relevant to understanding if transfer occurs and if so under what conditions.

FUTURE DIRECTIONS FOR TRANSFER RESEARCH

Socrates once said, there are no final answers – only better questions – and this section of the chapter is written in that spirit. Our review of the last 20 years of transfer research is encouraging on several fronts. In particular, researchers have made progress in several areas, particularly the development of models of what is meant by transfer and empirical tests of the individual differences, pretraining readiness, and posttraining climate that impact on the transfer of training to the job.

At the same time, the challenge of transfer persists and there are at least three areas where the existing body of research is still in its infancy and which we believe constitute timely, important and exciting future directions: (1) exploring the 'personalization' of transfer by trainees, (2) examining transfer experiences as *episodes* in organizational life, and (3) applying different *models of change* to understand transfer phenomena.

The Personalization of Transfer Research: Transfer as a Personal Choice

As noted earlier, much of the traditional research on training transfer has focused on factors such as training design and external factors such as supervisory support. More recently, however, researchers have gravitated toward individual-level factors which include personality characteristics and the motivation to learn. The practical implication is that if we can improve trainee 'readiness', and perhaps also enhance supervisory support, we will have a greater probability of transfer. While this assumption is intuitively appealing, such a view tends to present the trainee as a passive rather than an active player in his or her own behavior in relation to on the job after training. Yet, we know that individuals come into training with all sorts of differences in terms of their goals, expectations, needs, and attitudes toward training. As one example, Ford and Noe (1987) showed that attitudes about the quality of *past* training experiences in a company affected the extent to which the individuals stated a need for new training.

It makes sense, then, that in addition to (or in spite of) the influence of various factors on transfer effects, the decision to transfer ultimately resides with each individual trainee. From an active learning perspective, we can view trainees as making personal choices to transfer, or not to transfer, as the case may be. The choice might more commonly be what elements or aspects to transfer and what to leave behind. In this way, individual trainees customize or personalize the training process to fit their own conception of needs and wants from the experience.

This issue of customization or personalization of training transfer has to date been relatively ignored in the training literature. However, research by Yelon and his colleagues (Yelon, Reznich and Sleight, 1997; Yelon and Sheppard, 1999; Yelon *et al.*, 2004) has begun to shine some light on this personalization process. Using qualitative methods, the authors interviewed medical professionals, in relatively autonomous positions, about their intentions to transfer learning from recent educational programs. They then followed them up to see what they actually transferred and why. In essence, the medical personnel were encouraged to tell their own story – similar to a learning history approach taken by organizational learning researchers (e.g. Kleiner and Roth, 1997). An analysis of the stories revealed that some trainees came into the training program with a clear agenda of what they wanted to learn so they could immediately apply the skills to their job – others had only a vague idea of what they might want to apply – and still others came into the training with little thought of what to do with the material The stories also revealed individuals who saw at some point during training something they could immediately apply to their job or could envisage using it at some later time when a clear opportunity arose. Based on these stories, Yelon et al. (2004) developed a model of decision making leading to the intention to transfer. The key decision criteria were (1) how credible the information was, (2) how practical the skills were, and (3) the extent to which the knowledge or skill was needed. Yelon and his colleagues related these decision criteria and transfer intentions back to momentary observations made by the trainees during training and its interaction with how the material in training was presented (e.g. ideas, modeling, examples, practice). The qualitative data from the stories clearly showed that individuals actively customized or personalized the training – intending to transfer only parts of what was trained and coming up with their own strategies for how to apply the new knowledge and skills. The customized transfer 'choices' differed substantively across trainees.

The research by Yelon and his colleagues focused on trying to understand *why individuals* transfer trained knowledge and skills. A related research stream on decision making and choice focuses on why individuals do *not* make a decision or choice of action (Steel, 2007). For example, Steel (2007) argues that nonaction often has value, especially when it is uncertain what the outcome will be if a choice to act is made. He notes that people tend to favor tasks that are more pleasant in the short term, even if they are detrimental to themselves in the long term. Hence, the more intrinsically unpleasant a task is, the more likely people are to avoid doing it, leading to procrastination – voluntarily delaying an intended course of action despite expecting to be worse off for the delay.

The literature on choice and procrastination could help us understand why trainees may have good *intentions* to transfer but ultimately do not make a choice to actually try to apply the new skills on the job. Steel (2007) provides the results of a meta-analysis to offer a number of individual difference factors that might affect the extent of procrastination including fear of failure, low self-confidence, self-handicapping, impulsiveness and present time orientation (where thoughts of the future do not weigh heavily in decisions as instead the individuals pursue immediate gratification and thus neglect or ignore longer term responsibilities). Similarly, Van Hooft et al. (2005) have noted that procrastination, defined as the delay in starting or completing an intended course of action, can be viewed as a moderator in the relation between implementation intention and behavior. Individuals characterized by high levels of this trait may have good intentions to transfer but never get around to actually trying out new skills or knowledge. Or during the learning phase the more trainees dislike the learning task, the more they will consider it effortful or anxiety producing which in turn will lead the trainees to procrastinate – that is, delaying any attempt to transfer new skills to the job.

Anderson (2003) also provides a convincing case for why not making a decision or choice is a likely outcome in many situations. As he notes 'the experience of postponing certain choices is universal yet often appears to work against individual goals. Delays transform into lost opportunities and adhering to the status quo is frequently unjustified given advantageous alternatives. Still individuals persist in seeking default no action, no change options' (p. 139). Therefore, Anderson views decision avoidance as a pattern of behavior in which individuals seek to avoid the responsibility for making a decision by delaying or choosing options they perceive to be a nondecision (cf. Janis and Mann, 1977). Research is cited that highlights the tendency to avoid making a choice by postponing it or by seeking an easy way out that involves no action or no change. This research stream contends that in general, people prefer no change (status quo bias), no action (omission bias – preference for options that do not require action), inaction inertia, and choice deferral.

Anderson presents a number of principles that lead to no decisions that have implications for understanding training transfer. For example, positive prior outcomes (such as belief that my performance on the job has been good) increase the tendency to select the status quo option. Anticipation of regret (e.g. worrying that trying out a new skill may not succeed or make one look silly) is likely to favor inaction and maintaining the routine behavior that was occurring before training. For example, decision makers tend to associate action with more regret than inaction – this could have important implications for understanding lack of transfer efforts. In addition, speeded decisions produce more inaction inertia as well as higher regret ratings such that attempts to force individuals to immediately decide to apply trained skills may backfire without adequate discussion and support.

Interestingly, the research suggests that people choose not to defer if they expected feedback about the future opportunities and explicitly considered regret that may occur if they have not pursued a certain course of action such as trying out new behaviors. Finally, Anderson uses prospect theory and the loss aversion model to note that people tend to weight potential losses greater than potential gains of the same amount. Hence, the utility of potential 'rejoicing' experienced as a result of taking action (i.e. applying skills) would be less than that for potential increased regret if the action is not successful (i.e. anticipated problems with successfully trying out new skills). This situation would lead to an increased preference for the omission option (i.e. preference for the option that does not require action).

In the light of Anderson's work, research on training transfer could be enhanced in the future by considering transfer as a conscious choice that individuals make. One could study why transfer is attempted, how choices are made to personalize or customize training received or why a choice is made not to try and transfer a trained skill to the job. There are exciting new avenues for pursing these research questions that can lead to a greater understanding of the transfer process.

Exploring Training as an Organizational Episode

Most traditional research on transfer has taken an 'all things equal' perspective which suggests that people enter and leave training experiences under roughly the same conditions. Moreover, the term 'training' has generally connoted a one-dimensional and uniform experience. For example, prior to 1988 it was common (and it is still frequently the case) that research articles reported only that participants 'went through training', or 'participated in a training program', or 'received a certain number of days of training', or, more recently, 'completed an online learning module', with little further description of the nature of the context or overall trainee experience.

Of course, for people in organizations, training is not a uniform or isolated event but more aptly described as an *episode* – a series of cumulative stimuli and the cognitions associated with those experiences (Baldwin and Magjuka, 1997). All training episodes occur among many other organizational episodes experienced by those employees. Today's training episodes occur in greatly varying organizational contexts with learning stimuli no longer limited to classroom-based, instructor-led stimuli. We contend that transfer research would benefit from a significant shift that underscores the importance of the organizational context and the new learning realities of today.

Organizational Context

A considerable amount of writing in the organizational literature has suggested that the context or environment in which interventions take place will have profound effects on the outcomes of those interventions. Although some systematic consideration of the context of training interventions has begun (e.g. Latham and Crandall, 1991; Rouiller and Goldstein, 1993; Tracey, Tannenbaum and Kavanagh, 1995), such research continues to be slow to emerge. Organizational training takes place amid individuals doing their jobs, functioning in teams, and being exposed to a host of other organizational activities unrelated to the training in question. Participants have learned organizational rules that guide their behavior in that everyday context, and their reaction to different training episodes (i.e. episodic stimuli) will reflect their interpretation of the appropriate rules to apply.

For example, consider the seemingly straightforward activity of setting training performance goals. The focus of most goal-setting research has been on the objective characteristics of effective goals. There has been relatively little interest in examining the interpretation of goals by the trainee. Goal-setting studies have rarely considered the influence of the situation, the location within a training process, or the cumulative experience of training participants.

From an episodic perspective, when managers formulate performance goals, the act potentially communicates more to respondents than numerical targets and behavioral strategies. The communicated signal attached to goals may be positive or negative. When goals are formulated, one signal to employees may be that management has a clear idea concerning the desired outcome and is willing to assume some responsibility for the accomplishment of the established goals. However, it could also be the case that employees interpret the provision of goals in a less favorable fashion as just 'wishes' with no accountability or consequences for lack of accomplishment. The general point is that the motivating influence of any training design element is partially contingent on the trainees' accumulated experience with that design element in other settings.

The lesson for transfer researchers is to more explicitly address the social environment and organizational context of training activities. This does not mean abandoning the core of transfer research. Rather, it means more careful attention to variables that have been either ignored or controlled. Rather than generating additional ways to exclude these variables/questions from study, our research needs to explicitly explore how these variables may interact with training design to facilitate or inhibit transfer outcomes. The challenge is to identify and investigate the factors that combine to increase transfer effectiveness, using criteria such as robustness, parsimony and designability.

A robustly designed training intervention yields the highest level of predictable outcomes reliably and over time. Based on existing evidence, successfully inducing a high level of trainee self-efficacy prior to training would constitute a robust design strategy. A parsimonious design includes the fewest design elements. For example, if goal setting is shown to overwhelm other posttraining interventions, then simply using goal setting may be the most parsimonious strategy. Designability refers to the ease with which a training administrator can adopt recommendations for training design within reasonable time and budget constraints. It appears that certain labeling strategies may be exceptionally high in designability. A significant change in company reward or evaluation systems would be a less designable change.

An episodic perspective leads to a host of research questions that remain relatively unexplored. For example, what types of organizational rewards and disincentives affect motivation to transfer and get the attention of trainees? Do various constituencies interpret similarly the meaning of the same contextual elements? Within any single organization, are there any systematic differences in the ways subgroups (managers vs. professionals vs. clerical staff) react to the different design elements? Do different training cohorts affect trainee expectations and motivation?

To address such questions, we need a more concerted attempt to categorize, investigate and report contextual variables that may influence transfer. We contend that organizational context factors can easily overwhelm the effects of the best planned and delivered training, while a favorable context can enhance even suboptimal training interventions. In fact, we suspect that much prior transfer research would be subject to reinterpretation if contextual factors and trainee perceptions had been measured and reported.

The E-learning Reality

An episodic perspective reveals a second gap in the extant transfer research concerning the nature of the 'training' stimuli itself. That is, while it may have once been the case that training was synonymous with instructor-led, classroom experiences, today's learning episodes are typically much different. Indeed, it is hardly provocative to suggest that conceptions of what constitutes training have now changed dramatically from a generation ago. Just as CDs and DVDs and iPods have changed the way music is delivered and consumed, so too has the Internet, wireless technology and portable video capability transformed the way learners experience training. For example, recent estimates suggest that over 30% of all corporate training is now technology based rather than instructor led (Paradise, 2007).

Unfortunately, the present review suggests that transfer research has been slow to adapt to these learning realities. More specifically, only a very few of the 140 empirical studies we collected focused on training that would be considered outside the traditional structured, instructor-led, face-to-face, classroom education model. One notable exception is a recent study by Kirkman *et al.* (2006) who investigated transfer outcomes from computer-assisted (i.e. technology based) team training among 40 geographically dispersed *teams* in a high-technology company.

The authors found that the relation between teams' average training proficiency and team performance was complex and moderated by several factors. In particular, teams' average training proficiency had a positive association with customer satisfaction when teams were higher, rather than lower, in both trust and technology support and when team leaders had longer, rather than shorter, levels of tenure within their specific team. A key direction for future research, then, is to fully acknowledge that learning is no longer a synonym for classroom instruction and the traditional tenets of training excellence – great coursework and stimulating trainers – are no longer sufficient.

Nontraditional, e-learning coursework has many apparent advantages that can theoretically facilitate transfer. It presents great opportunities for the customization of learning and the creation of so-called J^3 learning (just for me, just in time, and just enough). Learners across the globe can have access to the best instruction available, they can set their own pace and schedule; discussions can continue after formal training sessions, using e-mail and e-discussion groups; and learners can gain access to immediate feedback (Horton, 2000; Schwann, 1997). E-learning can also save organizations time and money. One study found e-learning to be 40–60% less expensive than training delivered in the traditional classroom setting (Becker, 1999).

In theory, e-learning provides for minimization of transfer concerns – users have direct access to the information they need, when they need it (Filipczak, 1996). However, we know from many other technological advances that technology by itself is rarely the answer – and that is the case with transfer. The limited evidence suggests that e-learning does not eliminate the transfer challenge, only changes it. For example, some work on self-directed e-learning suggests that it can be *less* effective than other forms of instruction, particularly so for low-ability learners (Kraiger and Jerden, 2007). Furthermore, most of the organizational cost savings for training fail to report any transfer metrics; that is, e-learning may well cost less to administer the same training content but data are still elusive with respect to the overall impact (transfer) or effectiveness of those expenditures relevant to learning outcomes.

As we pursue a more concerted focus on transfer from e-learning it is worth noting the seemingly self-evident, but often neglected, reality that all e-learning initiatives are not the same. Carliner (1999) has presented a useful typology that categorizes e-learning in four ways: (1) *online training and education* where the trainee develops specific knowledge and skills by interacting with a computer, (2) *performance support*; that is, computer aided support to workers as they perform their jobs (e.g. a customer service representative may have a list of diagnostic questions pop-up onscreen as a guide during a customer interaction), (3) *knowledge management* or attempts to capture, store and organize information from employees and make the information available to others throughout the organization, and (4) *online collaboration* which are situations where people work together online from different locations (this form of e-learning is seen often in coaching, mentoring or tutoring relationships). The overall point is that we have heretofore too rarely acknowledged the reality that e-learning is multidimensional and future transfer research will benefit from more precision in observing and reporting the nature of the e-learning stimuli under investigation.

Beyond e-learning, it is also worth noting the research by the Center for Creative Leadership and others which continues to find that much of what gets referenced by people as their most critical training occurs *outside* of any structured learning environment – digital or otherwise (McCauley *et al.*, 1994). Such things as challenging assignments, good mentors and an organizational climate of success are factors that rank higher. Indeed, every situation that contributes to growth and development of an individual has a learning dimension to it. Unfortunately, the continuing focus on structured training has led to a conspicuous void in the literature regarding on-the-job tutoring and mentoring, action learning, or job rotation programs, though all signs suggest that such activities are increasingly employed in today's progressive firms (Paradise, 2007).

Given the increasing pressure to realize greater gains from organizational learning initiatives, a further key direction for transfer research is to explicitly acknowledge the wide variance in contemporary learning experiences and design accordingly investigations consistent with that reality. As these new forms of training emerge and evolve, the transfer literature would benefit enormously from more qualitative data such as observation, open-ended interviews and even participant observation (Mertens, 2005; Patton, 2002). Our more general prescription is to expand beyond classroom training design issues toward a more systematic consideration of the increasingly wider range of training stimuli and, indeed, the increasingly wider range of intra and extraorganizational contexts in which training experiences are embedded.

Implications of Organizational Change Research for Understanding Training Transfer

The key issue with transfer is change – changes in knowledge, skills, and attitudes as a function of training – which lead ultimately to changes in behavior and performance on the job (Goldstein and Ford, 2002). Despite the fundamental reality that change is embedded in any training transfer study, there have been only limited attempts to incorporate organizational change theories into training transfer research.

The organizational development and change field has evolved from a focus on humanistic beliefs and values (e.g. McGregor's Theory X and Y) into an integrated framework of theories and practices that are useful for understanding the dynamic aspect of change from individual, team, and organizational levels of analysis (Porras and Robertson, 1992). Organizational development is defined as planned change in order to align people and systems to improve individual and organizational effectiveness. Organizational change efforts typically involve altering the way individuals do their work. The theories and practices of OD, then, have important, but underappreciated, implications for expanding our understanding of training transfer because transfer is fundamentally about changes in behavior –altering how individuals do their work.

Nonetheless, the conventional assumptions underlying organizational change research are often quite different from the assumptions underlying training transfer research. First, organizational change theories challenge assumptions of the linearity of change, whereas transfer research has typically embraced an assumption of linearity. Second, the organizational change literature has tended to ask process questions of how individuals change, whereas transfer research has tended to focus on external factors that may impact on individuals' on-the-job behaviors. Third, organizational change perspectives have looked at the unintended consequences of change processes, whereas transfer research has focused on intentional outcomes. Methodologically, change research has focused on measurement issues over time and incorporating time into theories, whereas transfer research has tended to ignore issues of time.

The Nonlinearity of Transfer

The transfer literature has tended to make an unstated assumption that behavioral change is a linear process. One indicator of this assumption is the meta-analytic reviews that have correlated learning scores gathered in training sessions with posttraining transfer 'scores' (e.g. Alliger *et al.*, 1997). The language of linear change is embedded in the training literature in other ways. For example, Alliger *et al.* (1997) note the need to examine the extent to which utility-based reactions to training correlate more or less strongly with on-the-job application of trained skills than do affect-type reaction measures.

Organizational development and change models challenge assumptions of linearity. A basic framework for thinking about change comes from Lewin (1947) who framed change around three phases of unfreezing, moving, and refreezing (see also Schein, 2004). A key component of unfreezing is how ready the individuals are to change. Moving requires the adoption or altering of attitudes and behaviors to be consistent with the expectations of the change effort. Institutionalization or sustainability occurs with refreezing – where the change in behavior becomes a stable part of the employee's day-to-day activities. The assumption underlying this change perspective is that these are dynamic processes that are not well captured by linear perspectives.

As noted by Amis, Slack and Hinings (2004), organizations that enter programs of change (and individuals affected by the change process) will encounter 'delays, reversals, and oscillations' – especially in more contentious areas that have a significant impact on the way people operate. Similarly, Gersick (1988) discussed punctuated equilibrium models of change. From this perspective, groups do not go through a predictable set of stages but instead develop through formation, maintenance and sudden revision of the framework for performance. The patterns suggest not a linear progression but a major shift at some point (e.g. the halfway point of a project team's life). This notion of times of incremental change coupled with periods of more substantial change has been discussed at the individual, group, and organizational levels (e.g. see Gersick, 1991).

What if transfer researchers loosened the assumption of linearity of change? For example, consider an organization that is training all personnel in the popular 'six-sigma' approach to quality processes. It is likely that individuals who are trained will make fits and starts in trying to apply the principles and techniques. Other individuals may watch and wait and see if the new initiative has 'legs' before trying out the new processes. In both cases, one might not see much behavioral change on a day-to-day basis until some turning point – punctuated equilibrium points where all of a sudden behaviors have definitely changed for a number of people who have been trained. In this case, the time of measurement becomes critical – before the sudden shift one would think that change has been agonizingly slow – measurement after would show great success (i.e. transfer) for the six-sigma program. In this case, the shift in behavior may not be direct but seen as it unfolds over time (see Brown and Eisenhardt, 1998).

Transfer as a Change Process

Bartunek and Moch (1987) provide a theory of first, second and third order change that supports the notion of nonlinearity of change, while also adding more of a framework on what is actually changed as a function of a new initiative. First order change is the reinforcement of present understandings in the organization. In this case, the change effort and the changes in attitudes and behaviors do not question underlying cultural assumptions of the organization. Second order change is the conscious modification of existing schemata in an organization (shared meanings or frames of reference for the organization). Third order change occurs when individuals can recognize that a change in schemata is necessary for organizational survival. This framework highlights that the depth of a change intervention that is needed depends on what type of change one is interested in achieving. Second order change requires a change in schemata and thus sets a higher bar for considering a change initiative as a success. In addition, second order change suggests a major shift in behavior while first order change does not.

Zell (2003) discusses organizational change as a process of death, dying and rebirth. Zell discusses how change is a graduate process as individuals work through their resistance to change. In working through resistance, individuals can go through five stages (based on work of Kubler-Ross, 1969): (1) denial, (2) anger, (3) bargaining, (4) depression, and (5) acceptance. This perspective contends that resistance to change is ultimately maladaptive but that individuals may or may not eventually progress through the stages to acceptance. This change framework provides an affective perspective to change. Zell's approach to understanding change suggests that an individual may be resistant to the required change in behavior that is the goal of the training because they do not feel that the change is necessary. If so, the individual will begin to feel a number of different emotions that may impact whether behavioral change will actually occur.

Bridges (2003) argues that it is not the 'changes' *per se* that are the problem; rather, it is the transitions and how individuals manage the transition from one form of behavior to a new or altered behavior pattern. According to this view, change is situational – such as attending a training program at a particular location. Transition is psychological as individuals come to terms with the new situation and what it requires to be successful. Hence, getting people through the transition is essential if the expected change is actually to work as planned. Bridges contends that managing transitions is a process of helping individuals move through three phases: (1) letting go of old ways of doing things, (2) going through the in between time when the old is gone but the new is not fully functional (called the neutral zone), and (3) coming out of transition to a new beginning where the altered behaviors make senses and begin to work for the individual. There are key implications for understanding training transfer from these three perspectives. The notion of schemata leads to asking about what the objectives of training are – how much of a change is expected in terms of an individual's mental model as well as that of the collective. The issue of stages of acceptance provides a more affective approach rather than a strict cognitive perspective that pervades the field of training and work in training transfer and indeed cognition in organizations more generally (Ashkanasy and Ashton-James, 2005; Hodgkinson and Healey, 2008). The transfer literature focuses on the impact of changes in self-efficacy on behavioral change on the job but tends not to focus on emotional reactions to the intended change and how that might affect transfer. The issue of focusing on transitions suggests that training transfer research needs to examine more clearly the process of letting go of the old as well as studying the strategies that led individuals to more quickly let go of the past. For example, the work of Bridges points to the importance of clearly defining 'what is over and what is not over' with a change effort. This provides a clear implication that trainers and supervisors should clearly identify what skills gained in the past are still relevant to job performance despite the addition of new skill sets and consider how to manage appropriately the attendant emotional processes associated with the transition.

The transition framework also points to the need for transfer research to take seriously the neutral zone and the threats and opportunities that present themselves to trainees once going back to the job. Most training programs are not going to lead to full competency at the end of training – full competency will only occur with practice and experience on the job. We know very little about what trainees are doing, thinking, or feeling during transition through the neutral zone once back on the job. The change research on transitions would suggest that this period might lead to heightened levels of individual anxiety and decreases in motivation. Performance, at least in the short run, might actually become worse. As noted by Bridges at these points, some individuals will want to rush forward and other want to go back to the old ways of doing things. It is time to encourage short-range goals and checkpoints as well as experimentation and embracing setbacks as ways to improve toward the goals of the training program.

Transfer Over Time: Intentional and Otherwise

Although the mechanism or intervention to change is often seen as an event that occurs during a certain identifiable time frame, it is actually occurring continuously (Purser and Petranker, 2005). From this perspective, stability is a convention used to pin down an experience. Amis, Slack and Hinings (2004) discuss the pace of change and the sequence of change. Pace is viewed as the speed by which change is implemented (rapid, incremental, or slow). Sequencing deals with the question as to which part of the organization the change effort should be focused on and when (e.g. focusing first on people in high-impact jobs).

Other change researchers have concentrated on the readiness for change. Readiness has been defined as the extent to which individuals are prepared to participate in change activities and try new things (Holt et al., 2007a; Huy, 2001). Readiness, then, is reflected in the motives and aims of the individuals relevant to the proposed change. In addition, readiness has been defined as beliefs that the change being proposed is actually needed, is valued, and that the organization has the will and capability to actually change. If these beliefs are negative toward the change, resistance is highly likely. Holt et al. (2007b) reviewed the readiness literature and defined it as 'the extent to which an individual or collection of individuals is cognitively and emotionally inclined to accept, embrace, and adopt a particular plan to purposefully alter the status quo' (p. 326). They noted that readiness includes various attitudes and behaviors relevant to adopting the change strategy or in deciding to resist the change.

One implication of research on time and stability for training transfer is that a major change in behavior that seems to occur within a short time frame after a planned intervention like training may in fact have been developing for a long time. The change perspectives on pace and sequencing are not discussed in the transfer literature but have implications for understanding transfer at an organizational level. For example, one could ask whether the pacing for the training intervention – how fast or rapid the program is moved throughout the organization has an impact on transfer. Similarly, one could ask how the sequence of training program implementation in the organization might impact transfer results. Which groups are the first to be trained; or which departments/units go through the training and in what order – and does that matter in terms of transfer?

In addition, training research has focused on readiness for training – a concept that focuses on the extent to which individuals have the knowledge and skill levels to benefit from the training – as well as the concept of motivation to learn – are they ready to learn? Less attention has been focused on how ready the individual is to change their behavior patterns once back at work – to what extent the individual is cognitively and emotionally inclined to accept, embrace and adopt a particular training plan that alters the status quo. We need research that focuses on the forces for and against change (or for and against maintaining the status quo). Crucially, the organizational development and change frameworks and models discussed above have the potential to shed light on this issue.

CONCLUSION

Questions concerning transfer of training are not new. In fact, they were among the first issues addressed by early psychologists such as Thorndike and Woodworth (1901). However, until fairly recently, the majority of research attention has been focused on the design and delivery of learning events. The research literature is much different today than in 1988 when we put forth the challenge for researchers to 'take into account a variety of factors and linkages that, to date, have not been adequately examined' (Baldwin and Ford, 1988, p. 98). Indeed, much progress has been made in examining transfer from a broader and more dynamic perspective. The future looks bright for greater understanding and the successful management of transfer and, with a concerted focus on some new directions, our hope is that the next 20 years will be as fruitful as the past two decades have been. We look forward to our 2028 review!

REFERENCES

Alliger, G. M., Tannenbaum, S. I., Bennett, W., Jr et al. (1997). A meta-analysis of the relations among training criteria. *Personnel Psychology*, 50, 341–58.

Amis, J., Slack, T. & Hinings, C. (2004). The pace, sequence, and linearity of radical change. *Academy of Management Journal*, 47, 15–39.

Anderson, C. J. (2003). The psychology of doing nothing: forms of decision avoidance result from reason and emotion. *Psychological Bulletin*, 129, 139–67.

Ashkanasy, N. M. & Ashton-James, C. E. (2005). Emotion in organizations: a neglected topic in I/O Psychology, but with a bright future. In G. P. Hodgkinson & J. K. Ford (Eds), *International Review of Industrial and Occupational Psychology*, Vol. 20 (pp. 221–68). Chichester: John Wiley & Sons, Ltd.

Axtell, C. M., Maitlis, S. & Yearta, S. K. (1997). Predicting immediate and longer-term transfer of training. *Personnel Review*, 26 (3), 201–13.

Baldwin, T. T. (1992). Effects of alternative modeling strategies on outcomes of interpersonal-skills training. *Journal of Applied Psychology*, 77 (2), 147–54.

Baldwin, T. T. & Ford, J. K. (1988). Transfer of training: a review and directions for future research. *Personnel Psychology*, 41, 63–105.

Baldwin, T. T. & Magjuka, R. J. (1991). Organizational training and signals of importance: linking pre-training perceptions to intentions to transfer. *Human Resource Development Quarterly*, 2, 25–36.

Baldwin, T. T. & Magjuka, R. J. (1997). Training as an organizational episode: pre-training influences on trainee motivation. In J. K. Ford, S. W. J. Kozlowski, K. Kraiger et al. (Eds), *Improving Training Effectiveness in Work Organizations* (pp. 193–221). Mahwah, NJ: Erlbaum.

Baldwin, T. T., Magjuka, R. J. & Loher, B. T. (1991). The perils of participation: effects of trainee choice on motivation and learning. *Personnel Psychology*, 44, 51–66.

Bandura, A. (1986). *Social Foundations of Thought and Action: A Social Cognitive Theory*, Englewood Cliffs, NJ: Prentice Hall.

Barnett, S. M. & Ceci, S. J. (2002). When and where do we apply what we learn? A taxonomy for far transfer. *Psychological Bulletin*, 128, 612–37.

Bartunek, J. & Moch, M. (1987). First, second, and third order change and organizational development interventions: a cognitive approach. *Journal of Applied Behavioral Science*, 23, 483–500.

Bates, R. A. (2003). Managers as transfer agents. In E. F. Holton & T. T. Baldwin (Eds), *Improving Learning Transfer in Organizations* (pp. 243–70). San Francisco: Jossey-Bass.

Becker, D. (1999). Training on demand. *TechWeek*, 11, 16–22.

Bridges, W. (2003). *Managing Transitions: Making the Most of Change*, Cambridge, MA: Perseus Publishing.

Brown, S. L. & Eisenhardt, K. M. (1998). *Competing on the Edge: Strategy as Structured Chaos*, Boston, MA: Harvard Business School Press.

Brown, T. C. (2005). Effectiveness of distal and proximal goals as transfer-of-training interventions: a field experiment. *Human Resource Development Quarterly*, 16, 369–87.

Burke, L. A. & Baldwin, T. T. (1999). Workforce training transfer: a study of the effect of relapse prevention training and transfer climate. *Human Resource Management*, 38 (3), 227–41.

Burke, M. J., Sarpy, S. A., Tesluk, P. E. & Smith-Crowe, K. (2002). General safety performance: a test of a grounded theoretical model. *Personnel Psychology*, 55, 429–57.

Campbell, J. P. (1971). Personnel training and development. *Annual Review of Psychology*, 22, 565–602.

Campbell, J. P. (1989). The agenda for training theory and research. In I. L. Goldstein (Ed.), *Training and Development in Organizations* (pp. 469–86). San Francisco: Jossey-Bass.

Carliner, S. (1999). *An Overview of On-line Learning*, Amherst, MA: HRD Press.

Carlson, D. S., Bozeman, D. P., Kacmar, K. M. *et al.* (2000). Training motivation in organizations: an analysis of individual level antecedents. *Journal of Managerial Issues*, 12 (3), 271–87.

Cheng, E. W. L. & Ho, D. C. K. (2001). A review of transfer of training studies in the past decade. *Personnel Review*, 30, 102–18.

Colquitt, J. A., LePine, J. A. & Noe, R. A. (2000). Toward an integrative theory of training motivation: a meta-analytic path analysis of 20 years of research. *Journal of Applied Psychology*, 85 (5), 678–707.

Cox, B. D. (1997). The rediscovery of the active learner in adaptive contexts: a developmental-historical analysis of transfer of training. *Educational Psychologist*, 32, 41–55.

Cromwell, S. E. & Kolb, J. A. (2004). An examination of work-environment support factors affecting transfer of supervisory skills training to the workplace. *Human Resource Development Quarterly*, 15, 449–71.

Eddy, E. R. & Tannenbaum, S. I. (2003). Transfer in an e-learning context. In E. F. Holton & T. T. Baldwin (Eds), *Improving Learning Transfer in Organizations* (pp. 161–94). San Francisco: Jossey-Bass.

Facteau, J. D., Dobbins, G. H., Russell, J. E. A. *et al.* (1995). The influence of general perceptions of the training environment on pretraining motivation and perceived training transfer. *Journal of Management*, 21 (1), 1–25.

Filipczak, B. (1996). Training on the Intranets: the hope and the hype. *Training*, 33 (9), 24–32.

Ford, J. K. & Kraiger, K. (1995). The application of cognitive constructs to the instructional systems model of training: Implications for needs assessment, design, and transfer. In C. L. Cooper & I. T. Robertson (Eds), *International Review of Industrial and Organizational Psychology*, Vol. 10 (pp. 1–48). Chichester: Wiley.

Ford, J. K. & Noe, R. A. (1987). Self-assessed training needs: the effects of attitudes towards training, managerial level, and function. *Personnel Psychology*, 40, 39–53.

Ford, J. K., Quinones, M. A., Sego, D. J. & Sorra, J. S. (1992). Factors affecting the opportunity to perform trained tasks on the job. *Personnel Psychology*, 45, 511–27.

Ford, J. K. & Weissbein, D. A. (1997). Transfer of training: an updated review and analysis. *Performance Improvement Quarterly*, 10 (2), 22–41.

Gaudine, A. P. & Saks, A. M. (2004). A longitudinal quasi-experiment on the effects of posttraining transfer interventions. *Human Resource Development Quarterly*, 15 (1), 57–76.

Gersick, C. (1988). Time and transition in work teams: toward a new model of group development. *Academy of Management Journal*, **31**, 9–41.

Gersick, C. (1991). Revolutionary change theories: a multi-level exploration of the punctuated equilibrium paradigm. *Academy of Management Review*, **16**, 10–36.

Gist, M. E., Bavetta, A. G. & Stevens, C. K. (1990). Transfer training method – its influence on skill generalization, skill repetition, and performance-level. *Personnel Psychology*, **43** (3), 501–23.

Gist, M.E, Stevens, C.K & Bavetta, A. G. (1991). Effects of self-efficacy and post-training intervention on the acquisition and maintenance of complex interpersonal skills. *Personnel Psychology*, **44**, 837–61.

Goldstein, I. L. (1980). Training in work organizations. *Annual Review of Psychology*, **31**, 229–72.

Goldstein, I. & Ford, J. K. (2002). *Training in Organizations*, 4th edn, Belmont, CA: Wadsworth.

Gully, S. M., Payne, S. C., Koles, K. L. K. & Whiteman, J. K. (2002). The impact of error training and individual differences on training outcomes: an attribute-treatment interaction perspective. *Journal of Applied Psychology*, **87** (1), 143–55.

Hazucha, J. F., Hezlett, S. A. & Schneider, R. J. (1993). The impact of 360-degree feedback on management-skills development. *Human Resource Management*, **32** (2–3), 325–51.

Heimbeck, D., Frese, M., Sonnentag, S. & Keith, N. (2003). Integrating errors into the training process: the function of error management instructions and the role of goal orientation. *Personnel Psychology*, **56** (2), 333–61.

Heslin, P. A., VandeWalle, D. & Latham, G. P. (2006). Engagement in employee coaching: the role of managers' implicit person theory. *Personnel Psychology*, **59**, 871–902.

Hodgkinson, G. P. & Healey, M. P. (2008). Cognition in organizations. *Annual Review of Psychology*, **59**, 387–417.

Holladay, C. L. & Quinones, M. A. (2003). Practice variability and transfer of training: the role of self efficacy generality. *Journal of Applied Psychology*, **88**, 1094–103.

Holt, D. T., Armenakis, A. A., Field, H. S. & Harris, S. G. (2007a). Readiness for organizational change: the systematic development of a scale. *Journal of Applied Behavioral Science*, **43**, 232–55.

Holt, D. T., Armenakis, A. A., Harris, S. G. & Field, H. S. (2007b). Toward a comprehensive definition of readiness for change: a review of research and instrumentation. In W. Pasmore & R. Woodman (Eds), *Research in Organizational Change and Development*, Vol. 16 (pp. 289–336). New York, NY: JAI Press.

Holyoak, K. (1991). Symbolic connectionism: toward third generation theories of expertise. In K. A. Ericsson & J. Smith (Eds), *Toward a General Theory of Expertise* (pp. 301–36). Cambridge: Cambridge University Press.

Horton, W. (2000). *Designing Web-Based Training*, New York: John Wiley & Sons, Inc.

Huy, Q. (2001). Time, temporal capability, and planned change. *Academy of Management Review*, **26**, 601–23.

Janis, I.L. and Mann, L. (1977) *Decision Making: A Psychological Analysis of Conflict, Choice, and Commitment*. New York: Free Press.

Karl, K. A. & Ungsrithong, D. (1992). Effects of optimistic versus realistic previews of training programs on self-reported transfer of training. *Human Resource Development Quarterly*, **3**, 373–84.

Kirkman, B. L., Rosen, B., Tesluk, P. E. & Gibson, C. B. (2006). Enhancing the transfer of computer-assisted training proficiency in geographically distributed teams. *Journal of Applied Psychology*, **91** (3), 706–16.

Kirwan, C. & Birchall, D. (2006). Transfer of learning from management development programmes: testing the Holton model. *International Journal of Training and Development*, **10** (4), 252–68.

Kleiner, A. & Roth, G. (1997). How to make experience your best teacher. *Harvard Business Review*, **75** (5), 172–7.

Kozlowski, S. W. J., Gully, S. M., Brown, K. G. *et al.* (2001). Effects of training goals and goal orientation traits on multidimensional training outcomes and performance adaptability. *Organizational Behavior and Human Decision Processes*, **85** (1), 1–31.

Kraiger, K. (2001). *Creating, Implementing and Managing Effective Training and Development: State-of-the-art Lessons for Practice*, San Francisco: Jossey-Bass.

Kraiger, K. & Ford, J. K. (2007). The expanding role of workplace training: themes and trends influencing training research and practice. In L. Koppes (Ed.), *Historical Perspectives in Industrial and Organizational Psychology*. Mahwah, NJ: LEA.

Kraiger, K., Ford, J. K. & Salas, E. (1993). Application of cognitive, skill-based, and affective theories of learning outcomes to new methods of training evaluation. *Journal of Applied Psychology*, **78** (2), 311–28.

Kraiger, K. & Jerden, E. (2007). A new look at learner control: meta-analytic results and directions for future research. In S. M. Fiore & E. Salas (Eds), *Where Is the Learning in Distance Learning? Towards a Science of Distributed Learning and Training* (pp. 65–90). Washington, D.C.: APA Books.

Kubler-Ross, E. (1969). *On Death and Dying*, New York: Macmillan.

Latham, G. P. & Crandall, S. (1991). Organizational and social issues. In J. Morrison (Ed.), *Training for Performance: Principles of Applied Human Learning* (pp. 259–85). Chichester: John Wiley & Sons, Ltd.

Lewin, K. (1947). Frontiers in group dynamics, concept, method and reality in social science; social equilibria and social change. *Human Relations*, **1**, 5–41.

Lintern, G., Sheppard, D. J., Parker, D. L. *et al.* (1989). Simulator design and instructional features for air-to ground attack: a transfer study. *Human Factors*, **31**, 87–99.

Martocchio, J. J. (1992). Microcomputer usage as an opportunity – the influence of context in employee training. *Personnel Psychology*, **45** (3), 529–52.

Mathieu, J. E. & Martineau, J. W. (1997). Individual and situational influences on training motivation. In J. K. Ford, S. W. J. Kozlowski, K. Kraiger et al. (Eds), *Improving Training Effectiveness in Work Organizations* (pp. 193–221). Mahwah, NJ: Erlbaum.

Mathieu, J. E., Tannenbaum, S. I. & Salas, E. (1992). Influences of individual and situational characteristics on measures of training effectiveness. *Academy of Management Journal*, **35**, 828–47.

May, G. L. & Kahnweiler, W. M. (2000). The effect of a mastery practice design on learning and transfer in behavior modeling training. *Personnel Psychology*, **53** (2), 353–73.

McCauley, C. D., Ruderman, M. N., Ohlott, P. J. & Morrow, J E. (1994). Assessing the developmental components of managerial jobs. *Journal of Applied Psychology*, **79** (4), 544–60.

Mertens, D. M. (2005). *Research and Evaluation in Education and Psychology*, 2nd edn, Thousand Oaks, CA: Sage.

Naquin, S. S. & Holton, E. F., III. (2002). The effects of personality, affectivity, and work commitment on motivation to improve work through learning. *Human Resource Development Quarterly*, **13**, 357–76.

Noe, R. A., Sears, J. & Fullenkamp, A. M. (1990). Relapse training: does it influence trainees' post training behavior and cognitive strategies? *Journal of Business and Psychology*, **4** (3), 317–28.

Paradise, A. (2007). *ASTD State of the Industry Report*, Alexandria, VA: American Society of Training and Development.

Patton, M. (2002). *Qualitative Research and Evaluation Methods*, 3rd edn, Thousand Oaks, CA: Sage.

Porras, J. I. & Robertson, P. J. (1992). Organization development: theory, practice, and research. In M. D. Dunnette & L. M. Hough (Eds), *Handbook of Industrial and Organizational Psychology*, 2nd edn, Vol. 3 (pp. 719–822). Palo Alto, CA: Consulting Psychologists Press.

Purser, R. & Petranker, J. (2005). Unfreezing the future: exploring the dynamic of time in organizational change. *Journal of Applied Behavioral Science*, 41, 182–203.

Quinones, M. (1995). Pretraining context effects: training assignment as feedback. *Journal of Applied Psychology*, 80, 226–38.

Ree, M. J. & Earles, J. A. (1991). Predicting training success: not much more than g. *Personnel Psychology*, 44, 321–32.

Richman-Hirsch, W. L. (2001). Posttraining interventions to enhance transfer: the moderating effects of work environments. *Human Resource Development Quarterly*, 12 (2), 105–19.

Rouiller, J. Z. & Goldstein, I. L. (1993). The relationship between organizational transfer climate and positive transfer of training. *Human Resource Development Quarterly*, 4, 377–90.

Russ-Eft, D. (2002). A typology of training design and work environment factors affecting workplace learning and transfer. *Human Resource Development Review*, 1, 45–65.

Salas, E., Milham, L. M. & Bowers, C. A. (2003). Training evaluation in the military: misconceptions, opportunities, and challenges. *Military Psychology*, 15, 3–16.

Schein, E. (2004). *Organizational Culture and Leadership*, 3rd edn, San Francisco: Jossey-Bass.

Schmidt, R. A. & Bjork, R. A. (1992). New conceptualizations of practice: common principles in three paradigms suggest new concepts for training. *Psychological Science*, 3, 207–17.

Schwann, S. (1997). Media characteristics and knowledge acquisition in computer conferencing. *European Psychologist*, 2 (3), 277–85.

Schwoerer, C. E., May, D. R., Hollensbe, E. C. & Mencl, J. (2005). General and specific self-efficacy in the context of a training intervention to enhance performance expectancy. *Human Resource Development Quarterly*, 16 (1), 111–29.

Smith, E., Ford, J. K. & Kozlowski, S. (1997). Building adaptive expertise: implications for training design strategies. In M. Quinones & A. Ehrenstein (Eds), *Training for a Rapidly Changing Workplace*. Washington, D.C: APA.

Smith-Jentsch, K. A., Jentsch, F. G., Payne, S. C. & Salas, E. (1996). Can pre-training experiences explain individual differences in learning? *Journal of Applied Psychology*, 81, 110–6.

Steel, P. (2007). The nature of procrastination: a meta-analytic and theoretical review of quintessential self-regulatory failure. *Psychological Bulletin*, 133, 65–94.

Swezey, R. W., Perez, R. S. & Allen, J. A. (1991). Effects of instructional strategy and motion presentation conditions on the acquisition and transfer of electromechanical skill. *Human Factors*, 33, 309–23.

Tannenbaum, S. I., Mathieu, J. E., Salas, E. & Cannon-Bowers, J. A. (1991). Meeting trainees' expectations: the influence of training fulfillment on the development of commitment, self-efficacy, and motivation. *Journal of Applied Psychology*, 76, 759–69.

Taylor, P. J., Russ-Eft, D. F. & Chan, D. W. L. (2005). A meta-analytic review of behavior modeling training. *Journal of Applied Psychology*, 90 (4), 692–709.

Thorndike, E. L. & Woodworth, R. S. (1901). The influence of improvement in one mental function upon the efficiency of other functions. *Psychological Review*, **8**, 247–61.

Tracey, J. B., Tannenbaum, S. I. & Kavanagh, M. J. (1995). Applying trained skills on the job: the importance of the work environment. *Journal of Applied Psychology*, **80** (2), 239–52.

Tziner, A., Haccoun, R. R. & Kadish, A. (1991). Personal and situational characteristics influencing the effectiveness of transfer of training improvement strategies. *Journal of Occupational Psychology*, **64** (2), 167–77.

Van Hooft, E. A. J., Born, M. P., Taris, T. W. *et al.* (2005). Bridging the gap between intentions and behavior: implementation intentions, action control, and procrastination. *Journal of Vocational Behavior*, **66**, 238–56.

Warr, P. & Bunce, D. (1995). Training characteristics and the outcomes of open learning. *Personnel Psychology*, **48** (2), 347–75.

Wexley, K. N. (1984). Personnel training. *Annual Review of Psychology*, **35**, 519–51.

Xiao, J. (1996). The relationship between organizational factors and the transfer of training in the electronics industry in Shenzhen, China. *Human Resource Development Quarterly*, **7**, 55–73.

Yelon, S. L. & Ford, J. K. (1999). Pursuing a multidimensional view of transfer. *Performance Improvement Quarterly*, **12**, 58–7.

Yelon, S. L., Reznich, C. B. & Sleight, D. A. (1997). Medical fellows tell stories of application: a grounded theory on the dynamics of transfer. *Performance Improvement Quarterly*, **10**, 134–55.

Yelon, S. L. & Sheppard, L. M. (1999). The cost-benefit transfer model: an adaptation from medicine. *Performance Improvement Quarterly*, **12**, 79–94.

Yelon, S., Sheppard, L., Sleight, D. & Ford, J. K. (2004). Intentions to transfer: how do autonomous professional become motivated to use new ideas? *Performance Improvement Quarterly*, **17**, 82–103.

Zell, D. (2003). Organizational change as a process of death, dying and rebirth. *Journal of Applied Behavioral Science*, **39**, 73–96.

Chapter 3

FIFTY YEARS OF PSYCHOLOGICAL CONTRACT RESEARCH: WHAT DO WE KNOW AND WHAT ARE THE MAIN CHALLENGES?

Neil Conway and Rob B. Briner

School of Management and Organizational Psychology,
Birkbeck, University of London, UK

INTRODUCTION

Since its inception, the psychological contract concept has been viewed as an important idea for understanding the employment relationship and, more generally, workplace behavior (Conway and Briner, 2005; Guest, 2004a; Levinson *et al.*, 1962; Rousseau, 1995; Schein, 1965, 1980). Over the past 20 years, however, it has particularly captured researchers' attention as shown by the rapid increase in the number of journal articles, now several hundred, published on the subject. It has also over the same period had considerable appeal to managers and practitioners. A popular definition of the psychological contract is 'individual beliefs, shaped by the organization, regarding terms of an exchange agreement between the individual and their organization' (Rousseau, 1995, p. 9) where beliefs refer to an employee's interpretation of explicit and implicit promises. The psychological contract is used to explain employee behavior in two ways: By exploring how reciprocal promises oblige employees to do things for their employer (e.g. Coyle-Shapiro and Kessler, 2002c; Rousseau, 1990), and considering how employees react when they believe promises made to them are broken (Conway and Briner, 2002a; Robinson, 1996; Robinson and Rousseau, 1994).

There are a number of reasons for this upsurge of interest in the psychological contract. First, the psychological contract has highly intuitive links with employment contracts. Employment contracts will have explicit terms and conditions akin to explicit promises. These terms will also be open to

International Review of Industrial and Organizational Psychology, 2009, Volume 24.
Edited by G. P. Hodgkinson and J. K. Ford. Copyright © 2009 John Wiley & Sons, Ltd

interpretation by parties to the contract, which will lead to inferred and implicit understandings of the employment relationship. Furthermore, the unfolding employment relationship will lead to additional implicit perceptions derived from observing the other party's behavior (Rousseau, 1995; Kalleberg and Rogues, 2000). Second, the psychological contract can be useful for understanding how macro and micro changes to the employment relationship affect employees' experience of work. The psychological contract has been used to examine the impact of a wide range of different types of change such as the effects of downsizing (Feldheim, 2007), outsourcing (Ågerfalk and Fitzgerald, 2008; Koh, Ang and Straub, 2004), shifts from collective to individual employee representation (Calo, 2006), transitions to market economies (Kaše and Zupan, 2007), and moves to temporary contracts (Guest, 2004b) on employees' attitudes and behavior. Research typically considers how the various types of organizational and extra-organizational change alters each party's perceived obligations or violate previous promises and, in turn, how such psychological contract changes affect employee attitudes and behaviors. Third, while psychological contract theory shares some features with other employment or social exchanges approaches – such as equity and justice, organizational support and leader–member exchange – it also contributes uniquely to our understanding of the exchange through, for example, the concept of breach (Conway and Briner, 2005). Fourth, the psychological contract is about a set of ongoing, dynamic reciprocal processes, where its terms are actively renegotiated, fulfilled or breached, on a daily basis by both parties to the contract (Levinson et al., 1962; Schein, 1980). This distinguishes the psychological contract from many other organizational psychology theories that tend to focus on simple cause–effect relationships or include attitudinal constructs that provide little insight into everyday work experience and behavior.

Psychological contract research has progressed considerably since Millward and Brewerton's (2000) last review in this series. During this period, there has been a major review monograph (Conway and Briner, 2005), and, of course, a significant increase in the number of theoretical and empirical journal articles. Psychological contract studies have been conducted across many different occupational groups and national contexts and these generally support the main predictions of psychological contract theory. To illustrate the increasing academic interest, a recent meta-analysis looking at the specific issue of the effects of breach on work-related outcomes incorporated 51 separate studies, 43 (84%) of which were published between 2000 and 2006 (Zhao et al., 2007). Since 2000 there have also been several detailed critiques of the psychological contract (Conway and Briner, 2005; Cullinane and Dundon, 2006; Meckler, Drake and Levinson, 2003), contributing new insights to earlier critical accounts (Arnold, 1996; Guest, 1998). While none of these critiques recommend abandoning the idea, they do, taken collectively, represent a very wide-ranging assessment of the numerous limitations of existing research, covering issues such as definitional ambiguity, concept redundancy, inadequate explanatory power, the use of tired and inappropriate methodologies, and the lack of practical application. In our view, many of the limitations identified in these critiques are important and need to be taken seriously in order for the field to develop. Our main aims, therefore, are to critically review psychological contract theory and research, identify key challenges, and suggest research priorities.

We begin with a history of psychological contract research (which by coincidence has its 50th birthday last year, if we take Menniger's work, 1958, as the initial work), and then consider its definition. Next, we review significant theoretical and empirical developments in its two main research streams, namely, the contents of the psychological contract, and psychological contract breach. We then discuss the limitations associated with existing methods for researching the psychological contract. Finally, we present the main challenges associated with the psychological contract concept and consider how current research is responding to these challenges.

HISTORY OF THE PSYCHOLOGICAL CONTRACT CONCEPT

The history of psychological contract research can be organized in relation to Rousseau's (1989) seminal reconceptualization (Roehling, 1996). Psychological contract research prior to Rousseau's (1989) article was characterized by around half a dozen notable studies in which researchers from somewhat different disciplines tended to use their own definition and conceptualization of the psychological contract. Research during the Rousseau period has to a very large extent embraced and adopted her reconceptualization. It has focused on a small number of psychological contract concepts (i.e. promises, contents, and breach), being conducted largely from within the disciplines of organizational psychology and organizational behavior, and generated a large number (around 100) of mainly quantitative empirical studies. However, while research during this period has, in terms of quantity, dwarfed that conducted in the pre-Rousseau period, the early studies remain important in many respects – not least by shedding light on current confusions and disagreements about the psychological contract (Conway and Briner, 2005; Cullinane and Dundon, 2006; Guest, 1998; Meckler, Drake and Levinson, 2003; Roehling, 1996).

The Pre-Rousseau Period

During this period, the psychological contract concept was developed mainly in a number of key works including those by Argyris (1960), Menninger (Menninger, 1958; Menninger and Holzman, 1973), Levinson et al. (1962) and Schein (1965, 1980). Other texts published during this period and aimed more generally at the employer–employee exchange have influenced psychological contract research, such as March and Simon's (1958) contributions–inducements model. There have also been some philosophical texts exploring tacit and explicit agreements (Cabot, 1933), which, although not ever cited as directly influencing psychological contract research, present similar ideas.

Menninger (1958) explored the explicit and implicit contract between psychotherapist and patient, although he did not use the term 'psychological contract' until his later work (see Menninger and Holzman, 1973). Menninger was particularly interested in how unconscious motives influenced psychological contract behavior (see Sills, 2006, for recent debates and advances in the use of psychological contracts in counseling and psychotherapeutic settings).

Argyris (1960) first used the term 'psychological work contract' to refer to the unspoken agreement between foreman and employees in a US factory:

> Since the foremen realize the employees in this system will tend to produce optimally under passive leadership, and since the employees agree, a relationship may be hypothesized to evolve between the employees and the foreman which might be called the 'psychological work contract'. The employee will maintain high production, low grievances, etc., if the foremen guarantee and respect the norms of the employee informal culture (i.e. let the employees alone, make certain they make adequate wages, and have secure jobs). This is precisely what the employees need. (Argyris, 1960, p. 97.)

While Argyris pays little attention to the psychological contract beyond this particular observation, we can still see within it some of the defining features of later research, such as the necessity of an exchange of some kind, and the source of the unspoken belief, arising from observing consistent behavior over time.

Levinson et al. (1962) provide the most extensive and forensic analysis of psychological contracts. In contrast to other work from this period – which did relatively little to elaborate the psychological contract concept – Levinson et al. (1962) produced an entire book devoted to using the psychological contract to better understand the well-being of employees, drawing on interview data from 874 employees at a US utility plant. This text offers considerable insight into the links between psychological contracts and, for instance, reciprocity, workplace and role change, boundaries between work and nonwork, and trajectories of the psychological contract change over life stages.

Levinson et al. (1962) were the first writers to use the specific phrase 'psychological contract' and defined it as

> a series of mutual expectations of which the parties to the relationship may not themselves be even dimly aware but which nonetheless govern their relationship to each other ... The psychological or unwritten contract is a product of mutual expectations. These have two characteristics: (a) they are largely implicit and unspoken, and (b) they frequently antedate the relationship of person and company. (Levinson et al., 1962, pp. 21–22.)

Expectations have a strong obligatory quality, explaining their ability to govern the behavior of parties to the contract, and why employees will feel violated if they are not fulfilled. The psychological contract is viewed as a dynamic process being 'affirmed, altered or denied in day-to-day work experience' (Levinson *et al.*, 1962, p. 21).

A key idea here is the role of – largely unconscious – psychological needs and how they affect and define the psychological contract. According to this account, individuals are motivated to enter into and to change psychological contracts in order to better meet needs for affection, dependence, aggression, growth and development. In exchange for the employer fulfilling these needs, the employee will deploy effort to contribute to the needs of the company. Needs are therefore the driving force behind reciprocation: 'It is as if both employees and company are saying to one another, "You must, for I require it"' (Levinson *et al.*, 1962, p. 36), where reciprocation is 'the process of fulfilling a contractual relationship in which both parties seek continuously to meet their respective needs' (Levinson *et al.*, 1962, p. 38). Fulfilled psychological contracts explain mental health and well-being, whereas the failure to reciprocate leads to unfulfilled needs and subsequent reactions of frustration, anger and hostility. As Meckler, Drake and Levinson (2003) observe, it is here that Levinson *et al.* (1962, p. 104) introduce the notion of violation as occurring 'when the changing expectations of one party are imposed on and threaten the state of interdependence and the balance in psychological distance achieved by the other'. This definition has been eclipsed by more recent definitions of violation by Rousseau (1989) and Morrison and Robinson (1997). Finally, needs also explain the highly individuated nature of psychological contracts, as each party has their own distinctive needs and makes contributions toward the needs of the other party according to their knowledge, skills and abilities.

Turning to Schein's book *Organizational Psychology* (1965, 1970, 1980), the psychological contract 'implies that the individual has a variety of expectations of the organization and that the organization a variety of expectations of him. . . . Expectations such as these are not written into any formal agreement between employee and organization, yet they operate powerfully as determinants of behavior' (Schein, 1965, p. 11), where both employee and manager 'forge their expectations from their inner needs, what they have learned from others, traditions and norms which may be operating, their own past experience, and a host of other sources' (Schein, 1980, p. 24). Therefore, like Levinson, Schein also believed that needs (along with social learning and other unspecified sources) play a vital role in understanding the origins and development of the psychological contract, emphasizing the subjective and unconscious nature of influences on the psychological contract.

Schein regarded the psychological contract concept as a central way of understanding the employment relationship:

By way of conclusion, I would like to underline the importance of the psychological contract as a major variable of analysis. It is my central hypothesis that whether a person is working effectively, whether he generates commitment, loyalty, and enthusiasm for the organization and its goals, and whether he obtains satisfaction from his work, depend to a large measure on two conditions: 1. The degree to which his own expectations of what the organization will provide him and what he owes the organization matches what the organization's expectations are of what it will give and get. 2. Assuming there is agreement on expectations, what actually is to be exchanged – money in exchange for time at work; social-need satisfaction and security in exchange for work and loyalty; opportunities for self-actualization and challenging work in exchange for high productivity, quality work and creative efforts in the service of organizational goals; or various combinations of these and other things. (Schein, 1965, pp. 64–65.)

Schein therefore clearly states two mechanisms linking the psychological contract to outcomes. The first is *matching*, which inspired one of the few empirical studies of this period (see Kotter, 1973) and also much more recent studies (e.g., see Dabos and Rousseau, 2004). In line with Schein's predictions, Kotter (1973) found that the smaller the discrepancy between employee and employer expectations, the more likely employees report job satisfaction, productivity and reduced turnover. The second mechanism linking the psychological contract to outcomes proposed by Schein is the extent to which the exchange leads to need satisfaction echoing the positions taken by both Argyris and Levinson.

Like Levinson and colleagues, Schein also viewed the psychological contract as being highly dynamic and constantly renegotiated. However, this process of reciprocation and renegotiation was viewed somewhat differently. For Levinson, the unfolding reciprocation process was something rather hit-and-miss and potentially painful as while both parties are seeking to adjust their psychological contract to better satisfy their own needs they may at the same time thwart the needs of the other party (Meckler, Drake and Levinson, 2003). Schein, on the other hand, saw continual renegotiation as being influenced by explicit communication channels and enacting power, 'unfolding through mutual influence and mutual bargaining to establish a workable psychological contract' (Schein, 1965, p. 65).

In contrast to previous work, Schein gave more attention to the organization's side of the psychological contract and, in particular, how this can be expressed through the channels of organizational culture and line management assumptions (e.g. Theory X/Theory Y). These insights have clearly informed later work on the employer's perspective (e.g. Guest and Conway, 2002b).

Despite the conviction of these prominent scholars, their work generated very little empirical interest. To our knowledge, with the exception of Argyris and Levinson, the only published empirical studies in work settings on the psychological contract in the pre-Rousseau period were those by Kotter (1973) and Portwood and Miller (1976). There was also only a very small number of other articles discussing the psychological contract in relation to various organizational processes, such as career counseling (Baker and Berry, 1987), graduate recruitment (Herriot, 1988), organizational consulting (Boss, 1985), and understanding absence culture (Nicholson and Johns, 1985). Indeed, during this period, the psychological contract appeared to receive more attention as a means of understanding teacher–student relationships (Anderson, 1987; Holloman, 1972; Kolb, Rubin and McIntyre, 1984; Lobuts and Pennewill, 1984) than the employment relationship.

This apparent lack of interest is surprising. Perhaps, it indicates that Argyris, Schein and Levinson's efforts at conceptualizing the psychological contract were not sufficiently precise, leading to uncertainty about what 'beliefs' (e.g. expectations, obligations or needs) were part of the psychological contract. It may also be that researchers were deterred from exploring the concept by the emphasis on unconscious processes during a period in organizational research that was characterized by advances in cognitive theories, such as goal setting (Locke and Latham, 1990), and a more general decline in the popularity of the notion of 'needs' and unconscious processes. Furthermore, the mechanisms put forward for how the psychological contract affected outcomes – namely, matching expectations and thwarting or fulfilling needs – were perhaps too similar to popular and well-explored concepts of that time such as met expectations and need–satisfaction theories. It is clear that in spite of the considerable conceptual groundwork undertaken during this period, very few researchers were interested in building on this foundation.

The Rousseau Period

Rousseau has undoubtedly had the greatest influence on psychological contract research. In her initial and later work with colleagues, she has redefined the psychological contract (Rousseau, 1989), introduced and reconceptualized key psychological contract concepts such as breach and violation (Rousseau, 1989; Robinson and Rousseau, 1994), identified terms for organizing the content of psychological contracts (i.e. transactional and relational psychological contracts (Rousseau, 1990), and developed and validated now widely used measures of psychological contracts (Rousseau, 1990, 2000).

Rousseau's initial article (1989) is viewed as seminal and responsible for reinvigorating scholarly interest in the topic. She added clarity and precision to what she referred to as 'vaguely defined' concepts characterizing previous psychological contract research (p. 137). Virtually all of the several hundred psychological contract articles published since this seminal work adopt her definition. She defined the psychological contract as 'an individual's beliefs regarding the terms and conditions of a reciprocal exchange agreement between that focal person and another party. Key issues here include the belief that a promise has been made and a consideration offered in exchange for it, binding the parties to some set of reciprocal obligations' (Rousseau, 1989, p. 123).

Rousseau's definition broke with previous work in two major ways. The first was the emphasis on the promissory nature of psychological contract beliefs. Whereas previous research referred to psychological contract beliefs in a rather vague manner and emphasized their unconscious origins, Rousseau emphasized a more specific type of belief in the form of promises, making the distinction between explicit and implicit promises. Explicit promises refer to employee interpretations of verbal and written agreements, whereas implicit promises refer to employee interpretations of consistent and repeated patterns of exchange with the employer. Critically, both types of promise derive from observations of behavior, as made clear in a slightly later work: 'The key element in communicating a promise in a contract is a behavioral event' (Rousseau and McLean Parks, 1993, p. 6). An important implication of focusing on consciously accessible beliefs is that they are clearly amenable to questionnaire surveys, in contrast to previous conceptualizations based on unconscious processes, which did not lend themselves to straightforward empirical investigation.

The second break with tradition was to propose violation as a new mechanism linking the psychological contract to work-related attitudes and behavior. Violation was defined as the 'failure of organizations or other parties to respond to an employee's contribution in ways the individual believes they are obligated to do so' (Rousseau, 1989, p. 128).[1] Rousseau argued that perceived violation would damage relationships, leading to extreme emotional reactions such as outrage, the withdrawal of trust, commitment and behaviors crucial to the organization. Violation was also distinguished from related ideas such as unmet expectations and inequity.

Judging by the extent to which violation was used in frameworks linking the psychological contract to a wide range of attitudinal and behavioral outcomes, the concept of violation was extremely attractive to researchers. Its appeal might be due to its consistency with more general notions of contracts and the clear and obvious parallels between the violation of legal and psychological contracts. It is also much more understandable than the previous mechanisms (such as matching and thwarted needs) linking the psychological contract with outcomes. Like conscious promises, violation was also something that was consciously perceived by one party to the contract, thus also making it more amenable to empirical research than unconscious processes (needs) or processes requiring multiparty comparisons (matching).

Rousseau also emphasized that psychological contracts were held at the subjective and individual level and argued that it was this level of analysis that largely determined employee attitudes and behavior, rather than more complex interactions between two parties implied by previous conceptualizations. For instance, older conceptualizations of psychological contracts entailed perceived agreement, but for Rousseau whether employee and employer actually agreed about reciprocal promises was not seen as being of great importance.

---

[1] Rousseau's use of violation was later redefined by Morrison and Robinson (1997) to refer to psychological contract breach, and Morrison and Robinson defined violation as referring to emotional reactions that follow breach under certain conditions. This redefinition has been largely accepted in the field and will be used during the remainder of this chapter unless we refer specifically to Rousseau's early use of violation.

Alongside this, Rousseau also stated that organizations themselves could not have psychological contracts as such a notion would entail anthropomorphizing organizations and bring with it a range of problems, not least the problem of identifying how an organization could hold a set of subjective beliefs. One effect of this shift toward the individual subjective level was that later research would focus almost entirely on the employee's rather than the organization's or employer's perspective.

Rousseau did much to change and develop the psychological contract concept in particular ways that, on one hand, seemed to make it much more appealing and useful to researchers and thus her work had a major impact on the organizational behavior field. On the other hand, this reconceptualization inevitably meant that some potentially important features of the original conceptualizations were lost. So as well as the benefits of this reconceptualization, it is also important to consider the possible costs. We will return to this issue later.

In her initial and subsequent work, Rousseau established two main research agendas relating to the contents of psychological contracts (What are the contents? How are they formed? What are their consequences?) and violation of psychological contracts (What are the antecedents to and consequences of violation?). These two agendas could be mapped neatly onto the concurrent shifts in the social, economic and political forces affecting organizations at that time. How would the contents of psychological contract be shaped by such changes? Were such changes violating psychological contracts and what were the consequences of such violations? Understanding contents and violation (more recently referred to as breach) have dominated subsequent psychological contract research.

Conclusions

The psychological contract has been around for about 50 years and has considerable standing within organizational research. The history of the psychological contract may appear to suggest reasonable consensus and steady evolution over time. For instance, there are enduring fundamental ideas such as the subjective natures of psychological contracts and its basis in reciprocal exchanges. It is also apparent how research during the Rousseau period mirrors earlier formations. For example, the similarity of Schein's Theory X/Y management assumptions and Rousseau's transactional/relational psychological contract distinctions, Levinson *et al.*'s work on successful and unsuccessful reciprocity and its implications for well-being and later work on psychological contract fulfillment/breach, and Schein and Kotter's work on matching and more recent research on agreement and mutuality (e.g. Dabos and Rousseau, 2004).

However, in spite of some consistencies, the most striking feature of the history of the psychological contract concept is one of change and discontinuity in its meaning. We believe that such inconsistencies between the pre-Rousseau and the Rousseau period are at the heart of current confusion surrounding the psychological contract and have contributed to researchers' viewing the notion as 'all things to all people' (Roehling, 1996, p. 3). While Rousseau's conceptualization is currently the norm, it is clearly at odds with previous researchers' views and not without its own limitations. Some researchers argue that neglecting features emphasized in earlier definitions is to fundamentally overlook the true meaning of psychological contracts (Meckler, Drake and Levinson, 2003). It is suggested that the approach taken in the pre-Rousseau period was more valid as it viewed psychological contracts as ambiguous, unfolding on a momentary basis, and influenced by a wide range of unconscious forces. Comparing psychological contract research before and after Rousseau's initial article, therefore, raises a number of fundamentally unresolved controversies, such as what beliefs constitute psychological contracts (promise, obligation, expectation, need?) and the meaning of implicit beliefs (perceptions of predictable social behavior versus understandings derived from unconscious motives). How researchers interpret these terms is not a trivial issue. It determines the way in which they advance psychological contract theory and approach questions such as how psychological contracts form and how they operate.

CONTEMPORARY APPROACHES TO DEFINING THE PSYCHOLOGICAL CONTRACT

The most commonly used definition in contemporary psychological contract research is from Rousseau's (1995) book (stated earlier, we repeat it here): 'The psychological contract is individual beliefs, shaped by the organization, regarding terms of an exchange agreement between the individual and their organization' (Rousseau, 1995, p. 9). Beliefs are typically considered to consist of explicit and implicit promises. Despite the widespread use of this definition, it has also been noted by several commentators that contemporary researchers do in fact disagree about definitions and have different views about what it is the psychological contract refers to (Conway and Briner, 2005; Cullinane and Dundon, 2006; Guest, 1998; Meckler, Drake and Levinson, 2003). Indeed, some recent researchers have returned to definitions from the pre-Rousseau period, arguing that these earlier definitions more validly capture the 'true' meaning of the psychological contract (see, e.g., Meckler, Drake and Levinson, 2003, reprisal of Levinson and colleagues' work). In this section, we shall briefly unpack some of the key terms of Rousseau's definition, namely, what is meant by *beliefs*, *exchange agreement*, *parties* to the contract, and how organizations *shape* the contract.

What Beliefs Constitute Psychological Contracts?

What beliefs make up psychological contracts is probably the major area of disagreement. One major debate focuses on the differences between promises, obligations and expectations (Arnold, 1996; Guest, 1998; Conway and Briner, 2005). While earlier definitions by Argyris, Schein and Levinson emphasized expectations, psychological contract research since Rousseau has to a very large extent emphasized promises. Further complicating the picture, obligations have also been used throughout the history of the psychological contract and are often used interchangeably with the idea of promises (e.g. Rousseau, 1989; Morrison and Robinson, 1997).

As noted above, promises can be either explicit or implicit, but must be grounded in the employee's perceptions of the behavior of the other party with respect to what is exchanged between the employee and the employer (Rousseau and McLean Parks, 1993). Promises are thus viewed as having a more precise meaning and being more contractual than expectations, which are viewed as having a more general meaning:

> Expectations refer simply to what the employee expects to receive from his or her employer (Wanous, 1977). The psychological contract, on the other hand, refers to the perceived mutual obligations that characterize the employee's relationship with his/her employer. The psychological contract, unlike expectations, entails a belief in what the employer is obliged to provide, based on perceived promises of reciprocal exchange. (Robinson and Rousseau, 1994, p. 246.)

Expectations can, therefore, refer to anything the employee expects from their employer. They may arise from any number of sources (parental socialization, pre-employment experiences, previous employment experiences, etc.) and may have little to do with promises made between the employee and their current employer. Obligations are also viewed as having a more general meaning and may arise from employees' ideological beliefs about, for example, a just world. Expectations and obligations are only part of a psychological contract if they are the consequence of an explicit or implicit promise (Morrison and Robinson, 1997; Rousseau and McLean Parks, 1993).

While such attempts to differentiate promises, expectations and obligations are helpful, further clarity is needed. For example, the notion that expectations are part of psychological contracts if they arise from implicit promises means it is possible to trace almost every expectation one may have about work back to implicit promises, given that implicit promises have only been vaguely defined, for example, as 'based upon both inference and observation of past practices' (Rousseau, 1990, p. 390).

A second major issue is the extent the beliefs are consciously perceived. This debate is clearly captured in a recent exchange between Meckler, Drake and Levinson (2003) and Rousseau (2003).

Rousseau regards psychological contracts as an individual's perceptions of exchange behavior, implying that parties to psychological contracts individuals could, if asked to do so, consciously recall evidence of things the other party has said or done that amount to an explicit or implicit promise. This view is shared by a recent definition of the psychological contract offered by Guest, where he refers to psychological contracts as focusing on 'more or less explicit deals' (Guest, 2004a, p. 545).

In contrast, Meckler, Drake and Levinson (2003) reprise Levinson and colleagues earlier definition that emphasizes the unconscious origins of psychological contract beliefs. While both perspectives are consistent with other aspects of the psychological contract definition – its subjectivity, the exchange – the two types of belief are fundamentally different and imply completely different interpretations of the psychological contract and how it should be researched, understood and managed. These issues are of great importance because different beliefs imply different levels of psychological engagement (Guest, 1998) and also imply very different interpretations of other aspects of psychological contract theory (e.g. breach, negotiation).

In sum, the nature of psychological contract beliefs and the distinctions between different beliefs have not received sufficient attention.

What Does Exchange Agreement Mean?

There is a consensus among researchers that psychological contracts involve exchange. In promissory terms, psychological contracts are about conditional promises, or what are typically referred to as reciprocal promises. Unconditional promises (e.g. 'You have a job for life') are not part of psychological contracts. There is also agreement across definitions that the exchange can include anything exchanged between the two parties: 'It may have literally thousands of items . . . although the employee may consciously think of only a few' (Kotter, 1973, p. 92). However, in practice psychological contracts are typically viewed as being about the exchange or items core to the employment contract, such as the exchange of an employee's effort, creativity, flexibility, knowledge, skills and abilities in return for pay, opportunities for advancement, job security, status, and so on from the organization.

An important debate in this area relates to the specificity of the exchange. While we have some insights into the range of employee behaviors and employer rewards that form part of the general exchange, there is little clarity about the nature and indeed existence of specific links between individual items that form part of this exchange. For example, what specific employee behaviors are exchanged for, say, promotion?

In the psychological contract definition, exchange is also used in conjunction with agreement. While other types of contracts require actual verifiable agreement, such as legal contracts (Cheshire, Fifoot and Furmston, 1991), actual agreement is not necessary for psychological contracts; what matters is whether a party to a psychological contract perceives agreement: 'Agreement exists in the eye of the beholder and not necessarily in fact' (Rousseau and McLean Parks, 1993, p. 3).

In an early critique, Arnold (1996) noted the definitional ambiguity of agreement and questioned whether agreement, or mutuality as it is sometimes referred to, refers to a strong form of mutuality, where there is perceived agreement over the existence, terms, and exchange linkages in the psychological contract, or whether perceived agreement is of a weaker form of mutuality, acknowledging that a contract exists, but nothing more. Both strong and weak forms of agreement raise some challenging issues for how the psychological contract is defined. If psychological contracts entail a strong form of mutuality, then it seems improbable that such a clear understanding of a contract's terms could be perceived without some outward sign of agreement. Alternatively, if psychological contracts are defined by a weak form of mutuality, can this reasonably be considered to be a contract, as the perceived terms and details of the exchange remain unspecified? Can someone have a contract with an organization, without knowing its terms? In summary, strong forms of agreement are conceptually incompatible with the implicit nature of psychological contracts, whereas weak forms of agreement are incompatible with the contractual nature of psychological contracts.

Who or What Are the Parties to Psychological Contract?

While most psychological contract research focuses on work settings, psychological contracts will inevitably emerge when any two individuals develop a relationship involving an ongoing exchange of tangible and intangible things. This is illustrated by the application of the psychological contract into other relationship dyads such as teacher–student relationships in classrooms (Anderson, 1987; Holloman, 1972; Kolb, Rubin and McIntyre, 1984; Lobuts and Pennewill, 1984), students and their professor (Taras and Steel, 2007; Wade-Benzoni, Rousseau and Li, 2006), tenants and landlords (Radford and Larwood, 1982), service providers and customers (Schneider and Bowen, 1999), salesperson and customer relationships during product return transactions (Autry, Hill and O'Brein, 2007), supplier–buyer relationships in the motor industry (Kingshott, 2006), customer relationships and corporate reputation (MacMillan et al., 2005, buyers and sellers in online market places (Pavlou and Gefen, 2005), and IT outsourcing interfirm relationships (Koh, Soon and Straub, 2004).

In work contexts, psychological contract definitions and research generally refer to the individual employee's perspective of their relationship with the organization. There are two important issues relating to the meaning of 'organization' in psychological contract definitions.

The first is how employees cognitively represent the organization as the other party to their psychological contract. In simple forms of employee–employer relationships where there is an obvious and single individual employer (e.g. small organizations), it is relatively straightforward to represent the employer. However, what happens in larger organizations, where there is no single individual that encapsulates or represents the employer? Researchers have argued that employees somehow aggregate psychological contract messages communicated from principals, agents, and practices that variously represent the organization. Drawing heavily on early writing by Levinson (Levinson et al., 1962; Levinson, 1965), it is thought that employees aggregate these differing perceptions through a process of anthropomorphizing the organization in order to arrive at a view of the organization as if it were a coherent single entity (Eisenberger et al., 1986; Levinson et al., 1962; Morrison and Robinson, 1997; Rousseau, 1989; Schein, 1965; Sims, 1994).

The second issue relates to whether organizations can actually hold psychological contracts with an employee. Most definitions, such as those by Rousseau and colleagues, emphasize that psychological contracts are held by individual employees. Organizations cannot have psychological contracts:

> The organization, as the other party in the relationship, provides the context for the creation of a psychological contract, but cannot in turn have a psychological contract with its members. Organizations cannot 'perceive', though their individual managers can themselves personally perceive a psychological contract with employees and respond accordingly. (Rousseau, 1989, p. 126.)

One problem with the position that organizations cannot have psychological contracts is that the same researchers who adopt this perspective also assume that employees make the mistake of anthropomorphizing the organization as part of their psychological contract. In other words, while these researchers take the position that organizations cannot have a psychological contract, they assume that employees will perceive the opposite to be the case (i.e. that the organization does indeed hold such contracts with themselves and their fellow colleagues). Nevertheless, with few exceptions (see Guest and Conway, 2002b; Tsui and Wang, 2002), most research focuses on the employee's rather than the employer's perspective.

In summary, most psychological contract research follows Rousseau's emphasis on the employee's experience and tends to assume employees treat the organization, via a process of anthropomorphizing, as a single entity.

To What Extent Are Psychological Contracts 'Shaped' by Organizations?

There is little agreement between researchers about the extent to which psychological contracts are shaped by organizations. Some definitions, particularly those from earlier work, state that psychological contracts are shaped by a very wide range of forces and appear to prioritize no single source. For example, Schein (1980, p. 24) states that psychological contracts arise from employees 'inner needs, what they have learned from others, traditions and norms which may be operating, their own past experience, and a host of other sources'. In contrast, more recent definitions influenced by Rousseau strongly emphasize the organization's role in shaping psychological contracts (Roehling, 1996). This view emphasizes that employee psychological contract beliefs must be grounded in the behavior of the employee's current organization; beliefs arising from elsewhere are not part of the psychological contract.

These opposing viewpoints closely reflect different ideas about where psychological contracts originate. Do they arise from relatively explicit contractual behavior by the employer, or are psychological contracts more open to highly idiosyncratic sensemaking and unconscious processes? At present, the answer to this question is unclear. However, given that Rousseau and colleagues use terms such as 'shaping', this suggests that beliefs are only somewhat determined by the organization's actions, and we can conclude that psychological contracts are more than likely open to many influences, reflecting their highly subjective nature.

In conclusion, definitions of all the key terms within the psychological contract are contested. We return to these debates toward the end of our review when we consider in more detail challenges facing the psychological contract concept.

REVIEWING THE MAIN RESEARCH STREAMS: WHAT DO WE KNOW?

Since the origins of the psychological contract concept (Menninger, 1958; Levinson *et al.*, 1962), researchers have made the distinction between the content of the psychological contract (i.e. What is exchanged?) and the process (e.g. How is the exchange regulated? How does the exchange break down?). The content/process distinction can be used to organize almost all psychological contract research. The content/process distinction has also been used to label theories in other areas, such as work motivation (e.g. Campbell and Pritchard, 1976), but it is perhaps particularly relevant to research examining contracts, as contracts must contain terms and guide behavior over time by requiring parties to fulfill terms. In this section, we will review findings that examine the antecedents and consequences of both the contents and processes of psychological contracts. It should be noted that although we discuss antecedents and consequences, these are largely theoretical assertions, as most studies in the field use cross-sectional designs and cannot therefore examine causality empirically. We will return to this limitation later.

The Contents of Psychological Contracts

Defining and Categorizing the Contents of Psychological Contracts

The contents of psychological contracts have been defined as 'expectations of what the employee feels she or he owes and is owed in turn by the organization' (Rousseau, 1990, p. 393). Consistent with the subjective emphasis of the psychological contract, the notion of contents does not refer to what is actually exchanged, but the employee's perceptions of implicit and explicit promises relating to the exchange of things the employee does for the organization in return for things the employee gets back. Employee inputs into the exchange are frequently referred to as contributions, whereas the organization's inputs are referred to as inducements; drawing on March and Simon's (1958) early contributions–inducements model. However, it should be noticed that whether or not these inputs are actually contributions or inducements is an empirical question which is rarely examined. Hence, using such terms is in most cases based on assumptions about the motives and mechanisms underlying these inputs.

The contents of psychological contracts contain two different types of information (Conway and Briner, 2005). The first type concerns what is exchanged – What is in the list of items each party brings to the deal? The second type of information is much more elaborate and concerns the precise linkages between items that the employee and employer input into the deal. This information is arguably more important as it provides a much clearer basis for understanding reciprocity and prediction; unfortunately, however, most research into the contents only addresses the first type of information.

Early research in this area sought to establish empirically the typical items that form the contents of psychological contracts, and whether it was possible to categorize the content in some way. By far the most enduring and popularly used way of categorizing contents has been the transactional/relational distinction.

Rousseau (1990) again provides one of the earliest and most important studies on contents by establishing a core set of psychological contract content items and the transactional/relational distinction that would go on to dominate later research. She asked human resource managers about the obligations they sought from and made to graduate recruits during selection. A sample of MBA students was surveyed and the results of a factor analysis were interpreted along the lines of the legal scholar MacNeil's (1974, 1980) transactional/relational distinction. Transactional psychological contracts are defined as promises of exchange where the terms are specific, explicit, take place over a short time frame, and are likely to entail the exchange of tangible resources. In contrast, relational psychological contracts are amorphous, implicit and highly subjective, take place over no clear time frame, and entail the exchange of intangible socio-affective resources. Correlational analysis found that employee promises of working overtime, engaging in voluntary extra-role activities, and giving notice before quitting were associated with employer promises of high pay, performance-based pay, training and development items (interpreted as the transactional exchange) and employee promises of loyalty, being prepared to commit to a minimum stay within the organization, and willingness to accept a transfer requested by the organization were associated with job security (interpreted as the relational exchange).

The transactional/relational distinction has been used by many researchers examining psychological contract contents (e.g. Bunderson, 2001; Coyle-Shapiro and Kessler, 2000; De Cuyper and De Witte, 2006; Grimmer and Oddy, 2007; Hui, Lee and Rousseau, 2004; Millward and Hopkins, 1998; Raja, Johns and Ntalianis, 2004; Robinson, Kraatz and Rousseau, 1994; Robinson and Rousseau, 1994; Rousseau, 1990, 1995). Two measures are currently in common usage: the first is Rousseau's (2000) Psychological Contract Inventory (PCI) and is an updated version of her earlier measure (Rousseau, 1990); the second is the Psychological Contract Scale (PCS) (Millwood and Hopkins, 1998).

It should be noted that much work takes place outside of the transactional/relational distinction. A prominent example is Guzzo, Noonan and Elron's (1994) survey of expatriate workers. Forty-three items derived from the participating company's human resource policies were used to assess the three broad areas of financial inducements, general support, and family-oriented support. This is one of the few content studies that made efforts to contextually derive its content measure, an approach that is highly consistent with the theoretical assumptions about the nature of psychological contracts and a strategy that resulted in a more convincing representation of the contents of expatriate workers' psychological contracts.

A second prominent study by Herriot, Manning and Kidd (1997) collected qualitative accounts from 184 employees and 184 managers (the latter in an attempt to capture the organization's perspective) using a convenience, snowball sample across numerous organizations. The sample was designed to be nationally representative of UK organizations. Respondents were required to recall occasions on which the organization and employee had fallen short of or exceeded expectations. Responses were content analyzed into distinct themes reflecting a wide range of content not readily reducible to a small number of dimensions. The findings also indicated substantial differences between employee and employer perspectives, with employees more likely to report traditional industrial relations content items such as fair pay and a pleasant working environment whereas employers were more likely to identify relationship items such as respectful treatment and recognition for special contributions.

Evaluation of Contents Measurement Instruments
and Distinctions of Associated Constructs

First, if we focus on the early key studies (Guzzo, Noonan and Elron, 1994; Herriot, Manning and Kidd, 1997; Millward and Hopkins, 1998; Rousseau, 1990), rather than studies that derive their approach and measures from these works, there is actually little agreement about the beliefs constituting psychological contracts. Rousseau's (1990) questionnaire items feature the belief 'obligations' (the PCI refers to 'commitment or obligation'; Rousseau, 2000). The Guzzo, Noonan and Elron (1994) measure asks respondents to report what they believed the organization 'should' provide. The critical incident approach adopted by Herriot, Manning and Kidd (1997) features the expression 'how you would expect your organization to treat you or your colleagues'. Millward and Hopkins (1998) ask respondents about a range of beliefs using terms such as 'expect', 'feel', 'chance' (as in likelihood), 'prefer' and 'commitment'. These studies are therefore probably examining somewhat different constructs depending on how the psychological contract is defined and operationalized. If we were to strictly follow the most recent psychological contract definitions – that emphasize promises – then none of these questionnaires operationalizes precisely the notion of psychological contracts.

Second, there is little agreement about the content items across studies. The lists differ substantially in terms of the number of items and the vital qualifying details and item wording (e.g. high pay, pay for performance, fair pay, pay commensurate with market rates, etc.). This variation is consistent with ideas that the contents of psychological contracts are potentially vast and could relate to anything (Kotter, 1973; Schein, 1980), and that the terms of psychological contracts are defined with respect to the local context, as part of an unfolding relationship. However, such variation also implies that it is possibly a mistake to search for a small number of generalizable dimensions.

Third, psychological contract contents research has almost entirely overlooked the key defining feature of exchange. Questionnaire measures consist of independent lists of employee and employer promises where there is no a priori linking of employee and employer inputs. Researchers use correlational analyses and infer the items form an exchange; however, the exchange is not explicitly measured. It could be the case that items included in these lists are relatively unconditional promises or simply conditions of employment and therefore a very minor or indeed nonelement of the contents. For example, organizational benefits that apply across the entire workforce – such as pensions, holiday entitlement, and fringe benefits – are not in any meaningful way conditional on an individual employee's contributions. To our knowledge, Millwood and Hopkin's (1998) PCS is the only measure that includes several items detailing and exchange (e.g. 'I have a reasonable chance of promotion if I work hard'). In other words, while exchange is a central feature of the definition of the psychological contract – and indeed all contracts – research into psychological contract contents fails to assess this exchange.

Fourth, both the logical and empirical support for the transactional/relational distinction is limited. Definitions of transactional and relational contracts refer to features of terms in a contract – implicit versus explicit, short-term versus long-term, and so on – where these features could apply to any item. For example, pay is typically treated as part of a transactional contract; however, it is easy to imagine how pay and particularly qualities of the pay arrangement (such as its fairness) are highly implicit. Therefore, the meaning of any content item is defined by the context of the exchange, and consequently, it would not be reasonable to expect any particular patterning of items across multiple contexts or studies. This is supported by findings showing that training is associated with either, both or neither transactional and relational psychological dimensions (Arnold, 1996; Coyle-Shapiro and Kessler, 2000). Policy capturing studies provide evidence that the exchange is messy, relational and transactional items being exchanged within the same contract (see Rousseau and Anton, 1991). Although there has been some empirical support for the transactional/relational distinction (e.g. Hui, Lee and Rousseau, 2004), other studies have failed support this distinction (for a review, see Taylor and Tekleab, 2004). Although the search for very simple dimensional accounts of complex constructs seems to appeal to many researchers we can also ask, given what we know about the sensitivity of the psychological contract contents to a range of individual, organizational, cultural and other contexts, whether such an approach is sensible here.

Fifth, all studies assume promises to be consciously accessible and therefore relatively explicit. This is most clearly demonstrated by the typical study that uses questionnaire checklists, but is also a feature of more qualitative approaches. Such an approach is clearly at odds with definitions that emphasize psychological contracts as highly implicit. Such beliefs are not simultaneously consciously accessible, employees become aware of them as they experience, engage in, and reflect upon events at work (Meckler, Drake and Levinson, 2003). If we accept this argument, then questionnaire checklists are unlikely to be valid indicators of contents as a consequence of the limited conscious access respondents have to psychological contract beliefs.

Antecedents of the Contents of Psychological Contracts

In this section, we consider the factors that variously shape employee perceptions of promises and obligations. We do so under headings reflecting the sources of promises, namely, factors outside the organization, organizational and employment contract factors, and individual and social factors.

Factors Outside the Organization (Extra-Organizational Factors)

There are obviously a very wide range of possible factors outside the workplace, such as pre-employment work-related experiences, exposure to the experience of work via family and friends, and media, along with experiences gained from belonging to other institutions that communicate psychological contracts, such as schools (e.g. Anderson, 1987; Holloman, 1972; Kolb, Rubin and McIntyre, 1984; Lobuts and Pennewill, 1984). Violation during previous employments has also been found to influence the degree of trust and cynicism toward a new employer (Pugh, Skarlicki and Passell, 2003).

A second set of factors relate to nonwork experiences, where events such as parenthood, marriage, problems in relationships outside of work, and so on, may affect an employee's ability to contribute at work and change their expectations about what they want from work. Millward's (2006) longitudinal qualitative analysis of women during maternity leave and return to work shows that the transition to motherhood has profound effects on identity and psychological contracts, in this case affecting women's preference for and the perceived reasonableness of psychological contract terms. Outside of these studies, we are unaware of other research in this area; clearly, there is much more that needs to be known about how factors outside work shape psychological contracts in work.

Organizational Factors and Employment Contract Factors

A major way organizations shape psychological contracts is through their human agents, such as managers, communicating messages to employees. Some research suggests that line managers are a particularly important communication channel. In some cases, for example, managers may help clarify organizational communications (Guest and Conway, 2000), whereas in others they may exaggerate what the organization can offer, leading to subsequent psychological contract breach (Grant, 1999; Greene, Ackers and Black, 2001).

Organizations also communicate psychological contracts through policy documents and various practices, particularly human resource practices (Rousseau, 1995; see also the special issue of *Human Resource Management*, Fall 1994). Survey studies have found that in organizations with more human resource practices, both employees (Guest and Conway, 1998; Westwood, Sparrow and Leung's, 2001) and employers (Guest and Conway, 2002b) perceive that more promises have been made. There is also some evidence that individual HR practices (D'Annunzio-Green and Francis, 2005) and bundles of practices (Conway and Monks, 2008) may influence psychological contract perceptions. For instance, in a survey of staff in the Irish health service (nurses, community care, and administration), Conway and Monks (2008) found that what they referred to as 'basic' HR practices – communications, staffing and rewards – were more strongly associated with the psychological contract than practices characterizing more sophisticated HR systems, such as team working and career development. Clearly, there are opportunities for more detailed research in this area to examine when, how and to what extent individual and bundles of HR practices, such as recruitment, induction and performance appraisals, influence psychological contract perceptions.

A qualitative study of police workers emphasized how promises were implicitly communicated. Dick (2006) found that police workers promissory beliefs about moving from full-time to part-time work were informed by their idiosyncratic inferences from structural practices such as industrial tribunals, actions of the HR department, the government department responsible for policing, as well as the views of coworkers who had already made the transition. This study also revealed how the meaning of HR policies and practices toward part-time working is socially constructed by workers using and contesting the practices, illustrating the dynamic interplay between employees enacting their psychological contract and social norms regarding practices.

There has been a growing interest in the extent to which employment contracts, particularly so-called nonstandard contracts such as temporary, fixed-term and part-time work, influence psychological contracts (e.g. Beard and Edwards, 1995; Claes, 2005; Conway and Briner, 2002b; Coyle-Shapiro and Kessler, 2002b; De Cuyper and De Witte, 2006; Druker and Stanworth, 2004; Guest, 2004b; Guest and Conway, 2000). Most studies compare the psychological contracts of employees on nonstandard employment contracts to those of permanent full-time workers. A common assumption is that being employed on a nonstandard contract results in more transactional and less relational psychological contracts, and that such an arrangement is associated with negative outcomes. While there is some support for this hypothesis (De Cuyper and De Witte, 2006; Millward and Hopkins, 1998), a number of studies find that employees on temporary contracts prefer and indeed choose more transactional psychological contracts and report positive outcomes (Guest, 2004b). Studies in this area more generally show that while the psychological contract is a useful explanatory variable for understanding the experience of employees on nonstandard employment contracts, the assumptions sometimes made about the psychological contract contents or preferences of these groups have not always been supported empirically. Perhaps a more promising research direction is to move away from transactional/relational distinctions toward examining other features of psychological contracts, such as stability, scope, tangibility, focus, time frame, particularism, multiple agency and volition (McLean Parks, Kidder and Gallagher, 1998).

Individual and Social Factors

Although only a small number of studies have examined the effects of individual differences on psychological contract contents, they already suggest a wide range of influencing factors, including occupational and exchange ideologies (Bunderson, 2001; Coyle-Shapiro and Neuman, 2004), personal and social identities (Hallier and Forbes, 2004), work values (De Vos, Buyens and Schalk, 2005), and personality (Raja, Johns and Ntalianis, 2004). It is suggested that individual differences shape psychological contracts by influencing employees' choice of tasks and how they construe and enact contract terms (Raja, Johns and Ntalianis, 2004).

Social interaction and social comparison among coworkers are viewed as having a major impact on shaping psychological contracts. However, with the exception of a series of studies by Ho and colleagues (Ho, 2005; Ho and Levesque, 2005; Ho, Rousseau and Levesque, 2006), there is little empirical research in this area. The study most relevant to the formation of psychological contracts conducted a network analysis of employees from a start-up company and found that social capital accrued through structural hole brokering and being part of cohesive social networks was associated with employees reporting more transactional obligations (Ho, Rousseau and Levesque, 2006).

Psychological contract formation has also been explored through longitudinal studies of socialization processes (Thomas and Anderson, 1998; De Vos, Buyens and Schalk, 2005). In a study of British Army recruits, Thomas and Anderson (1998) found that newcomer proactivity in the form of information seeking about one's role, interpersonal support, organizational practices, and social relationships resulted in stronger expectations of what employees felt they should receive from the army. De Vos, Buyens and Schalk's (2005) study of over 900 Belgian employees found that employees seek contract-related information that is congruent with their values. For instance, employees valuing economic rewards sought information about financial promises. These studies illustrate that employees are not merely passive receivers of organizational communications regarding psychological contracts; they also actively shape their psychological contracts through information seeking behavior consistent with personal values.

The final factor we consider is the extent to which psychological contract breach affects the contents of psychological contracts. Longitudinal research strongly suggests that psychological contract breach leads to employees rebalancing or redressing the deal by lowering their obligations to their employer (Coyle-Shapiro and Kessler, 2002a; Robinson, Kraatz and Rousseau, 1994). Similarly, employers have also been found to lower their obligations to employees who are perceived to have not fulfilled their obligations (Coyle-Shapiro and Kessler, 2002a). Studies also find that the effects of breach differ across the transactional/relational distinction. Breaches can be more damaging to relational than transactional psychological contracts (Grimmer and Oddy, 2007) and may lead to employees shifting from a relational to a transactional psychological contract (Lester, Kickul and Bergmann, 2007).

Consequences of the Contents of Psychological Contracts

Most empirical studies exploring psychological contract contents have looked at how contents are formed rather than the consequences of the contents of psychological contracts. This trend may well indicate that psychological contract breach, rather than contents, has much stronger theoretical links with outcomes.

Empirical studies adopt two main approaches to examining the consequences of contents. The first posits that the contents of psychological contracts influence outcomes through social exchange. Put simply, the employer does something for the employee and the employee feels obliged to do something in return. Support for the social exchange approach is mixed, in that it is somewhat contradictory. One study finds small correlations between employee perceptions of employee and employer obligations (Rousseau, 1990) and another finds no association (Coyle-Shapiro and Kessler, 2002c). One study finds small positive associations between employee perceptions of their employer's transactional and relational promises and organizational citizenship behavior (Hui, Lee and Rousseau, 2004), another finds positive associations between relational promises and employee attitudes (job satisfaction, organizational commitment, and intention to quit), but negative associations between transactional promises and the same outcomes (Raja, Johns and Ntalianis, 2004), and another study finds very little direct or no associations between employee perception of employer promises and attitudes and self-reported behavior (Coyle-Shapiro and Kessler, 2000). In short, there is limited support for the social exchange model suggesting, at best, that the norm of reciprocity has only small effects.

The second approach toward examining the consequences of psychological contract contents involves the use of variants of Schein's (1965) matching hypothesis. Shore and Barksdale (1998) argue that the extent to which employee and employer obligations 'balance' matters in terms of explaining outcomes. Employer–employee relationships can be either balanced (consisting of mutually high, or mutually low obligations) or imbalanced in terms of employees feeling over- or underobligated. A study of MBA students found that balanced, mutually high obligations were associated with positive employee attitudes.

Dabos and Rousseau (2004) explored mutuality (i.e. agreement) between researchers and directors (i.e. employers) at US universities. Mutuality was defined as 'the degree to which the two parties agree on their interpretations of promises and commitments each party has made and accepted (i.e. agreement on what each party owes the other)' (p. 53). Agreement was defined and operationalized as the actual agreement between employee and employer promises, which is, therefore, somewhat at odds with the notion that matching is about the subjective perception of agreement. Mixed support was found for the effects on attitudes of agreement between employee and employer promises and only quite weak support for links to more objective individual performance outcomes.

Contents: Conclusions and Challenges

In general, relatively few studies have examined the factors that shape and the consequences of the contents of psychological contracts, with some areas, such as understanding factors outside of work and factors that predate an employee's current organization having been almost completely ignored. This neglect is surprising, given Levinson et al.'s (1962) view that key influences on the psychological contract frequently antedate the current employer.

Nevertheless, our brief review reveals that almost anything can in principle influence employees' beliefs about their psychological contract. However, very little is known about the relative importance of such factors or how these factors interact. For example, there is reasonable support for the idea that HR practices communicate psychological contracts but at the same time individuals differ in terms of how proactively they seek out HR practices (Sturges *et al.*, 2002, 2005) suggesting that both individual differences and structural factors interact to shape psychological contract beliefs.

Some antecedents to psychological contracts no doubt communicate promises to employees in explicit and implicit ways. However, the extent to which these factors operate at an implicit level is not well understood. Survey methods typically gather information about promises in general and do not typically request participants to make distinctions between explicit and implicit promises. We have to assume that questionnaires are to a very large extent accessing consciously accessible and therefore largely explicit promises. There is also little understanding about how agents behave when communicating implicit promises.

There are also concerns about the usefulness of proposed mechanisms linking the contents to outcomes. A major issue is that the social exchange and mutuality are very likely to be confounded with psychological contract breach as, for example, mutual high obligations are actually a reflection of ongoing fulfillment, yet breach is rarely analyzed in conjunction with these mechanisms and therefore we have no way of knowing whether effects found for, say, mutuality, are in fact due to psychological contract breach/fulfillment. Indeed, employees are only expected to reciprocate if employers fulfill their obligations and therefore the study of the contents of psychological contracts relies on psychological contract fulfillment. This concern is further supported by the findings of a longitudinal study which showed that breach predicts the content of psychological contracts, but the contents of psychological contracts are unrelated to breach (Lester, Kickul and Bergmann, 2007). Research suggests that mutuality and social exchange approaches to understanding the effects of the contents of psychological contracts may not be that important in terms of explaining outcomes and thus require further conceptual development.

Breach and Violation of Psychological Contracts

Psychological contract breach – and in particular the consequences of breach – has by far received the most empirical attention in psychological contract research. Breach provides the most compelling idea for linking the psychological contract to outcomes. Furthermore, the consequences of breach is the only area in which there are a reasonable number of studies showing fairly consistent findings, in contrast to the smattering of studies with variable results examining the contents of psychological contracts.

Psychological contract breach occurs 'when one party in a relationship perceives another to have failed to fulfill promised obligation(s)' (Robinson and Rousseau, 1994, p. 247), whereas violation refers to the extreme affective reactions that follow breach on certain occasions. Early studies tended to use breach and violation interchangeably until Morrison and Robinson (1997) argued for the distinction that has now become accepted. Psychological contract fulfillment is viewed as the opposite of breach, as the definition of breach suggests. However, as we shall discuss later, there are reasons to believe that fulfillment and breach operate quite differently in terms of their effects on outcomes.

Most empirical studies of psychological contract breach consist of quantitative questionnaire surveys, around 90% of which use cross-sectional designs (Conway and Briner, 2005). Again, this means relatively little can be concluded about causality. Although there is no single standard measure of psychological contract breach, they tend to be very similar, typically asking respondents to report the extent to which their organization has kept its promises. Measures take one of two forms, the first being a checklist of specific content items (e.g. pay, promotion, and training) where lists vary in terms of length and the specific wording of items. Checklists occasionally operationalize dimensions of psychological contract, such as transactional and relational contracts. The second form of measure requires respondents to provide a global assessment of psychological contract fulfillment (e.g. 'So far my employer has done an excellent job of fulfilling its promises to me'; Robinson and Morrison, 2000). In this section, we examine the antecedents to and consequences of breach. In addition, we examine recent challenges to the breach concept.

Antecedents to Breach

Antecedents to breach, rather unsurprisingly, resemble antecedents to contents. One likely cause of breach is the inadequate provision of human resource practices, which studies have consistently found to be associated with employees perception of breach. This relationship has been found in cross-sectional and longitudinal quantitative studies, and in qualitative case studies (Grant, 1999; Greene, Ackers and Black, 2001; Guest and Conway, 1997, 1998, 1999, 2000, 2001, 2002a, 2004). Psychological contract fulfillment has also been found to be positively associated with specific HR practices, such as organizational socialization practices and tactics (Dulac et al., 2008; Robinson and Morrison, 2000) and both formal (e.g. training to develop career) and informal (e.g. informal career advice) career management practices offered by the organization (Sturges et al., 2005).

Unsupportive relationships at work have been associated with breach, with several studies finding negative relationships between perceived organizational support and leader–member exchange and breach (Dulac et al., 2008; Sutton and Griffin, 2004; Tekleab, Takeuchi and Taylor, 2005). Researchers explain these findings by suggesting that employees in supportive relationships allow leeway and flexibility around delivery, trust the other party to deliver in the long run, are more likely to forgive discrepancies, and are less inclined to monitor and therefore may not even detect employer breaches.

Morrison and Robinson (1997) draw the useful distinction between when organizations break promises to employees due to deliberately *reneging* and breach arising from *incongruence* (i.e. misunderstandings). This distinction is useful both for understanding why breach actually occurs and also for considering whether employees make similar attributions when trying to make sense of breach. However, very few studies have examined reneging or incongruence. Two studies that collected paired employee–employer perceptions of psychological contract breach suggest that discrepant psychological contracts are common (Lester *et al.*, 2002; Truong and Quang, 2007). Truong and Quang (2007) sampled 220 MBA students in employment and their HR managers in Vietnam and found a correlation of only 0.36 between employee's and HR manager's perception of the organization's obligations, and a correlation of 0.39 between employee and HR manager's perception of the fulfillment of obligations. Furthermore, and perhaps unsurprisingly, employers perceived higher fulfillment of obligations by the organization. Finding similar results, in an earlier study, Lester *et al.* (2002) sampled 134 employee–line manager dyads from MBA students and telecommunications employees from the United States and found that supervisor and employee views differ about extent of breach, with employees as one might expect more likely to report breach. Employees were also more likely to attribute breach to the organization's intentional reneging, whereas supervisors more likely to attribute breach to situations beyond the organization's control. Unfortunately, neither of these studies examined the extent to which discrepant views led to breach, nor did they consider the extent of subjective agreement (the above comparisons are based on actual agreement).

Studies have begun to explore how individual differences affect breach. Edwards *et al.* (2003) carried out a series of experiments and questionnaire surveys and found that the ideology of self-reliance – the tendency of workers to take responsibility for their own welfare and employability and not to rely on the organization – reduced the extent to which employees perceived redundancy programs as psychological contract breach. Raja, Johns and Ntalianis (2004) found mixed results for associations between personality traits and perceived breach. Neuroticism, conscientiousness, and locus of control were related to perceived breach, whereas extra-version, equity sensitivity and self-esteem were not.

The final antecedent to breach considered here is social comparison processes. Ho (2005) argues that when employees compare themselves inequitably to coworkers, they are more likely to perceive breach. Building on this work, O'Neill, Halbesleben and Edwards (2007) consider two types of social comparisons; firstly, where employees compare themselves to others (referred to as *other-referent*), and, secondly, where employees compare their current experiences to their own previous, anticipated future, or ideal experiences (referred to as *self-referent*). Both types of comparisons are associated equally with breach and found to be triggered by changes to HR policies and practices. Social comparison processes may also explain other studies that consistently find differences in psychological contract breach reported by groups that are known to compare themselves to one another, such as part-time and full-time workers (Conway and Briner, 2002b; Gakovic and Tetrick, 2003; Millward and Hopkins, 1998) and temporary and permanent contract workers (De Cuyper and De Witte, 2006). Self-referent comparisons may be a key factor in explaining findings from studies that show factors outside the current employer, such as experiencing breach in former employment relationships and the perceived attractiveness of alternative employment, influence breach (Robinson and Morrison, 2000).

In summary, research on the antecedents to psychological contract breach has yielded some encouraging findings and suggests some likely processes for understanding how employees interpret workplace events as breach. However, rather like the antecedents of psychological contract contents, there is currently little breadth or depth of findings associated with any single factor, or a good understanding of the relative importance of factors and how they interact with each other.

Consequences of Breach

According to psychological contract theory, employee perceptions of psychological contract breach will result in negative outcomes for the employee and the organization. Employees are believed to suffer extreme emotional reactions, develop negative attitudes toward the organization, and withdraw various forms of positive behavior following breach.

Many questionnaire surveys have examined the consequences of breach. Employee perceptions of breach (i.e. when their organization has failed to deliver on its promises) have been found to associate with the following:

- *Negative affective outcomes.* Negative emotions, such as anger, violation and depression (e.g. Conway and Briner, 2002b), and reduced psychological well-being (e.g. Conway and Briner, 2002a).
- *Negative attitudes toward the organization.* Decreased levels of trust in the organization (e.g. Robinson, 1996; Grimmer and Oddy, 2007; Deery, Iverson and Walsh, 2006), reduced organizational commitment (e.g. Lester *et al.*, 2002; Turnley and Feldman, 1999b; Grimmer and Oddy, 2007), reduced job satisfaction (e.g. Tekleab and Taylor, 2003), and the development of cynical attitudes toward the organization (e.g. Johnson and O'Leary-Kelly, 2003).
- *Withdrawal intentions and behaviors.* Lowering obligations toward the organization (e.g. Robinson, Kraatz and Rousseau, 1994; Coyle-Shapiro and Kessler, 2002a), decreased levels of performance, including self-reported knowledge sharing and innovation (Thompson and Heron, 2006), self-reported in-role performance (e.g. Restubog, Bordia and Tang, 2006; Robinson, 1996; Turnley and Feldman, 1999b, 2000), supervisor-rated in-role performance (e.g. Lester *et al.*, 2002; Restubog, Bordia and Tang, 2006),

and various organizational citizenship or extra-role behaviors (e.g. Robinson, 1996; Robinson and Morrison, 1995; Turnley and Feldman, 2000), intentions to leave and in some cases actually leaving the organization (e.g. Tekleab and Taylor, 2003; Turnley and Feldman, 1999b; Robinson and Rousseau, 1994; Robinson, 1995, 1996).

- *Abusive behavior toward others.* Supervisors perceiving breach by the organization in turn abuse direct reports (as reported by the supervisors direct reports) (Hoobler and Brass, 2006), and self-reported workplace deviant behaviors toward colleagues and the organization (Restubog, Bordia and Tang, 2007).

Two recent meta-analyses of mostly cross-sectional studies summarize the impact of breach on work outcomes (Bal, De Lange and Jansen, 2007; Zhao *et al.*, 2007). The two studies, unsurprisingly, arrive at very similar results for the direct effects of breach on outcomes. Zhao *et al.* (2007) incorporated the results of 51 studies in their meta-analyses and found that breach shared an average observed effect size (correlation) of 0.43 with violation (based on 11 studies), 0.53 with mistrust (based on 9 studies), −0.45 with job satisfaction (based on 28 studies), −0.32 with organizational commitment (based on 20 studies), 0.34 with the intention to quit (based on 22 studies), −0.11 with organizational citizenship behavior (OCB) (based on 21 studies), and −0.20 with in-role performance (based on 16 studies). However, the average correlation with actual turnover was just 0.05 (based on 5 studies).

The effects of breach have been compared with meta-analytic findings for other concepts. Zhao *et al.* (2007) compare the effects of breach with those found from a meta-analysis of met expectations (Wanous *et al.*, 1992) and note that breach has larger effects on outcomes (about 0.15 of a correlation index). Conway and Briner (2005) compare the average effects of breach on outcomes with those found for organizational justice from a meta-analysis (Cohen-Charash and Spector, 2001) and find that breach and justice have very similar patterns of associations with outcomes, justice being marginally stronger. From this, we can conclude that psychological contract breach is as important in terms of its associations with outcomes as other popularly assessed indicators of the employment relationship.

One immediately striking finding from across these studies is that breach has much stronger associations with attitudes than it does with (largely self-reported) behavior. Most of the studies included in the meta-analyses use cross-sectional, self-report designs. An exception is the findings between breach and actual turnover reported in Zhao *et al.*'s (2007) meta-analyses, where no association was found. How does the use of more rigorous designs affect the strength of relationship between breach and other behavioral outcomes? A small number of studies examining the consequences of breach have collected longitudinal data and objective behavioral measures obtained from organizational records. These studies find breach has a correlation with job performance between −0.20 and −0.34 (Bunderson, 2001; Conway and Coyle-Shapiro, 2006; Sturges et al., 2005), and breach variously has a correlation with absence of 0.17 (Sturges et al., 2005) and 0.04 (Deery, Iverson and Walsh, 2006). These studies also suggest that breach has markedly lower associations with behaviors than attitudes, where relationships are almost nonexistent for absence and turnover; however, more longitudinal designs drawing on objective behavioral data are required before drawing firm conclusions.

Finally, how do researchers explain the effects of breach? Many possible types of explanation have been suggested including discrepancy approaches (e.g. discrepancy between promises and delivery mirroring negative evaluations such as job dissatisfaction or unmet expectations; Zhao et al., 2007), trust explanations (e.g. breach destroying trust and thus negating further rounds of reciprocation; Robinson and Rousseau, 1994), balance ideas such as rebalancing obligations and inequity (e.g. the organization fails to deliver its side of the deal and therefore the employee readjusts what they are prepared to offer; Turnley et al., 2003), breach depriving employees of rewards (e.g. Robinson and Rousseau, 1994), breach impeding progress toward goals (e.g. Conway and Briner, 2002a), retaliation (e.g. breach involving a loss of face that inspires revenge; Zhao et al., 2007), and breach communicating to the employee that the organization does not value its contribution and therefore the employee adopts a more transactional approach toward the organization (Coyle-Shapiro and Conway, 2005).

We could find no consistent pattern for how these explanations were used across outcomes or studies. The large number of explanations demonstrates the flexibility of the breach idea, but it also shows a lack of parsimony and precision and raises concerns as to exactly how the mechanisms underlying these explanations actually work – particularly as some may help explain both the effects and the causes of breach (e.g. low trust). There is a further concern that several of these explanations – including impeding goals, inequity, loss of face and feeling unvalued – do not relate to the psychological contract as such and, therefore, that these explanations sit somewhat outside psychological contract theory, thus making it difficult to incorporate them in a coherent account of the effects of psychological contract breach.

Researchers rarely explore the mechanisms and processes through which breach affects outcomes. Tests for mediators, which is one way of inferring simple mechanisms, between breach and outcomes mostly draw on negative affect and rebalancing obligations (e.g. Grimmer and Oddy, 2007; Restubog, Bordia and Tang, 2006; Tekleab, Takeuchi and Taylor, 2005; Thompson and Heron, 2006; Turnley and Feldman, 2000; Zhao et al., 2007). These studies have produced mixed findings. For example, affective commitment has been found to fully (Thompson and Heron, 2006), partially (Grimmer and Oddy, 2007; Turnley and Feldman, 2000), and nonmediate (Sturges et al., 2005) links between breach and outcomes, with stronger mediating effects for discretionary rather than in-role behavior (Restubog, Bordia and Tang, 2006), and mediation varying across psychological contract type (Grimmer and Oddy, 2007). Turnley and Feldman (2000) found job satisfaction to partially mediate the relationship between breach and intentions to quit, whereas Tekleab *et al.* (2005) found job satisfaction to fully mediate the same relationship. Furthermore, mediation is often tested using data from cross-sectional designs and therefore such findings are unlikely to be particularly robust.

Moderators of the Breach–Outcomes Relationship

Zhao *et al.* (2007) also consider whether the type of breach measure (global versus composite) and the content of the breach (transactional versus relational) moderate responses to breach. Measures of global breach had slightly higher correlations with outcomes than composite measures of breach. Transactional breach had somewhat smaller correlations for four out of the five outcomes compared with relational contract breach. In the other meta-analysis of breach, Bal, De Lange and Jansen (2007) examined age as a moderator, with the expectation that older workers would react less intensely to breach than younger workers, as older workers have been found to have more realistic expectations and are better at emotion regulation (Carstensen, Isaacowitz and Charles, 1999). The results were puzzling as older workers reacted less negatively to breach in relation to trust and organizational commitment, but more negatively in relation to job satisfaction.

Outside of these meta-analyses, a number of other studies consider moderators of the breach–outcome relationship, where these moderators include the perceived importance of the promise (Conway and Briner, 2002a), attributions of reneging versus breach being outside the organization's control (Conway and Briner, 2002a; Turnley and Feldman, 1999b; Turnley *et al.*, 2003; Robinson and Morrison, 2000), the procedural, distributive, or interactive justice of the breach (Kickul, Lester and Finkl, 2002; Kickul, Lester and Finkl, 2002; Lo and Aryee, 2003; Robinson and Morrison, 2000; Thompson and Heron, 2005; Turnley and Feldman, 1999a), personal ideologies (Bunderson, 2001), national culture (Grimmer and Oddy, 2007; Kickul, Lester and Belgio, 2004), personality traits (Ho, Weingart and Rousseau, 2004; Raja, Johns and Ntalianis, 2004; Restubog, Bordia and Tang, 2007), and supportive relationships such as leader–member exchange and perceived organizational support (Dulac *et al.*, 2008; Restubog and Bordia, 2006).

The analyses of moderators show that there are many possible moderators, but those examined so far have tended to be restricted to the same variables also studied in relation to antecedents to the contents and breach of psychological contracts. There are also some important gaps, such as the need for more studies that examine whether the implicit/explicit distinction moderates breach effects. These studies examining moderators are difficult to integrate because they often use different sets of outcomes. However, where it has been possible to compare across such studies, findings for the moderator effects have tended to be small, frequently nonsignificant, and inconsistent. For example, Ho, Weingart and Rousseau (2004) used a scenario-based experiment with an undergraduate sample and found that the personality traits of agreeableness and neuroticism moderated some negative emotional responses to breach; Raja, Johns and Ntalianis (2004) examined the extent to which six personality traits moderated the effects of breach on violation, where only the locus of control acted as a moderator. A potential moderator examined in both studies was neuroticism; however, it was only found to moderate outcomes in one of these studies (i.e. Ho, Weingart and Rousseau, 2004). Another example of contradictory findings and theorizing across studies is in connection with the moderating role of supportive relationships with managers, the latter having been variously found to weaken (Dulac *et al.*, 2008) and strengthen (Restubog and Bordia, 2006) reactions to breach. Dulac *et al.* (2008) argue that supportive relationships buffer the effects of breach by inclining employees to forgive, whereas Restubog and Bordia (2006) argue that the effects of breach will be exaggerated in supportive relationships as it indicates betrayal. Of course, one could argue that the moderators examined thus far depend on yet more moderators, but it is probably more an indication of the weak theory. In general, moderator effects appear more likely to be found when the proposed relationship is highly self-evident and therefore, not very illuminating (e.g. the effects of breach are stronger for important as opposed to unimportant promises; employees with tendencies to feel entitled to receive things react more strongly to breach than employees with benevolent tendencies).

Challenges to the Breach Concept

Much of the appeal and value of the breach concept lies in the simple idea that breach has a straightforward negative relationship with outcomes. This simple prediction is, however, increasingly being questioned in the light of challenges relating to whether breach has any value over and above related concepts, whether there are substantively different ways of breaking promises, whether there are many nonlinear relationships between the breach–fulfillment continuum and outcomes and whether this varies across the content of the promise and across outcomes, and challenges to how breach is measured. These challenges raise serious concerns about breach – the heart of psychological contract theory – questioning its value, parsimony, and the appropriateness of examining psychological contract breach using typical methods and designs (i.e. cross-sectional, self-report surveys).

How does Breach Differ from Related Constructs?

The first issue is the extent to which psychological contract breach contributes to our understanding of the employment exchange beyond the many other exchange constructs, such as perceived organizational support, leader–member exchange, organizational justice notions, and trust. As we have noted above, these exchange concepts are often used to explain the effects of breach on outcomes. There is also considerable empirical overlap; breach is often found to be highly intercorrelated with these exchange constructs and to share similar associations with outcomes and antecedents.

The main theoretical distinction between breach and the other exchange ideas is that breach refers to the discrepancy between what was promised and what was delivered, whereas perceived organizational support, leader–member exchange and fairness are fundamentally concerned with what employees get from the organization (i.e. delivery; Aselage and Eisenberger, 2003; Coyle-Shapiro and Conway, 2005). This distinction is helpful, but it overlooks the near certainty that perceptions of psychological contract fulfillment, support, and equity will co-occur with every case of delivery because they are all defined as part of the same ongoing exchange relationship and, therefore, employees will invariably evaluate what they receive in the light of expectations established from previous exchange encounters. While a small number of studies have tested the discriminant validity of measures of psychological contract breach, met expectations and justice (e.g. Robinson, 1996; Turnley and Feldman, 2000), they have done so in a limited way by, for example, including measures of breach and met expectations or justice that do not permit precise comparison, due (among other differences) to variations in the number of items and item content across measures.

The second issue relates to the problems associated with breach being defined as the discrepancy between what was promised and what was delivered. Breach therefore simultaneously captures the three concepts of promises made, rewards received, and the discrepancy between the two (i.e. breach) where any one of these concepts could possibly explain links between breach and outcomes (Arnold, 1996). To gain understanding of the unique explanatory power of breach, in future, researchers should carefully control for perceptions of promises made and rewards received. Given the importance, accuracy and clarity of Arnold's (1996) observation, it is quite surprising that we could only find one study that considers these three components together. This study found that the components of psychological contract fulfillment (particularly rewards) are more important in predicting OCBs than psychological contract fulfillment (Coyle-Shapiro and Conway, 2005). In other words, what matters to employees is what they actually get rather than the discrepancy between what they get and what they are told they will get.

Given the above theoretical and empirical overlaps, research is urgently needed to disentangle these concepts and understand their relative importance, or to gain a better understanding of how they may be part of a common unfolding or simultaneous process.

Are There Different Ways of Breaking a Promise?

The standard view of breach is that it simply refers to a broken promise regarding some aspect of work, without considering whether there are different

Table 3.1 Ways of psychological contract breach

Cassar and Briner's (2005) analysis of employee–employer relationships	Pavlou and Geffen's (2005) analysis of buyer–seller online relationships
Delay: Where the fulfillment of the promise occurs later than expected	*Product delivery delay*: Failure to send product in a timely manner
Different type or form of reward: What is delivered is of a different form from what has been promised	*Product misrepresentation*: Item delivered differs to one described in advertisement
Magnitude: What is delivered is less than what was promised	*Fraud*: Failure to deliver the product purchased
Inequity: What is received is less than or different from what others in similar positions are getting	*Product guarantees*: Offering a refund policy and then failing to acknowledge guarantee
Reciprocal imbalance: The employee perceives that they are giving far more to the organization than they are getting back in return	*Contract default*: Refusal to accept payment and to send product
	Payment policy: Refusal to follow payment policy and accept certain forms of payment

ways of breaking promises. Two recent studies examine this issue. Table 3.1 summarizes the five categories derived from Cassar and Briner's (2005) analysis of qualitative interviews with employees arrived and the six categories derived from Pavlou and Gefen's (2005) review of academic and practitioner literature relating to the psychological contract analysis of online buyer–seller relationships.

There are clearly some similarities in findings. Furthermore, Cassar (2004) finds that the breach types differentially relate to outcomes. These studies clearly show that there is more than one way to break a promise. Future research should explore different types of breach to examine how they affect outcomes, how they interact, and in what contexts they develop. Examining ways of breaking promises may have particular benefits for managing psychological contracts by highlighting more or less acceptable or repairable forms of breach and therefore providing options for organizations forced into breaching psychological contracts.

Limitations of Breach Measures

We have already noted several limitations of psychological contract questionnaires, for example, that they do not capture exchange, and that there is little agreement across measures in terms of the psychological contract belief referred to (e.g. promise, obligation, commitment, and expectation). In this section, we focus on the wording of items typically used to measure psychological contract breach. Conway and Briner (2005) provide an extensive analysis

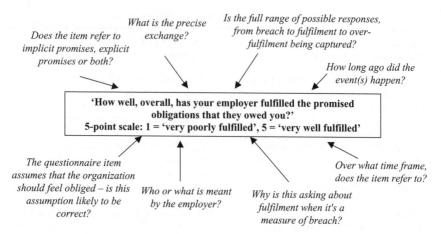

Figure 3.1   Key issues when measuring psychological contract breach.
Source: Understanding Psychological Contracts at Work: A Critical Evaluation of Theory and Research,
Conway, N. & Briner, R., Copyright © 2005 Oxford University Press.

of this issue; here we present their summary of the limitations in Figure 3.1. The figure focuses on an item used by Robinson and Rousseau (1994), which is illustrative of breach measures.

Taken together, these issues amount to a serious degree of measurement imprecision. Such imprecision is an inevitable feature of a questionnaire survey approach, which is largely restricted to asking general questions. Furthermore, given the underspecified nature of psychological contract theory, the degree of generality is perhaps not so much an item design fault as a design requirement of measures given the specificity of underlying theory. For instance, psychological contract theory gives no clear guidelines as to who or what represents the organization, what the exchange is, or the appropriate time lag between breach and its effects on outcomes. A questionnaire approach is also incompatible with examining implicit beliefs (which are unlikely to be immediately consciously accessible); however, if psychological contract measures were worded in terms of explicit promises, they would be at odds with most researchers' views that psychological contracts are predominantly about implicit beliefs. Many of the issues in Figure 3.1 apply equally well to promises made as they do to promises broken and are therefore relevant to measures of psychological contract contents.

The Nature of the Relationship Between Breach and Fulfillment and Outcomes

The traditional view of psychological contract researchers is that the breach–fulfillment continuum has linear effects on outcomes, where these effects are invariably negative for both employees (e.g. reduced job satisfaction) and for organizations (e.g. reduced employee effort) (Lambert, Edwards and

Cable, 2003). However, several recent studies challenge this traditional view. Conway and Briner's (2002a) diary study of psychological contracts found that broken promises generally had a stronger effect on daily mood than exceeded promises. Lambert, Edwards and Cable (2003) polynomial regression analysis of survey data found that promises exceeded on certain items (e.g. pay) associate positively with job satisfaction, whereas promises exceeded on other items (e.g. task variety) associate negatively with job satisfaction. These studies suggest that breach and fulfillment may not belong to a single continuum and that breach and fulfillment may have nonlinear effects on outcomes that may vary according to the content of the item.

Other research challenges the notion that breach invariably results in negative outcomes and, in contrast, suggests that breach may have some positive effects in the long run. Pavlou and Gefen (2005) found that buyers who experience breach making online purchases are less likely to experience breach with different sellers in subsequent transactions. The authors argue that this is because through the experience of breach, buyers learn how to become better purchasers, less naïve, and better at negotiating future exchanges in ways that will minimize the chances of breach. Ingram's (2007) study of undergraduate psychology students in employment found that breach is associated with forgiveness in trusting relationships.

In summary, the studies reviewed in this section present a far more complex picture of the relationship between breach, fulfillment and outcomes than that considered in traditional psychological contract breach research. Going forward, however, researchers need to gain a better understanding of why effects vary across outcomes, and to examine how effects may change over time.

Conclusions: Breach

What can we conclude from psychological contract breach studies? First, there are just too few studies to draw firm conclusions in many crucial research areas, such as the antecedents to breach and moderators of the breach–outcome relationship. Furthermore, when we move beyond psychological contract theory's most obvious prediction (the direct effects of breach on outcomes), there are remarkably few consistent findings; research is piecemeal, and effect sizes weak. Second, breach has much weaker links with work behavior than work attitudes, suggesting breach may not be very useful for understanding some forms of work behavior. Third, there are a large number of possible explanations for the effects of breach on outcomes, but few have been tested and those that have are not clearly supported. Fourth, there have been several major challenges to the breach concept. These challenges have added some depth of analysis to the breach idea, but they collectively introduce so much complexity about the where, when, and what of breach that the simple predictive use of breach becomes untenable, the initial parsimonious appeal of breach being diminished. Finally, there are very few rigorous empirical studies (e.g. ones incorporating longitudinal data, with behavioral, as opposed to self-report, outcomes) to draw firm conclusions, even concerning the consequences of breach. The dominant cross-sectional self-report method is in this context, and indeed most contexts, a very weak one.

METHODOLOGICAL CHALLENGES

Psychological contract researchers have used a number of different methods including questionnaires (e.g. Rousseau, 1990), scenarios (Edwards *et al.*, 2003; Rousseau and Anton, 1991), critical incident techniques (Herriot, Manning and Kidd, 1997), interviews (Argyris, 1960; Dick, 2006; Levinson *et al.*, 1962), diaries (Conway and Briner, 2002a), case studies (Grant, 1999; Greene, Ackers and Black, 2001), and analyses of publicly available documents (Pavlou and Gefen, 2005). But, by far, the most common method has been questionnaire surveys. Conway and Briner (2005) estimate that about 90% of the psychological contract empirical studies use questionnaire surveys (of this 70% are cross-sectional and 20% longitudinal surveys) and 10% of empirical studies are based on qualitative interview data.

The field's preoccupation with the survey method – along with its general use of single source data, MBA student samples, and elaborate statistical analyses – has led researchers to conclude that psychological contract research has fallen into a 'methodological rut' (Taylor and Tekleab, 2004, p. 279). The most glaring and disturbing feature of this rut is the mismatch between the survey method and psychological contract theory. As noted above, the psychological contract can be viewed in two interlinked ways, first, as an exchange process unfolding on a day-to-day basis and driven along by events, such as the communication or fulfillment of implicit or explicit promises, or interrupted by events, most notably psychological contract breach (e.g. Conway and Briner's (2002a) diary study). Because there is so little research into the psychological contract as an unfolding process, it is not clear how the psychological contract operates in this respect, in terms of what the key events may be, how the psychological contract changes, and how such changes affect immediate and longer term emotional, cognitive and behavioral responses, and so on. The second and most common way to view the psychological contract is as a 'state' that refers to an individual's global impression of the employer's promissory behavior over the course of the relationship. This 'state' is in effect the individual's subjective summation of all the events taking place under the first approach. The state of the psychological contract is subject to the antecedents and consequences discussed earlier.

Neither of the above approaches to the psychological contract – and certainly not the first approach – is adequately captured by questionnaire surveys. The survey approach falls short in three major ways. Firstly, Reis and Wheeler's (1991) wide-ranging and powerful critique shows that questionnaire surveys are an extremely weak method for capturing behavior and events related to social activity. The 'personalized impressions' obtained from respondents answering questionnaires have been 'percolated, construed, and reframed through various perceptual, cognitive, and motivational processes' (Reis and Wheeler, 1991, p. 271). They document numerous biases pertaining to each of these three processes that substantially affect how respondents select, recall, and aggregate past events, with the result that information obtained from questionnaires are likely to be invalid and unreliable indicators of everyday events and social behavior. In terms of psychological contract research, measures used to capture contents and breach are therefore an inaccurate record of what actually happened; instead, they are likely to reflect attitudes employees hold toward the organization. As such, these attitudes are similar to organizational commitment and job satisfaction. These limitations of the questionnaire approach to psychological contract research apply to surveys of workplace behavior more generally, irrespective of whether they are underpinned by cross-sectional or longitudinal research designs, and in the case of the latter, where the waves of data collection are separated by significant time periods.

Secondly, cross-sectional designs cannot examine causality. Therefore, while most psychological contract studies discuss hypotheses and results in terms of antecedents, consequences, mediators, outcomes, and so on, such statements are assumptions and not tested empirically to any rigorous degree. Any obtained correlation between, say, breach and a behavior may in part reflect reverse causality, a bidirectional relationship, or a spurious relationship due to an omitted variable. Establishing causality in psychological contract research – or for any exchange-based concept – is perhaps particularly problematic as inputs (antecedents) and outputs (consequences) to the psychological contract alternate as the exchange process unfolds over time.

The third limitation of surveys is that because they are only suitable for capturing respondents' consciously accessible perceptions and attitudes at the time of participation, they are unsuitable for measuring implicit beliefs and therefore psychological contracts. While there is some debate among researchers as to how consciously accessible psychological contract implicit beliefs are, ranging from being partly unconsciously formulated (Levinson et al., 1962) to much more conscious perceptions of social behavior (Rousseau, 1995), even researchers emphasizing conscious perceptions would recognize that employees are not simultaneously conscious of all such beliefs (Meckler, Drake and Levinson, 2003). If individuals cannot consciously recall the terms of their psychological contracts upon demand, then this leads to the sobering and perhaps depressing conclusion that all questionnaire studies to date are not measuring psychological contracts at all but are instead measuring only explicit contracts.

To conclude, the common approach of using surveys is fundamentally inappropriate to examining psychological contracts. The use of surveys has no doubt limited our understanding by, for example, leading to highly selective examinations of the features and concepts of the psychological contract (Hallier and Forbes, 2004). In future, researchers should choose a method capable of studying social processes over time. Later, we consider possible approaches to examining the psychological contract that are a better fit with its defined characteristics. While there are practical, career and other reasons why most researchers continue to use inappropriate methods and designs, we are in little doubt that insight into psychological contracts will not develop to any significant degree if we do not change how we research it.

FIVE CHALLENGES TO THE PSYCHOLOGICAL CONTRACT NOTION

In this section, we focus on the key challenges and therefore research priorities for the psychological contract concept. We restrict our analysis to issues relating to how the psychological contract has been defined, as any such challenges will clearly also apply to any related area of psychological contract theory. Table 3.2 summarizes a number of challenges arising from our earlier review of definitional problems, drawn from five major critiques of the psychological contract (Arnold, 1996; Conway and Briner, 2005; Cullinane and Dundon, 2006; Guest, 1998; Meckler, Drake and Levinson, 2003).

In the remainder of this section, we will focus on five of the challenges that we believe are most pressing to understanding the psychological contract, namely: What is meant by an implicit promise? What are the precise links between what employees offer and what they get back from the organization? How are psychological contracts negotiated? Who or what do employees perceive to be the other party to the contract? How can we begin to understand the psychological contract as a process?

What Is an Implicit Promise?

Understanding this issue is also the key to understanding the distinction between promises, obligations, expectations and needs. As mentioned already, while early researchers emphasized the implicit nature of psychological contracts (e.g. Kotter, 1973; Levinson *et al.*, 1962; Schein, 1965, 1980), there has been an increasing trend toward focusing on beliefs based on explicit deals (e.g. Guest, 2004a), possibly reflecting researchers' desire to remove any ambiguity about what the psychological contract refers to. The movement away from implicit promises toward merely interpreting explicit promises is in many ways unfortunate, as the implicitness of a psychological contract is the main way in which it is distinctive from, say, legal and employment contracts and from other exchange constructs that deal with explicit behavior, such as perceived organizational support (Eisenberger *et al.*, 1986) and leader–member exchange (Wayne, Shore and Liden, 1997). Furthermore, shifting the emphasis to more explicit contracts would lead to other aspects of the definition becoming marginalized or irrelevant, such as the subjectivity and dynamic nature of psychological contracts. For example, how can an explicit contract – with the likely requirement that both parties consent to it changing – evolve dynamically?

Table 3.2 A summary of challenges facing the psychological contract

Feature	Challenge	Authors
What beliefs make up the psychological contract?	Do psychological contracts consist of promises, obligations, or expectations? How do these terms differ and interrelate?	Arnold, 1996; Guest, 1998; Conway and Briner, 2005
	Should open and explicit promises still be referred to as psychological contract beliefs? Are they insufficiently psychological and more akin to a legal contract?	Guest, 1998
	Contemporary research focuses on behavioral contracts and therefore neglects the psychological underpinnings of psychological contracts of early research (most notably Levinson *et al.*, 1962).	Meckler, Drake and Levinson, 2003
	The perceptions-of-behavior approach neglects the vital role of psychological needs and the extent psychological contract beliefs are partly unconsciously formulated.	Meckler, Drake and Levinson, 2003
	What does implicit mean and what role does inference and interpretation play in terms of generating implicit promises? For example, what is the status of expectations that arise from inferences employees make from implicit promises?	Conway and Briner, 2005
Exchange	What are the specific links between employee obligations and employer obligations that form the exchange?	Conway and Briner, 2005
Agreement	Do psychological contracts require a strong (i.e. covering the existence, terms, and linkages between terms) or weak (i.e. that a contract exists, even if its terms are not known) form of agreement?	Arnold, 1996

(Continued)

Table 3.2   *(Countinued)*

Feature	Challenge	Authors
	If agreement is to be understood as subjective, is it still appropriate to refer to the psychological contract as a contract, which by legal definitions requires the outward appearance of agreement?	Guest, 1998; Cullinane and Dundon, 2006
	Changing most other types of contracts (e.g. legal contracts) is quite difficult and requires the consent of both parties: how is consent achieved when changing psychological contracts?	Cullinane and Dundon, 2006
Features of contracts	Lists of dimensions (e.g. stability, scope, tangibility, focus, and time frame) are intuitive rather than theoretical. Furthermore, they are largely descriptive rather than evaluative or construed as part of theory linking the psychological contract to outcomes.	Guest, 1998
Implicit negotiation	How are implicit psychological contracts negotiated?	Arnold, 1996
	How can we understand psychological contracts as an unfolding process?	Conway and Briner, 2005
How are psychological contracts shaped?	When do psychological contracts begin?	Guest, 1998
	How are organizations shaped by factors predating and outside the organization?	Conway and Briner, 2005
	Given that in most organizations there will be multiple contract makers sending mixed messages and the organization's prerogative is to do what it likes with employees – how and why do employees perceive and interpret promises in the first place?	Cullinane and Dundon, 2006
The agency problem	Can organizations have psychological contracts?	Guest, 1998; Conway and Briner, 2005; Cullinane and Dundon, 2006

Table 3.2   *(Countinued)*

Feature	Challenge	Authors
	If not (because of problems associated with anthropomorphizing organizations), who is the other party to an employee's psychological contract?	
	How do employees cognitively represent the organization as the other party to the contract? Do employees anthropomorphize the organization and, if so, how?	Conway and Briner, 2005

Implicit promises have been defined as 'interpretations of patterns of past exchange, vicarious learning (e.g. witnessing other employees' experiences) as well as through various factors that each party may take for granted (e.g. good faith or fairness)' (Robinson and Rousseau, 1994, p. 246), and beliefs 'based upon both inferences and observations of past practice' (Rousseau, 1990, p. 390). We believe there are two interrelated issues that need to be tackled in order to better understand implicit promise. The first issue is to develop understanding of what is meant by 'interpretation' and 'inference', mentioned in the above definitions. These terms have not been sufficiently defined. Taking 'inferences' as an example, the definition of implicit promises suggests that employees can make endless iterations of inferences, resulting in the contents of psychological contracts becoming unbounded and indistinguishable from other beliefs (e.g. expectations, desires, fantasies) (Conway and Briner, 2005). The second issue is addressing the extent to which implicit promises are consciously versus unconsciously based. Most recent research follows Rousseau and positions psychological contracts as perceptions of open and explicit behavior (and therefore accessible using questionnaire approaches) whereas Levinson and others (Kotter, 1973; Levinson *et al.*, 1962; Meckler, Drake and Levinson, 2003; Nuttall, 2004) view psychological contract beliefs as largely unconscious. Meckler, Drake and Levinson (2003) lament the move away from the psychological contract's clinical origins:

Although contemporary psychological contract literature insists on speaking primarily about conscious expectations in the employment relationship, the original clinically based conceptualization focused on understanding what are often *unconscious* needs for affection, dependency, and aggression and the personal identity or ego ideals that drive motivation and behavior ... [recent developments] grant too much importance to the social and unwritten-but-understood elements of the principle-agent contracts, with too little weight being given to the psychological elements. (Meckler, Drake and Levinson, 2003, p. 218.)

'Psychological elements' here are equated with unconscious beliefs (Rousseau, 2003). Implicit psychological contracts are partly unconscious because they derive from unconscious needs: 'An implicit psychological contract *results* when the individual and the organization achieve a mutually beneficial working arrangement that satisfies each other's psychological needs' (Meckler, Drake and Levinson, 2003, p. 222, our emphasis). It is the repeated patterns of exchange behavior between employees and organizations in their attempts to fulfill each other's needs that leads to the perception of implicit promises as described by Rousseau.

A further aspect of the unconscious quality of implicit promises that is not captured by the needs approach is that they develop through subtle conditioning processes as a result of the employee–employer interaction. This conditioning may not be consciously observed by the employee but may nevertheless affect their behavior.

To conclude, it is very difficult to find useful and clear definitions of implicit promises and related terms (e.g. inference). A major task facing psychological contract researchers is therefore to unpack and clarify the meaning of implicit promises. A problem is that the various definitions of implicit promises are not descriptions of a phenomenon as such, but complex propositions that also include where such beliefs come from (note the use of 'based upon' in Rousseau's definition, and 'results' in Mecklar *et al.*'s definition). One possibility is to develop some kind of taxonomy of implicit promises based on the origins of the promise (explicit social behavior, unconscious needs, and behavioral conditioning). In addressing this definitional challenge, researchers must somehow go beyond a prevailing paradox in this area, namely, that the more implicit a psychological contract becomes (whether in a Rousseau or Levinsonian sense), the less it resembles an exchange contract; however, the more the psychological contract becomes like an employment contract, the less psychological it becomes, unless we take the position that all contracts are psychological or at least contain substantial psychological elements.

What Are the Precise Links between What Employees Offer and What They Get Back from the Organization?

Currently, psychological contract theory provides very little guidance about the specific links between what employees offer and what the organization offers in return, as illustrated by the following quote:

> Contracts are agreements to exchange services for compensation. The rich array of possible exchanges (such as effort, learning, sacrificed opportunities elsewhere) and their duration (a day or infinity) create a variety of potential contracts between employee and employer. (Rousseau and Wade-Benzoni, 1995, pp. 293–294.)

Distinctions have, of course, been made between transactional and relational psychological contracts, but this distinction represents only a slight narrowing of the exchange with no specific links made within the distinctions. Furthermore, as mentioned above, factor analyses from empirical studies find that the distinction is not particularly reliable across studies (Taylor and Tekleab, 2004). Nor has the distinction become established in the way psychological contracts are measured.

When researchers discuss the exchange underlying psychological contracts, they often refer to literature on social exchange (e.g. Blau's (1964) classic text), although social exchange research has been equally vague about specifying any precise links:

> Social exchange generates an expectation of some future return for contributions; however the exact nature of that return is unspecified . . . social exchange does not occur on a quid pro quo or calculated basis (like economic exchanges) [they] are based on individual's trusting that the other parties to the exchange will fairly discharge their obligation in the long run. (Konovsky and Pugh, 1994, p. 657.)

As the quote by Konovsky and Pugh illustrates, social exchange theory makes no claims about precise links between what each party offers; it does, nonetheless, provide the insight that it is the receipt of something that instills an obligation to reciprocate, where the content and timing of the reciprocation are decided by the recipient and do not have to follow a consistent pattern. The lack of specificity in social exchange theory can perhaps be traced back to the origins of social exchange, particularly notions of gift exchange (Mauss, 1925). When someone receives a gift, there is unlikely to be an exact template specifying the nature of the return gift.

However, psychological contracts in employment do not involve the exchange of gifts and this lack of specificity regarding the nature of the exchange in regard of the psychological contract is potentially problematic for the advancement of psychological contract theory. Parties do things for one another because they want certain things in return, and where at least some of the returns desired are very apparent, such as pay for performance. One of the claims made by recent researchers is that psychological contracts operate like mental models that allow both parties to predict what they will get from the relationship, and in doing so provide employees with a sense of security and a feeling they can influence their own destinies in organizations (Rousseau, 2001a; Shore and Tetrick, 1994). However, if there is no consistent pattern of exchange over time, then there is no even semistable mental model, and psychological contract theory gives way to social exchange theory, such that when employers provide something to employees, they can be reasonably confident they will get something back, but far less confident about what or when.

Understanding the precise links between the things exchanged by each party is, therefore, important in order to distinguish psychological contract theory from social exchange theory. It is also important for the advancement of psychological contract theory more generally through, for example, being able to predict how an employee will react if a specific organizational input is withdrawn. Most empirical research on the psychological contracts tends to operationalize the general exchange, which is completely at odds with psychological contract theory that presents psychological contracts as mental models and cognitive schemas predicting how each party should behave (e.g. Rousseau, 2001a). It is difficult to conceive of reciprocal promises in terms of such very general exchanges. The challenge is to specify the exchange linkages. Existing attempts at exchange configurations are often cited – most notably Foa and Foa's (1980; see also Foa, 1971) resource exchange configuration – but have not attracted much research interest. These early efforts provide a starting point, but at this stage, it probably makes more sense to conduct research using more inductive approaches, given that workplaces exchanges are likely to be highly contextual and therefore not captured by Foa and Foa's general categories.

Who Is the Other Party to the Contract?

As mentioned earlier, there are two main issues here, namely, the question of how employees cognitively represent the organization and, following from this, the question of whether it is feasible for organizations to have psychological contracts.

The first issue involves understanding how employees integrate information from the various agents, principals and structural communicators to arrive at a perception of the organization as a single other party to the psychological contract. The main way researchers assume employees cognitively represent the organization is by embracing Levinson's (1965) work that argues employees anthropomorphize the organization:

> In a sense, the organization takes on an anthropomorphic identity as a party to the psychological contract. This personification of organizations is most likely facilitated by the fact that organizations have legal, moral and financial responsibilities for the actions of their agents, and by the fact that organizational policies and precedents provide continuity regardless of the specific agents involved. (Robinson and Morrison, 1995, p. 290.)

> For many individuals the organization now takes on a parental role as part of the unconscious psychological contract. (Meckler, Drake and Levinson, 2003.)

Levinson's (1965) thesis draws on the concept of transference from psychoanalysis to explain how employees perceive the organization as a parental surrogate. To our knowledge, the personification of the organization is endorsed by all psychological contract researchers. Levinson's anthropomorphism thesis is a highly provocative idea, but could also perhaps be described as the elephant in the room of psychological contract theory, as it must be one of its most uncritically accepted assumptions. To our knowledge, there is no empirical evidence that employees follow such a process to arrive at the perception of a single other party. Instead, it is an assumed fact from early writing. Some challenges associated with this idea are, first, that it has never been clearly explained how anthropomorphism to arrive at a single organization entity is or could be consistent with other writing that presents the organization as consisting of a network of agents, principals and practices communicating the psychological contract. For example, studies in related social exchange fields strongly suggest that individuals develop quite distinct relationships according to the foci (Lavelle, Rupp and Brockner, 2007). There has been little consideration of how the aggregation process is complicated by conflicting messages across agents, principles and practices. Second, the content or type of the parental surrogate has been insufficiently elaborated, although Levinson's original thesis saw organizations in caring paternal mode. Recent research on workplace familism may be a useful starting point for elaborating the role types (Aycan, 2006; Restubog and Bordia, 2006) as it offers an expanded view of parental roles. Aycan (2006), for example, explores the four parental styles of the benevolent, exploitative, authoritarian, and authoritative parent as possible roles assumed by managers toward their employees. Finally, the idea of anthropomorphizing nonhuman entities has been criticized for being imprecise and inappropriate (see Sullivan's (1995) critique of the 'selfish gene'). A clear challenge, then, is to unpack the assumption that employees anthropomorphize the organization and to empirically examine whether and how employees view organizations in this way. In short, we simply do now know who or what represents the other party to an employee's psychological contract.

Are there alternative theories to transference and anthropomorphism for understanding how agents' actions generalize to the organization? Pavlou and Gefen (2005) suggest using theories that explain how an individual's behavior may by used inductively to represent the social group they belong to, or how an individual's behavior is deducted from the social group he or she belongs to, such as perceived similarity (Piccoli and Ives, 2003), entitivity theory (Stewart, 2003), and balance theory (Heider, 1958). A further alternative is to take a bottom–up approach by focusing on psychological contracts employees develop with specific foci, such as line managers, role models and senior managers, how these may change over time, and to investigate whether the various psychological contracts can be integrated.

We now turn to the second issue of whether an organization can actually have a psychological contract. Taylor and Tekleab (2004) view developing the employer's perspective as the most important psychological contract research priority. It is well accepted that individual managers can perceive a psychological contract with employees; however, here we are interested in whether it is possible to conceptualize and operationalize an employer's perspective.

There has been relatively little research on the employer's perspective, despite the view that employers can hold psychological contracts has been a feature of psychological contract research from its inception (Argyris, 1960; Kotter, 1973; Levinson et al., 1962; Schein, 1965, 1980) to more recent work (Coyle-Shapiro and Kessler, 1998; Guest, 1998, 2004a; Guest and Conway,

2002b; Herriot and Pemberton, 1997; Shore and Coyle-Shapiro, 2003; Tsui and Wang, 2002). As Guest (1998, p. 675) has noted, 'The anxiety about [researchers] anthropomorphizing the organization is allowed to dominate and as a result the two-sided nature of the notion of exchange and a contract is neglected.' Researchers have operationalized the employer's psychological contract through specific agents (line manager, director, and HR manager), giving little consideration as to whether the agents adequately represent the organization's perspective, unless of course the other party is effectively the sole employer of the individual. Furthermore, researchers who study employer perspectives have yet to offer any convincing explanation of how the behaviors of different organizational representatives are aggregated such that employees perceive the organization as akin to another individual representing the other party to the psychological contract.

Tsui and colleagues (Tsui *et al.*, 1995, 1997) have proposed and tested four approaches an organization can take to managing employment relationships, namely, underinvestment in employees, overinvestment, mutual investment, and quasi-spot contracts. Interestingly, Tsui *et al.* (1997) state that their approach is not one based on the psychological contract as it only addresses one party's perspective, although a later study notes some close parallels between the two approaches (Tsui and Wang, 2002), and Guest (2004a) notes its potential to provide an employer's perspective. A problem with this sort of typological approach is that it is applied pretty much uniformly across employees belonging to the organization and therefore starts to resemble more of a social contract rather than an individualized psychological contract. A key challenge therefore in constructing an employer's perspective appears to be extending beyond the perspective of a single organizational party, but in so doing, maintaining an individualized relationship between the organization and the employee.

How Are Psychological Contracts Implicitly Negotiated?

Very little psychological contract research investigates how psychological contracts change. By far, the most common way of understanding psychological contract change has been through examining breach. However, we would not expect breach to be the *modus operandi* of psychological contracts; rather we would expect it to be ongoing fulfillment or negotiation. Whereas ongoing fulfillment does not involve change, negotiation clearly does.

Negotiation is viewed as central to psychological contracts (Herriot and Pemberton, 1995; Morishima, 1996; Rousseau, 1995); however, there is almost no research in this area. The two possible exceptions are Herriot and Pemberton's (1995, 1996, 1997) work on negotiation, which they refer to as 'psychological contracting', and Rousseau's (2001b, 2005) recent work on I-Deals. Psychological contracting is a prescriptive model that involves two parties engaging in the four stages of informing, negotiating, monitoring and renegotiating psychological contract terms (Herriot and Pemberton, 1997). Herriot and Pemberton (1997) argue that this process would lead to more explicit psychological contracts which in turn would lead to greater trust between employee and employer. Rousseau's work on I-Deals examines how certain employees, such as those with highly marketable knowledge and skills and therefore in a position of negotiating power, can proactively manage their psychological contract by presenting a case to their employer as to how their psychological contract should be customized. Psychological contracting and I-Deals are two very promising early attempts to examine negotiation; however, both approaches are geared toward explicit negotiation and therefore neither approach in its current form is very helpful for understanding how psychological contracts are implicitly negotiated. In both cases, the implicit psychological correlates to the concepts both models propose are not clear. Herriot and Pemberton (1997, p. 47) acknowledge that their process model is 'explicit contracting', whereas I-Deals currently involves activities such as employees drawing attention to their labor market value which would appear to have to involve explicit negotiation. Furthermore, both models make the questionable assumption that making psychological contracts explicit will lead to positive outcomes. In one of the few studies examining negotiation, Millward Purvis and Cropley's (2003) qualitative study of children's nannies and their employers (i.e. the child's parents) found that implicit negotiations led to more trusting relationships than explicit negotiations, as they permitted both parties more flexibility to shift the relationship in preferred directions, which would not have been possible under explicit psychological contracts, as such actions would probably be viewed as breach.

Attempts to conceptualize implicit negotiation again come from Rousseau (1995) describing implicit negotiation as 'contract drift' (p. 142) that remains within the 'spirit' (p. 154) of the contractual framework (referred to as 'accommodation', p. 153). It is only when drift exceeds one of the parties' 'zones of acceptance' (p. 144) that it constitutes a breach. Successful accommodation involves 'active participation in change by both parties' (p. 160). Though the terms – 'spirit of the contract', 'drift' and 'zone of acceptance' – have an intuitive appeal, they are ambiguous and require clarification. Furthermore, it is difficult to see how negotiations of this nature differ from low-level breach. For example, when does a negotiation exceed the 'zone of acceptance' to become breach? And if breach is defined by exceeding a zone of acceptance, then why isn't some sort of threshold included within the definition of psychological contract breach?

More fundamentally, it is not clear what the act of implicit negotiation entails. How do employees implicitly communicate that they want to negotiate their psychological contract? Is this an overt or covert behavior? Do negotiations involve an initial unprecedented action by the employee? How does the employee perceive that their employer has witnessed and accept the negotiation behavior? How do employees satisfy themselves that their efforts to implicitly negotiate their psychological contract have not violated the other party's psychological contract? Does the employer have to actively accept the negotiation, or can the employer passively consent? Does every employee and employer action constitute some form of psychological contract negotiation (cf. Schein's statement that psychological contracts are 'constantly renegotiated', 1980, p. 24)? To the extent that such actions do form a part of the ongoing negation process, which types of implicit negotiation can be considered as operating meaningfully over and above this 'background level' of negotiation? These are just some of the questions we need to start addressing to begin to develop an understanding of implicit negotiation.

Exploring the Psychological Contract as a *Process*

Psychological contracts are formed, negotiated, renegotiated, fulfilled, breached, repaired, grow into more relational psychological contracts, and so on, where each stage or activity is part of an ongoing process. Schein (1980, p. 24) views the psychological contract as being 'constantly renegotiated' where researching the psychological contract requires 'a systems approach capable of handling interdependent phenomena' (Schein, 1980, p. 65); Meckler, Drake and Levinson (2003, p. 225) describe the process as having 'an ongoing nature extending over time and multiple episodes. Implicit in this extended time frame is the provision of feedback cycles where both parties are adjusting to changes that may enhance as well as frustrate the satisfaction of their needs. Typically this feedback is not explicitly monitored nor carefully understood, so that mutual adjustments are haphazard and often painful to both parties.'

While researchers frequently mention the process nature of psychological contracts, there is currently little conceptual language for understanding this process and few if any empirical studies are designed to capture unfolding processes. In a recent review of developments in process approaches to organizational phenomena, Langley (1999) compared between variance and process theories. Variance theories typify current psychological contract research and are characterized by linear relationships between groups of independent and dependent variables, simplified causal relationships, and ignoring any precise temporal ordering. In contrast, process theories conceptualize the world in terms of discrete events and experiences located in time, attempt to shed light on the sequencing of these events, paying attention to multiple levels of analyses and the time intervals between events. In contrast to variance theories, process theories consider a wide range of experiences and outcomes. Psychological contract research does not meet any of these criteria, in that it tends to look at attitudes (not events), does not consider time issues, focuses on the employee's perspective, and restricts itself largely to looking at correlations between breach and a small number of attitudes and perceptions (e.g. job satisfaction, commitment and citizenship behavior).

While there have been some attempts to discuss psychological contract processes (e.g. Rousseau, 1995; Morrison and Robinson, 1997; Levinson et al.,

1962), there have been no attempts that approach process theorizing in the manner described by Langley (1999). In the first instance, psychological contract theory needs to incorporate the language and concepts of process theories, by integrating some its key ideas, such as how events are precisely located in time and space, feedback loops, multiple levels of analysis, variation in the speed and duration of unfolding events, vicious and virtuous circles, upward and downward spirals, thresholds, equilibriums shifts, selective attention, selective retention, anticipation and so on (cf. Langley, 1999; Masuch, 1985; Mintzberg, 1980; Pentland, 1999; Pettigrew, 1992; Van de Ven, 1992).

RESPONSES TO THE FIVE CHALLENGES

The challenges outlined above are those faced by the vast majority of psychological contract researchers. There are, however, several cases where researchers have begun to address some of these issues. We briefly and selectively identify and describe some of these studies to illustrate ways in which these challenges can be met.

First, attempts to develop a features-based analysis of psychological contracts might provide valuable descriptive insights into psychological contracts, how psychological contracts differ across individuals and offer alternatives to breach in terms of how psychological contracts affect outcomes. Suggested features of psychological contracts include stability, scope, tangibility, focus, time frame, particularism and volition (McLean Parks, Kidder and Gallagher, 1998; Rousseau and McLean Parks, 1993; Sels, Janssens and Van Den Brande, 2004). At present, there is little understanding as to how these features develop or affect outcomes. It is unlikely that each will demonstrate the same impact as breach, but these features may offer insight into understanding more specific experiences, such as instability leading to feelings of anxiety, focus leading to role clarity, and so on.

Second, there are small but clear signs that researchers are using more robust and varied designs, such as longitudinal studies with behavioral data (e.g. Pavlou and Gefen, 2005; Tekleab, Takeuchi and Taylor, 2005), diaries (Conway and Briner, 2002), and qualitative approaches (D'Annunzio-Green and Francis, 2005; Dick, 2006; Hallier and Forbes, 2004; Nadin and Cassell, 2007). Quantitative studies are also using more sophisticated statistical analyses, such as curve analyses (Lambert, Edwards and Cable, 2003) and network analyses (Ho, Rousseau and Levesque, 2006). Studies are also beginning to combine diverse sources of data; for example, Pavlou and Gefen (2005), in researching the marketplace rather than the workplace, integrate primary quantitative data with longitudinal quantitative and qualitative secondary data from online eBay and Amazon auctions. Such secondary data may not have the obvious face validity of psychological contract questionnaire measures, but instead offer more subtle, situated behavior, unaffected by researcher demands, that can be used to infer psychological contract processes.

The psychological contract has also been examined from perspectives outside the normative paradigm. Cullinane and Dundon (2006) take a critical approach, arguing that the psychological contract is a discursive artifact used by organizations to advance their own interests at the cost of neglecting workers by, for example, imposing deals that supposedly represent the interests of both parties but are, in fact, attempts to regulate how employees think about work. Cullinane and Dundon also deconstruct the psychological contract literature, arguing that it pursues a managerialist perspective of the employment relationship and undermines the study of traditional employment relations and its concerns, not least the interests of trades unions. Furthermore, the language of psychological contract theory, such as mutual obligations, reciprocity, and so on, is at odds with the fundamental power imbalance faced by most employees. From this perspective, the psychological contract is just another concept, in line with initiatives such as HRM (Legge, 1995), that seeks to advance capitalism. The effects of possible managerialist bias in psychological contract research deserves further exploration as taking a more employee-oriented perspective which also takes into account power may help meet some of the challenges outlined earlier.

The variety of approaches and analytical methods currently in use show clearly that psychological contracts and associated processes are amenable to a wide array of research approaches. Our general observation is that these alternative research methods and designs, irrespective of whether they take a more robust quantitative approach and/or a qualitative approach, tend to produce findings that challenge results from cross-sectional surveys. While the more robust designs are far fewer in number, we are inclined to treat them as more credible, as they offer much better quality evidence from an evidence-based practice perspective (Briner, 2000; Rousseau, 2006) and are more aligned to the psychological contract's theoretical assumptions.

CONCLUSIONS

We offer three main interrelated and somewhat stark conclusions. The first is that the psychological contract remains vaguely defined. We still do not know the meaning of several fundamental terms: What are the beliefs? What exactly is the exchange? Who or what represents the organization, how do employees arrive at a sense of it, and can it have a psychological contract as the other party to the relationship? Until some of the many challenges we have identified above relating to the definition key terms are addressed, we cannot ascertain the ultimate value of empirical studies as they may not be capturing psychological contracts. Such definitional limitations and gaps also mean that we know very little about how individuals, managers or organizations can manage psychological contracts.

Our second conclusion is that there is very little theory in this area. If we put aside breach, the remaining ideas are not so much theories or explanations, but categories and typologies – for example transactional/relational, implicit/explicit and matched/unmatched contracts – that do not form part of a coherent explanatory or predictive theory. Such typologies have some descriptive value, but tend to be used as part of speculative models, where such models do not tend to produce robust findings. Not surprisingly, therefore, they tend not to be adopted in subsequent research. Weak theory has no doubt contributed to the lack of cumulative evidence and indeed limited practical application of the concept. Our impression is that the field has grown somewhat beyond the idea of breach, but has yet to find a compelling idea to take its place. One possibility is to return to the contract metaphor, as several authors have recently attempted (D'Annunzio-Green and Francis, 2005; Grant, 1999; Pavlou and Gefen, 2005) and explore whether ideas from contract law – such as misrepresentation, frustration, remedy, guarantees and excuse – have meaningful psychological correlates.

Third and finally are the problems, mentioned throughout this chapter, with the dominant methodologies and designs used to research the psychological contract. Put simply, data from cross-sectional self-report studies do very little to advance our understanding of the psychological contract.

We began by noting that psychological contract research has grown exponentially in terms of the number of published articles since the last review in this series; however, this growth has not resulted in a significant or marked increase in conceptual clarification, theory development or good quality empirical evidence. We believe that psychological contract research should now focus on better understanding the unique contributions of the psychological contract concept to organizational psychology – its implicitness and how it guides everyday behavior through cycles of creation, maintenance, negotiation, and interruption. By doing so, the psychological contract may yet demonstrate its potential as key mechanism for understanding behavior at work.

REFERENCES

Ågerfalk, P. J. & Fitzgerald, B. (2008). Outsourcing to an unknown workforce: exploring opensourcing as a global sourcing strategy. *MIS Quarterly*, **32** (2), 385–409.

Anderson, E. S. (1987). The psychological contract: a method for increasing student satisfaction. *Journal of Marketing Education*, **9** (2), 25–29.

Argyris, C. (1960). *Understanding Organizational Behavior*. Homewood, IL: Dorsey.

Arnold, J. (1996). The psychological contract: a concept in need of closer scrutiny? *European Journal of Work and Organizational Psychology*, **5**, 511–20.

Aselage, J. & Eisenberger, R. (2003). Perceived organizational support and psychological contracts: a theoretical integration. *Journal of Organizational Behavior*, **24**, 491–509.

Autry, C. W., Hill, D. J. & O'Brien, M. (2007). Attitude toward the customer: a study of product returns episodes. *Journal of Managerial Issues*, **19** (3), 315–39.

Aycan, Z. (2006). Paternalism: towards conceptual refinement and operationalization. In K. S. Yang, K. K. Hwang & U. Kim (Eds), *Scientific Advances in Indigenous*

Psychologies: Empirical, Philosophical, and Cultural Contributions. Cambridge, MA: Cambridge University Press.

Baker, H. G. & Berry, V. M. (1987). Processes and advantages of entry-level career counseling. *Personnel Journal,* **66** (4), 111–21.

Bal, P. M., De Lange, A. H. & Jansen, P. G. W. (2007). Psychological contract breach and job attitudes: a meta-analysis of age as a moderator. *Journal of Vocational Behavior,* **72** (1), 143–58.

Beard, K. M. & Edwards, J. R. (1995). Employees at risk: contingent work and the psychological experience of contingent workers. In C. L. Cooper & D. M. Rousseau (Eds), *Trends in Organizational Behavior.* Chichester: John Wiley & Sons Ltd.

Blau, P. (1964). *Exchange and Power in Social Life.* New York: John Wiley & Sons, Inc.

Boss, R. W. (1985). The psychological contract: a key to effective organization development consultation. *Consultation: An International Journal,* **4** (4), 284–304.

Briner, R. (2000). Evidence-based human resource management. In L. Trinder & S. Reynolds (Eds), *Evidence-Based Practice: A Critical Appraisal* (pp. 184–211). London: Blackwell Science.

Bunderson, J. S. (2001). How work ideologies shape psychological contracts of professional employees: doctors' responses to perceived breach. *Journal of Organizational Behavior,* **22**, 717–41.

Cabot, R. C. (1933). *The Meaning of Right and Wrong.* New York: The Macmillan Company.

Calo, T. J. (2006). The psychological contract and the union contract: a paradigm shift in public sector employee relations. *Public Personnel Management,* **35** (4), 331–42.

Campbell, J. P. & Pritchard, R. D. (1976). Motivation theory in industrial and organizational psychology. In M. D. Dunnette (Ed.), *Handbook of Industrial–Organizational Psychology* (pp. 63–130). Chicago: Rand McNally.

Carstensen, L. L., Isaacowitz, D. M. & Charles, S. T. (1999). Taking time seriously. A theory of socioemotional selectivity. *American Psychologist,* **54**, 165–81.

Cassar V. (2004). Identifying and investigating the component forms of psychological contract violatio. London Univ. Dissertation.

Cassar, V. & Briner, R. B. (2005). Psychological contract 'breach': a multiple component perspective to an over-researched construct? *Revista de Psicología Social,* **20**, 125–36.

Cheshire, G. C., Fifoot, C. H. S. & Furmston, M. P. (1991). *Law of Contract,* 12th edn, London: Butterworths.

Claes, R. (2005). Organization promises in the triangular psychological contract as perceived by temporary agency workers, agencies, and client organizations. *Employee Responsibilities and Rights Journal,* **17** (3), 131–42.

Cohen-Charash, Y. & Spector, P. E. (2001). The role of justice in organizations: a meta-analysis. *Organizational Behavior and Human Decision Processes,* **86**, 278–321.

Conway, N. & Briner, R. B. (2002a). A daily diary study of affective responses to psychological contract breach and exceeded promises. *Journal of Organizational Behavior,* **23**, 287–302.

Conway, N. & Briner, R. B. (2002b). Full-time versus part-time employees: understanding the links between work status, the psychological contract, and attitudes. *Journal of Vocational Behavior,* **61**, 279–301.

Conway, N. & Briner, R. (2005). *Understanding Psychological Contracts at Work: A Critical Evaluation of Theory and Research.* Oxford: Oxford University Press.

Conway, N. & Coyle-Shapiro, J. (2006). *Reciprocity and the Psychological Contract.* Proceedings of the Annual Meeting of the Academy of Management Conference, Atlanta.

Conway, E. & Monks, K. (2008). HR practices and commitment to change: an employee-level analysis. *Human Resource Management Journal*, 18 (1), 72–89.

Coyle-Shapiro, J. & Conway, N. (2005). Exchange relationships: examining psychological contracts and perceived organizational support. *Journal of Applied Psychology*, 90 (4), 774–81.

Coyle-Shapiro, J. & Kessler, I. (1998). The psychological contract in the UK public sector: employer and employee obligations and contract fulfilment. Paper Presented at the Annual Meeting of the Academy of Management, San Diego.

Coyle-Shapiro, J. & Kessler, I. (2000). Consequences of the psychological contract for the employment relationship: a large-scale survey. *Journal of Management Studies*, 37, 903–30.

Coyle-Shapiro, J. & Kessler, I. (2002a). Exploring reciprocity through the lens of the psychological contract: employee and employer perspectives. *European Journal of Work and Organizational Psychology*, 11, 69–86.

Coyle-Shapiro, J. & Kessler, I. (2002b). A psychological contract perspective on organizational citizenship behavior. *Journal of Organizational Behavior*, 23, 927–46.

Coyle-Shapiro, J. & Kessler, I. (2002c). Contingent and non-contingent working in local government: contrasting psychological contracts. *Public Administration*, 80, 77–101.

Coyle-Shapiro, J. & Neuman, J. (2004). Individual dispositions and the psychological contract: the moderating effects of exchange and creditor ideologies. *Journal of Vocational Behavior*, 64, 150–64.

Cullinane, N. & Dundon, T. (2006). The psychological contract: a critical review. *International Journal of Management Reviews*, 8 (2), 113–29.

D'Annunzio-Green, N. & Francis, H. (2005). Human resource development and the psychological contract: great expectations or false hopes? *Human Resource Development International*, 8 (3), 327–344.

Dabos, G. E. & Rousseau, D. M. (2004). Mutuality and reciprocity in the psychological contracts of employees and employers. *Journal of Applied Psychology*, 89 (1), 52–72.

De Cuyper, N. & De Witte, H. (2006). The impact of job insecurity and contract type on attitudes, well-being, and behavioural reports: a psychological contract perspective. *Journal of Occupational and Organizational Psychology*, 79, 395–409.

De Vos, A., Buyens, D. & Schalk, R. (2005). Making sense of a new employment relationship: psychological contract-related information seeking and the role of work values and locus of control. *International Journal of Selection and Assessment*, 13 (1), 41–52.

Deery, S. J., Iverson, R. D. & Walsh, J. T. (2006). Toward a better understanding of psychological contract breach: a study of costumer service employees. *Journal of Applied Psychology*, 91, 166–75.

Dick, P. (2006). The psychological contract and the transition from full to part-time police work. *Journal of Organizational Behavior*, 27 (1), 37–58.

Druker, J. & Stanworth, C. (2004). Mutual expectations: a study of the three-way relationship between employment agencies, their client organisations and white-collar agency 'temps'. *Industrial Relations Journal*, 35 (1), 58–75.

Dulac, T., Coyle-Shapiro, J.A-M., Henderson, D. & Wayne, S. (2008). Not all responses to breach are the same: a longitudinal study examining the interconnection of social exchange and psychological contract processes in organizations. *Academy of Management Journal*, 51(6), 1079–1098.

Edwards, J. C., Rust, K. G., McKinley, W. & Moon, G. (2003). Business ideologies and perceived breach of contract during downsizing: the role of the ideology of employee self-reliance. *Journal of Organizational Behavior*, 24, 1–23.

Eisenberger, R., Huntingdon, R., Hutchison, S. & Sowa, D. (1986). Perceived organizational support. *Journal of Applied Psychology*, 71, 500–507.

Feldheim, M. A. (2007). Public sector downsizing and employee trust. *International Journal of Public Administration*, 30 (3), 249–70.

Foa, U. G. (1971). Interpersonal and economic resources. *Science*, 171, 345–51.

Foa, U. G. & Foa, E. B. (1980). Resource theory: interpersonal behavior as exchange. In K. J. Gergen, M. S. Greenberg & R. H. Willis (Eds), *Social Exchange: Advances in Theory and Research* (pp. 77–94). New York: Plenum.

Gakovic, A. & Tetrick, L. E. (2003). Perceived organizational support and work status: a comparison of the employment relationships of part-time and full-time employees attending university classes. *Journal of Organizational Behavior*, 24 (5), 649–66.

Grant, D. (1999). HRM, rhetoric and the psychological contract: a case of 'easier said than done'. *International Journal of Human Resource Management*, 10, 327–50.

Greene, A.-M., Ackers, P. & Black, J. (2001). Lost narratives? From paternalism to team-working in a lock manufacturing firm. *Economic and Industrial Democracy*, 22, 211–37.

Grimmer, M. & Oddy, M. (2007). Violation of the psychological contract: the mediating effect of relational versus transactional beliefs. *Australian Journal of Management*, 32 (1), 153–74.

Guest, D. (1998). Is the psychological contract worth taking seriously? *Journal of Organizational Behavior*, 19, 649–64.

Guest, D. (2004a). The psychology of the employment relationship: an analysis based on the psychological contract. *Applied Psychology*, 53, 541–55.

Guest, D. (2004b). Flexible employment contracts, the psychological contract and employee outcomes: an analysis and review of the evidence. *International Journal of Management Reviews*, 5/6, 1–19.

Guest, D. & Conway, N. (1997). *Employee Motivation and the Psychological Contract*. IPD Research Report, London: IPD.

Guest, D & Conway, N. (1998). *Fairness and the Psychological Contract*. IPD Research Report, London: IPD.

Guest, D. & Conway, N. (1999). *Organizational Change and the Psychological Contract*. IPD Research Report, London: IPD.

Guest, D. & Conway, N. (2000). *The Public Sector and the Psychological Contract*. IPD Research Report, London: IPD.

Guest, D. & Conway, N. (2001). *Public and Private Sector Perspectives on the Psychological Contract*. CIPD Research Report, London: CIPD.

Guest, D. & Conway, N. (2002a). *Pressure at Work and the Psychological Contract*. CIPD Research Report, London: CIPD.

Guest, D. & Conway, N. (2002b). Communicating the psychological contract: an employer perspective. *Human Resource Management Journal*, 12, 22–39.

Guest, D. & Conway, N. (2004). *Employee Well-being and the Psychological Contract*. CIPD Research Report, London: CIPD.

Guzzo, R. A., Noonan, K. A. & Elron, E. (1994). Expatriate managers and the psychological contract. *Journal of Applied Psychology*, 79, 617–26.

Hallier, J. & Forbes, T. (2004). In search of theory development in grounded investigations: doctors' experiences of managing as an example of fitted and prospective theorizing. *Journal of Management Studies*, 41 (8), 1379–1410.

Heider, F. (1958). *The Psychology of Interpersonal Relations*, Hillsdale, NJ: Lawrence Erlbaum.

Herriot, P. (1988). Graduate recruitment: psychological contracts and the balance of power. *British Journal of Guidance and Counselling*, 16 (3), 228–41.

Herriot, P. & Pemberton, C. (1995). *New Deals: The Revolution in Managerial Careers*. Chichester: John Wiley & Sons, Ltd.

Herriot, P. & Pemberton, C. (1996). Contracting careers. *Human Relations*, 49, 759–90.

Herriot, P. & Pemberton, C. (1997). Facilitating new deals. *Human Resource Management Journal*, 7, 45–56.

Herriot, P., Manning, W. E. G. & Kidd, J. M. (1997). The content of the psychological contract. *British Journal of Management*, 8, 151–62.

Ho, V. T. (2005). Social influences on evaluation of psychological contract fulfillment. *Academy of Management Review*, 30, 113–29.

Ho, V. T. & Levesque, L. L. (2005). With a little help from my friends (and substitutes): social referents and influence in psychological contract fulfillment. *Organization Science*, 16, 275–89.

Ho, V. T., Rousseau, D. M., & Levesque, L. L. (2006). Social networks and the psychological contract: structural holes, cohesive ties, and beliefs regarding employer obligations. *Human Relations*, 59 (4), 459–81.

Ho, V. T., Weingart, L. R. & Rousseau, D. M. (2004). Responses to broken promises: does personality matter? *Journal of Vocational Behavior*, 65 (2), 276–93.

Holloman, C. (1972). Human growth and development in the classroom. *Academy of Management Proceedings*, 304–8.

Hoobler, J. M. & Brass, D. J. (2006). Abusive supervision and family undermining as displaced aggression. *Journal of Applied Psychology*, 91 (5), 1125–33.

Hui, C., Lee, C. & Rousseau, D. M. (2004). Psychological contract and organizational citizenship behavior in China: investigating generalizability and instrumentality. *Journal of Applied Psychology*, 89, 311–21.

Ingram, K. (2007). Prosocial reactions to psychological contract violation: an interdependence theory perspective. Paper Presented at the Workshop on Research Advances in Organizational Behavior, University of Toulouse, France.

Johnson, J. L. & O'Leary-Kelly, A. M. (2003). The effects of psychological contract breach and organizational cynicism: not all social exchange violations are created equal. *Journal of Organizational Behavior*, 24, 627–47.

Kaše, R. & Zupan, N. (2007). Psychological contracts and employee outcomes in transition to market economy: a comparison of two Slovenian companies. *Problems and Perspectives in Management*, 5 (4), 16–27.

Kalleberg, A. & Rogues, J. (2000). Employment relations in Norway: some dimensions and correlates. *Journal of Organizational Behavior*, 21, 315–35.

Kickul, J., Lester, S. W. & Belgio, E. (2004). Attitudinal and behavioral outcomes of psychological contract breach: a cross-cultural comparison of the United States and Hong Kong Chinese. *International Journal of Cross-Cultural Management*, 4, 229–49.

Kickul, J., Lester, S. W. & Finkl, J. (2002). Promise breaking during radical organizational change: do justice interventions make a difference? *Journal of Organizational Behavior*, 23, 469–88.

Kingshott, R. P. J. (2006). The impact of psychological contracts upon trust and commitment within supplier–buyer relationships: a social exchange view. *Industrial Marketing Management*, 35 (6), 724–39.

Koh, C., Ang, S. & Straub, D. W. (2004). IT outsourcing success: A psychological contract perspective. *Information Systems Research*, 15 (4), 356–73.

Kolb, D. A., Rubin, I. M. & McIntyre, J. M. (1984). *Organizational Psychology: An Experimental Approach to Organizational Behavior*. Englewood Cliffs, NJ: Prentice-Hall.

Konovsky, M. A. & Pugh, S. D. (1994). Citizenship behavior and social exchange. *Academy of Management Review*, 37, 659–69.

Kotter, J. P. (1973). The psychological contract: managing the joining up process. *California Management Review*, 15, 91–99.

Lambert, L. S., Edwards, J. B. & Cable, D. M. (2003). Breach and fulfillment of the psychological contract: a comparison of traditional and expanded views. *Personnel Psychology*, 56, 895–934.

Langley, A. (1999). Strategies for theorizing from process data. *Academy of Management Review*, **24**, 691–710.

Lavelle, J. J., Rupp, D. E. & Brockner, J. (2007). Taking a multifoci approach to the study of justice, social exchange, and citizenship behavior: the target similarity model. *Journal of Management*, **33** (6), 841–66.

Legge, K. (1995). *Human Resource Management: Rhetorics and Realities*. Basingstoke: Macmillan.

Lester, S. W., Kickul, J. R. & Bergmann, T. J. (2007). Managing employee perceptions of the psychological contract over time: the role of employer social accounts and contract fulfillment. *Journal of Organizational Behavior*, **28** (2), 191–208.

Lester, S. W., Turnley, W. H., Bloodgood, J. M. & Bolino, M. C. (2002). Not seeing eye to eye: differences in supervisor and subordinate perceptions of and attributions for psychological contract breach. *Journal of Organizational Behavior*, **23**, 39–56.

Levinson, H. (1965). Reciprocation: the relationship between man and organization. *Administrative Science Quarterly*, **9**, 370–90.

Levinson, H., Price, C. R., Munden, K. J. & Solley, C. M. (1962). *Men, Management, and Mental Health*. Cambridge, MA: Harvard University Press.

Lo, S. & Aryee, S. (2003). Psychological contract breach in a Chinese context: An integrative approach. *Journal of Management Studies*, **40** (4), 1005–1020.

Lobuts, J. F. & Pennewill, C. L. (1984). Do we dare restructure the classroom environment? *Journal of Creative Behavior*, **18** (4), 237–46.

Locke, E. A. & Latham, G. P. (1990). *A Theory of Goal Setting and Task Performance*. Englewood Cliffs, NJ: Prentice Hall.

MacMillan, K., Money, K., Downing, S. & Hillenbrand, C. (2005). Reputation in relationships: measuring experiences, emotions and behaviors. *Corporate Reputation Review*, **8** (3), 214–32.

Macneil, I. R. (1974). The many futures of contract. *Southern California Law Review*, **47**, 691–816.

Macneil, I. R. (1980). *The New Social Contract*. New Haven, CT: Yale University Press.

March, J. E. & Simon, H. A. (1958). *Organizations*. New York: John Wiley & Sons, Inc.

Masuch, M. (1985). Vicious circles in organizations. *Administrative Science Quarterly*, **30**, 14–33.

Mauss, M. (1925). *The Gift*. Glencoe, Ill: Free Press. 1954 (Republished, New York: Norton, 1967). Transalation of Mauss (1925) by I. Cunnison.

Meckler, M., Drake, B. H. & Levinson, H. (2003). Putting psychology back into psychological contracts. *Journal of Management Inquiry*, **12**, 217–28.

Menninger, K. (1958). *Theory of Psychoanalytic Technique*. New York: Basic Books.

Menninger, K. & Holzman, P. S. (1973). *Theory of Psychoanalytic Technique*, 2nd edn, New York: Basic Books.

Millward, L. J. (2006). The transition to motherhood in an organizational context: an interpretative phenomenological analysis. *Journal of Occupational and Organizational Psychology*, **79** (3), 315–33.

Millward, L. J. & Brewerton, P. M. (2000). Psychological contracts: employee relations for the twenty-first century. In C. L. Cooper & I. T. Robertson (Eds), *International Review of Industrial and Organizational Psychology*, Vol. 15 (pp. 1–61). Chichester: John Wiley & Sons, Ltd.

Millward, L. J. & Hopkins, L. J. (1998). Organizational commitment and the psychological contract. *Journal of Social and Applied Psychology*, **28**, 16–31.

Millward Purvis, L. J. & Cropley, M. (2003). Psychological contracting: processes of contract formation during interviews between nannies and their 'employers'. *Journal of Occupational and Organizational Psychology*, **76**, 213–41.

Mintzberg, H. (1980). *The Nature of Managerial Work*. Englewood Cliffs, NJ: Prentice-Hall.

Morishima, M. (1996). Renegotiating psychological contracts: Japanese style. In C. L. Cooper & D. M. Rousseau (Eds), *Trends in Organizational Behavior*, Vol. 3 (pp. 139–58). Hoboken, NJ: John Wiley & Sons, Inc.

Morrison, E. W. & Robinson, S. L. (1997). When employees feel betrayed: a model of how psychological contract violation develops. *Academy of Management Review*, **22**, 226–56.

Nadin, S. & Cassell, C. (2007). New deal for old? *International Small Business Journal*, **25** (4), 417–43.

Nicholson, N. & Johns, G. (1985). The absence culture and the psychological contract – who's in control of absence? *Academy of Management Review*, **10**, 397–407.

Nuttall, J. (2004). Modes of interpersonal relationship in management organisations. *Journal of Change Management*, **4** (1), 15–29.

O'Neill, B. S., Halbesleben, J. R. B. & Edwards, J. C. (2007). Integrating employment contracts and comparisons: what one can teach us about the other. *Journal of Managerial Issues*, **19** (2), 161–85.

Pavlou, P. A. & Gefen, D. (2005). Psychological contract violation in online marketplace: antecedents, consequences, and moderating role. *Information Systems Research*, **16** (4), 372–99.

McLean Parks, J., Kidder, D. L. & Gallagher, D. G. (1998). Fitting square pegs into round holes: mapping the domain of contingent work arrangements onto the psychological contract. *Journal of Organizational Behavior*, **19**, 697–730.

Pentland, B. T. (1999). Building process theory with narrative: from description to explanation. *Academy of Management Review*, **24**, 711–24.

Pettigrew, A. (1992). The character and significance of strategy process research. *Strategic Management Journal*, **13** (Special Issue), 5–16.

Piccoli, G. & Ives, B. (2003). Trust and the unintended effects of behaviour control in virtual teams. *MIS Quarterly*, **27** (3), 365–95.

Portwood, J. D. & Miller, E. L. (1976). Evaluating the psychological contract: its implications for employee job satisfaction and work behavior. *Academy of Management Proceedings*, 109–13.

Pugh, S. D., Skarlicki, D. P. & Passell, B. S. (2003). After the fall: layoff victims' trust and cynicism in re-employment. *Journal of Occupational and Organizational Psychology*, **76** (2), 201–12.

Radford, L. M.and Larwood, L. (1982). A field study of conflict in psychological exchange: the California taxpayers' revolt. *Journal of Applied Social Psychology*, **12** (1), 60–69.

Raja, U., Johns, G. & Ntalianis, F. (2004). The impact of personality on psychological contracts. *Academy of Management Journal*, **47**, 350–67.

Reis, H. T. & Wheeler, L. (1991). Studying social interaction with the Rochester interaction record. *Advances in Experimental Social Psychology*, **24**, 269–318.

Restubog, S. L. D. & Bordia, P. (2006). Workplace familism and psychological contract breach in the Philippines. *Applied Psychology: An International Review*, **55**, 563–85.

Restubog, S. L. D., Bordia, P. & Tang, R. L. (2006). Effects of psychological contract breach on performance of IT employees: the mediating role of affective commitment. *Journal of Occupational and Organizational Psychology*, **79**, 299–306.

Restubog, S. L. D., Bordia, P. & Tang, R. L. (2007). Behavioural outcomes of psychological contract breach in a non-western culture: the moderating role of equity sensitivity. *British Journal of Management*, **18** (4), 376–86.

Robinson, S. L. (1995). Violations of psychological contracts: impact on employee attitudes. In L. E. Tetrick & J. Barling (Eds), *Changing Employment Relations: Behavioral and Social Perspectives* (pp. 91–108). Washington, DC: American Psychological Association.

Robinson, S. L. (1996). Trust and breach of the psychological contract. *Administrative Science Quarterly*, **41**, 574–99.

Robinson, S. L. & Morrison, E. W. (1995). Psychological contracts and OCB: the effect of unfulfilled obligations on civic virtue behavior. *Journal of Organizational Behaviour*, **16**, 289–98.

Robinson, S. L. & Morrison, E. W. (2000). The development of psychological contract breach and violation: a longitudinal study. *Journal of Organizational Behavior*, **21**, 525–46.

Robinson, S. L. & Rousseau, D. M. (1994). Violating the psychological contract: not the exception but the norm. *Journal of Organizational Behavior*, **15**, 245–59.

Robinson, S. L., Kraatz, M. S. & Rousseau, D. M. (1994). Changing obligations and the psychological contract: a longitudinal study. *Academy of Management Journal*, **37**, 137–52.

Roehling, M. V. (1996). The origins and the early development of the psychological contract construct. Paper Presented at the Annual Meeting of the Academy of Management, Cincinnati.

Rousseau, D. M. (1989). Psychological and implied contracts in organizations. *Employee Responsibilities and Rights Journal*, **2**, 121–39.

Rousseau, D. M. (1990). New hire perceptions of their own and their employer's obligations: a study of psychological contracts. *Journal of Organizational Behavior*, **11**, 389–400.

Rousseau, D. M. (1995). *Psychological Contracts in Organizations: Understanding Written and Unwritten Agreements*. Thousand Oaks, CA: Sage.

Rousseau, D. M. (2000). *Psychological contract inventory: Technical report (Technical Report Number 2)*, Pittsburgh, PA: Carnegie Mellon University.

Rousseau, D. M. (2001a). Schema, promise and mutuality: the building blocks of the psychological contract. *Journal of Occupational and Organizational Psychology*, **74**, 511–41.

Rousseau, D. M. (2001b). Idiosyncratic deals: flexibility versus fairness? *Organizational Dynamics*, **29** (4), 260–71.

Rousseau, D. M. (2003). Extending the psychology of the psychological contract. *Journal of Management Inquiry*, **12** (3), 229–38.

Rousseau, D. M. (2005). *I-Deals: Idiosyncratic Deals Employees Bargain for Themselves*. New York: M. E. Sharpe.

Rousseau, D. M. (2006). Is there such a thing as 'evidence-based management'? *Academy of Management Review*, **31** (2), 256–69.

Rousseau, D. M. & Anton, R. J. (1991). Fairness and implied contract obligations in job terminations: the role of contributions, promises and performance. *Journal of Organizational Behavior*, **12**, 287–99.

Rousseau, D. M. & McLean Parks, J. (1993). The contracts of individuals and organizations. *Research in Organizational Behavior*, **15**, 1–43.

Rousseau, D. M. & Wade-Benzoni, K. A. (1995). Changing individual and organizational attachments: a two-way street. In A. Howard (Ed.), *The Changing Nature of Work* (pp. 290–322). San Francisco: Jossey-Bass.

Schein, E. H. (1965, 1970, 1980). *Organizational Psychology*. Englewood Cliffs, NJ: Prentice-Hall.

Schneider, B. & Bowen, D. E. (1999). Understanding customer delight and outrage. *Sloan Management Review*, **41**, 35–45.

Sels, L., Janssens, M. & Van Den Brande, I. (2004). Assessing the nature of psychological contracts: a validation of six dimensions. *Journal of Organizational Behavior*, **25** (4), 461–88.

Shore, L. M. & Barksdale, K. (1998). Examining degree of balance and level of obligation in the employment relationship: a social exchange approach. *Journal of Organizational Behavior*, **19**, 731–45.

Shore, L. & Coyle-Shapiro, J. (2003). New developments in the employee–organization relationship. *Journal of Organizational Behavior*, **24**, 443–50.

Shore, L. M. & Tetrick, L. E. (1994). The psychological contract as an explanatory framework in the employment relationship. In C. L. Cooper & D. M. Rousseau (Eds), *Trends in Organizational Behavior* (pp. 91–103). New York: John Wiley & Sons, Inc.

Sills, C. (2006). *Contracts in Counselling and Psychotherapy*, 2nd edn, Thousand Oaks, CA: Sage.

Sims, R. R. (1994). Human resource management's role in clarifying the new psychological contract. *Human Resource Management*, **33**, 373–82.

Stewart, K. L. (2003). Trust transfer on the World Wide Web. *Organization Science*, **14** (1), 5–17.

Sturges, J., Guest, D., Conway, N. & Mackenzie Davey, K. (2002). A longitudinal study of the relationship between career management and organisational commitment among graduates in the first ten years of work. *Journal of Organizational Behavior*, **23**, 731–48.

Sturges, J., Conway, N., Liefooghe, A. & Guest, D. (2005). Managing the career deal: the psychological contract as a framework for understanding career management, organizational commitment and work behavior. *Journal of Organizational Behavior*, **26**, 821–38.

Sullivan, L. G. (1995). Myth, metaphor and hypothesis: how anthropomorphism defeats science. *Philosophical Transactions of the Royal Society of London Series: Biological Sciences*, **349**, 219–24.

Sutton, G. & Griffin, M. A. (2004). Integrating expectations, experiences, and psychological contract violations: a longitudinal study of new professionals. *Journal of Occupational and Organizational Psychology*, **77**, 493–514.

Taras, D. & Steel, P. (2007). We provoked business students to unionize: using deception to prove an IR point. *British Journal of Industrial Relations*, **45** (1), 179–98.

Taylor, S. M. & Tekleab, A. G. (2004). Taking stock of psychological contract research: assessing progress, addressing troublesome issues, and setting research priorities. In J. Coyle-Shapiro, L. Shore, M. S. Taylor & L. Tetrick (Eds), *The Employment Relationship: Examining Psychological and Contextual Perspectives* (pp. 253–83). Oxford: Oxford University Press.

Tekleab, A. G., Takeuchi, R. & Taylor, M. S. (2005). Extending the chain of relationships among organizational justice, social exchange, and employee reactions: the role of contract violations. *Academy of Management Journal*, **48**, 146–57.

Tekleab, A. G. & Taylor, S. M. (2003). Aren't there two parties in an employment relationship? Antecedents and consequences of organization–employee agreement on contract obligations and violations. *Journal of Organizational Behavior*, **24**, 585–608.

Thomas, H. D. C. & Anderson, N. (1998). Changes in newcomers' psychological contracts during organizational socialization: a study of recruits entering the British Army. *Journal of Organizational Behavior*, **19**, 745–67.

Thompson, M. & Heron, P. (2005). The difference a manager can make: organizational justice and knowledge worker commitment. *International Journal of Human Resource Management*, **16** (3), 383–404.

Thompson, M. & Heron, P. (2006). Relational quality and innovative performance in R&D based science and technology firms. *Human Resource Management Journal*, **16** (1), 28–47.

Truong, D. X. & Quang, T. (2007). The psychological contract in employment in Vietnam: preliminary empirical evidence from an economy in transition. *Asia Pacific Business Review*, **13** (1), 113–31.

Tsui, A., Pearce, J., Porter, L. & Hite, J. (1995). Choice of employee–organization relationship: influence of internal and external organizational factors. In G. Ferris (Ed.), *Research in Personnel and Human Resource Management*, Vol. 13 (pp. 117–51). Greenwich, CT: JAI Press.

Tsui, A., Pearce, J., Porter, L. & Tripoli, A. (1997). Alternative approaches to the employee–organization relationship: does investment in employees pay off? *Academy of Management Journal*, **40**, 1089–1121.

Tsui, A. S. & Wang, D. X. (2002). Employment relationships from the employer's perspective: current research and future directions. In C. L. Cooper & I. T. Robertson (Eds), *International Review of Industrial and Organizational Psychology* (pp. 77–114). Chichester: John Wiley & Sons, Ltd.

Turnley, W. H. & Feldman, D. C. (1999a). A discrepancy model of psychological contract violations. *Human Resource Management Review*, **9**, 367–86.

Turnley, W. H. & Feldman, D. C. (1999b). The impact of psychological contract violations on exit, voice, loyalty, and neglect. *Human Relations*, **52**, 895–922.

Turnley, W. H. & Feldman, D. C. (2000). Re-examining the effects of psychological contract violations: unmet expectations and job dissatisfaction as mediators. *Journal of Organizational Behavior*, **21**, 25–42.

Turnley, W. H., Bolino, M. C., Lester, S. W. & Bloodgood, J. M. (2003). The impact of psychological contract fulfillment on the performance of in-role and organizational citizenship behaviors. *Journal of Management*, **29**, 187–206.

Van de Ven, A. H. (1992). Suggestions for studying strategy process: a research note. *Strategic Management Journal*, **13** (Special Issue), 169–88.

Wade-Benzoni, K. A., Rousseau, D. M. & Li, M. (2006). Managing relationships across generations of academics: psychological contracts in faculty-doctoral student collaborations. *International Journal of Conflict Management*, **17** (1), 4–32.

Wanous, J. P. (1977). Organizational entry: newcomers moving from outside to inside. *Psychological Bulletin*, **84**, 601–18.

Wanous, J. P., Poland, T. D., Premack, S. L. & Davis, K. S. (1992). The effect of met expectations on newcomer attitudes and behaviors: a review and meta-analysis. *Journal of Applied Psychology*, **77**, 288–97.

Wayne, S. J., Shore, L. M. & Liden, R. C. (1997). Perceived organizational support and leader–member exchange: a social exchange perspective. *Academy of Management Journal*, **40**, 82–111.

Westwood, R., Sparrow, P. & Leung, A. (2001). Challenges to the psychological contract in Hong Kong. *International Journal of Human Resource Management*, **12**, 621–50.

Zhao, H., Wayne, S. J., Glibkowski, B. C. & Bravo, J. (2007). The impact of psychological contract breach on work-related outcomes: a meta-analysis. *Personnel Psychology*, **60**, 647–80.

Chapter 4

SECURITY IN ORGANIZATIONS: EXPANDING THE FRONTIER OF INDUSTRIAL–ORGANIZATIONAL PSYCHOLOGY*

Edward G. Bitzer, III

Department of Psychology, Colorado State University, Fort Collins, Co, USA

Peter Y. Chen

Department of Psychology, Colorado State University, Fort Collins, CO, USA

Roger G. Johnston

Argonne National Laboratory, Argonne, IL, USA

Prior to recent terrorist attacks (such as those of 11 September 2001 in the United States, 11 March 2004 in Madrid, and 7 July 2005 in London), law enforcement and intelligence agencies around the globe were aware of increasing security threats directed toward critical infrastructure and systems. In the wake of these events, aggressive efforts have been made to protect strategic assets against vulnerabilities. However, vulnerabilities can threaten more than critical infrastructure and related strategic assets. For example, organizations and their constituencies also face a number of security threats which can be inferred from the definition of security as the act of safeguarding a state, organization, or people against danger (Simpson and Weiner, 1989). Indeed, virtually every organization is faced with a variety of threats that can have

---

* The chapter is solely the responsibility of the authors and does not necessarily represent the official views of CCRT, NIOSH, Argonne National Laboratory, or the US Department of Energy.

International Review of Industrial and Organizational Psychology, 2009, Volume 24.
Edited by G. P. Hodgkinson and J. K. Ford. Copyright © 2009 John Wiley & Sons, Ltd

potential adverse consequences for the organization, its members, and even the broader society.

A particular area that has received much needed attention over the past few years has been directed at the threats that human-caused events, whether intentional or unintentional, can create. For instance, it has been shown that 75% of employees steal from their employer at least once (McGurn, 1988) and almost 95% of US businesses have reported experiencing some theft or fraud (Case, 2000). In addition, one study found that nearly 25% of organizations surveyed reported some type of physical attack against an on-the-job employee during the course of a 3-year period (Rigdon, 1994), and 37% of US workers (approximately 54 million people) have experienced repeated mistreatment during their work life including, but not limited to, verbal/nonverbal abuse, threatening, humiliation, or intimidation (Workplace Bullying Institute, 2007). Furthermore, the recent widespread adoption of information technology has introduced organizations to a number of new potential security threats including electronic espionage, denial of service attacks, and even identity theft. A variety of recent media reports highlight such problems and underscore the need to protect both computer networks (Marquand and Arnoldy, 2007) as well as information stored on electronic media (Seper, 2007).

Theft, violence, and computer hacking are just three examples from a long list of security threats that confront organizations. In light of the potentially severe impacts, any one of these security threats can present; organizations are increasingly viewing strong security as an operational necessity that is vital to their long-term interests. According to a recent report published by the Federal Reserve Bank of New York (Hobijn and Sager, 2007), it has been estimated that total government and private sector expenditures designated for security in the United States have risen from $56 billion in 2001 to almost $100 billion in 2005. Rapid increases in expenditures are also occurring in other countries. For instance, it has been estimated that security expenditures pertaining to information technology security products and services in the United Kingdom were about £2.3billion in 2006, which had increased by 26.9% from the prior year (IT Security Market Report, 2007).

Much of the investment has been used for research and development of security hardware and software including global positioning systems, radio frequency identification tags, and data encryption algorithms (e.g. Warner and Johnston, 2002, 2006). There is no doubt that this type of hardware can help strengthen security. However, Pond (2002) has pointed out that many security challenges have contributing factors related to human and organizational characteristics. Understanding these human and organizational characteristics would significantly augment high-tech equipment to address root causes of insecurity.

Based on the theory of open systems, security behaviors and practices in organizations can be affected by two main subsystems in the workplace: physical-related systems and human-related systems. Physical-related systems emphasize aspects of security such as the use of GPS (global positioning system) and GPS spoofing countermeasures (Warner and Johnston, 2002) or tamper-indicating seals. Human-related systems, on the other hand, emphasize employee and organization characteristics such as human motivation, security policies and procedures, as well as the priority organizations place on security.

Without question, the use of well-designed physical-related security systems to prevent security threats is vital to ensuring security at work. Nevertheless, the expected positive effects could be drastically undercut if human-related systems are not taken into consideration. The logic behind this argument extends from past safety research. Empirical evidence has shown that hazard-free working conditions alone do not prevent the occurrence of accidents if organizations prioritize productivity ahead of safety (Snyder *et al.*, 2008). Additionally, organizations' safety policies are unlikely to decrease injuries or accidents if management cares little about the workers' well-being (Huang *et al.*, 2004). Furthermore, it has been shown that workers often prefer conventional tools over ergonomically designed hand tools due to an incompatibility between the physical and human-related systems (Dartt and Rosecrance, 2008).

With this in mind, this chapter on organizational security focuses on three main topics. First, we discuss what workplace security behaviors are (e.g. securing sensitive information or preventing the introduction of prohibited devices in controlled locations) and contrast them with other similar constructs including safety behaviors (e.g. Burke *et al.*, 2002; Hofmann, Morgeson and Gerras, 2003) as well as counterproductive workplace behaviors such as aggression (Chen and Spector, 1992; Spector, 1975; Snyder *et al.*, 2004). Second, factors that may influence security behaviors are reviewed. Finally, we discuss possible directions for future research with the hope that industrial–organizational psychologists, organizational behavioral scientists, and human resource management professionals expand current research and practice to the field of security.

SECURITY BEHAVIORS

Workplace security behaviors, which can be viewed as a subset of job performance, are goal-oriented actions under employees' control (Campbell *et al.*, 1993) which are essential for organizational survival and relevant to the organization's goals. These behaviors include both intentional as well as unintentional acts. Likewise, since they are conceptualized within the context of job performance, security behaviors can be categorized as either positive or negative on the basis of the outcomes that result. If organizational or individual assets are safeguarded as a result of a behavior, that behavior is viewed as positive. If a behavior threatens such assets, the behavior is considered to be negative.

Security behaviors include both job-specific tasks (e.g. security officers conduct vulnerability assessments) and non-job-specific tasks (e.g. employees lock file cabinets before leaving offices). In other words, these behaviors can be considered as part of a technical core which are required by one's job (e.g. security guards conduct patrols or computer programmers develop network firewalls), or activities that directly or indirectly support the technical core and are common to many or all employees within an organization such as an employee reminding a coworker to turn off a cell phone in a controlled environment. The former is often referred to as task performance; while the latter is often considered context performance as articulated by Borman and Motowidlo (1993). In the present review, we do not focus on job-specific security behaviors, which are part of a technical core (e.g. the ability to investigate a security breach or skills necessary to conduct vulnerability assessments). Instead, we concentrate on non-job-specific security behaviors that are common to many or all of the employees within an organization. These common security behaviors are rarely discussed within the security industry or in the literature related to fields such as organizational behavior, human resources management, or industrial/organizational psychology. In the following sections, we compare and contrast security behaviors with two other similar concepts: counterproductive behaviors and safety behaviors. Following that, we examine what non-job-specific security behaviors are.

Distinctions between Security Behaviors and Counterproductive Behaviors

While reviewing security behaviors, one would undoubtedly wonder about similarities between security behaviors and counterproductive behaviors. The latter are related to, and in some cases overlap with, security behaviors. The concept of counterproductive workplace behaviors (CWBs) was initially proposed by Spector (1975), and refers to a set of distinct behaviors that are deliberately done in order to harm an organization and/or organizational stakeholders such as clients, coworkers, customers, and supervisors (Spector and Fox, 2005). Counterproductive behavior is a broad concept that encompasses perhaps as many as 85 different types of behaviors (Gruys, 1999). From an organization's perspective, CWBs include actions such as abuse against others, production deviance, sabotage, theft, and withdrawal. Despite the inclusion of a wide range of behaviors, or perhaps because of it, attempts have been made to develop a way to categorize CWBs. For example, they can be classified on the basis of three conceptual dimensions: direct (yell at a coworker) or indirect (ruin a coworker's reputation by spreading rumors), active (e.g. making threats) or passive (e.g. withholding information needed by a coworker), and directed toward organizations or individuals (Snyder et al., 2004).

Over the years, CWBs have been studied under a wide variety of labels including aggression (e.g. Douglas and Martinko, 2001), deviance (e.g. Bennett and Robinson, 2000), retaliation (Skarlicki and Folger, 1997), revenge (e.g. Bies and Tripp, 2005), antisocial workplace behavior (Giacalone and Greenberg, 1997), and bullying (Einarsen et al., 2003). However, all of these terms generally share three common threads. First, research in CWBs focuses on organizational members as perpetrators. Second, CWBs are traditionally viewed as intentional acts meant to harm other employees or the organization. Third, different CWBs may be committed for a variety of reasons. This suggests that the concept of CWBs is not a unitary one (Spector *et al.*, 2006) and therefore these should be considered as causal indicators instead of effect indicators at the conceptual level (Bollen and Lennox, 1991).

Considering the various forms of CWBs, one might argue that workplace security is merely a subset of the CWB concept. However, CWBs and security behaviors are not synonymous. First, research on CWBs, by definition, focuses on perpetrators within an organization. In contrast, security research focuses on security violations or incidents caused by the actions of organizational insiders, organizational outsiders, or a combination of insiders and outsiders. Furthermore, CWBs are typically defined as intentional acts. While security violations such as espionage are clearly the result of intentional behavior, security violations also result from unintentional behaviors driven by negligence or inadequate knowledge.

Distinctions between Security Behaviors and Safety Behaviors

Another construct related to security behaviors is that of safety behaviors. Similar to CWBs, there are various forms of safety behaviors. Specifically, safety behaviors can be separated into general safety behaviors (Burke *et al.*, 2002) and safety citizenship behaviors (Hofmann, Morgeson and Gerras, 2003). General safety behaviors are the actions that individuals perform with the goal of reducing injuries and illness. Examples of these behaviors include using personal protective equipment, engaging in work practices that reduce risk, communicating health and safety information, and exercising employee rights and responsibilities. In contrast to general safety behaviors, safety citizenship behaviors are actions that are beyond what is formally expected, including volunteering for safety committees, raising safety concerns during planning sessions, protecting fellow crew members from safety hazards, attending safety meetings, and trying to improve safety procedures

In some cultures, such as in Russia, there is no distinction between safety and security which is reflected linguistically by the fact that the same word is used to represent both concepts (Khripunov, 2005). And while the English language does have separate words for the two concepts, many English language thesauri list safety and security as synonyms (Kipfer, 2007). But the relationship between the two concepts is more than just a linguistic one. For example, safety and security programs are both largely compliance based or rules driven. In addition, the causes of both safety and security events can often be traced back to a number of individual (e.g. motivation) or organizational (e.g. organizational climate) factors. Finally, some incidents such as workplace violence (e.g. shootings or robbery) are difficult to categorize as either a safety or security problem.

Nonetheless, the construct of safety behaviors is conceptually distinct from security behaviors on several grounds. First, occupational safety research and related legislation (e.g. Occupational Safety and Health Act, 1970) have mainly focused on establishing safe and healthy working conditions for employees by reducing illness as well as fatal and non-fatal injuries resulting from inadequate working conditions (e.g. over time) or working procedures (e.g. repetitive motions). Compared to security threats, which can be directed at either the organization or the individual, safety threats such as hazard exposures are almost exclusively directed at individual workers.

Second, unsafe behaviors are rarely done intentionally to harm organizations or even individuals. Threats to workplace safety are not typically the result of intentional acts by employees nor caused by a malicious adversary; rather, they are often dictated by characteristics of organizations and job tasks (NORA Organization of Work Team, 2002), hazardous exposures (e.g. welding fumes, pesticides, noise, repetitive motions), and individuals (e.g. risk perceptions and attitudes). Security incidents, on the other hand, can be committed intentionally or unintentionally, with or without an adversary. Finally, security officers and safety officers perform different tasks with different tools and equipment as evidenced from job analysis (O*NET, 2006, 2008).

In sum, despite the distinctions between security behaviors and the constructs of CWBs and safety behaviors, results and conclusions from research on these topics may have applicability to understanding organizational security. For example, Spector et al. (2006) found that security-related CWBs such as abuse against others tend to relate more strongly to job stressors than psychological strains. Hollinger (1986) also reported that theft, which is clearly a security issue, is more common among younger employees with less tenure and less commitment to the organization. Clearly, some of the extant research on the antecedents in CWBs (cf. Snyder et al., 2004 for a comprehensive review) and safety behaviors (e.g. Sampson, Chen and DeArmond, 2008; Snyder et al., 2008; Zohar and Luria, 2005) would likely provide fruitful insights into the study of security behaviors.

Taken as a whole, the review above suggests that there is certainly a relationship, and in some cases an overlap, between security behaviors and both CWBs and safety behaviors. However, the ways in which the latter two concepts have historically been operationalized seem to provide sufficient grounds to justify viewing security behaviors as a distinct behavioral domain. Within this domain, we propose that security behaviors can be categorized on the basis of three characteristics: the perpetrator, the intent, and the target. First, the perpetrator can either be an organizational outsider, an organizational insider, or a combination of both outsiders and insiders. Second, security behaviors (whether positive, indifferent, or negative) can be either intentional or unintentional, and intentional security behaviors (particularly those that are negative) can be either malevolent or benign. Finally, security behaviors can affect either the organization (as in the case of espionage) or the organization's employees (as in the case of workplace violence).

ANTECEDENTS OF SECURITY BEHAVIORS

Assuming a degree of individual control, ones' security behaviors – much like job performance – are influenced by three primary determinants: declarative knowledge about security (e.g. knowledge of security regulations and procedures), procedural knowledge and skills (e.g. skills to execute behaviors such as self-management skills to protect workplace security), and motivation to perform the required behavior. However, the assumption that individuals have complete control over their behavior is not realistic, particularly within the context of the workplace. Therefore, it is prudent to consider those factors beyond ones' control that might positively or negatively affect the determinants, and in turn impact security behaviors. Clearly, there are a variety of factors that might be considered. However, we limit our discussion to organizational characteristics because we believe antecedents of this type are the most likely to be outside an employee's control. And among all the potential organizational characteristics from which to choose, there has been indirect evidence to suggest that antecedents of security behaviors might include job characteristics, organizational justice, and security climate.

Job Characteristics

Job characteristics such as organizational constraints, workload, role ambiguity, and role conflict likely play some role in affecting employees' motivation to comply with security regulations and policies. Organizational constraints are situational obstacles at work that prevent workers from performing their duties. These constraints include things such as incomplete or poor information as well as interruptions by coworkers. Constraints such as these have already been linked to poor performance, frustration, and job dissatisfaction (Peters *et al.*, 1988), CWBs such as sabotage and theft (Chen and Spector, 1992; Fox and Spector, 1999; Storms and Spector, 1987), as well as safety behaviors (Sampson, DeArmond and Chen, 2008). Chen and his colleagues (Chen and Spector, 1992; Sampson, DeArmond and Chen, 2008) have also demonstrated that ambiguous job information (e.g. as a result of miscommunication) as well as conflicting job demands or requests from managers (e.g. production quotas and workload vs. safety or security) are associated with CWBs and safety behaviors. Finally, the lack of control over one's environment has been found to be related to increased absence (Rentsch and Steel, 1998) and sabotage (Klein, Leong and Silvia, 1996).

Organizational Justice

In addition to job characteristics, the experience of injustice at work may affect the determinants of security behaviors. The feeling of unjust treatment or perceptions of unfairness in the workplace resulting from issues such as pay and promotion decisions have been found to trigger deviant or aggressive behaviors (Fisher and Baron, 1982; Geddes and Baron, 1997; Greenberg and Scott, 1996; Neuman and Baron, 1998), retaliation (Navran, 1991; Skarlicki and Folger, 1997), lateness (Hollinger, Slora and Terris, 1992), and theft (Greenberg, 1990).

While perceptions of injustice have consistently predicted CWBs, it is not entirely clear how different causes of these perceptions might be related to targets of aggressive actions such as a supervisor or coworker. Empirical research has suggested that there may be different mechanisms responsible for different aggressive acts (Spector *et al.*, 2006), and it is believed that perpetrators of aggressive behaviors tend to target those they feel are the source of injustice (Spector and Fox, 2005). However, supervisors and managers are often viewed as representatives of the organization (Levinson, 1965; Rhoades and Eisenberger, 2002), so it is possible that negative security behaviors might be directed at these individuals even if the source of injustice is viewed to be the organization. Likewise, injustice from supervisors may lead to negative security behaviors against the supervisor personally and against the organization. What is clear from these findings, however, is the important roles supervisors and managers can play in preventing intentional as well as unintentional negative security behaviors.

Security Climate

Among all plausible antecedents described above, security climate likely plays an important role in shaping security behaviors. Extending from the definition of general organizational and safety climate to the strategic outcome of security, security climate can be defined as a security characteristic of an organization that is manifested in employees' shared perceptions of the organization's security policies, practices, and procedures.

It has frequently been suggested that efforts to improve security should focus much more on organizational factors such as security climate as a way to augment physical-related security systems. For instance, General Eugene Habiger, retired commander of US strategic nuclear forces and security advisor to the US Department of Energy, contended that 'good security is 20% equipment and 80% culture' (cited in Bunn and Wier, 2004, pp. 48–50). The International Atomic Energy Agency (IAEA), an agency of the United Nations responsible for monitoring nuclear security and safeguards programs among member nations, has also repeatedly issued statements urging members to foster a good security culture as a supplement to existing efforts to protect nuclear assets (e.g. IAEA, 2001; IAEA, 2002; IAEA, 2003). In addition, in 2005 the presidents of the United States and Russia issued a joint statement that acknowledges the importance of nuclear security culture and commits to developing greater understanding and application of the construct (White House, 2005).

Second, security climate has received very little research attention in fields such as industrial–organizational psychology even with the increasing interest on the topic in the security literature. Given the scarcity of research, it is not surprising that the construct of security climate is not well understood. The confusion that exists in the security literature is evident in the preceding paragraph. Despite the recognized distinctions between the concepts of culture and climate (Ostroff, Kinicki and Tamkins, 2003), the term 'security culture' is ubiquitous in discussions that actually refer to security climate. Much more troublesome than the misuse of terminology, however, is the fact that a clear conceptualization of security climate and its components has only recently been articulated (Bitzer, 2009).

Security climate is expected to impact security behaviors and as a result security incidents on the basis of two general assumptions about employees within an organization (Schneider, 1975): (1) employees desire, create, and maintain order in their workplace and (2) an ordered workplace helps employees determine what appropriate behaviors in a given situation are. In essence, employees comprehend order through rules or procedures regarding security. They then adjust their actions to follow the order created by their perceptions of these rules and procedures at work. In this way, employees are able to act in a way that supports the goals of the organization, which are reflected in the strong security climate. As a result, enhanced security behaviors are expected in an organization with a strong security climate.

The above expectation has been supported by research where organizational climate was applied to safety as well as customer service (e.g. Schneider, White and Paul, 1998; Zohar and Luria, 2005). In the context of security, a recent study (Bitzer, 2009) found that security climate (e.g. supervisors promote good security practices; employees are willing to report security) predicted the frequency of security incidents as well as employee self-reporting of security incidents such as when an employee directly involved in a security event reports the occurrence to the organization. While these results are encouraging, much more work is needed. This is particularly true in light of the calls to use security climate in high-risk organizations operating in the nuclear field.

What Does Security Climate Entail?

On the basis of Zohar's (2003) conceptualization of climate, security climate reflects employees' appraisal of security policies, procedures, and practices, indicated by desired role behaviors (e.g. management reacts quickly to resolve security violation or invest resources in security training). Over the years, climate researchers have proposed many climate dimensions including structure, reward, risk, warmth, support, standards, conflict, identity, democraticness, supportiveness, innovativeness, peer relations, pressure, and so on (Ostroff, Kinicki and Tamkins, 2003).

Among the various organizational climate dimensions that have been proposed, management commitment or support has been consistently identified as one of the key components of changing, shaping, and establishing climate (Campbell et al., 1970; Flin et al., 2000; Hemingway and Smith, 1999; Ho, 2005; Seo et al., 2004; Smith-Crowe, Burke and Landis, 2003; Tracey and Tews, 2005; Waters, Roach and Batlis, 1974; Weyman, Clarke and Cox, 2003; Zohar and Luria, 2005). For example, Flin et al. found that of the 18 scales of safety climate included in their review, 72% contained some measure of management commitment or support for safety. This result was supported by Seo et al. who found that among the 16 studies reviewed nearly two-thirds operationalized management commitment as a dimension of safety climate.

Management commitment/support for security is important because it can influence an employee's perceptions of how important security is to the organization. Clarke (1999) found that the discrepancy between managers' espoused values that are officially endorsed and enacted values or those that are put into practice through actual behavior about safety was a driving factor in the development of employee perceptions of a safety program. And it is reasonable to believe that the same may be true within the realm of security. One possible explanation for such an effect comes from Hofmann and colleagues (Hofmann and Morgeson, 1999; Hofmann, Morgeson and Gerras, 2003) who have suggested a social exchange model as the theoretical mechanism underlying the importance of management commitment. According to these authors, when employees perceive strong management commitment to safety they return that commitment with safety compliance as part of the social exchange.

Effects of management support or commitment on security behaviors might also be explained by role modeling. Greenberg and Scott (1996) have suggested that at least some employee theft may be attributed to the fact that employees mimic behaviors modeled by their supervisors or managers. They argued that if a manager engages in activities such as theft, employees would likely perceive that managers are not committed to security and therefore it is not important for them to be concerned with it. Although there is a lack of empirical evidence testing the above proposition, such a suggestion is supported by assertions from a number of other experts on employee theft (e.g. Cherrington and Cherrington, 1985; Greenberg, 1997; Hollinger, 1989).

Research has suggested that certain management practices convey their commitment to security, which in turn influences employees' security behaviors. For instance, inappropriate security behaviors such as employee theft diminish when managers regularly communicate to employees about the importance of security (Carter et al., 1988). In addition, it has been suggested that when managers conduct regular security audits they are displaying their commitment to security, and this practice can lead to a reduction of employee theft behaviors as well as an increase in management's awareness of the problem (Jones and Terris, 1983). Finally, a limited amount of theoretical work in the field of nuclear security also suggests that management support for security plays an important role in building security climate. For example, Khripunov, Nikonov and Katsva (2004) contend that managers 'can use their positions of power to...encourage new and different assumptions and patterns of thinking among their colleagues' (pp. 45–46).

Additionally, coworker support for security might be an important dimension of security climate. Theoretical support for this comes from the theory of reasoned action and the theory of planned behavior (Fishbein and Ajzen, 1975; Ajzen, 1985, 1991). Both of these theories propose that an individual's behavior is impacted by social influence in the form of both subjective norms as well as normative beliefs. On the one hand, subjective norms consist of perceptions that a behavior, in this case a behavior either supportive of or detrimental to security, is expected by important and respected people that surround an individual. On the other hand, normative beliefs are an individual's perception about a behavior (again, one either supportive of or detrimental to security) that is influenced in part by the judgments of the significant others that surround the individual. Taken together, subjective norms and normative beliefs can exert social influence from one's coworkers. These social influences can then impact an individual's perceptions, as well as behaviors, related to security.

In addition to management commitment, it has been suggested that perceptions of organizational policies and procedures are a key component of climate (Rentsch, 1990). Zohar (1980) found that, along with management support, employees' perceptions of safety procedures were an important aspect of an organization's safety climate. In addition, Coyle, Sleeman and Adams (1995) found that employees' perceptions of company safety policies accounted for the second largest percentage of variance in safety climate among clerical and service organizations in Australia. Similarly, Diaz and Cabrera (1997) found that perceptions of organizational policies explained the greatest percentage of variance in safety climate among employees working in the airline industry.

Limited research in the field of security also suggests that security policies and procedures are often judged by employees in terms of their relevance (Are they necessary?), their effectiveness (Do they actually improve security?), and their user-friendliness (Are they understandable and not overly cumbersome to implement?). Thus, Khripunov, Nikonov and Katsva (2004) suggested that security policies and procedures should be up to date, succinct, clear, and user-friendly.

EXPAND THE FRONTIER: WHAT IS NEXT?

It is undoubtedly important to have advanced physical-related security systems to protect organizations from security threats. However, it is reasonable to argue that when employees lack adequate declarative knowledge, procedural skills and – perhaps most important – motivation to use and maintain these systems, even the best equipment and technology are worth little more than the raw materials they are made of. With this in mind, we foresee several avenues for future research.

The first challenge is to systematically identify a taxonomy of security behaviors that are common to most or all employees. Identification of the taxonomy is critical because different forms of security behaviors may have distinct underlying mechanisms such as caused by different antecedents under different contexts, as suggested in CWB literature (Spector *et al.*, 2006) and the performance literature (Van Scotter, Motowidlo and Cross, 2000).

The second challenge for research and practice is to identify antecedents and understand determinants of security behaviors that are common to most or all employees. Theoretical models of job performance (e.g. Borman and Motowidlo, 1993; Campbell *et al.*, 1993) and reviews of performance management (e.g. Motowidlo, 2003) provide invaluable insights regarding plausible individual antecedents (e.g. attitudes, risk perception, personality) and organizational antecedents (e.g. communication, leadership, error culture) which may affect security knowledge, security skills, and motivation to engage in security behaviors.

An additional challenge for researchers and practitioners is to understand contextual as well as individual factors that are associated with unintentional negative security behaviors, and developing strategies to reduce unintentional negative security behaviors. As pointed out earlier, some security violations are the result of unintentional acts such as engaging in a conversation with a colleague in an unsecured area where an unauthorized person could listen in. Research aimed at identifying factors leading to such behaviors could lead to their reduction.

Given that security violations have relatively low base rate, the challenge for practitioners is how to maintain vigilance of negative security behaviors and provide performance feedback and recognition for positive security behaviors. Research focusing on daily feedback, recognition, communication (e.g. Hofmann and Stetzer, 1996; Zohar and Luria, 2003) and error management (Van Dyck *et al.*, 2005) has shown positive impacts on safety and organizational performance, and their findings may shed light on ways of maintaining security vigilance.

Ultimately, we argue that the top priority for improving security behaviors is to understand what contributes to organizational security, although we recognize that there are many plausible organizational factors that may influence behaviors in general, and security behaviors in particular. As yet, evidence from safety climate (e.g. Zohar and Luria, 2005) as well as some initial findings on security (Bitzer, 2009) suggests that security climate can be improved. To that end, we would suggest a number of possible areas for future security climate research. One area that merits additional investigation is further exploration of the facet structure of climate for security. The safety climate field, despite over 25 years of research, is still in the process of refining the underlying dimensions of the construct. Therefore, it would be presumptuous to claim that a definitive set of all relevant dimensions of security climate could have been identified at this early stage. Without a doubt, additional research designed to test the dimensions that have been proposed is necessary to accurately identify the true facets underlying climate for security. The nature of future research is needed not only to verify the existence of these dimensions, but also to explore whether other facets not already proposed might be important components of climate for security.

Another line of research in the field of security climate that needs attention is the development and validation of measurement tools designed specifically to assess climate for security. The development of measures specific to climate for security would make it easier for future researchers attempting to further explore the nature of the concept, and the development of such a measure would allow organizations to establish baselines and track the development of their own climate for security in a meaningful way.

Future efforts to study organizational security might also consider the question of generalizability. Research aimed at addressing organizational security needs to take work settings and industry types into consideration. For example, financial institutions, retail organizations, and hospitals all face important security issues. However, the nature of the issues these organizations face, such as the kinds of adversaries they are confronted with and the threats these adversaries pose, are likely to vary significantly from each other and from other types of organizations.

As mentioned above, the IAEA has repeatedly stressed the importance of organizational factors at nuclear facilities. Such calls underscore the importance of a next area for future research. Specifically, there is a need for cross-cultural research on security behaviors. Different nations have different perspectives and processes when developing security regulations. Therefore, it would be interesting to see if there are differences in how and why security behaviors, regulations, practices and security climate develop in different nations. It has been stated that different cultures tend to view the concept of security differently (Khripunov, 2005). Furthermore, Hofstede (1983) has suggested that nations can vary on an individualism–collectivism continuum. According to this theory, the prevailing view in individualistic cultures is that each person is responsible for himself or herself and commitment to the group is secondary. On the other hand, collectivistic cultures tend to demand loyalty to the group in exchange for the benefits that membership affords.

The final area for potential future research is to examine how the presence of a security climate might affect other types of climates as well as how it might interact with other climates and impact organizational outcomes. As suggested recently by Zohar (2008), organizational climate contains multiple facets such as ethical climate (Parboteeah and Kapp, 2008), customer service climate (Schneider, 1990), and violence climate (Spector et al., 2007). It is possible that some of these climates would likely covary because they reflect different yet related organizational characteristics. On the basis of Zohar's multi-climate framework, security climate may interact with ownership climate, which indicates whether organizations encourage workers to commit extra-role activities such as vigilance or focus on workers' compliance on every security regulation. Under the high security climate and high ownership climate, workers would show extra-role or citizenship security behaviors. In contrast, workers would comply with security regulations as required when security climate is high and ownership climate is low.

Another example would be the relationship between security climate and climate for innovation. On the one hand, a strong security climate might lead employees to be cautious about widely disseminating sensitive information. However, innovative climates tend to exhibit a free flow of information. Given that these two perspectives appear to be at odds, it is likely that these climates would affect each other such that a strong security climate would hinder a strong innovative climate, or vice versa.

Finally, although we recognize that there are many plausible organizational factors that may influence behavior in general and security behavior in particular, we argue that the top priority for improving security behaviors is to understand key organizational factors such as management support for security in shaping security behaviors. Evidence from the safety literature (e.g., Zohar and Luria, 2005) has suggested that management's concern such as frequently exhibiting verbal exchanges about security issues would build strong security climate over time, which may predict various aspects of security performance. In light of this chapter, we believe that better understanding the antecedents and determinants of security behaviors could be an important, and long overdue, addition to the field of security.

ACKNOWLEDGEMENTS

This chapter is based in part on the dissertation of Edward G. Bitzer, III, which was directed by Peter Y. Chen. Preparation of this chapter was partially supported by the Center for Construction Research and Training (CCRT) as part of a cooperative agreement with the National Institute for Occupational Safety and Health (NIOSH, grant no. OH008307).

REFERENCES

Ajzen, I. (1985). From intentions to actions: a theory of planned behavior. In J. Kuhl & J. Beckman (Eds), *Action-Control: From Cognition to Behavior* (pp. 11–39) Heidelberg: Springer.

Ajzen, I. (1991). The theory of planned behavior. *Organizational Behavior and Human Decision Processes*, **50** (2), 179–211.

Bennett, R. J. & Robinson, S. L. (2000). Development of a measure of workplace deviance. *Journal of Applied Psychology*, **85**, 349–60.

Bies, R. J. & Tripp, T. M. (2005). The study of revenge in the workplace: conceptual, ideological, and empirical issues. In S. Fox & P. E. Spector (Eds), *Counterproductive Workplace Behavior: Investigations of Actors and Targets* (pp. 83–105) Washington, DC: APA.

Bitzer, E. G. (2009). An exploratory investigation of organizational security climate in a highly regulated environment. Colorado State Univ. Dissertation.

Bollen, K. & Lennox, R. (1991). Conventional wisdom on measurement: a structural equation perspective. *Psychological Bulletin*, 110, 305–14.

Borman, W. C. & Motowidlo, S. J. (1993). Expanding the criterion domain to include elements of contextual performance. In N. Schmitt, W. C. Borman & Associates (Eds), *Personnel Selection in Organizations* (pp. 71–98) San Francisco: Jossey-Bass.

Bunn, M. & Wier, A. (2004). *Securing the Bomb: An Agenda for Action*, Commissioned by the Nuclear Threat Initiative, http://www.nti.org/cnwm (accessed 5 July 2005).

Burke, M. J., Sarpy, S. A., Tesluk, P. E. & Smith-Crowe, K. (2002). General safety performance: a test of a grounded theoretical model. *Personnel Psychology*, 55, 429–57.

Campbell, J. P., Dunnette, M. D., Lawler, E. E. & Weick, K. E. (1970). *Managerial Behavior, Performance, and Effectiveness*, New York: McGraw-Hill.

Campbell, J. P., McCloy, R. A., Oppler, S. H. & Sager, C. E. (1993). A theory of performance. In N. Schmitt, W. C. Borman & Associates (Eds), *Personnel Selection in Organizations* (pp. 35–70) San Francisco: Jossey-Bass.

Carter, N., Holmström, A., Simpanen, M. & Melin, L. (1988). Theft reduction in a grocery store through product identification and graphing of losses for employees. *Journal of Applied Behavior Analysis*, 21, 385–89.

Case, J. (2000). *Employee Theft: The Profit Killer*, Del Mar, CA: John Case & Associates.

Chen, P. & Spector, P. (1992). Relationships of work stressors with aggression, withdrawal, theft and substance use: an exploratory study. *Journal of Occupational and Organizational Psychology*, 65 (3), 177–184.

Cherrington, D. J. & Cherrington, J. O. (1985). The climate of honesty in retail stores. In W. Terris (Ed.), *Employee Theft: Research, Theory and Applications* (pp. 27–39) Park Ridge, IL: London House.

Clarke, S. (1999). Perceptions of organizational safety: implications for the development of a safety culture. *Journal of Organizational Behavior*, 20, 185–98.

Coyle, I. R., Sleeman, S. D. & Adams, N. (1995). Safety climate. *Journal of Safety Research*, 26 (4), 247–54.

Dartt, A. & Rosecrance, J. (2008). *Field Evaluation of an Ergonomically Designed Hand Tool*. NORA Symposium: Public Market for Ideas and Partnerships, Denver, CO.

Diaz, R. I. & Cabrera, D. D. (1997). Safety climate and attitude as evaluation measures of organizational safety. *Accident Analysis and Prevention*, 29, 643–50.

Douglas, S. & Martinko, M. (2001). Exploring the role of individual differences in the prediction of workplace aggression. *Journal of Applied Psychology*, 86 (4), 547–59.

Einarsen, S., Hoel, H., Zapf, D. & Cooper, C. L. (2003). The concept of bullying at work: the European tradition. In S. Einarsen, H. Hoel, D. Zapf & C. L. Cooper (Eds), *Bullying and Emotional Abuse in the Workplace*. New York: Taylor & Francis.

Fishbein, M. & Ajzen, I. (1975). *Belief, Attitude, Intention, and Behavior: An Introduction to Theory and Research*, Reading, MA: Addison-Wesley.

Fisher, J. D. & Baron, R. M. (1982). An equity-based model of vandalism. *Population and Environment: Behavioral and Social Issues*, 5, 182–200.

Flin, R., Mearns, K., O'Connor, P. & Bryden, R. (2000). Measuring safety climate: identifying the common features. *Safety Science*, 34, 177–92.

Fox, S. & Spector, P. (1999). A model of work frustration-aggression. *Journal of Organizational Behavior*, 20 (6), 915–931.

Geddes, D. & Baron, R. A. (1997). Workplace aggression as a consequence on negative performance feedback. *Management Communication Quarterly*, 10, 433–54.

Greenberg, J. (1990). Employee theft as a reaction to underpayment inequity: the hidden cost of pay cuts. *Journal of Applied Psychology*, 75, 561–68.

Greenberg, J. (1997). A social influence model of employee theft: beyond the fraud triangle. *Research on Negotiations in Organizations*, 6, 29–51.

Greenberg, J. & Scott, K. S. (1996). Why do workers bite the hands that feed them? Employee theft as social exchange process. *Research in Organizational Behavior*, 18, 111–56.

Gruys, M. L. (1999). The dimensionality of deviant employee performance in the workplace.University of Minnesota Dissertation.

Hemingway, M. A. & Smith, C. S. (1999). Organizational climate and occupational stressors as predictors of withdrawal behaviors and injuries in nurses. *Journal of Occupational and Organizational Psychology*, 72, 285–99.

Ho, M. (2005). Safety climate and occupational injury: an examination of climate dimensions and injury outcomes. The Johns Hopkins Univ. Dissertation. Retrieved 5 June 2007, from ProQuest Digital Dissertations database (Publication No. AAT 3155623).

Hobijn, B. & Sager, E. (2007). What has homeland security cost? An assessment: 2001–2005 [Electronic version]. *Current Issues in Economics and Finance*, 13, 1–7.

Hofmann, D. A. & Morgeson, F. P. (1999). Safety-related behavior as a social exchange: the role of perceived organizational support and leader-member exchange. *Journal of Applied Psychology*, 84, 286–96.

Hofmann, D. A., Morgeson, F. P. & Gerras, S. J. (2003). Climate as a moderator of the relationship between leader-member exchange and content specific citizenship: safety climate as an exemplar. *Journal of Applied Psychology*, 88, 170–78.

Hofmann, D. & Stetzer, A. (1996). A cross-level investigation of factors influencing unsafe behaviors and accidents. *Personnel Psychology*, 49 (2), 307–339.

Hofstede, G. (1983). Dimensions of national cultures in fifty countries and three re-gions. In J. B. Deregowski, S. Dziurawiec & R. C. Annis (Eds), *Expiscations in Cross-Cultural Psychology* (pp. 335–55) Lisse: Swets and Zeitlinger.

Hollinger, R. C. (1986). Acts against the workplace: social bonding and employee deviance. *Deviant Behavior*, 7, 53–75.

Hollinger, R. C. (1989). *Dishonesty in the Workplace: A Manager's Guide to Preventing Theft*, Park Ridge, IL: London House.

Hollinger, R. C., Slora, K. B. & Terris, W. (1992). Deviance in the fast-food restaurant: correlates of employee theft, altruism, and counterproductivity. *Deviant Behavior: An Interdisciplinary Journal*, 13, 155–84.

Huang, Y. H., Chen, P. Y., Krauss, A. D. & Rogers, D. A. (2004). Quality of the execution of corporate safety policies and employee safety outcomes: assessing the moderating role of supervisor support and the mediating role of employee safety control. *Journal of Business and Psychology*, 18, 483–506.

International Atomic Energy Agency: Board of Governors (2001). *Nuclear Verification and Security of Material: Physical Protection Objectives and Fundamental Principles*. GOV/2001/41, August, Vienna, Austria.

International Atomic Energy Agency: Board of Governors/General Conference (2002). *Measures to Strengthen International Cooperation in Nuclear, Radiation, Transport and Waste Safety: Implementation of the Revised Action Plan for the Safety and Security of Radiation Sources*. GOV/2002/35/Add. 1-GC46/11/Add. 1, September, Vienna, Austria.

International Atomic Energy Agency: General Conference (2003). *Nuclear Security: Measures to Protect against Nuclear Terrorism*. GC47/17, August, Vienna, Austria.

IT Security Market Report (2007). Research and Markets, Dublin, Ireland.

Jones, J. W. & Terris, W. (1983). Predicting employees' theft in home improvement centers. *Psychological Reports*, **52**, 187–201.

Khripunov, I. (2005). Nuclear security: attitude check. *Bulletin of the Atomic Scientists*, **61**, 58–64.

Khripunov, I., Nikonov, D. & Katsva, M. (2004). Nuclear industry framework. In Khripunov, I. & Holmes, J. (Eds), *Nuclear Security Culture: The Case of Russia* (pp. 45–46). Athens, GA: University of Georgia, Center for International Trade and Security.

Kipfer, B. A. (ed.) (2007). *Roget's New Millennium Thesaurus*, 1st edn, v 1.3.1, http://thesaurus.reference.com/browse/security (accessed 9 April 2007).

Klein, R.L., Leong, G. B. & Silvia, J. A. (1996). Employee sabotage in the workplace: a biopsychosocial model. *Journal of Forensic Sciences*, **41**, 52–55.

Levinson, H. (1965). Reciprocation: the relationship between man and the organization. *Administrative Science Quarterly*, **9**, 370–90.

Marquand, R. & Arnoldy, B. (2007). China emerges as leader in cyberwarfare. *Christian Science Monitor*, 14 September, W1.

McGurn, S. (1988). Spotting the thieves who work among us. *Wall Street Journal*, 27 March, 16A.

Motowidlo, S. (2003). Job performance. In W. C. Borman, D. R. Ilgen & R. J. Klimoski (Eds), *Handbook of Psychology: Industrial and Organizational Psychology*, Vol. 12 (pp. 39–53). Hoboken, NJ: John Wiley & Sons Inc.

Neuman, J. H. & Baron, R. A. (1998). Workplace violence and workplace aggression: evidence concerning specific forms, potential causes, and preferred targets. *Journal of Management*, **24**, 391–419.

Navran, F. J. (1991). Silent saboteurs. *Executive Excellence*, **8**, 11–13.

NORA Organization of Work Team (2002). *The Changing Organization of Work and the Safety and Health of Working People*. US Department of Health and Human Services, DHHS (NIOSH) Publication No. 2002-226.

Occupational Safety and Health Act (1970). *Occupational safety and Health Act of 1970*, http://www.osha.gov/pls/oshaweb/owasrch.search_form?p_doc_type=OSHACT

O*NET Online (2006). *Summary report for: 29-9011.00 – occupational health and safety specialists*, http://online.onetcenter.org/link/summary/29-9011.00 (accessed 13 October 2008).

O*NET Online (2008). *Summary report for: 33-9032.00 – security guard*, http://online.onetcenter.org/link/summary/33-9032.00 (accessed 13 October 2008).

Ostroff, C., Kinicki, A. J. & Tamkins, M. M. (2003). Organizational culture and climate. In I. B. Weiner (Series Ed.) and W. C. Borman, D. R. Ilgen & R. J. Klimoski (Vol. Eds), *Handbook of Psychology: Vol. 12. Industrial and Organizational Psychology* (pp. 565–93). Hoboken, NJ: John Wiley & Sons, Inc.

Parboteeah, K. & Kapp, E. (2008). Ethical climates and workplace safety behaviors: an empirical investigation. *Journal of Business Ethics*, **80** (3), 515–29.

Peters, L., O'Connor, E., Eulberg, J. & Watson, T. (1988). An examination of situational constraints in Air Force work settings. *Human Performance*, **1** (2), 133–44.

Pond, D. J. (2002). *Enhanced Security Through Human Error Reduction (ESTHER)*, *LA-UR-02-815*, Los Alamos, NM: Los Alamos National Laboratory.

Rentsch, J. R. (1990). Climate and culture: interaction and qualitative differences in organizational meanings. *Journal of Applied Psychology*, **75**, 668–81.

Rentsch, J. R. & Steel, R. P. (1998). Testing the durability of job characteristics as predictors of absenteeism over a six-year period. *Personnel Psychology*, **51**, 165–89.

Rhoades, L. & Eisenberger, R. (2002). Perceived organizational support: a review of the literature. *Journal of Applied Psychology*, **87**, 698–714.

Rigdon, J. E. (1994). Companies see more workplace violence. *Wall Street Journal*, 12 April, B1.

Sampson, J. M., DeArmond, S. & Chen, P. Y. (2008). *Interactive Effects of Safety Constraints, Safety Uncertainty, and Verbal Exchanges*. Paper presented at the 23rd Annual Conference of the Society for Industrial and Organizational Psychology, April, San Francisco, CA.

Schneider, B. (1975). Organizational climates: an essay. *Personnel Psychology*, **28**, 447–79.

Schneider, B. (1990). The climate for service: an application of the climate construct. In B. Schneider (Ed.), *Organizational Climate and Culture* (pp. 383–412). San Francisco: Jossey Bass.

Schneider, B., White, S. S. & Paul, M. C. (1998). Linking service climate and customer perceptions of service quality: test of a causal model. *Journal of Applied Psychology*, **83**, 150–63.

Seo, D. C., Torabi, M. R., Blair, E. H. & Ellis, N. T. (2004). A cross-validation of safety climate scale using confirmatory factor analytic approach. *Journal of Safety Research*, **35**, 427–45.

Seper, J. (2007). Ten of 160 missing FBI laptops had sensitive data. *The Washington Times*, 13 February, A3.

Simpson, J. & Weiner, E. (eds) (1989). *Oxford English Dictionary*, 2nd edn, Oxford: Oxford University Press. http://0-dictionary.oed.com.catalog.library.colostate.edu/cgi/entry/50218187?single=1&query_type=word&queryword=security&first=1&max_to_show=10 (accessed 15 October 2007).

Skarlicki, D. P. & Folger, R. (1997). Retaliation in the workplace: the roles of distributive, procedural, and interactional justice. *Journal of Applied Psychology*, **82**, 434–43.

Smith-Crowe, K., Burke, M. J. & Landis, R. S. (2003). Organizational climate as a moderator of safety knowledge-safety performance relationships. *Journal of Organizational Behavior*, **24**, 861–76.

Snyder, L. A., Chen, P. Y., Grubb, P. L. *et al.* (2004). Workplace aggression and violence: causes, consequences, and interventions. In P. L. Perrewe & D. C. Ganster (Eds), *Research in Occupational Stress and Well Being*, Vol. 4 (pp. 1–65). Amsterdam: Elsevier/JAI.

Snyder, L. A., Krauss, A. D., Chen, P. Y. *et al.* (2008). Occupational safety: application of the job demand-control-support model. *Accident Analysis and Prevention*, **40**, 1713–23.

Spector, P. E. (1975). Relationships of organizational frustration with reported behavioral reactions of employees. *Journal of Applied Psychology*, **60**, 635–37.

Spector, P. E., Coulter, M. L., Stockwell, H. G. & Matz, M. W. (2007). Perceived violence climate: a new construct and its relationship to workplace physical violence and verbal aggression, and their potential consequences. *Work and Stress*, **21**, 117–30.

Spector, P. E. & Fox, S. (2005). A model of counterproductive work behavior. In S. Fox & P. E. Spector (Eds), *Counterproductive Workplace Behavior: Investigations of Actors and Targets* (pp. 151–74). Washington, DC: APA.

Spector, P. E., Fox, S., Penney, L. M. *et al.* (2006). The dimensionality of counterproductivity: Are all counterproductive behaviors created equal? *Journal of Vocational Behavior*, **68**, 446–60.

Storms, P. L. & Spector, P. E. (1987). Relationships of frustration with reported behavioural reactions: the moderating effect of locus of control. *Journal of Occupational Psychology*, **60**, 227–34.

Tracey, J. B. & Tews, M. J. (2005). Construct validity of a general training climate scale. *Organizational Research Methods*, **8**, 353–74.

Van Dyck, C., Frese, M., Baer, M. & Sonnentag, S. (2005). Organizational error management culture and its impact on performance. *Journal of Applied Psychology*, **90**, 1228–40.

Van Scotter, J. R., Motowidlo, S. J. & Cross, T. C. (2000). Effects of task performance and contextual performance on systemic rewards. *Journal of Applied Psychology*, **85**, 526–35.

Warner, J. S. & Johnston, R. G. (2002). A simple demonstration that the global positioning system (GPS) is vulnerable to spoofing. *The Journal of Security Administration*, **25**, 19–28.

Warner, J. S. & Johnston, R. G. (2006). *Limitations and Vulnerabilities of RFID and Contact Memory Devices*. Talk given at the 7th Security Seals Symposium, 28 February to 2 March, Santa Barbara, CA.

Waters, L. K., Roach, D. & Batlis, N. (1974). Organizational climate dimensions and job-related attitudes. *Personnel Psychology*, **27**, 465–76.

Weyman, A., Clarke, D. D. & Cox, T. (2003). Developing a factor model of coal miners' attributions on risk-taking at work. *Work and Stress*, **17** (4), 306–20.

White House: Office of the Press Secretary (2005). Joint statement by President Bush and President Putin on *Nuclear Security Cooperation*, http://www.whitehouse.gov/news/releases/2005/02/20050224-8.html (accessed 26 May 2005).

Workplace Bullying Institute (2007). *US Workplace Bullying Survey*, http://bullyinginstitute.org/zogby2007/wbi-zogby2007.html (accessed 28 December 2007).

Zohar, D. (1980). Safety climate in industrial organizations: theoretical and applied implications. *Journal of Applied Psychology*, **65** (1), 96–102.

Zohar, D. (2003). Safety climate: conceptual and measurement issues. In J. C. Quick & L. E. Tetrick (Eds), *Handbook of Occupational Health Psychology* (pp. 123–42). Washington: American Psychological Association.

Zohar, D. (2008). A multi-level multi-climate approach for safety climate. In P. Y. Chen (Chair) *New Developments in the Conceptualization of Safety Climate*. Presented at the 7th International Conference on Occupational Stress & Health, Washington, DC, USA.

Zohar, D. & Luria, G. (2003). The use of supervisory practices as leverage to improve safety behavior: a cross-level intervention model. *Journal of Safety Research*, **34**, 567–77.

Zohar, D. & Luria, G. (2005). A multilevel model of safety climate: cross-level relationships between organization and group-level climates. *Journal of Applied Psychology*, **90**, 616–28.

Chapter 5

SENSEMAKING IN VIRTUAL TEAMS: THE IMPACT OF EMOTIONS AND SUPPORT TOOLS ON TEAM MENTAL MODELS AND TEAM PERFORMANCE

Anat Rafaeli, Shy Ravid and Arik Cheshin

Technion, Industrial Engineering and Management, Haifa, Israel

INTRODUCTION

Consider a virtual software development team responsible for developing a web-based tool for a client. Their task is to create a completely new tool that will be custom made according to the client's specifications. The development team meets face-to-face periodically, but most of the time each member of the team works independently. Members of this virtual team typically communicate through electronic media, such as e-mail, chat or shared documents. Initially, different members may hold different mental models about the attributes of the final product and about the development process. But as the project progresses these mental models must somehow converge in order for the project to be successfully completed. They somehow coalesce into a team mental model.

Building on this example, we integrate research in social psychology on sensemaking with research on team mental models and suggest that the evolution of a shared mental model concerning the project's goals and work processes relies on a recursive triangulation of two cycles: a direct cognitive cycle, in which the sensemaking process is influenced by, but also leads to, the team mental model; and an indirect, emotional cycle, in which individual intuition and emotions influence the sensemaking of team members and the emergent team mental model. We suggest that support tools hold critical influences over both of these cycles, helping to shape the sensemaking and the emotions of the team. We argue that the effects of support tools become particularly important when teams act in a virtual environment in which interactions are mediated by these tools.

International Review of Industrial and Organizational Psychology, 2009, Volume 24.
Edited by G. P. Hodgkinson and J. K. Ford. Copyright © 2009 John Wiley & Sons, Ltd

We develop this argument by following the example of a virtual team working on the development of new software. We begin with an analysis of the idea and importance of team mental models, and the influence of the sensemaking process on the evolution of such models. We then shift our focus to the interplay between emotions and sensemaking at two levels of analysis (individual and team). Finally, we touch upon the effects of support tools on this interplay.

MENTAL MODELS AND SHARED MENTAL MODELS

People navigate their social and organizational environment by developing mental models. These models comprise mental descriptions of system purpose and form, and explanations of system functioning and system states; a model can also include predictions of future system states (Rouse and Morris, 1986, p. 351). Mental models translate reality into internal representations, and these translations guide the way people cope with requirements posed by reality (Park and Gittleman, 1995, p. 303). In this chapter, we analyze the evolution of mental models in virtual teams where communication among members must rely on technological means.

As implied in the opening vignette, some sharing of mental models is critical to the functioning of virtual teams. Team members have their own individual mental models that represent their understanding of the team's goals and characteristics, and the connections between their own work and collective actions (Marks *et al.*, 2002). Individual mental models also include prescriptions about the roles and behavior patterns required from each member for successful completion of the collective team's tasks (Marks *et al.*, 2002). So what happens when team members' mental models diverge? Resolving disagreements may be difficult even for actual, physical teams, where members can meet to iron out differences and compare or exchange ideas. How much more so, then, in virtual teams, which are prone to failures in knowledge sharing (Cramton, 2001; Cramton, Orvis and Wilson, 2007; Gratton, Voigt and Erickson, 2007).

Cramton (2002) suggested that key reasons for the problems frequently encountered by virtual teams include the inadequate sharing of knowledge, uneven distribution of information, differences of opinion on what information is considered salient, differences in teammates' rates of progress, and uncertainty about the meaning of electronic silence. We suggest that these limitations add up to limited (or perhaps, at times, non-existent) overlap of the members' individual mental models. Thus, a key factor determining the effectiveness of a virtual team is the extent to which members' individual mental models come to share elements or overlap with the mental models of other members.

When the individual mental models of different team members are similar, a *team mental model* can be argued to exist. A team mental model can be defined as a 'shared, organized understanding and mental representation of the key elements of the team's relevant environment' (Mohammed and Dumville, 2001,

p. 90). Some authors have spoken of 'shared mental models' (cf. Cannon-Bowers, Salas and Converse, 1993; Jeffery, Maes and Bratton-Jeffery, 2005; Kraiger and Wenzel, 1997; Marks *et al.*, 2002). We prefer the term 'team mental model' because, though we accept that such models are created through a process of sharing, we see the model as a quality of the team. When team members share a highly crystallized mental model, they work with a single understanding of each member's roles and responsibilities, and a single set of expectations about the team's needs, goals and constraints (Cannon-Bowers, Salas and Converse, 1993; Weick and Roberts, 1993).

Put differently, team mental models comprise the agreed-upon or convergent understanding that team members hold about the team and its tasks, including their circumstances, constraints and context (Feldman and Rafaeli, 2002). Team mental models both are derived from, and help team members formulate, collective explanations and expectations about the team's work processes; they facilitate communication and coordination of team activities, which in turn help develop and sustain situational awareness (Cannon-Bowers and Salas, 1997; Jeffery, Maes and Bratton-Jeffery, 2005; Kraiger and Wenzel, 1997; Salas, Cannon-Bowers and Blickensderfer, 1993; Stout, Cannon-Bowers and Salas, 1996). A key challenge for the creation of team mental models in virtual teams is the limited and constrained communication inherent to these bodies, and consequently, the limited opportunities for members to share and exchange elements of their individual mental models (Gibson and Gibbs, 2006; Mohrman, Klein and Finegold, 2003; Rico *et al.*, 2008). This challenge exists with regard to multiple elements or aspects of mental models, because of the limited and constrained communication in virtual teams.

TYPES OF TEAM MENTAL MODELS

Previous research has identified several types of team mental models. Cannon-Bowers, Salas and Converse (1993), for example, differentiated between four types. *Task models* comprise information regarding the task to be performed and related procedures, strategies, and environmental constraints. *Equipment models* refer to the tools and equipment required to accomplish the task. *Team attribute models* encompass information about the knowledge and preferences, skills, tendencies and abilities of other team members. Finally, the *team interaction model* outlines how team members work with each other. The latter is particularly challenging in virtual teams, where aspects of individual performance (e.g. specific responsibilities assigned to each member) may be clear, but issues arising from interpersonal interactions may be murky and difficult to resolve.

Other scholars have suggested somewhat different, but conceptually compatible typologies. Kraiger and Wenzel (1997) suggested that team mental models comprise three elements: *knowledge, behavior,* and *attitudes.* By *knowledge,* they refer to organized and structured assumptions about the task, process, or reactions to the environment. By *behavior*, they mean team members' mutual expectations, and *attitude* encompasses interpretations and affective reactions of the team, its behavior in relation to its environment.

Marks *et al.* (2002) offered a broader conceptualization of team mental models, distinguishing between *task-work* and *teamwork*. They defined 'task-work' as 'a team's interactions with tasks, tools, machines, and systems' (Bowers, Braun and Morgan, 1997, p. 90). Task-work represents *what* it is that teams are doing. In contrast, teamwork describes *how* teams are doing whatever they are doing (Marks *et al.*, 2002). Continuing this line of thought, Mathieu *et al.* (2000) argued that in order to be successful, team members should be able to perform task-related functions while also working well together as a team, that is, they connect the performance of 'task-work' to effective 'teamwork'. These dynamics, which operate at the team level, depend on the level of similarity between the individual models of different members. Here as well, virtual teams are challenged by the limited opportunities to examine the extent of similarity.

What happens when mental models of individual members of a virtual team are not shared? Cronin and Weingart (2007) conceptualized this situation as involving *representational gaps*, which they defined as 'inconsistencies between individuals' definitions of the team's problem' (Cronin and Weingart, 2007, p. 761). They note several ways in which such gaps can cause harm: Gaps can impede social and work processes, decrease coordination, create conflict, and, most importantly, lead to the misuse or misunderstanding of information. Representational gaps are particularly likely to occur in virtual teams, where the representations of individual members typically develop in completely different settings, and contextual effects can create completely different interpretations of the team (Griffith, Mannix and Neale, 2003).

Thus, multiple and different mental models may coexist in the minds of multiple team members, with individual members of a team themselves likely to hold not one, but multiple mental models (Klimoski and Mohammed, 1994). Furthermore, teams are likely to contain multiple models representing the multiple members of the team. Virtual teamwork in particular occurs against a backdrop of confusing and potentially dissimilar or even incompatible mental models. An important question, therefore, is whether and how individual models converge into a team mental model, and whether and how the shared team mental model influences the outcomes and effectiveness of the team (Gibson and Cohen, 2003). As we elaborate next, the critical issue is the extent to which mental models of different team members are similar, meaning that they have shared or overlapping elements.

TEAM MENTAL MODELS, TEAM PERFORMANCE AND TEAM OUTCOMES

The extent to which the individual mental models of different members are similar can be viewed as an indicator of the extent to which team members work toward common objectives and have a shared vision of how their team will function. According to Mathieu *et al.* (2000), the existence of a team mental model allows coordinated actions and helps different members be 'in sync'. This statement implicitly assumes that the existence of a team mental model implies similarity among members' individual mental models. Recognizing this assumption is critical, as otherwise individual members may take for granted that their own mental model is shared by others (cf. Hinds and Weisband, 2003, p. 30).

In virtual teams, a failure to synchronize the mental models of individual members may create process loss and ineffective team processes (Rico *et al.*, 2008). When the individual mental models of virtual team members coincide or overlap, members can anticipate or predict the activities and needs of others; this allows them to adapt to changing demands, and the team's effectiveness is enhanced (Cannon-Bowers, Salas and Converse, 1993; Mathieu *et al.*, 2000; Rico *et al.*, 2008). For example, Lim and Klein (2006) report on a field study in which teams whose members structured and organized their knowledge in a similar fashion found it easy to coordinate their activities. And Cannon-Bowers, Salas and Converse (1993) noted that in order to adapt effectively to changing demands, team members must predict what their other members are going to do and what they need in order to do it.

Indeed, a spate of both theoretical reviews and empirical studies connect team mental models to team effectiveness (Marks, Zaccaro and Mathieu, 2000; Mathieu *et al.*, 2000; Mathieu *et al.*, 2005; Rentsch and Klimoski, 2001; Stout *et al.*, 1999). For example, Marks, Zaccaro and Mathieu (2000) found that the development of team mental models enhanced team communication and team performance. Marks *et al.* (2002) describe experimental studies that show team mental models to be associated with improved backup behaviors of team members and improved performance. And Mathieu *et al.* (2005) showed that team processes partially mediate the relationships between the team mental model and team task performance. These effects appear to be particularly salient when team coordination and effectiveness are critical, which occurs primarily with complex or unpredictable tasks (Cannon-Bowers, Salas and Converse, 1993; Marks, Zaccaro and Mathieu, 2000).

A key question opened up by this analysis, however, is what it means that 'a team has a mental model'. A related question is how team mental models can be evaluated. These critical questions have received scant research attention, and clearly deserve a closer look.

Evaluations of a team mental model can refer to two aspects: (1) the *accuracy or quality* of the model for the goals or tasks the team performs; and (2) the *similarity or overlap* between the models held by different individual members.[1] In one of the few published discussions on this question, Marks, Zaccaro and Mathieu (2000) argued that these factors (accuracy and similarity) interact in their effects on team performance. They further argued that the relationship

---

[1] Different concepts can be used to refer to this idea – we use the concepts of similarity, overlap and convergence of mental models interchangeably.

between similarity and performance is stronger when teams hold mental models that are of relatively poor fit to the task; that is, when the members' individual mental models are all highly accurate, or well fit to the task, small differences between them become less important. This suggests that the two features (accuracy and similarity) are not fully independent, since with certain (e.g. highly accurate) models, similarity does not need to be sought or assessed. Striving for similarity becomes essential when the individual mental models of some team members are more accurate than the mental models of others.

In order for a team to develop a highly accurate (sometimes referred to as high-quality) team mental model, the sensemaking of different individuals must somehow be managed and navigated toward the more accurate model. This process depends on sensemaking of individual team members, but regards the extent of similarity of the emergent mental model that the sensemaking performed by different team members evokes. However, different team members may continue to hold differing individual mental models, even as a team continues to work toward a common model. This is particularly likely in a virtual team where individuals work independently and only periodically have the opportunity to compare their own assumptions (i.e. mental models) to those of others (Hinds and Weisband, 2003).

Thus, individual mental models (relating to the team's tasks, attributes of members, or team processes – i.e. the 'what' and the 'how' of the team's work) may continue to govern the behavior of team members, even if a certain team mental model has emerged. A full assessment of a mental model of a virtual team must therefore begin with an assessment of the types of mental models held by members of the team. It must then continue with an assessment of (i) the accuracy or appropriateness of each of these models, and (ii) the extent of these models' similarity.[2]

Conducting such an assessment is complicated, however, and is another issue that has received insufficient research attention. Mathieu et al. (2005, p. 53), among the few to approach this question, suggested the following steps: (1) Assess the mental models held by a wide range of team members; (2) Cluster the models identified into similar types; (3) Determine the member quality or expertise that relates to the identified model; and (4) Consider the identified quality or expertise as a critical issue for indexing the team mental model.

Using this process in an empirical study, Mathieu et al. (2005) showed that the quality of both task and the team-process models were positively related to subsequent team process and task performance. In this study, team process partially mediated the relationship between the quality of the team mental model and team outcomes. In an earlier study (Mathieu et al., 2000),

---

[2] As noted earlier, teams can have multiple types of models, such as a task model and an interpersonal model. Some elements of the models may be shared by all members and some may be maintained only by some or even one of the members. Likewise, some elements of each model may be accurate and some inaccurate.

the quality of the model fully mediated the relationship. In other words, a convergent and accurate team mental model creates an effective team process which in turn leads to effective teamwork and task performance. Similarly, Lim and Klein (2006) reported on a field study that assessed teams with regard to their teamwork and task-work. Similarity of members' individual mental models of teamwork and task-work predicted team performance.

However, as Lim and Klein (2006) note, except for the few studies described above, far too little research has explored the antecedents of similarity, accuracy or convergence in team mental models. Based on our review of available work, we call for additional examination of the impact of quality (accuracy and similarity) of a team mental model on team performance. We offer the prediction that team mental models characterized by greater accuracy and greater similarity allow members to anticipate how others will act and what support they will require, thus enhancing coordination and trust and reducing conflicts.

A key question this prediction opens up is how and under what conditions teams are likely to develop team mental models that can be characterized by greater accuracy or similarity. We contend next that collective team sensemaking is a critical prerequisite to these important outcomes.

SENSEMAKING

Each member comes to the team with certain conceptions, which are likely to be based on prior experiences and to be somewhat detached from the current project context. As they begin to work on the project, team members interact and learn about the conceptions of others, while also conveying their own. Through such interactions, team members also develop a mental picture of the environment in which they are working and may come to identify various constraints on the project work. Gradually, members develop a more refined understanding of the project, the project team, and the project environment; this acquired learning leads them to revise their individual mental models of the project and the team. Through recurring interactions the mental models held by different team members are likely to converge, leading to the evolution of a team mental model. This model may be more or less accurate for the task at hand, and may be more or less accepted by different team members. The extent of accuracy and the extent of agreement depend on various features of the people involved, but also on the tools and processes that they use as a team.

Sensemaking – a concept introduced by Weick (1979, 1995) – is a critical term for understanding the emergence of individual understandings, or individual mental models, and their interplay with team mental models. Weick's analysis portrays organizational work as a stream of ongoing and unpredictable experiences in which people search for answers to the basic question of 'what's the story?' (Weick, Sutcliff and Obstfeld, 2005, p. 410). The cumulative answers to this question (which Weick labeled 'Interpretation') lead to the development of cognitive mental models of a given work situation (Weick and Daft, 1983). Thus, as Hill and Levenhagen (1995) note, sensemaking is the process of the development of mental models. And as Nosek and McNeese

(1997) explain, sensemaking is what allows decision makers to update their metal models and construct their knowledge of a given situation, which ultimately influences behavior.

The connection between sensemaking and team mental models has received some empirical research attention. For example, sensemaking was suggested to explain the development and communication of a new vision (which can be viewed as a new mental model) of a given business environment. Hill and Levenhagen (1995) specifically suggested that people first hold intuitive (affective-based) models of a given business environment, and then refine this view into formalized individual mental models as they learn more about the business. The refinement and formalization process relies on verbal or physical metaphors, which help individuals to articulate the parameters or elements of a situation (Weick, 1979).

The idea of sensemaking raises the important point that people are active agents in the creation of perceptions and assumptions that become the constraints and opportunities for their own thinking. Such constraints and opportunities are also important for other people with whom an individual works, as members of the team may be influenced by or come to adopt the assumptions held by others. People are not necessarily cognizant of the sensemaking process, since retrospective sensemaking can occur; in retrospective sensemaking, people can know what they are doing (and others may know what they have done) only after it was already done as well (Weick, 1995). For example, certain conceptions and actions may promote or stall an issue, but people may realize that such promotion or stalling occurred only after the fact. Leadership or other forms of guidance are essential influences over sensemaking, because people are likely to be overwhelmed by too much information, and spelling out values or priorities can help clarify the appropriate course of action (Dutton and Jackson, 1987; Weick, 1995).

In virtual teams, the sensemaking process takes place against the backdrop of a unique set of challenges. Information regarding the work context of team members is not easily available to members of a virtual team (Cramton, 2001; Hinds and Weisband, 2003), and members are often in ignorance of others' actions (Gutwin and Greenberg, 2002), which can lead to attribution errors. Cramton, Orvis and Wilson (2007), for example, reported that members of virtual teams are more likely to make internal dispositional attributions, opposed to members of collocated teams that tend to make situational attributions, about the negative behavior of team partners. Cramton, Orvis and Wilson (2007) attributed this to situation invisibility in virtual teams, and the limitations this imposes on information sharing[3]. Such attributions

---

[3] Sharing information about the work context of individual members can help develop mutual understanding (Fussell and Krauss, 1992) and help establish common norms of behavior of different (and geographically distant) team members (Hinds and Bailey, 2003). It may also help reduce conflicts in a virtual team (cf. Hinds and Mortensen, 2005).

in virtual teamwork are a key part of what Weick defined as the interpretation element of sensemaking, and they set the stage for and influence the later stage of sensemaking – enactment.

Available analyses of mental models and sensemaking have focused primarily on the cognitive part of the process. Yet, as Hill and Levenhagen (1995, p. 1071) note, mental cycles are born in the minds of individuals as ineffable concepts with emotive content. Consistent with Weick's (1995) analysis, various episodes in a team effort are likely to evoke new emotions – making them, as Weiss and Cropanzano (1996, p. 93) put it, 'affective events', which in turn are likely to lead to modifications in team members' original mental models.

Another element that can provide a basis for shared understandings and a common pattern of meanings – that is, a team mental model – is the use of common work tools. Such tools can help promote communication and the sharing of information among different team members, helping to define the mental models in a virtual team and to improve their accuracy. We will discuss these tools later in this chapter.

The process of repeated sensemaking and emotion cycles continues to refine and ultimately defines the team mental model and team performance. In the remainder of this chapter, we describe and analyze this process in greater detail. A critical feature of the process that must be recognized up front is its recursiveness: Team mental models influence the sensemaking and the emotions of team members, but at the same time are also influenced by them (Jeffery, Maes and Bratton-Jeffery, 2005). Built into the idea of sensemaking is active and continuous change in the team mental model: A virtual team working on a given task will face and interpret a new situation by calling on the existing mental model or models. The new situation *ignites* sensemaking, leading to *interpretations* that determine team members' behavior, or *enactment* of the new situation.

The results of a given sensemaking episode – the interpretations and behaviors it evokes – provide new information to team members. This new information ignites a new sensemaking process, in which members examine and compare their own assumptions and behaviors to those of others. The new sensemaking process will likely lead to modification of the team mental model, as different members come to see aspects of their mental model as inappropriate, or learn about how others view things. Such learning ignites further sensemaking, and through interpretation and enactment produces further refinement in the team mental model.

Thus, multiple team members are both influenced by and influential over the emergent team mental model. The team mental model is as much a product of the task at hand as it is a product of the interactions among team member. Individual team members working on their specific tasks are engaged in individual-level sensemaking, which leads to personal understandings and personal mental models as eloquently described by Weick and his colleagues (Weick, 1979, 1990, 1995). At the team level, individual mental models coalesce into a team mental model, which influences the way the team works and the team outcomes (Donellon, Gray and Bougon, 1986; Klimoski and Mohammed, 1994).

However, the socially inspired process of sensemaking in a virtual team implicitly presumes a flow of communication and amicable social relations among team members. The diversity of team members, or the distance between members of a virtual team, may hamper such relations. Dahlin, Weingart and Hinds (2005), for example, found that when teams are functionally diverse, integration of information – which they define as the making of logical links between items of information – is more difficult to achieve. Such creation of linkages between individual information bits is paramount to the creation of a team mental model. In a similar vein, when relations are stressed, untrusting or conflict-ridden, the sensemaking process is impeded (cf. Dunn and Schweitzer, 2005), which would influence the emergent team mental model.

EMOTION AND SENSEMAKING

Team members working on a project encounter a bug in the system they have developed, and one member expresses frustration and anger. Other members interpret this to mean that they are being held responsible for the problem, and they get angry as well. The resulting social disconnect among team members makes each one more resistant to accepting suggestions or ideas for change from his or her fellows; in other words, members remain committed to their own initial mental models. This reduces the synchronization of the mental models of different team members and increases the risk of errors or inaccuracies in the product.

The link between sensemaking and emotion has been discussed explicitly in only a handful of studies (Maitlis, Vogus and Lawrence, 2008; Myers, 2007; Rafaeli and Vilnai-Yavetz 2004). Yet, as Maitlis, Vogus and Lawrence (2008) aptly noted, emotion has always been hinted at as the motivation behind sensemaking in all its stages: the ignition, the interpretation and the enactment. Recently, Rhee (2007) has stated that the mechanisms behind the influence of group emotion on performance are still mostly unexamined. In this theoretical chapter, we suggest that sensemaking and group mental models are one of the mechanisms that link between group emotions and performance.

As suggested by our brief illustrative story, the relationship between affect and emotion is reciprocal and dynamic. Specifically, three complementary dynamics can connect emotion to sensemaking:

(1) *Emotion (and in particular arousal[4]) is a cause of sensemaking.* Sensemaking is triggered when a situation involves something out of the ordinary (like the bug in the vignette above) – an event or action that attracts attention through being puzzling, startling or unexpected (Weick, 1990, 1995; Weick, Sutcliff

---

[4] Arousal is commonly presumed to be a key aspect of emotion, meaning that the level of arousal differentiates between different emotions (cf. Russell and Feldman-Barrett, 1999; Russell and Pratt, 1980).

and Obstfeld, 2005). Such events create arousal, which we recognize as curiosity or a need to interpret what has happened (Gioia and Thomas, 1996; Maitlis, Vogus and Lawrence, 2008; Weick, 1995). Being central to emotion (cf. Russell and Feldman-Barrett, 1999; Russell and Pratt, 1980), arousal connects emotion to sensemaking. High-arousal emotions (e.g. fear, anger, or frustration, but also joy and happiness) can be presumed to inspire a search for interpretations, thus evoking the sensemaking cycle described above.

(2) *Emotions serve as information that influences sensemaking.* Emotions can serve as an intrinsic cue about how one should judge a situation (Schwartz and Clore, 1983); emotions thus act as a source of information (Albarracin and Kumkale, 2003). Schwartz and Clore (1983, 2007) explicitly identified the *feeling-as-information* model, which suggests that people interpret the environment in part by reading their own affective states. Emotions influence not only how people interpret the environment but also the type of information processing tactics they employ (Chartrand, van Baaren and Bargh, 2006) and the decisions they make (Forgas, 1998).

In our opening story, the anger and frustration expressed by one member of the team was interpreted by others to be an implicit accusation, and an act of disassociation from responsibility for the problem. In other words, in the sensemaking process, the emotions of others can be considered information regarding those others' goals, inclinations, reactions, and likely future behaviors (Ashkanasy and Ashton-James, 2005; Ashkanasy, Hartel and Zerbe, 2000; Rafaeli and Sutton, 1989; Riggio, 2001), and can also influence the emotions and attributions of other team members (Hareli and Rafaeli, 2008). Sensemaking goes wrong when emotions are misinterpreted; the anger of the person in our vignette could have been directed at himself, or at people outside the team, rather than at the other team members.

The valence[5] of the emotion that a situation evokes – whether positive or negative – will influence how the situation is interpreted (Russell and Pratt, 1980; Russell and Feldman-Barrett 1999; Watson, Clark and Tellegen, 1988), feeding behaviors and attitudes such as trust, cooperation, self-defense or aggression. An event might cause excitement (a positive emotion) or fear (a negative emotion), each leading to a specific set of interpretations and actions (Hareli and Rafaeli, 2008): evoked fear would lead to retreat from the situation, while evoked happiness and excitement would likely prompt greater connection. These behaviors are part of the enactment of the way the situation is interpreted, meaning they are part of the sensemaking process.

In other words, negative feelings such as anger, guilt, or anxiety are likely to be interpreted as a cue that there is some kind of a problem, and therefore to inspire more focused processing (or intensive sensemaking) (Tiedens

---

[5] Valence is the second critical aspect of emotion, distinguishing between positive emotions (e.g. happiness, joy or calmness) and negative emotions (e.g. anger, guilt, anxiety or sadness) (cf. Russell and Feldman-Barrett, 1999; Russell and Pratt, 1980).

and Linton, 2001). However, feelings of threat or risk have been shown to stifle thinking and create rigidity (Staw, Sandeland and Dutton, 1981), making people less likely to revise their mental model of a situation. Note also that negative emotions do not necessarily inspire greater accuracy: sadness has been shown to impair the accuracy of various judgments (Ambady and Gray, 2002).

In contrast, positive feelings (happiness, joy or calmness) are subconsciously viewed as cues that everything is going well and that there is no need to be on guard (Loewenstein et al., 2001). In such cases, the unconscious tendency is not to engage in deep processing but rather to continue with the present course of action, or even expand into new terrain (Fredrickson, 2001, 2003). Thus, individuals experiencing positive emotions are likely to be open to new ideas and to allow expansions of the team mental model.

The extent to which emotions influence sensemaking may depend on the nature of the mental effort people invest in a situation (cf. Forgas, 1990, 1995). Forgas' analysis focused primarily on the individual level, but has been found relevant for the team level. For example, Forgas (1990) reported on a laboratory experiment that showed group affect to influence group judgments. In this study, the valence of the affect of group members (positive or negative) was related to the extent to which groups adopted decisions that were more extreme than individual decisions (Moscovici and Zavalloni, 1969). When team affect was positive, decisions were positively polarized (meaning that they were more positive than when the same judgments were made by individuals alone). Negative affect did not evoke a parallel negative polarization effect, and Forgas (1990) suggested that the asymmetry may be due to the influence of negative affect on communication within the group. Since negative affect decreases communication, it did not influence the group outcome.

Similarly, Forgas and George's analysis (2001) suggests that team emotion influences the way teamwork unfolds, since teamwork is likely to involve situations that are relatively abstract and interpersonally complex. Extending Forgas and George's findings, in teams that handle more complex information and more complex processing, the influences of affect over the team sensemaking process are likely to be stronger.

Part of the information conveyed by emotion relates to the emotions felt by other people in the team. Emotions tend to be 'contagious' (Barsade, 2002; Hatfield, Cacioppo and Rapson, 1994), spreading between different members of the same team (Barsade, 2002) and converging in groups that work together (Totterdell et al., 1998; Totterdell, 2000). Such contagion and convergence in team emotion occur even among members of virtual teams who interact only through electronic and verbal channels (Rafaeli, Cheshin and Israeli, 2007).

For people working together in a team, others' emotions may therefore become events that convey information and trigger sensemaking. Emotions are social entities (Hareli and Rafaeli, 2008), meaning that not only the emotions one feels but also the emotions one observes in others provide cues regarding one's surroundings. The frustration and anger expressed by one member in our example above is a signal to others that there may be a real problem which needs to be addressed, adding an important element to the team mental model. If no one had expressed these emotions, team members might have converged on the assumption that the identified bug was 'not really a problem'.

Most profoundly, emotions ignite interpretations regarding communication. Positive emotions attract and connect people within a virtual team, while negative emotions create exclusion and social distance between team members (cf. Ratner, 2000). For this reason, emotion can be assumed to ignite interpretations about the extent of cohesiveness of the team (Lawler and Yoon, 1996). Barsade (2002) found that displays of positive affect by one member were enough to create more cooperation and greater success within co-located teams, and Rafaeli, Cheshin and Israeli (2007) extended these findings to virtual teams. When team emotions are positive, people may feel a greater sense of affinity to other team members, increasing their willingness to listen to and learn from other people and causing their mental models to converge. Positive team affect, therefore, can be predicted to create what Cannon-Bowers and Salas (1997) and Marks et al. (2002) labeled as the group mental model about teamwork. Thus, individual emotions and team emotions can influence the quality of the emergent group mental model regarding group process and teamwork. However, research on the nature of these linkages is lacking.

(3) *Emotional reactions to certain interpretations of a situation trigger future sensemaking.* Interpretations of events are known to be a source of emotion (Ortony, Clore and Collins, 1988; Smith and Ellsworth, 1985). Sensemaking can therefore evoke certain emotions, which would then influence subsequent sensemaking following the two dynamics discussed above. For example, a person who blames a problem on the supposed negligence of a colleague might feel anger, whereas someone taking the responsibility on himself would feel guilt (Smith and Ellsworth, 1985); each emotional state will lead to a further, different sensemaking process. Sensemaking itself is likely to bring about a sense of composure or relief (Pennebaker, 2000) simply by virtue of resolving a question or bringing understanding to a situation (Weick, 1995). Moreover, the particular type of understanding produced by sensemaking of a situation – the content of the inferences – might itself evoke emotion. To illustrate, organizational layoffs are likely to trigger some anxiety: people may feel not only a sense of relief if they are not laid off, but also sorrow about losing their peers and fear about what the future may hold (Maitlis and Ozcelik, 2004). Each of this series of situations – the initial layoffs, learning that one still has a job but that others have left, and the realization that one may still be laid off in the future – evokes emotions.

In virtual teams, the interpretation of events was shown by Cramton, Orvis and Wilson (2007) to create attributions about teammates, which can evoke emotions toward these teammates. Suppose, for example, a teammate is said to not have completed assigned work; attributing this to laziness would likely lead to anger (Smith and Ellsworth, 1985). But if it was known that this teammate had recently experienced a death in the family, fellow team members might feel sympathy rather than anger.

Virtual teams may also experience series of events as in the example of layoffs above, in which case a series of emotions may unfold (Ashforth and Humphrey, 1995; Weiss and Cropanzano, 1996). Indeed, as noted by Ashforth, Keriner and Mel (2000), routine work is saturated with transitions between events. Each transition creates a general sense of arousal, which, as noted earlier, would ignite interpretations and enactment and inspire modifications of a former mental model. Subsequent events would then continue to refine the content of the mental model (e.g. Do team members think their fellows will do their share of the work? Do they trust the other people in the team?), the accuracy of the mental model (e.g. Will team members actually do their share of the work? Are team members indeed trustworthy?), and the similarity or agreement between different members regarding the mental model (e.g. How many people trust other members of the team?).

Since members of virtual teams often rely on electronic means of communication, they have limited access to information about other team members, and misattributions are likely to occur (Cramton, Orvis and Wilson, 2007). Communication patterns that 'screen out' certain members from team interactions constrain their social information and interpersonal exchanges, which can make the influence of emotional content more or less efficient and accurate (Gibson and Earley, 2007).

In short, here as well a reciprocal and dynamic relationship exists, this time between emotion and sensemaking: emotions evoked by interpretations of a situation guide further interpretations, which in turn guide individual actions, creating a new reality that can ignite new interpretations, in a process that Hareli and Rafaeli (2008) labeled 'emotion cycles'. These cycles are critical to emergent team mental models; they operate behind the scenes and influence the sensemaking process through which team mental models develop. The accuracy of a team mental model will be influenced by the emotions in the team, as will the degree to which the mental model is shared, since certain emotions are more likely to inspire attraction, communication and sharing.

Thus far we have argued that the development of a team mental model depends on the sensemaking of team members, which itself both arises from and triggers the emotions of team members. A question this analysis begs is what can be done to improve the sensemaking process to evoke more positive emotions and more accurate team mental models. In the final leg of our argument, we suggest that the work tools used by a team can facilitate the sensemaking of team members toward the emergence of a more accurate and more convergent team mental model.

TOOLS TO SUPPORT SENSEMAKING AND THE DEVELOPMENT OF TEAM MENTAL MODELS

Members of our virtual team work in three geographical locations. They have developed a routine of weekly virtual update meetings in which each member reports on his or her progress and problems, and they maintain a project wiki in which they can all add or edit entries. They also use shared documents that describe their work plans and progress. These documents are saved on-line which makes them available for periodical retrieval, reading and updating by members of the team. These tools provide members with a clear sense of the goals and progress of the project and of the views and progress of other team members. Members learn about how others view things, and adapt their assumptions and expectations accordingly.

Multiple tools and procedures can support team efforts. Generally, support tools need to be assessed according to the extent to which they allow or facilitate collaboration among multiple team members. Virtual teams may suffer from insufficient shared experiences and less information sharing, most likely leading to less shared understanding (Hinds and Weisband, 2003). We suggest two key categories of tools that we believe can promote more effective construction of a team mental model: communication tools and information-sharing tools.

Communication Tools

Communication is a key to team sensemaking, since team members need a window into other members' thoughts and perceptions in order to adapt their own, individual mental models (Hill and Levenhagen, 1995; Nosek and McNeese, 1997; Urch Druskat and Pescosolido, 2002; Weick, Sutcliff and Obstfeld, 2005). Communication among team members has been argued explicitly to facilitate the development of a team mental model (Jeffery, Maes and Bratton-Jeffery, 2005). Through communication with other team members, people can learn about the thoughts and perceptions of other members of their team, which provides a window into the individual mental model of other members. Without communication, people continue to work within their own, personal mental models, and no similarity or convergence of the individual models will occur.

Communication tools influence the cues and information available about the mental models held by other people. Daft and Lengel (1986) proposed a theory on the *information richness of communication tools,* in which they connect the characteristics of different communication tools to the ambiguity or accuracy of the information they can convey. Media richness, according to Daft and Lengel (1986), is based on the quality of information conveyed by an interaction, which is assessed through four parameters: availability of multiple cues, use of natural language, availability of feedback, and availability of a personal focus.

Following Daft and Lengel (1986), communication tools that are 'rich', such as Web conferencing and video conferencing, allow use of natural language, provide feedback, and allow for personalization. Tools low in richness, such as asynchronized text (e.g. letters or e-mail) fail to provide one or more of these and, according to Daft and Lengel (1986), create greater ambiguity. Thus, media-rich tools improve communication and increase the probability of an accurate understanding between different team members, while media-poor tools increase the likelihood of inaccurate interpretations and flawed mental models. Supporting this analysis, Straus (1996), for example, found that virtual teams that relied on text-based electronic media exchanged about half of the words of teams communicating verbally and face-to-face. The social information that is left out of such messages was argued by Cramton and Orvis (2003) to be critical for the development of a team mental model.

With richer communication tools, less time is needed to resolve disagreements or misunderstandings. Rich communication tools enable a transfer of information that improves awareness of the real-time activities of others. For instance, use of rich communication tools enables collaborative partners to easily view or even create together the same work plans, flow charts, or product sketches. Such shared viewing is known to improve the evolution of shared understanding of the issues under discussion (Damian and Zowghi, 2003; Gutwin and Greenberg, 2002; Larsson, 2003). Similarly, Bell and Kozlowski (2002) propose that as complexity, dynamicity and challenge of tasks increase, teams will adapt richer media.

Since sensemaking and the development of a team mental model necessarily rely on the availability of information to different team members, the richness of the communication media that team members can use, and the frequency with which such tools are used, clearly influences the quality of the emergent team mental model. Rich communication can improve clarity and understanding among team partners, thus improving the similarity or congruence of the team mental model (Cramton, 2001).

Consistent with this analysis, Cramton, Orvis and Wilson (2007) have shown the downside of communication media that are low in richness. People interacting through computer-mediated communication were shown in their studies to maintain a dispositional rather than a situational interpersonal attribution. Dispositional attributions tend to stifle team cohesion and members' willingness to adapt their conceptions to those of others, suggesting that low-richness communication tools are not likely to benefit the team mental model. For example, unlike the vignette described in our opening of this section, in a team relying on communication with low richness, individuals are likely to conclude that team members located at another location are unreliable and uncommitted to a joint project, even if local technological failure do not allow other members to make progress. In addition, with media-poor communications, feedback is limited and delayed (Byron, 2008), leading to increased ambiguity and misunderstandings which can stifle sensemaking and hamper the quality of the team mental model. In this vein, a team's ability to exchange ideas, to plan, and to reach consensus was shown by Kayworth and Leidner (2000) to improve when the information richness of the support tools they used became richer. Finally, work teams that rely primarily upon tools low in communication richness are less likely to use relational communication and thus less likely to perceive each other accurately (Walther, Anderson and Park, 1994) – and therefore less likely to narrow the gaps between their respective mental models. Similarly, the use of leaner communication tools may impede the emergence of an accurate mental model because of the lack of feedback. Byron (2008), for example, suggests that the lack of synchronic feedback when using e-mail is due to less information available to team members, which hampers the accuracy of the interpretations of the situation. This is true, especially when a team's task is complex, rich communication tools are essential to help teams converge on a high-accuracy mental model (DeLuca and Valacich, 2006). In this vein, a team's ability to exchange ideas, to plan, and to reach consensus was shown by Kayworth and Leidner (2000) to improve when the information richness of the support tools they used increased.

However, research on the extent to which (and under what conditions) rich communication tools improve the sensemaking process and the quality of emergent team mental models is very limited. Especially lacking is empirical research. The key question identified by our analysis is what communication tools are likely to make a team mental model more accurate or appropriate for the team task, and which communication tools would induce more sharing or more convergence of the team mental model.

Information-Sharing Tools

A second category of tools that can promote the development of high-quality team mental models comprises technologies that enable the sharing of work plans, progress reports and budget plans without rich communication. This category includes repositories in which shared files are stored and maintained, organizational Wikis that allow sharing of discussions, documents and other textual information, organizational portals, Web-based project management tools, and so on.

Effective teamwork relies on suitable use of information sharing (Cramton and Orvis, 2003). Information-sharing tools ensure that team members are working toward the same plans and goals and have access to updated information on the project (cf. Orlikowski, 2002). They also allow team members to work on the same artifacts (such as source codes or documents). Thus, information-sharing tools can enhance the ability of team members to understand *what* others are working on, as well as *how* or *why* they are working on it. In other words, information-sharing tools help people obtain a closer understanding of the mental model of other team members, namely the way other people view the team effort and context (Mohrman, Klein and

Finegold, 2003), including the team goals (Bolstand and Endsley, 1999) and work processes (Cramton, 2001). These dynamics are particularly critical in virtual teams, where remote teammates have a hard time observing and obtaining important situational information about other members.

For example, information-sharing tools can allow team members to see the work charts of the team, which include an indication of the progress of all the members of the team in the joint project. Such a view of all team members affords a better understanding for members of the rate of progress, constraints and progress of all other members, and of the team as a whole. Such an understanding improves the chances that different team members will develop a similar view on the project. At the same time, a development of a common understanding through information-sharing tools decreases the chances of some major flaws in the individual and team mental model because the perspectives of all team members are integrated.

Thus, information-sharing tools improve a team's ability to develop a high-quality team mental model. Tools that open up information so that it is available to everyone make it more likely that individual sensemaking takes place within a common framework or context (Larsson, 2003). When the sensemaking of individuals is based on the same information base, they are likely to interpret the work structure and processes in more or less the same way (Damian, Lanubile and Mallardo, 2006). And ensuing enactments – behaviors following a certain interpretation – are also likely to be more in sync, because the point of departure of everyone involved is the same. Information-sharing tools thus also increases the accuracy of perceptions, because the information stored reflects the knowledge of all team members (Damian and Zowghi, 2003), and offers an archive of common knowledge that can be reviewed and corrected by all (Myers, 2007). Successful leadership of virtual teams can assist in the sensemaking process by creating explicit structure and routines for the team tasks (Bell and Kozlowski, 2002).

Information sharing has advantages even over rich communication in that the former allows information shared earlier to be easily accessed at any point throughout the project's life. (This is the critical difference between simply holding an electronic discussion over an unresolved issue and storing inputs from multiple exchanges about this issue on an electronic board which allows people to view multiple posts.) In this vein Hinds and Weisband (2003), for example, recommend using online team spaces and sharing information about day-to-day activities to facilitate shared understanding in virtual teams.

Project management tools such as Microsoft Project standardize project work by providing templates and guidelines for action. Such tools help establish a shared perspective on a project and its plans, status, and deliverables by providing a common framework and set of work practices. Hence, the use of project management tools can enhance the development of similar understandings (Engwall, Kling and Werr, 2005), or greater similarity between individual mental models. The use of such tools also improves accuracy of the team mental model because it helps team members understand who is working on what part of which system, where, when, and how, and increases the probability of correcting misaligned individual efforts (Orlikowski, 2002). Such tools also help develop a common language (Engwall, Kling and Werr, 2005) or a standard glossary (Smite, 2006) for a work team, both of which enhance the shared understandings among members of the project team.

The use of team support tools further reduces the probability of coordination faults or uneven distribution of information (Hinds and Mortensen, 2005; Cramton, 2001). Similar to the case that our opening story portrayed, Orlikowski (2002) argued that use of information-sharing tools that enable collaborative planning can improve team coordination and can help team members overcome their respective adaptation difficulties. Such tools also allow easier and quicker resolution of conflicts (cf. Qureshi, Liu and Vogel, 2006).

In short, information-sharing tools enhance coordination and synergy of virtual teams, which can help improve the quality (accuracy and similarity) of the team mental model. Both models regarding the team task – the *what* (goals, constraints, and tools) – and models regarding the team processes – the *how* – are likely to be more accurate and more similar when information-sharing tools are put to good use. However, here as well, the empirical research on which we could rely for our analysis is very limited. We use this platform to call for additional research on whether, when, and how the use of information-sharing tools can lead to more refined and focused sensemaking. Particularly essential is research on the influence of the use of these tools over the quality of the emergent team mental model and ensuing team performance.

SUPPORT TOOLS AND EMOTIONS

One of the team members, Lucy, believes that she has put in effort and achieved results above and beyond her assigned role. Another team member, John, posts a notice on the team forum stating that the Lucy has done a good job but there is a lot more work to be done. Paul posts a notice to the effect that the deadline is approaching and there is a need for intensive effort from all team members. Lucy feels that her efforts have not been sufficiently recognized and that she is not getting the respect she deserves. The other members of the team feel anxious and stressed by the approaching deadline despite the fact that the project is going as planned. Lucy relieves her frustration by withdrawing from the team and paying more attention to her own work. The other members get angry at Lucy, and a general air of alienation takes over the team, causing them to lose their stamina and fall behind schedule. A member who realizes what is happening suggests a two-day retreat in which members can air their concerns.

The effects of team support tools – both communication tools and information-sharing tools – on sensemaking and ensuing mental models may also occur through their effect on emotion. These effects have received the least amount of research attention, but they are another critical leg of our argument, an additional channel of influence over sensemaking and team mental models.

Drawing on a very limited body of literature, we briefly suggest the effects of communication tools and information-sharing tools over emotion separately.

Communication tools and emotion. Expressing and understanding emotions has been argued to be heavily reliant on non-verbal cues (such as facial expressions, direct gaze, tone of voice, etc.) (cf. Critchley *et al.*, 2005; Ekman, Friesen and Ancoli, 1980; Kock, 2005; Mehrabian, 1972). Communication tools vary in the degree to which they enable non-verbal cues; yet even where these are limited, emotions are still argued to have an effect (cf. Byron and Baldridge, 2005). Research suggests that users of text-based support tools communicate emotions to others, intentionally or not (Thompsen and Foulger, 1996; Walther and D'Addario, 2001). And, emotion plays a role in how people interpret various messages, and the judgments they make (Forgas, 1995).

In regard to sensemaking, it has been found that in the absence of clear cues about the emotions of others, individuals are likely to fill in seeming gaps with information that they draw from a cognitive schema (Brewer and Treyens, 1981; Meindl, Stubbart and Porac, 1996). Studies have shown that individuals can and do express emotions in text-based support tools (e-mail and instant messenger), though attempts to convey emotions are often misinterpreted (Byron, 2008). Findings regarding the interpretations of emotions in text-based communication suggest a severe risk of miscommunication. Byron and Baldridge (2005), for example, found that the interpretation of emotions could be highly inaccurate, with the same cues at times perceived as representing completely different, and potentially contradictory emotions (e.g. the length of a message was perceived as indicating both happiness and anger).

Yet there is some indication that verbal exchanges can offer valuable and relatively accurate emotion information. Hancock, Landrigan and Sliver (2007) reported that individuals had no difficulty expressing negative and positive affect in a text-based medium and that the affect was accurately perceived by recipients. Hancock, Landrigan and Sliver (2007) also showed that how messages were delivered (or how an emotion was displayed) differed significantly as far as amount of text, the use of affective terms, punctuation and even the pauses between responses. Additional confirmation that people can infer emotion from text is afforded by the high degree of agreement typically observed when raters are asked to identify the affect in texts (Bestgen, 1994; Mossholder *et al.*, 1995).

However, the fact that people can identify affect in text does not mean that the affect which textual communications create in team members is a valid representation of the sender's intent. E-mail is an example of a communication tool that is very commonly used and that relies on text-based communication with very limited non-verbal cues. Byron (2008) provided a theoretical examination of the emotional influences of e-mail, and noted two important biases in e-mail reading, which she labeled *neutrality* and *negativity*. In the *neutrality effect*, Byron refers a *decrease* in perceptions of *positive* emotions in texts; in the *negativity effect*, Byron refers to an *increase* in the perceived *intensity* of negative emotions in texts. Offering some empirical support for the negativity effect,

Walther and D'Addario (2001) found that negative cues tend to override other cues in computer-mediated communication.

A key problem with most forms of communication open to virtual teams is the lack of traditional non-verbal cues. One category of cues that is available and can be used to express – or at least attempt to express – emotion is para-verbal cues. In spoken language, para-verbal refers to tone of voice and intonation (e.g. speaking in a loud voice conveys more anger). In written text, para-verbal cues may include the use of punctuation, use of capital letters, and emoticons. Initial research indicates that the use of these cues is inconsistent in text-based communication (Rezabek and Cochenour, 1998; Witmer and Katzman, 1997), since norms regarding the use of para-verbal cues in writing have not yet developed. It appears, therefore, that such cues cannot be reliably used by team members to interpret the emotions of their teammates, or to judge the appropriateness of their own emotional reactions.

In short, research findings are only beginning to accumulate and thus far offer insufficient understanding of the relationship between communication tools and emotion. With more text-based communication, some biases seem to exist, but not a lot more can be said. Going back to the relationship between emotion and sensemaking, there does appear to be another channel whereby communication tools influence sensemaking: Clearly, some dynamics connect the type of communication channels and tools used to the emotions that team members feel. But findings are too preliminary and limited, and another call for additional research is in place.

Information-sharing tools and emotion. When members of a virtual team are limited to computer-mediated communication, they are deprived not only of non-verbal emotional cues, but also of cues about the social context or social status of other members of the team, and the lack of these cues can have a substantial influence over social interactions among team members (Owens, Neale and Sutton, 2000; Sproull and Kiesler, 1986). The effects of status differences that typically guide and govern social interactions can be erased, for example, if people do not have any information about social status. People may also draw various conclusions about other members, forming various attributions. However, these attributions may suffer from biases: A lack of context and interaction information was argued by Cramton (2001) and Kankanhalli, Tan and Wei (2007) to increase the extent to which people make personal attributions in interpretations of conflict situations. With more personal, rather than situational attributions, the nature of emotions elicited is likely to be different, as are ensuing emotion-sensemaking and sensemaking-mental model cycles.

For example, if a problem arises in a virtual team, people are likely to draw inferences and make attributions for the reason or cause of the problem. While the real reason may be situational or contextual reasons (e.g. technology failure, staff shortage), a lack of rich-media communication is likely to lead people to make personal attributions (e.g. poor motivation or poor ability of the team members in whose domain the problems occurred). Following these personal attributions, emotions of anger are more likely to surface, rather than empathy or solidarity that an understanding of the situational causes may have evoked.

Members of virtual teams are likely to hold uneven information about various issues, in addition to the cultural and organizational differences that set them apart. These multiple differences are likely to lead to different interpretations of the same project issues (cf. Cramton, 2001; Hinds and Weisband, 2003). Such conflicting interpretations may escalate to interpersonal conflicts that involve negative emotions. Lacking awareness of the activities and constraints of others reduces the sharing of common contexts and can lead to different interpretations of events related to task execution (Gutwin and Greenberg 2002; Hinds and Mortensen, 2005). This may cause misattribution of faults to a person instead of a situation, and again may result in negative interpersonal emotions. According to Myers (2007), the fact that in virtual communication interactions are available for review and replication creates a situation in which every interaction gets a lot of attention, and some might come to seem more important than they actually are. This can lead to escalation of conflicts that in face-to-face communication might have been resolved faster and more easily.

At the same time, the use of information-sharing tools can reduce the probability that negative emotions will arise. This is when information-sharing tools are used in a way that evens out coordination faults or uneven distribution of information (Cramton, 2001; Hinds and Mortensen, 2005). Information-sharing tools that ensure complete visibility of information to all team members are a means to increasing collaboration and trust among team members. By increasing collaboration and trust, a more positive emotional atmosphere is created in the team. By keeping people well informed about the progress, constraints and plans of their teammates are viewed through a context and situational lens, rather than a personal lens. By encouraging the adoption of a project or team-level view, information-sharing tools help ensure that problems are more likely to be constructively solved by creating individual sensemaking processes that evoke a more accurate individual mental model and inspire higher similarity in the team mental model.

SUMMARY

A summary of our analysis is depicted in Figure 5.1.

At the core of our argument is the relationship between team performance and the development of a team mental model of the team-task and team-processes. The team mental model, as depicted in Figure 5.1, is composed of the mental models of individual team members, and is developed in a recursive cycle in which individual sensemaking of team situations involve ignition of a need to make sense of a situation, interpretation of the situation, and enactment of an understanding (a new mental model) of the team and the situation.

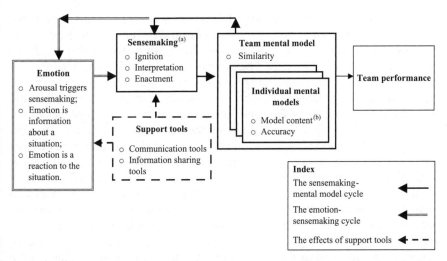

Figure 5.1 Team mental models in virtual teams: the dynamics of sensemaking, emotion and support tools. (a) Sensemaking is an individual-level cognitive process that produces individual-level mental models. The bold arrows in the figure depict the active and continuous recursive influence between the individual and team mental models created by the dynamic sensemaking process: Members of a virtual team working on a given task face and interpret new situations by calling on existing mental models. Each new situation *ignites* a sensemaking process, which leads to *interpretations* that determine members' behavior or *enactment* of the new situation. The result of each sensemaking effort creates a new context for all team members, that likely leads to some modification of the individual and team mental model. People may learn about inappropriate aspects of the model, or about how others view things, and such learning ignites further sensemaking. Through interpretation and enactment, people further refine their individual mental model, which influences the emergent team mental model. This cyclical process is a critical element of teamwork, and a critical influence over team performance. (b) Models with different content may inhabit a team; models can refer to the 'what' the team does and/or models that refer to 'how' the teamwork is done. Assessments of the team mental model must identify the different types of models and then assess the degree to which each is appropriate as well as the degree to which it is shared by different members of the team.

Individual and team mental models refer to a certain set of assumptions about the content of the team task, and about teamwork processes. They also need to be assessed according to the accuracy of these assumptions given the way the team task is construed by various stakeholders. In addition, since a team mental model necessarily refers to some hybrid of the mental models of individual members, it (the team mental model) needs to be assessed according to the degree of similarity between the mental models of different individual team members. So as Figure 5.1 depicts, both individual and team mental models are to be assessed according to the content they embed and the accuracy of this content. A unique feature of the team mental model is the extent of similarity in it, meaning the extent to which the mental models of different individual members and the emergent hybrid of these individual models are similar to each other. With a team mental model that holds greater similarity, team processes can be expected to flow more smoothly and to suffer from less conflict.

Thus, sensemaking is an individual-level cognitive process that produces individual-level mental models. The cycle of bold arrows in Figure 5.1 depicts the recursive and continuous change of individual and team mental model created by the dynamic sensemaking process: Members of a virtual team working on a given task constantly face and interpret situations – occurrences in the flow of teamwork – by calling on existing mental models. Each new situation ignites the sensemaking process, leading to interpretations that determine team members' behavior or enactment of the new situation. One sensemaking effort – ignition, interpretation and enactment – provides a new mental frame for all team members, that likely leads to some modification of the individual and team mental models. People may learn about inappropriate aspects of their previous model, or about how others view things. Such learning ignites further sensemaking, and through continuous ignition, interpretation and enactment, people continue to refine their individual mental model, which influences the emergent team mental model. The recursive sensemaking process is a critical foundation of teamwork, and a critical influence over team performance.

As Figure 5.1 further depicts, we posit an additional cycle of influence over team sensemaking – an emotion cycle, depicted in a double-arrow in Figure 5.1. This cycle refers to various emotional influences over sensemaking. As the figure summarizes, the influences can be of three types. First, high-arousal emotions (e.g. anger, irritation, delight, or excitement) can create a trigger for sensemaking. Second, individually felt emotions can serve as cues or information about the situation at hand. A feeling of anger, for example, may create a sense that someone else has failed, which may ignite a sensemaking cycle in which identification of blame or responsibility is sought, and accordingly, interpretations and enactment are taken. Thirdly, certain interpretations may evoke emotions that themselves color the nature of a sensemaking cycle. Understanding that someone else has failed, for example, may evoke irritation, which can create impatience and abrupt rather than detailed processing of a situation.

A third body of influence over the sensemaking process – depicted in the broken arrow in Figure 5.1 – regards the tools used to support the work of a virtual team. In particular, our analysis highlighted the importance of rich communication tools and information-sharing tools. Effective support tools can promote effective team effort by facilitating individual sensemaking that takes into consideration the perspectives of other people in a virtual team, which increases the extent of accuracy of the emergent team mental model. With the use of information rich and information-sharing support tools, interactions among team members help remove inaccuracies in each member's mental models, and help create a more accurate and more convergent (i.e. with high similarity) team mental model, which is a critical antecedent to effective team performance.

REFERENCES

Albarracin, D. & Kumkale, T. (2003). Affect as information in persuasion: a model of affect identification and discounting. *Journal of Personality and Social Psychology*, **84** (3), 453–69.

Ambady, N. & Gray, H. (2002). On being sad and mistaken: mood effects on the accuracy of thin-slice judgements. *Journal of Personality and Social Psychology*, **83** (4), 947–61.

Ashforth, B. E. & Humphrey, R. H. (1995). Emotions in the work place: a reappraisal. *Human Relations*, **48**, 97–125.

Ashforth, B. E., Kreiner, G. E. & Mel, F. (2000). All in a day's work: boundaries and micro role transitions. *Academy of Management Review*, **25** (3), 472–91.

Ashkanasy, N. M. & Ashton-James, C. E. (2005). Emotion in organizations: a neglected topic in I/O Psychology, but with a bright future. In G. P. Hodgkinson & J. K. Ford (Eds), *International Review of Industrial and Occupational Psychology*, Vol. 20 (pp. 221–68). Chichester: John Wiley & Sons, Ltd.

Ashkanasy, N. M., Hartel, C. E. & Zerbe, W. J. (2000). Emotions in the workplace: research, theory, and practice. In N. M. Ashkanasy, C. E. Hartel & W. J. Zerbe (Eds), *Emotions in the Workplace: Developments in the Study of the Managed Heart* (pp. 1–18). Westport, CT: Quorum Books.

Barsade, S. G. (2002). The ripple effect: emotional contagion and its influence on group behavior. *Administrative Science Quarterly, December*, **47**, 644–75.

Bell, B. S. & Kozlowski, S. W. J. (2002). A typology of virtual teams – implications for effective leadership. *Group and Organization Management*, **27** (1), 14–49.

Bestgen, Y. (1994). Can emotional valence in stories be determined by words? *Cognition and Emotion*, **7**, 21–36.

Bolstand, C. A. & Endsley, M. R. (1999). Shared mental models and shared displays: an empirical evaluation of team performance. *Proceedings of the 43rd Meeting of the Human Factors and Ergonomics Society, 1999*.

Bowers, C. A., Braun, C. C. & Morgan, B. B., Jr (1997). Team workload: its meaning and measurement. In M. T. Brannick, E. Salas & C. Prince (Eds), *Team Performance and Measurement: Theory, Methods, and Applications* (pp. 85–108). Mahwah, NJ: Erlbaum.

Brewer, W. F. & Treyens, J. C. (1981). Role of schemata in memory for places. *Cognitive Psychology*, **13**, 207–30.

Byron, K. (2008). Carrying too heavy a load? The communication and miscommunication of emotion by e-mail. *Academy of Management Review*, **33** (2), 309–27.

Byron, K. & Baldridge, D. C. (2005). Toward a model of nonverbal cues and emotion in email. *Academy of Management Proceedings*, B1–B6. *Academy of Management Best Conference Paper*.

Cannon-Bowers, J. A. & Salas, E. (1997). Teamwork competencies: the intersection of team member knowledge, skills, and attitudes. In H. F. O'Neil (Ed.), *Workforce Readiness: Competencies and Assessment* (pp. 151–74). Hillsdale, NJ: Lawrence Erlbaum and Associates.

Cannon-Bowers, J. A., Salas, E. & Converse, S. A. (1993). Shared mental models in expert team decision making. In N. J. Castellan, Jr (Ed.), *Current Issues in Individual and Group Decision Making* (pp. 221–46). Hillsdale, NJ: Erlbaum.

Chartrand, T. L., van Baaren, R. B. & Bargh, J. A. (2006). Linking automatic evaluation to mood and information processing style: consequences for experienced affect, impression formation, and stereotyping. *Journal of Experimental Psychology-General*, **135** (1), 70–77.

Cramton, C. D. (2001). The mutual knowledge problem and its consequences for dispersed collaboration. *Organization Science*, 12 (3), 346–71.

Cramton, C. D. (2002). Finding common ground in dispersed collaboration. *Organizational Dynamics*, 30 (4), 356–67.

Cramton, C. D. & Orvis, K. L. (2003). Overcoming barriers to information sharing in virtual teams. In C. B. Gibson & S. G. Cohen (Eds), *Virtual Teams that Work, Creating the Conditions for Virtual Team Effectiveness* (pp. 214–29). San Fransisco: Jossey-Bass.

Cramton, C. D., Orvis, K. L. & Wilson, J. M. (2007). Situation invisibility and attribution in distributed collaborations. *Journal of Management*, 33 (4), 525–46.

Cronin, M. A. & Weingart, L. R. (2007). Representational gaps, information processing, and conflict in functionally diverse teams. *Academy of Management Review*, 32 (3), 761–73.

Critchley, H. D., Rotshtein, P., Nagai, Y. *et al.* (2005). Activity in the human brain predicting differential heart rate responses to emotional facial expressions. *Neuroimage*, 24 (3), 751–62.

Daft, R. L. & Lengel, R. H. (1986). Organizational information requirements, media richness and structural design. *Management Science*, 32, 554–71.

Dahlin, K. B., Weingart, L. R. & Hinds, P. J. (2005). Team diversity and information use. *Academy of Management Journal*, 48 (6), 1107–23.

Damian, D., Lanubile, F. & Mallardo, T. (2006, May 20–28). *The Role of Asynchronous Discussions in Increasing the Effectiveness of Remote Synchronous Requirements Negotiations. Paper presented at the ICSE'06, Shanghai, China.*

Damian, D. E. & Zowghi, D. (2003). Requirements engineering challenges in multi-site software development organizations. *Requirements Engineering Journal*, 8, 149–60.

DeLuca, D. & Valacich, J. S. (2006). Virtual teams in and out of synchronicity. *Information Technology and People*, 19 (4), 323–44.

Donellon, A., Gray, B. & Bougon, M. (1986). Communication, meaning and organized actions. *Administrative Sciences Quarterly*, 31, 43–55.

Dunn, J. R. & Schweitzer, M. E. (2005). Feeling and believing: the influence of emotion on trust. *Journal of Personality and Social Psychology*, 88, 736–48.

Dutton, J. E. & Jackson, S. E. (1987). Categorizing strategic issues: links to organizational action. *Academy of Management Review*, 12 (1), 75–90.

Ekman, P., Friesen, W. V. & Ancoli, S. (1980). Facial signs of emotional experience. *Journal of Personality and Social Psychology*, 39, 1125–34.

Engwall, M., Kling, R. & Werr, A. (2005). Models in action: how management models are interpreted in new product development. *R&D Management*, 35 (4), 427–39.

Feldman, M. S. & Rafaeli, A. (2002). Organizational routines as sources of connections and understandings. *Journal of Management Studies*, 39 (3), 309–31.

Forgas, J. P. (1990). Affective influences on individual and group judgements. *European Journal of Social Psychology*, 20, 441–53.

Forgas, J. P. (1995). Mood and judgment: the affect infusion model (AIM). *Psychological Bulletin*, 117 (1), 39–66.

Forgas, J. P. (1998). On feeling good and getting your way: mood effects on negotiator cognition and bargaining strategies. *Journal of Personality and Social Psychology*, 74 (3), 565–77.

Forgas, J. P. & George, M. J. (2001). Affective influences on judgments and behavior in organizations: an information processing perspective. *Organizational Behavior and Human Decision Processes*, 86 (1), 3–34.

Fredrickson, B. L. (2001). The role of positive emotions in positive psychology. *American Psychologist*, 56 (3), 218–26.

Fredrickson, B. L. (2003). The value of positive emotion. *American Scientist*, 91 (4), 330.

Fussell, S. R. & Krauss, R. M. (1992). Coordination of knowledge in communication: effects of speakers' assumptions about what others know. *Journal of Personality and Social Psychology*, **62**, 378–91.

Gibson, C. B. & Cohen, S. G. (2003). *Virtual Teams That Work, Creating the Conditions for Virtual Team Effectiveness*. San Francisco: Jossey-Bass.

Gibson, C. B. & Earley, P. C. (2007). Collective cognition in action: accumulation, interaction, examination, and accommodation in the development and operation of group efficacy beliefs in the workplace. *Academy of Management Review*, **32** (2), 438–58.

Gibson, C. B. & Gibbs, J. L. (2006). Unpacking the concept of virtuality: the effects of geographic dispersion, electronic dependence, dynamic structure, and national diversity on team innovation. *Administrative Science Quarterly*, **51**, 451–95.

Gioia, D. A. & Thomas, J. B. (1996). Identity, image and issue interpretation: sensemaking during strategic change in academia. *Administrative Science Quarterly*, **41**, 370–403.

Gratton, L., Voigt A. & Erickson, T. (2007). Bridging faultlines in diverse teams. *Mit Sloan Management Review*, **48** (4): 22–29.

Griffith, T. L., Mannix, E. A. & Neale, M. A. (2003). Conflict and virtual teams. In S. G. Cohen & C. B. Gibson (Eds), *Virtual Teams that Work, Creating the Conditions for Virtual Team Effectiveness* (pp. 335–52). San Fransisco: Jossey-Bass.

Gutwin, C. & Greenberg, S. (2002). A descriptive framework of workspace awareness for real-time groupware. *Computer Supported Cooperative Work*, **11**, 411–46.

Hancock, J. T., Landrigan, C. & Silver, C. (2007). Expressing emotion in text-based communication. *Proceedings of CHI 2007, New York*, ACM Press.

Hareli, S. & Rafaeli, A. (2008). Emotion cycles: on the social influence of emotion in organizations. *Research in Organizational Behavior*, **28**, 35–59.

Hatfield, E., Cacioppo, J. & Rapson, R. L. (1994). *Emotional Contagion*. New York: Cambridge University Press.

Hill, C. R. & Levenhagen, M. (1995). Metaphors and mental models: sensemaking and sensegiving in innovative and entrepreneurial activities. *Journal of Management*, **21** (6), 1057–74.

Hinds, P. J. & Bailey, D. E. (2003). Out of sight, out of sync: understanding conflict in distributed teams. *Organization Science*, **14** (6), 615–32.

Hinds, P. J. & Mortensen, M. (2005). Understanding conflict in geographically distributed teams: the moderating effects of shared identity, shared context, and spontaneous communication. *Organization Science*, **16** (3), 290–307.

Hinds, P. J. & Weisband, S. P. (2003). Knowledge sharing and shared understanding in virtual teams. In C. B. Gibson & S. G. Cohen (Eds), *Virtual Teams that Work, Creating the Conditions for Virtual Team Effectiveness* (pp. 21–36). San Fransisco: Jossey-Bass.

Jeffery, A. B., Maes, J. D. & Bratton-Jeffery, M. F. (2005). Improving team decision-making performance with collaborative modeling. *Team Performance Management*, **11**, 40–50.

Kankanhalli, A., Tan, B. C. Y. & Wei, K. K. (2007). Conflict and performance in global virtual teams. *Journal of Management Information Systems*, **23** (3), 237–74.

Kayworth, T. & Leidner, D. (2000). The global virtual manager: a prescription for success. *European Management Journal*, **18** (2), 183–94.

Klimoski, R. & Mohammed, S. (1994). Team mental model – construct or metaphor. *Journal of Management*, **20** (2), 403–37.

Kock, N. (2005). Media richness or media naturalness? The evolution of our biological communication apparatus and its influence on our behavior toward e-communication tools. *IEEE Transactions on Professional Communication*, **48**, 117–30.

Kraiger, K. & Wenzel, L. H. (1997). A framework for understanding and measuring shared mental models of team performance and team effectiveness. In M. T. Brannick, E. Salas & C. Prince (Eds), *Team Performance Assessment and Measurement: Theory Methods and Applications* (pp. 63–84). Hillsdale, NJ: Lawrence Erlbaum and Associates.

Larsson, A. (2003). *Making Sense of Collaboration: The Challenge of Thinking Together in Global Design Teams*. Paper Presented at the GROUP 2003, Sanibel Island, FL, USA.

Lawler, E. J. & Yoon, J. (1996). Commitment in exchange relations: test of a theory of relational cohesion. *American Sociological Review*, 61, 89–108.

Lim, B. C. & Klein, K. J. (2006). Team mental models and team performance: a field study of the effects of team mental model similarity and accuracy. *Journal of Organizational Behavior*, 27 (4), 403–18.

Loewenstein, G. F., Weber, E. U., Hsee, C. K. & Welch N. (2001). Risk as a feeling. *Psychological Bulletin*, 127 (2), 267–86.

Maitlis, S. & Ozcelik, H. (2004). Toxic decision processes: a study of emotion in organizational decision making. *Organization Science*, 15 (4), 375–93.

Maitlis, S., Vogus, T. & Lawrence, T. (2008). Emotion and sensemaking in organizations. Western Academy of Management Annual Meeting, Oakland, CA.

Marks, M. A., Sabella, M. J., Burke, C. S. & Zaccaro, S. J. (2002). The impact of cross-training on team effectiveness. *Journal of Applied Psychology*, 87 (1), 3–13.

Marks, M. A., Zaccaro, S. J. & Mathieu, J. E. (2000). Performance implications of leader briefings and team-interaction training for team adaptation to novel environments. *Journal of Applied Psychology*, 85, 971–86.

Mathieu, J. E., Heffner, T. S., Goodwin, G. F. et al. (2005). Scaling the quality of teammates mental models: equifinality and normative comparisons. *Journal of Organizational Behavior*, 26, 37–56.

Mathieu, J. E., Heffner, T. S., Goodwin, G. F. et al. (2000). The influence of shared mental models on team process and performance. *Journal of Applied Psychology*, 85, 273–83.

Mehrabian, A. (1972). *Nonverbal Communication*. Chicago: Aldine-Atherton.

Meindl, J. R., Stubbart, C. & Porac, J. F. (1996). *Cognition Within and Between Organizations*. London: Sage.

Mohammed, S. & Dumville, B. C. (2001). Team mental models in a team knowledge framework: expanding theory and measurement across disciplinary boundaries. *Journal of Organizational Behavior Special Issue: Shared Cognition*, 22 (2), 89–106.

Mohrman, S. A., Klein, J. A. & Finegold, D. (2003). Managing the global new product development network: a sense-making perspective. In S. G. Cohen & C. B. Gibson (Eds), *Virtual Teams that Work, Creating the Conditions for Virtual Team Effectiveness* (pp. 37–58). San Fransisco: Jossey-Bass.

Moscovici, S. & Zavalloni, M. (1969). The group as a polarizer of attitudes. *Journal of Personality and Social Psychology*, 12, 125–35.

Mossholder, K. W., Settoon, R. P., Harris, S. G. & Armenakis, A. A. (1995). Measuring emotion in open-ended survey responses: an application of textual data analysis. *Journal of Management*, 21, 335–55.

Myers, P. (2007). Sexed up intelligence or irresponsible reporting? The interplay of virtual communication and emotion in dispute sensemaking. *Human Relations*, 60 (4), 609–36.

Nosek, T. J. & McNeese, M. D. (1997). Augmenting group sense making in ill-defined, emerging situations: experiences, lessons learned and issues for future development. *Information Technology and People*, 10 (3), 241–52.

Orlikowski, W. J. (2002). Knowing in practice: enacting a collective capability in distributed organizing. *Organization Science*, **13** (3), 249–73.

Ortony, A., Clore, G. L. & Collins, A. (1988). *The Cognitive Structure of Emotions*. New York: Cambridge University Press.

Owens, D. A., Neale, M. A. & Sutton, R. I. (2000). Technologies of status management: status dynamics in email communications. In M. A. Neale, E. A. Mannix & T. L. Griffith (Eds), *Research on Groups and Teams, Technology*, Vol. 3 (pp. 205–230). Greenwich, CT: JAI Press.

Park, O. & Gittleman, S. S. (1995). Dynamic characteristics of mental models and dynamic visual displays. *Instructional Science*, **23**, 303–20.

Pennebaker, J. W. (2000). Telling stories: the health benefits of narrative. *Literature and Medicine*, **19**, 3–18.

Qureshi, S., Liu, M. & Vogel, D. (2006). The effects of electronic collaboration in distributed project management. *Group Decision and Negotiation*, **15**, 55–75.

Rafaeli, A., Cheshin, A. & Israeli, R. (2007). Anger contagion and team performance. Paper Presented at the Annual Meeting of the Academy of Management, Philadelphia.

Rafaeli, A. & Sutton, R. I. (1989). The expression of emotion in organizational life. In L. L. Cummings & B. M. Staw (Eds), *Research in Organizational Behavior*, Vol. 11 (pp. 1–42). Greenwich, CT: JAI Press.

Rafaeli, A. & Vilnai-Yavetz, I. (2004). Emotion as a connection of physical artifacts and organizations. *Organization Science*, **15** (6), 671–86.

Ratner, C. (2000). A cultural–psychological analysis of emotions. *Culture and Psychology*, **6**, 5–39.

Rentsch, J. R. & Klimoski, R. J. (2001). Why do great minds think alike? Antecedents of team member schema agreement. *Journal of Organizational Behavior*, **22**, 107–20.

Rezabek, L. L. & Cochenour, J. J. (1998). Visual cues in computer-mediated communication: supplementing text with emoticons. *Journal of Visual Literacy*, **18**, 210–15.

Rhee, S. Y. (2007). Shared emotions and group outcomes: the role of group member interactions. In E. A. Mannix, M. A. Neal & C. P. Anderson (Eds), *Research on Managing Groups and Teams, Affect and Groups*, Vol. 10 (pp. 65–95). Oxford: Elsevier Science.

Rico, R., Sanchez-Manzanares, M., Gil, F. & Gibson, C. (2008). Team implicit coordination processes: a team knowledge-based approach. *Academy of Management Review*, **33** (1), 163–84.

Riggio, R. E. (2001). Interpersonal sensitivity research and organizational psychology: theoretical and methodological applications. In J. A. Hall & F. J. Bernierri (Eds), *Interpersonal Sensitivity: Theory and Measurement* (pp. 305–18). Mahwah, NJ: Erlbaum.

Rouse, W. B. & Morris, N. M. (1986). On looking into the black-box – prospects and limits in the search for mental models. *Psychological Bulletin*, **100** (3), 349–63.

Russell, J. A. & Feldman-Barrett, L. (1999). Core affect, prototypical emotional episodes, and other things called emotions: dissecting the elephant. *Journal of Personality and Social Psychology*, **76** (5), 805–19.

Russell, J. A. & Pratt, G. (1980). A description of the affective quality attributed to environments. *Journal of Personality and Social Psychology*, **38** (2), 311–22.

Salas, E., Cannon-Bowers, J. A. & Blickensderfer, E. L. (1993). Team performance and training research: emerging principles. *Journal of the Washington Academy of Sciences*, **83**, 81–106.

Schwarz, N. & Clore, G. L. (1983). Mood, misattribution, and judgments of wellbeing: informative and directive functions of affective states. *Journal of Personality and Social Psychology*, **45**, 513–23.

Schwarz, N. & Clore, G. L. (2007). Feelings and phenomenal experiences. In E. T. Higgins & A. Kruglanski (Eds), *Social Psychology: Handbook of Basic Principles*, 2nd edn (pp. 385–407). New York: Guilford Press.

Smite, D. (2006). Requirements management in distributed projects. *Journal of Universal Knowledge Management*, 1 (2), 69–76.

Smith, C. & Ellsworth, P. (1985). Patterns of cognitive appraisal in emotion. *Journal of Personality and Social Psychology*, 48, 813–38.

Sproull, L. & Kiesler, S. (1986). Reducing social context cues: electronic mail in organizational communication. *Management Science*, 32, 1492–512.

Staw, B. M., Sandelands, L. E. & Dutton, J. E. (1981). Threat rigidity effects in organizational behavior: a multilevel analysis. *Administrative Science Quarterly*, 26, 501–24.

Stout, R. J., Cannon-Bowers, J. A. & Salas, E. (1996). The role of shared mental models in developing team situational awareness: implications for training. *Training Research Journal*, 2, 85–116.

Stout, R. J., Cannon-Bowers, J. A., Salas, E. & Milanovich, D. M. (1999). Planning, shared mental models, and coordinated performance: an empirical link is established. *Human Factors*, 41, 61–71.

Straus, S. G. (1996). Getting a clue: the effects of communication media and information distribution on participation and performance in computer mediated and face-to-face groups. *Small Group Research*, 27, 115–42.

Thompsen, P. A. & Foulger, D. (1996). Effects of pictographs and quoting on flaming in electronic mail. *Computers in Human Behavior*, 12, 225–43.

Tiedens, L. Z. & Linton, S. (2001). Judgment under emotional certainty and uncertainty: the effects of specific emotions on information processing. *Journal of Personality and Social Psychology*, 81 (6), 973–88.

Totterdell, P. (2000). Catching moods and hitting runs: mood linkage and subjective performance in professional sport teams. *Journal of Applied Psychology*, 85 (6), 848–59.

Totterdell, P., Kellett, S., Teuchmann, K. & Briner, R. B. (1998). Evidence of mood linkage in work groups. *Journal of Personality and Social Psychology*, 74 (6), 1504–15.

Urch Druskat, V. & Pescosolido, A. T. (2002). The content of effective teamwork mental models in self-managing teams: ownership, learning and heedful interrelating. *Human Relations*, 55, 283–314.

Walther, J. B., Anderson, J. F. & Park, D. (1994). Interpersonal effects in computer-mediated interaction: a metaanalysis of social and anti-social communication. *Communication Research*, 21, 460–87.

Walther, J. B. & D'Addario, K. P. (2001). The impact of emoticons on message interpretations in computer-mediated communication. *Social Science Computer Review*, 19, 324–47.

Watson, D., Clark, L. A. & Tellegen, A. (1988). Development and validation of brief measures of positive and negative affect: the PANAS scales. *Journal of Personality and Social Psychology*, 54 (6), 1063–70.

Weick, K. E. (1979). *The Social Psychology of Organizing*, 2nd edn, New York: Random House.

Weick, K. E. (1990). The vulnerable system: an analysis of the Tenerife air disaster. *Journal of Management*, 16, 571–93.

Weick, K. E. (1995). *Sensemaking in Organizations*. Thousand Oaks, CA: Sage.

Weick, K. E. & Daft, R. L. (1983). The effectiveness of interpretation systems. In K. S. Cameron & D. A. Whetten (Eds), *Organizational Effectiveness: A Comparison of Multiple Models* (pp. 71–93). New York: Academic Press.

Weick, K. E. & Roberts, K. H. (1993). Collective mind in organizations – heedful interrelating on flight decks. *Administrative Science Quarterly*, **38** (3), 357–81.

Weick, K. E., Sutcliff, K. M. & Obstfeld, D. (2005). Organizing and the process of sensemaking. *Organization Science*, **16** (4), 409–21.

Weiss, H. M. & Cropanzano, R. (1996). Affective events theory: a theoretical discussion of the structure, causes and consequences of affective experiences at work. In R. I. Sutton & B. M. Staw (Eds), *Research in Organizational Behavior* (pp. 93–133). Greenwich, CT: JAI Press.

Witmer, D. & Katzman, S. L. (1997). On-line smiles: Does gender make a difference in the use of graphic accents? *Journal of Computer-Mediated Communication*, **2**, http://www.ascusc.org/jcmc/vol2/issue4/witmer1.html.

Chapter 6

TEAM PERFORMANCE IN DYNAMIC TASK ENVIRONMENTS

Verlin B. Hinsz, Dana M. Wallace and Jared L. Ladbury

Department of Psychology, North Dakota State University, North Dakota, USA

Organizations continue to explore ways of effectively pursuing their objectives and visions for their futures. One perspective on how organizations can be more effective is to develop strategies and technologies that enhance the ways in which members of the organizations collaborate and coordinate as they perform dynamic and complex tasks. Modern organizations look different from their predecessors in numerous ways (Hinsz, 2001). They are more dependent on emerging technologies. The tempo of organizational actions has increased. Organizational members perform tasks that are much more sophisticated and complex. Moreover, the members are increasingly working in groups and teams (Cohen and Bailey, 1997; Devine *et al.*, 1999). Thus, technology, tempo, tasks, and teams are defining features of modern organizations. However, research has not provided many comprehensive approaches for understanding how teams perform technologically sophisticated and complex tasks in rapidly changing environments.

In this chapter, we offer perspectives for conceptualizing team performance in complex and dynamic task environments. Initially, we describe what is meant by dynamic task environments and particularly those that are addressed with team performance. In this way, we highlight what makes dynamic task environments unique in modern organizational settings. We review selected research related to team performance in dynamic task environments. This selective review motivates us toward a conceptualization of team performance in dynamic task environments that integrates notions from a variety of theoretical approaches. The literature review and the conceptualization also reveal that interdependence, coordination, and cross-level effects (individual-to-team, team-to-individual) are characteristic features of team performance in dynamic task environments. We discuss some implications of research related

International Review of Industrial and Organizational Psychology, 2009, Volume 24.
Edited by G. P. Hodgkinson and J. K. Ford. Copyright © 2009 John Wiley & Sons, Ltd

to various central topics included in the conceptual framework. Several examples of this research illustrate that cross-level effects can be some of the most powerful for team performance, and some of the more interesting topics for future research. Finally, we discuss how multiple teams acting in concert may be important in future research on team performance in dynamic task environments.

Dynamic Task Environments

There are a number of perspectives on dynamic task environments and related research appears in an array of journals. Much of the recent research on dynamic task environments has followed three general traditions. Researchers have tended to study the impact of cognitive factors on performance in dynamic tasks (Araujo, Davids and Serpa, 2005; Gonzalez, Thomas and Vanyukov, 2005) or the effects of different types of feedback on improved functioning in a dynamic task environment (Diehl and Sterman, 1995; Gonzalez, 2005; Paich and Sterman, 1993; Qudrat-Ullah, 2007). Much research has also focused on decision making aspects of dynamic task environments following the naturalistic decision making tradition (Zsambok and Klein, 1997).

Although a variety of perspectives contribute to the research on dynamic task environments, there appears to be consistency in the explicit and implicit definitions used for dynamic tasks. The classic work by Edwards (1962) serves as the origin for ways of defining dynamic tasks. A broad definition is that dynamic tasks require multiple responses in a changing environment (Araujo, Davids and Serpa, 2005; Qudrat-Ullah, 2007; Reimer, Park and Hinsz, 2006). A narrower definition adds that the responses made must effect a change in the environment, thus resulting in many potential feedback loops (Brehmer, 1992; Gonzalez, 2005). Thus, the common themes of dynamic task environments are that they involve *responses* to *changes* in the *task environment*. Implicitly, these responses are made in anticipation of desired changes in the task environment. It is this narrower view of dynamic tasks that best fits our view and other perspectives of team performance in dynamic task environments.

An example of a dynamic task environment and individual-level performance is that of a currency trader in the spot market. A currency trader needs to know about events as they unfold and their impact on the currencies being traded. For example, the Japanese Prime Minister resigns, the European Bank holds its interest rates, a gold mining firm in Canada announces a major expansion, a storm hits oil fields in the North Sea, a governor in the US Federal Reserve states that inflation is the main concern, a major South African wholesaler begins dumping diamonds on the market, China and Taiwan begin unification negotiations, and there is new evidence that the rate of global warming was underestimated. All of these events, which are news when they occur, have to be factored in with the movement of traded and related currencies to effectively manage currency risk and produce a profit. Note that this is just one example reflecting the conditions of responding to changes in a dynamic task environment.

Similarly, we can consider dynamic task environments involving team performance in which two or more members must interact interdependently on a task to achieve a common goal. Teams often have a history of previous interaction and anticipate future interactions. Team members also generally share an identity as a team. In team performance situations, the responses are interdependent and involve an aggregation of member efforts. In many teams, the members have specific roles that dictate how the member is to behave and contribute to achieving the goal. Underlying these views of team performance is the important characteristic of interdependence among team members. Interdependence can be seen in terms of frequency, duration and intensity of the interactions among team members, particularly with regard to the goals and associated task. Consequently, dynamic task environments influence the nature of interactions among team members, but most importantly they define the task as one that is undergoing dramatic change and the team responses need to adjust to those changes to achieve desired goals.

Team performance in dynamic task environments involves more than responses to changes in the environment. When teams perform a task in a dynamic environment, there can be accompanying changes within the team members. The team members can learn about the task environment to adopt new responses and develop knowledge and skills that improve the members' responses. These changes allow the members to more effectively adapt to changes in the task environment. Moreover, dynamic task environments often lead to changes in team membership (i.e. turnover). Members can enter and leave the team, replacing individuals who fulfill specific roles as well as take knowledge and skills with them (Levine and Choi, 2004). Moreover, as the team spends more time acting together, the team may develop and change in terms of team interaction (i.e. frequency, intensity, and duration). As a consequence, the nature of the interdependence also changes in dynamic tasks. Teams are expected to change the environment in dynamic tasks, but the team can also reformulate or reframe the task. Therefore, dynamic task environments can involve changes beyond the team responses. Teams performing dynamic tasks are changing along many dimensions including the team, the team members, their interactions, their perception of the task, the task environment and the larger context it inhabits.

There are many examples of dynamic task environments faced by teams. Shortly we will review some of the research literatures that point to firefighters, military command and control teams, and uninhabited aerial vehicle (UAV) ground control station teams as examples. Emergency response teams for police, disaster, fire, and medical emergencies serve as additional examples. Many team sports also reflect dynamic task environments. Top management teams confronting intense instability, change, and uncertainty in their organization would also be considered a team facing a dynamic task environment (Edmondson, Roberto and Watkins, 2003). In fact, many teams of which we are aware perform tasks in dynamic environments. In this chapter, our focal unit is the team (cf., Hitt et al., 2007), and particularly teams that operate in work organizations rather than social units or sports teams which, although each fascinating, are outside the scope of our examination.

Perspectives on Team Performance in Dynamic Task Environments

A multitude of perspectives exist for team performance and effectiveness (Ilgen et al., 2005; Kozlowski and Ilgen, 2006; Marks, Mathieu and Zaccaro, 2001). For teams to be effective in contributing to the welfare of organizations, they have to be adaptive to changing circumstances (Kozlowski et al., 1999). Adaptive teams and organizations are now considered necessary in competitive environments (Burke et al., 2006; Kozlowski et al., 1999). Recent conceptualizations consider the regulatory processes that help explain member and team actions in relation to events in the environment (Chen and Kanfer, 2006; DeShon et al., 2004; Marks et al., 2001). The fast-paced tempo of responding to changes matches aspects of this regulatory approach (McGrath and Argote, 2001). Also, a multilevel approach to teams has arisen, with the individuals, social interactions of members, teams, and teams within the organizational context as different levels (Chan, 1998; Chen and Kanfer, 2006; Hitt et al., 2007; Kozlowski et al., 1999). Consequently, current perspectives on effective teams emphasize that they be responsive to changes, have the structure necessary to anticipate changes, incorporate the skills, knowledge, ability, resources and resilience to act in their dynamic environments, and that they respond appropriately to change without hostility, resistance, or rigidity. We can see that team performance in dynamic task environments is an important consideration of these current perspectives of team effectiveness.

The multiple perspectives of dynamic team performance have not been limited to industrial and organizational psychology (Kozlowski and Bell, 2003). Team performance in dynamic task environments are also described in human factors (McNeese, Salas and Endsley, 2001), sports psychology (Reimer, Park and Hinsz, 2006), cognitive engineering (Letsky et al., 2008), health care (Hirokowa, DeGroyer and Vaide, 2007; Tschan et al., 2006), and social psychology (Arrow, McGrath and Berdahl, 2000). As a consequence, the research literature on team performance on dynamic tasks is widely dispersed. In response, we offer a selective review that shows the diversity of approaches to the consideration of team performance on dynamic tasks. Some of this research appears in earlier reviews of teams and team performance (Ilgen et al., 2005; Kozlowski and Ilgen, 2006) and some is unique to this selective review.

A Selective Literature Review

Because of the importance of teams for military functions, much of dynamic team performance research has focused on teams in military settings. In many of these research efforts, the teams perform dynamic tasks in synthetic (simulated) task environments (Schiflett *et al.*, 2004). For example, several studies have examined team performance in command and control synthetic task environments. Command and control involves both the decision making and information processing aspects of many teams. Some of this research has focused more on the information processing aspects of command and control (Cooke *et al.*, 2007; Hinsz and Wallace, in press) while other research has focused on decision making (Hedlund, Ilgen and Hollenbeck, 1998).

For over 20 years, researchers have examined team performance in dynamic task environments at Michigan State University (see http://www.bus. msu.edu/mgt/lab/). The team effectiveness lab there has published over 30 articles that refer to various aspects of performance in dynamic task environments. Among many developments, this research has resulted in a multilevel theory of team decision making (Ilgen *et al.*, 1995) and structural contingency theory of teams in organizations (Hollenbeck *et al.*, 2002). This research program involves a series of studies that have used a dynamic resource allocation command and control synthetic task environment (Humphrey *et al.*, 2004). As an example, Moon *et al.* (2004) examined how structural changes influence team performance. In particular, when teams changed from a functional to a divisional structure they had better performance than other teams that moved from a divisional to a functional structure. An important finding was that measures of the coordination level within the teams mediated the effects of shifts between functional and divisional structures. Research in this program has examined individual differences and helping behaviors as well as many other topics involved in team performance in dynamic task environments.

Research on team performance in command and control environments has been conducted by many others. Shebilske, Levchuk and Freeman (in press) have examined dynamic task performance in a synthetic command and control task environment. Much of Shebilske's research examines team training factors that enhance task performance on dynamic tasks (e.g. Shebilske *et al.*, 1999). Cooke and colleagues consider communication, training, and team cognition influences in a dynamic simulated task environment of operators of UAVs (Cooke *et al.*, 2007; Cooke, Gorman and Kiekel, 2008; Cooke *et al.*, 2006). Similarly, Hinsz, Ladbury and Park (2008; Ladbury, Hinsz and Park, 2007) have also conducted research looking at team performance in a dynamic simulated task environment of UAV operators. Hinsz, Ladbury and Park (2008) use combinations-of-contributions theory to examine how cognitive abilities and personality factors of team members are combined to predict team performance. In an Airborne Warning and Control Station (AWACS) dynamic task environment, Hinsz and Wallace (in press) investigated how teams presented with overwhelming information can discriminate among and remember attributes of targets. They found teams did not differ from individuals when both were subjected to a dynamic task situation with an extremely challenging display of critical information.

Another viewpoint on dynamic team task environments is emergency and disaster response teams. An eloquent discussion of the importance of effective decision making and leadership with teams facing dynamic tasks is provided by Useem, Cook and Sutton (2005). They discuss a case study of firefighters operating in teams in a major forest fire. This case illustrates the importance of effective leadership, utilizing member knowledge, appropriate communication, and the essential nature of coordination for team performance that can result in dire consequences. Similarly, Clancy et al. (2003) examined the effectiveness of different command styles on the performance of teams battling forest fires in a synthetic task environment (FIRECHIEF; Omodei, Taranto and Wearing, 1999). Majchrzak, Jarvenpaa and Hollingshead (2007) considered how these types of disaster response teams might develop and use transactive knowledge systems. Such a transactive knowledge system can reflect a potentially beneficial distribution of information among team members so they can cope with quickly changing events. The team members would need to have expert knowledge distributed to the proper members, these members are assigned to relevant tasks, and all members know this knowledge distribution and task assignment. The potential impact of transactive knowledge systems for team performance in dynamic tasks is yet to be demonstrated, and the benefits may not always emerge (Wallace and Hinsz, in press).

Other research on dynamic task environments has examined sports teams (e.g. Feltz and Lirgg, 1998; Myers, Feltz and Short, 2004). Reimer, Park and Hinsz (2006) have considered how sports teams coordinate their action and cognitions. Similar to Useem, Cook and Sutton (2005), Reimer, Park and Hinsz (2006) also discuss the role of leadership in terms of coaches that influence team performance, which receives considerable attention in the sports team literature (e.g. Feltz and Lirgg, 2001). Some additional research is emerging on medical teams in dynamic task environments. Tschan et al. (2006) examined emergency room teams and considered how coordination within the team helps them deal with a patient suffering from cardiac arrest. Similarly, Tschan et al. (2008) examined dynamic decision making in emergency room teams presented with a potentially fatal case that could be made worse if the wrong treatment was applied. Helmreich and Schaefer (1994) also considered errors in emergency room teams that influenced patient care.

Across the literatures just described, coordination stands out as an important factor in team performance on dynamic task environments (e.g. Moon et al., 2004; Reimer, Park and Hinsz, 2006; Tschan et al., 2006; Useem, Cook and Sutton, 2005). Park, Hinsz and Ladbury (2006) provide a theoretical perspective on coordination in dynamic task environments involving teams. Rico *et al.* (2008) also consider coordination a critical feature of team performance. Like others (e.g. Wittenbaum, Merry and Stasser, 1996), Rico *et al.* (2008) theorize about the implicit or tacit coordination that drives many aspects of team interaction and process. From a different perspective, Steiner (1972) argues that two factors contribute to the failure of team performance to achieve its potential. One factor is the coordination losses that arise with task-performing groups and teams when they attempt to work together. The other factor is the motivation losses that emerge in interacting groups and teams (e.g. Shepperd, 1993). In the research highlighted above, motivation losses are not believed to contribute much to poor performance for many of the tasks, although they can remain a substantial problem. Coordination losses are the issue that is frequently addressed with interventions in dynamic team task environments because they are believed to represent the greatest problem in teams achieving their potential.

A different issue that arises from the research on team performance in dynamic task environments is the way it is conceptualized. Although important efforts have been made in conceptualizing dynamic team performance (e.g. Chen and Kanfer, 2006; Ilgen *et al.*, 2005; Kozlowski and Ilgen, 2006), these conceptualizations are generally less specific and provide less concrete implications than the topic deserves. This lack of specificity is likely a result of the diversity of perspectives and settings in which team performance in dynamic task environments is considered. Consequently, the conceptualization presented here is developed and draws upon various theoretical approaches and attempts to integrate notions from the diverse perspectives applied to team performance in dynamic task environments.

Overview of the Conceptual Framework

Our framework is based upon a number of theoretical and conceptual bases. Because the objective is to develop models of team performance in dynamic task environments, the models rely substantially upon our understanding of individual action in dynamic environments. In particular, a dynamic model of performance for goal-directed behavior is useful. However, for considerations of team performance in dynamic environments, it is necessary to go beyond the actions of individuals to consider (a) the actions of teams as functioning units, (b) the ways that individual-level phenomena influence team processes and action, and (c) the ways that team interactions and actions influence individual-level actions. These additional considerations reflect the nature of interdependence among members that influences effective team performance.

Our conceptual framework also rests upon recent theoretical developments that consider groups and teams as complex, adaptive, and dynamic systems (e.g. Arrow, McGrath and Berdahl, 2000; Kozlowski and Ilgen, 2006). These theoretical developments extend traditional research on teams' onetime performance in task environments to situations in which the team members adapt to changes in the task environment and changes in the other team members. As we come to consider teams and organizations as being responsive and adaptive to dynamic changes in their environments, it is also important to recognize that individual members of the organization will change as well. These changes in the individuals mean that their teammates will likely need to adapt to the changes of the individuals with whom they interact. Thus, teams can be seen as dynamic collectives that also respond socially to the rapidly changing aspects of the situations they face.

Teams performing dynamic tasks also need to consider and anticipate changes in the task. This anticipation by teams develops from the expectations members have as part of their experiences with the task and in the team (Hinsz, 2004). These expectations also provide team members with a basis for understanding future team performance on the task. Our understanding of teams implies that we need to appreciate the cognitive responses to task performance as well as the expectations that members have about their interactions with the task. To show how the nature of the team, task, and team members all contribute to team performance on dynamic tasks, our conceptual framework relies upon a hierarchy of embedded systems (cf., Kozlowski et al., 2001). The embedded systems aspect of the conceptual framework is an elaboration of control and systems models of individual performance on dynamic tasks. The emphasis upon individual performance of dynamic tasks sets the stage for considering the greater complexity that arises for team performance situations. Thus, the development of our conceptual framework begins with a description of a model of individual task performance on dynamic tasks.

A Model of Individual Performance in Dynamic Task Environments

There is a well-developed literature regarding the performance of individuals on dynamic tasks (e.g. Karoly, 1993; Wickens, 1992) that can serve as foundations upon which to build a team-based model. One constraint we impose on the type of model is a focus on goal-directed behavior leading to performance. Most regulatory approaches and other models of task performance place an emphasis on the actions an individual makes in pursuit of goals (DeShon et al., 2004; Klein, 1989; Marks et al., 2001). Similarly, teams generally engage in goal-directed behavior (Hinsz, 1995a). Clearly, the performance of individuals on the dynamic tasks of interest involves the pursuit of some objectives or mission. In the same way, the performance of teams may depend on the degree to which members pursue goals related to the team's objectives.

Control theory provides a general approach to performance in dynamic environments that focuses on goal-directed behavior (i.e. Carver and Scheier,

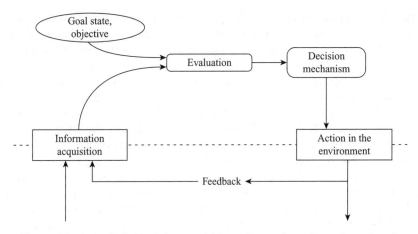

Figure 6.1 A simple feedback-loop model for actions performed on a dynamic task.

1981, 1998; Klein, 1989; Lord and Kernan, 1989; Powers, 1973; Rasmussen, Pejtersen and Goodstein,1994). Figure 6.1 presents a general version of a simple feedback-loop model of goal-directed behavior related to task performance. The representation in Figure 6.1 is an extension of control-systems theoretical approaches and closely resembles that of Lord and Kernan (1989) in their model of motivation for goal-directed behavior for task performance.

The simple feedback-loop model presented in Figure 6.1 divides the realm of interest into the portion that is in the human task performer (above the dotted line) and a portion in the environment in which the task exists (below the dotted line). In this system, the person acquires relevant information from the environment. This information is usually relevant to some objective or desired goal state. A comparison between the state of the environment as perceived and the desired goal state occurs, and an evaluation of any discrepancies is made. If the evaluation uncovers a discrepancy that requires action, the decision mechanism then determines the type of action that is required. The action can be of various kinds. The decision mechanism may indicate a behavioral change regarding the nature of the action is necessary (e.g. intensity, direction, persistence). The decision mechanism may also mandate cognitive changes on the part of the actor (e.g. a change in the goal, a change in a frame of reference, redirection of the search for information). These decisions are then translated into actions on the part of the person in the environment. These actions and other events will then result in changes in the environment, which will serve as new information that may be acquired (feedback).

The actions the individual produces are generally directed toward the task of interest. These actions should influence the task and contribute to the critical performance outcomes that are assessed. The model presented in Figure 6.1 implies that the action has an impact on the task resulting in the performance outcomes that can be measured. It is important to understand that the relation between action and performance outcomes is complex and indirect (Kanfer, 1992). Consequently, Figure 6.1 represents this as a relationship without a direct link, but with the actions having an impact in the task environment.

A limitation of this feedback-loop model is that it does not clearly indicate how individuals process information. For most tasks in modern organizations, the processing of information has important influences on actions and eventual performance (Walsh, 1995). There are a number of similarities between the ways information is processed and the simple feedback-loop model. Both begin with information that is acquired in the context of a goal or objective. Moreover, both information processing and the feedback model end with a response or action. Preceding the action, both involve information in reaching a decision of how to act. In addition, both information processing and the feedback-loop model indicate that actions influence the environment in a way that contributes feedback as a source of information.

The specific aspects of information processing (e.g. working memory) do not play a primary role in the following discussion; therefore an action-control model of performance on dynamic tasks is presented in Figure 6.2. Figure 6.2

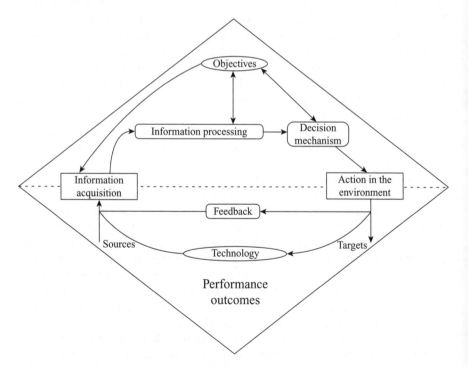

Figure 6.2   An action-control model for individuals performing dynamic tasks.

indicates that the processing of information is one component of an overall model that examines the action of the individual in a dynamic environment. The objectives and information acquired play a role in controlling the actions of the individual on the task, and the actions are influenced by a decision mechanism. Figure 6.2 also indicates that outcomes arise from the individual's actions in the environment. Specifically, these are outcomes associated with performing the dynamic task. These outcomes are meant to reflect those that are intended as a function the individual acting in the environment, but unintended outcomes are implied as well.

Multiple sources of information and multiple targets of action are shown in the Figure 6.2 representation. The actions of an individual on a dynamic task can be directed toward a host of targets (e.g. coworkers, technological devices). Moreover, the information used in performing the task can come from a variety of sources (e.g. displays, coworkers). The dotted line in Figure 6.2 can be considered the interface between the human task performer and a technological system used to perform the task. Figure 6.2 serves as the representation of individual performance (termed the action-control model) upon which a model of team performance is developed.

Action-Control in Dynamic Task Environments

To place the model of individual performance on dynamic tasks in a more specific context, consider action-control models as they reflect the actions of the individual team members of an UAV. UAVs have attracted much attention due to their usefulness in the US military's involvement in Bosnia and Kosovo, more recently in the campaigns in Afghanistan and Iraq (New Breed, 2001), and are expected to serve greatly expanded functions in future U.S. military operations and strategy (Unmanned Aircraft Systems Roadmap, 2005). Additionally, UAVs offer a unique opportunity to examine the theoretical implications of the models we describe in a complex, goal-directed, interdependent, and dynamic environment.

According to a task analysis of the US Air Force's Predator UAV (Hall and Gugerty, 1997), there are three conceptual functions or roles that individual team members perform to operate the reconnaissance UAV from the ground-control station: the pilot, the camera operator, and the communications and mission planning manager. The pilot is the individual that flies the vehicle. The camera operator is responsible for the acquisition of data about a target from cameras and other data sensors. The communications and mission planning manager is responsible for planning the mission and exchanging information with external centers and agents. Much like teams in other dynamic situations, one member is responsible for transporting people and material, another is responsible for collecting important information, and a third is responsible for making plans and communicating with others (e.g. stakeholders).

Let us presume that the UAV is on a mission to acquire data in a nonhostile area. Each member of the team has individual objectives for task performance. The manager sketches out the schedule of targets and briefs the pilot and camera operator about mission parameters. The manager monitors how well each target is acquired in reference to criteria specified by external agents. Given the understanding of the mission, the pilot then attempts to maneuver the UAV efficiently so that it safely maintains the appropriate flight path within the specific territory and air space constraints. Because the mission is largely defined by the targets to be acquired, the pilot also has to arrange the flight path so that the camera operator can get optimal photographs of the target. Consequently, the camera operator is dependent upon the pilot to get his equipment to a proper heading to take optimal photographs, and is also dependent on the manager for specification of the data to be acquired. Likewise, the manager is dependent upon the camera operator to provide optimal photographs so that the mission can progress. Moreover, the manager relies upon the pilot to inform him if there are constraints that require a change to the schedule of targets (i.e. strong head winds, potential cloud obstruction). Consequently, the UAV task environment has three roles that are highly interdependent, requiring coordination and collaboration among the team members to accomplish their mission (Park, Hinsz and Ladbury, 2006).

The UAV task environment is also dynamic. Changes in wind speed and direction or cloud cover can interfere with a planned schedule for acquiring targets. External agents can ask for more information about a target, which would require another pass over the target, perhaps at a different angle or from a different direction. The UAV team can be asked to acquire photos or data of new targets introduced while the UAV team is performing its mission. These ad-hoc targets often require the manager to adapt the schedule of targets, as well as initiate changes in the objectives that the pilot and camera operator would have. The UAV task environment is very dynamic in nature and requires the team members to adapt to a number of situational changes.

This simple description of the UAV task environment suggests that the team members performing the tasks are highly interdependent. Team members must coordinate their actions and should have effective collaboration strategies to optimally and successfully complete their missions (Park, Hinsz and Ladbury, 2006). Moreover, the activities of a UAV ground control station team reflect the characteristics of modern teams in that they must be adaptive and work in technologically sophisticated environments that are dynamic. The functions of each of the team members could be represented by an action-control model (Figure 6.2); however, such a representation would not reflect the interaction among team members. It is important to realize that the interdependent nature of team members' tasks suggests that the conceptualization needs to illustrate the ways in which the members work together as a team to complete the mission. The interdependent nature of the ways team members function as an interacting team are better represented by Figure 6.3.

Coordination
network

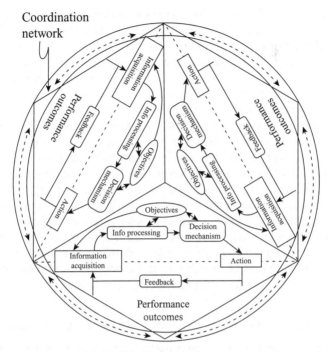

Figure 6.3   A model of team member interactions and interdependence for dynamic tasks including the coordination network indicating the flow of information and interactions among team members.

A Model of Team Member Interactions in a Dynamic Task Environment

Figure 6.3 shows a team as a functioning unit that incorporates the team members and their functions. The representation in Figure 6.3 is applicable to dynamic task environments in which a number of interdependent team members interact. The hexagon in Figure 6.3 is divided into three diamonds that each represent a team member within a three-person group. Each of the diamonds intersects with the other two diamonds to demonstrate that there is an interrelation and interdependence between the activities of one member with the other team members. Moreover, the space outside of the hexagon inside the rectangle is meant to represent the environment and context in which the team performs its functions. This model provides a basis upon which to consider how the team members interact with each other and interact with their task environments in pursuit of objectives.

The model of team member interactions can also be expanded to indicate the flow of information and interactions. Figure 6.3 provides a representation of the team members encircled by a coordination network (Arrow, McGrath and Berdahl, 2000). This coordination network demonstrates that the actions of one member of the team can influence the other members of the team. Similarly, the actions of others can serve as important information for the team members in pursuit of their particular task objectives. Consequently, the coordination network can represent the flow of information, communication, and interactions among the team members. In a sense, the coordination network binds the team members to each other as they perform their individual functions as well as collaborate in effort to achieve the team's objectives.

Although the illustration of team member interactions in Figure 6.3 is two dimensional in nature, one can also envision links between aspects of the functions of each of the team members as arcs in the third dimension between the member action-control models (diamonds). For instance, the feedback one member receives from his actions may be directly relevant to the objectives of another team member. Likewise, the feedback that results from one member's actions could be information acquired by another team member. Moreover, an action by one member might be information for another. The strategies involved in collaboration among the team members may be represented by a collection of arcs among the team members.

A Hierarchy of Action-Control Models for Team Performance

Up to this point, the models of team performance have been developed from the individual level of analysis. However, the conceptualization described here also allows for the consideration of a team as an entity in itself. In this regard, the development of this model of team performance incorporates a multilevel perspective that is useful for understanding team effectiveness (Chan, 1998; Chen and Kanfer, 2006; Kozlowski and Ilgen, 2006). Figure 6.4 demonstrates that the processes the team performs as it pursues its goals can be conceived as an action-control model as well. In this case, the overarching mission of the team is specified instead of the objectives of each of the team members, although they will be interrelated. Moreover, the information processing at this level reflects the ways in which the information is processed collaboratively. In addition, the decision mechanism here reflects the consensus that is achieved about how the tasks will be conducted and the strategies involved. This action-control model of team performance uses the team as the level of analysis, with a focus on team-level performance outcomes in addition to the team member measures of performance.

The general action-control model of task performance was used at both the team-member and team-in-entirety levels. This homology (Chen, Bliese and Mathieu, 2005; Kozlowski and Ilgen, 2006) and parallelism (Chen and Kanfer, 2006) is intentional so that the similarities in the levels of the hierarchy and of the nature of performance in the dynamic task environment are shown. Figures 6.2–6.4 demonstrate that team performance in dynamic task environments can be represented at multiple levels. The lowest level (local) is that of the team

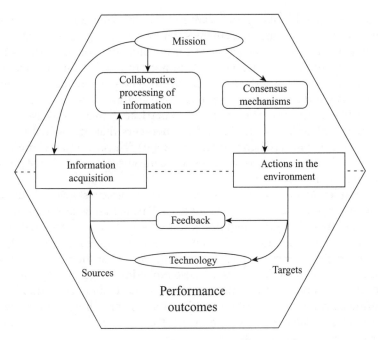

Figure 6.4   A team-level action-control model for performance of dynamic tasks.

member performing specific functions, independent of the activities of the other team members, as in Figure 6.2. The next highest level (local collective) indicates that the different team members can be seen as performing their tasks in the same environment, although there is no interaction implied among the members. The local collective level could be illustrated by a collection of models (Figure 6.2) with one model for every member of the team. The second from highest (local integrated) level illustrates the interactions that occur among the team members as they perform their tasks, as illustrated in Figure 6.3. Coordination and collaboration among the team members are the focus of this level. Finally, the top level (global) represents the actions of the team as a functioning unit as it pursues its mission (as presented in Figure 6.4).

A host of relations between the different levels in this hierarchy are implied. That is, the activities at the team level would influence the actions in the interaction level that may influence the action at the team member level (i.e. downward influence). Likewise, relations that represent upward influence would also arise. The actions of team members on their tasks would influence the interactions among the team members that may impact the activities of the team as a whole. These top-down and bottom-up influences of the different levels also suggest that reciprocal influences are quite likely among the levels in the hierarchy (Klein and Kozlowski, 2000). The relations across levels harbor some of the greatest influences in team performance and some of the most intriguing questions. For instance, many situations involve goals that are defined for the team as a whole as well as goals for the individual member (Crown and Rosse, 1995). In this case, it is not only important to know how the team goal influences the activities of the members but also how the member preferences for team goals and actions influence team goals (Hinsz, 1995a). There is some evidence that cross-level effects are asymmetrical in that teams are likely to have greater influence on the individual members than individual members have on team activities (Chen and Kanfer, 2006). We return to the importance of cross-level effects later as we consider central topics in this hierarchy of action-control models.

The multilevel view of team performance on dynamic tasks can be conceived as a hierarchy of the action-control models. This hierarchy also indicates that the different models represented in Figures 6.2–6.4 can be considered embedded systems. The individual performing a task is one system (Figure 6.2). The individual is also a team member interacting with other members as a system (Figure 6.3). The team interaction is also embedded in the team as an acting system itself. Moreover, the team interacts and has an impact on the dynamic environment which can also be considered a system. Thus, the hierarchy of action-control models can be seen as a set of embedded systems related to performance of dynamic tasks.

The hierarchy of action-control models illustrated in Figures 6.2–6.4 is intended to illustrate a conceptualization of team performance in dynamic task environments. This conceptualization suggests that team performance in a dynamic task environment may be considered a hierarchy of embedded subsystems that exist at multiple levels of analysis. The series of figures and the models they represent illustrate the complexity and nature of dynamic task environments that many teams will confront. Considering these illustrations as representations of the models relating the hierarchy of embedded systems, it is possible to consider a number of research topics that can contribute to an understanding of team performance in dynamic task environments.

Central Topics in the Study of Team Performance in Dynamic Task Environments

The description of the hierarchy of embedded action-control models offers representations of how team members interact and perform their functions. These models also provide a basis for considering a number of topics relevant for understanding team interaction and performance in dynamic task environments. Focusing on each of the models might be helpful for directing efforts toward a better understanding of team interaction and performance. Additionally, examining each of the constructs that are central to each of the models (e.g. feedback) might provide a basis for better understanding individual and team task performance. A literature review and integrative analysis could be conducted for each of the aspects of the models illustrated in Figures 6.3 and 6.4 (e.g. coordination network, feedback), and some of these integrative reviews exist (e.g. consensus mechanisms; Laughlin and Hollingshead, 1995). Yet, even examining the constructs will not provide a complete overview of the relevant topics because many of the constructs reflect processes (e.g. coordination) that go beyond those listed in the models. Nevertheless, we next explore select constructs and processes that arise when considering the hierarchical models of team performance on dynamic tasks. By shining a spotlight on each of the following topics some research issues relevant for understanding team performance in dynamic task environments are highlighted.

The central topics discussed below also draw attention to several common themes. One of these themes is the defining role that interdependence has on team performance and how interdependence appears to become more critical for team functioning as task environments become more dynamic. Similarly, coordination is a process that has been common for much of the research we have referenced. Coordination is likewise a process that impacts the central constructs and processes (e.g. coordination network). Additionally, the topics discussed below often involve cross-level effects. It is the cross-level effects within the hierarchy of models that are often the most compelling and puzzling. The cross-level effects also inspire many research questions of interest. So, the following discussion of central topics will reiterate the nature and importance of coordination, interdependence, and cross-level effects for team performance in dynamic task environments.

Information acquisition

The acquisition of information by team members in pursuit of objectives raises a number of issues. One issue is that team members can direct other members' attention to specific information. Using an UAV example, the manager influences the information that might receive attention by the pilot and camera operator. Also, in teams, the team members themselves become sources of information (Figure 6.4). Many factors also influence information attended to and acquired in teams (Hinsz, Tindale and Vollrath, 1997). In the self-regulation literature, self-focused attention is an individual difference variable related to information acquisition. Mullen (1987) extended the consideration of self-focus to members' attention in group settings showing that a distinctive status of a member in a team can influence how team members conceive of themselves, how other team members conceive of them, and how the team members contribute to task performance.

The acquisition of information in teams can also relate to conflicts between team members because they can have different objectives and must share finite resources. In UAV missions, only one of the cameras can be used at a time: either the belly camera used by the camera operator or a nose camera used for the pilot's view. Because both cameras cannot be used simultaneously, the pilot and camera operator must arrange to share the resource (Levine, 1998). These limitations in camera use demonstrate that team members must effectively allocate a shared resource to acquire the information that may be critical for each to meet their individual objectives. Team situations that involve shared resources for gathering information (e.g. firefighters) and resource allocation (e.g. Moon et al., 2004) are common in dynamic task environments. Shared resources and resource allocation illustrate again how interdependence and coordination are features of dynamic team task environments.

Time pressure is another feature of dynamic task environments that can influence the acquisition of information by team members (e.g. Judge and Miller, 1991). Time pressure tends to restrict the variability and amount of information that team members acquire (Karau and Kelly, 1992; Kelly and Karau, 1999; Kelly and Loving, 2004). If team members are expected to acquire unique information they are to share with the rest of the team, then time pressure might restrict the information acquired and the critical information will not be made available to the rest of the team. Moreover, there is evidence that involvement in teams leads the members to focus on more homogeneous and less diverse information (Hinsz, Tindale and Vollrath, 1997). By having this narrower focus of information, it is possible that team members would not share the perspectives that might be necessary for adapting to changes in dynamic task environments such that teams would not achieve their objectives.

Objectives

The objectives and goals team members have for performing tasks is a topic with a rich literature (Locke and Latham, 2002; O'Leary-Kelly, Martocchio and Frink, 1994; Weldon and Weingart, 1993; Zander, 1971). Some questions that might be raised concern: how potential conflicts among the objectives of the separate team members might be resolved. For example, how can interdependence in team member goals and objectives be coordinated to support the most effective performance? The literature on goal interdependence (cf., Mitchell and Silver, 1990; O'Leary-Kelly, Martocchio and Frink, 1994; Saavedra, Earley and Van Dyne, 1993) can serve as a foundation upon which to develop strategies to reduce goal conflict among interdependent team members while simultaneously taking advantage of the properties of goals to enhance the performance of the team members (Crown and Rosse, 1995).

Research on goal setting also provides an avenue to consider motivation in team performance. Because goal setting is an effective technique for enhancing individual performance, it has also been implemented at the team level to influence team performance. Much research on goal setting in groups and teams has been conducted (e.g. Crown and Rosse, 1995; Hinsz, 1995a) and reviewed (O'Leary-Kelly, Martocchio and Frink, 1994; Weldon and Weingart, 1993). Similar to regulatory approaches that consider the influence of goals and motivation on individual performance (e.g. Lord and Kernan, 1989), DeShon et al.

(2004) shows how regulatory approaches can be useful for team motivation and performance on dynamic tasks (see also Chen and Kanfer, 2006). Important questions arise as to how to motivate members toward common, team goals rather than individual goals that might be more concrete and instrumental for personal rewards. Also, how can member goals be aligned and coordinated to arrange a strategy so that the team achieves common goals as well as member goals? The relationships between member and team goals reflect cross-level effects. An additional issue that teams need to resolve is who determines what the goals will be, which involves decision making in teams.

Decision mechanism

The decision mechanism aspect of action-control models is a central topic for team performance. One issue that has emerged is the delineation of processes by which team decisions are reached regarding the cognitive and behavioral strategies to be used for team performance (Hinsz, 1999; Hollenbeck *et al.*, 1995; Kerr and Tindale, 2004; Tindale, Kameda and Hinsz, 2003). How are behavioral and cognitive strategies of members integrated to direct the actions of the team? How do team members come to agree on and make trade-offs regarding their plans and strategies? These questions highlight a few of the issues that arise when considering the interrelations among the team members' decisions regarding the nature of their interactions and task performance.

Another way that the cognitive strategies can be considered is in terms of shared cognitions for team action (Hinsz, Tindale and Vollrath, 1997; Cannon-Bower and Salas, 2001). As team members think about their strategies for action, they have to coordinate their actions with other team members. This implies that team members need to have coordinated cognitions (Reimer, Park and Hinsz, 2006). Research has begun to consider team cognition and its influence on team performance (Salas and Fiore, 2004). Likewise, coordinated cognitions can also be considered team cognitions (Cooke *et al.*, 2003). The cognitions that team members share for deciding how to act reflect the cross-level effects between members and the team (Hinsz, Tindale and Vollrath, 1997). Our understanding of team performance will be enhanced if we have better representations of how members think about their tasks, their teammates, and the ways in which the members' actions will result in the desired levels of team performance (Cannon-Bowers, Salas and Converse, 1993; Hinsz and Magnan, 2006).

Information processing

Related to the research on cognition in teams is the processing of information in teams (Hinsz, 2001; Hinsz, Tindale and Vollrath, 1997). One popular topic is shared mental models and their impact on team interaction and performance (Cannon-Bowers and Salas, 2001; Hinsz, 1995b, 2004; Klimoski and

Mohammed, 1994; Langan-Fox, Code and Langfield-Smith, 2000; Mathieu *et al.*, 2000). The mental models of team members performing complex, dynamic tasks also relate to situation awareness and shared situation awareness (Artman, 2000; Endsley, 1995; Stout, Cannon-Bowers and Salas, 1996). Mental models are complex networks of beliefs that individuals hold about the functioning of complex systems (Hinsz, 1995b). In the dynamic task environments, a number of complex systems are implied: the team task being performed, the technology the team members use while performing the task, and the team itself as a complex system (Hinsz, 1995b, 2004). Consequently, to understand the impact of shared mental models it is important to recognize that multiple mental models play a role in the effectiveness of teams performing dynamic tasks.

An aspect of information processing in teams is the biases that might be prevalent among the team members. A shared bias to perceive a specific situation in an ineffective fashion (e.g. shared pessimism about successfully completing a task) could mean that more in-depth analysis of the situation is not attempted and the team fails to completely fulfill its mission. Research on information-processing biases in groups suggests that biases can be exaggerated in team responses (Hinsz, Tindale and Nagao, 2008). Groups also appear to use biased strategies for integrating information, which can lead to improper consideration of the available information (Hinsz, Tindale and Nagao, 2008). Teams generally process information in an effective fashion (Hinsz, 2001). Yet under specific conditions, the biases and improper strategies of team members can be exaggerated which results in suboptimal task performance (Hinsz, Tindale and Vollrath, 1997). Other research shows how effective information processing by team members can result in extraordinary performance that achieves desired goals (Letsky *et al.*, 2008).

Actions

The actions of team members working together are a critical issue for team performance. One related topic is how the behaviors of each team member facilitate or hinder the activities of the other team members (Harris and Barnes-Farrell, 1997). If the actions of the members are not coordinated, then there are performance losses relative to optimal performance (Steiner, 1972). An important issue becomes how to coordinate the behaviors of the different team members to maximize performance and achieve effective interaction in terms of who does what, when, where, and how (Arrow, McGrath and Berdahl, 2000; Park, Hinsz and Ladbury, 2006; Reimer, Park and Hinsz, 2006). From a human factors perspective, technological aids (e.g. adaptive interfaces) could be investigated to serve as levers to enhance the actions of the team members in the performance of their tasks (Kozlowski and Ilgen, 2006). Similarly, collaborative behaviors such as aiding and assisting that occur in teams (Marks *et al.*, 2002; Porter *et al.*, 2003) could also be levers for enhancing performance of teams on dynamic tasks.

Considering actions in team performance also raises a number of conceptual questions. For instance, what is assessed as team performance? Is the performance a unitary response provided by the team? Or is it an aggregation of member actions after some level agreement among member responses is shown (e.g. intraclass correlation)? Neither aggregated nor unitary responses are a gold standard of team performance measurements, and each result from different task environments. Many of these issues arise as multilevel analyses are conducted to consider factors at both the individual and team level (Klein and Kozlowski, 2000). A somewhat related issue is definition of the criteria for evaluating team performance (Brodbeck, 1996). A variety of different criteria for team performance are often suggested, such as productivity, satisfaction of members, meeting expectations, viability of the group (Hackman, 1987), accuracy of response, time to response, and acceptance of response by members (Vroom, 1969). Much more consideration needs to be given to what should be the criteria for evaluating performance on dynamic tasks by teams who are supposed to work interdependently and adaptively.

Feedback

Although the role of feedback on performance for individual task performers has received considerable attention, much less research has addressed collective or team feedback (Hinsz, Tindale and Vollrath, 1997; Robinson and Weldon, 1993). One interesting and important question is the amount and distribution of feedback provided to the team members regarding their individual task performance and the team's overall task performance. For example, should each member of the team receive feedback about the consequences of other team members' actions, or will this produce information overload, or even dissension among the team members. A number of issues arise for feedback in team performance because feedback is critical for learning and skill acquisition on tasks. These issues become even more critical when the tasks are dynamic and complex, and members must respond adaptively to changes in the situation.

If we recognize that many teams will suffer from information overload when they are provided feedback about all the outcomes being assessed with complex tasks, then it becomes clear that the information that is the focus of feedback needs to be specified. Who or what should provide the feedback? Should feedback be automated? Should only authorities be provided control over the dissemination of feedback? Because of the dynamic nature of the feedback, when should feedback be given? Should feedback be provided continuously, at fixed intervals (e.g. quarterly), or only at the request of the team members? What categories of feedback content should be provided so that the appropriate outcomes are influenced? As is apparent, when providing feedback to teams that are performing dynamic tasks, a host of issues arise concerning who provides what feedback to whom in what way, when, where, and for what purpose. This feedback to the team and its members then becomes information and communications that flows through the coordination network.

Coordination network

The coordination network adds new views on factors that influence team performance. Because the coordination network includes the task relationships among the members as well as the information that is communicated and discussed among the team members, much of the way strategies are developed and implemented can be seen as consequences of the coordination network. One example is in terms of the strategies that teams implement to coordinate activities to enhance performance. A task analysis of AWACS weapons directors (Fahey et al., 1997) suggests that they meet before the start of a mission to negotiate contracts about how tasks and responsibilities will be shared and coordinated. These contracts appear to be important features of the weapons director teams, and likely contribute to the team effectiveness. Research suggests that teams rarely structure their interactions (Hackman, 1987), even though teams are known to abhor a vacuum (Hinsz, 1995a). Thus, one way of enhancing team performance would be to establish a structure in which team members meet to negotiate arrangements regarding how tasks and responsibilities would be coordinated. These negotiated arrangements might enhance shared situation awareness (Endsley and Jones, 2001) as well as contribute to better teamwork strategies (cf., Rentsch and Hall, 1994; Stout et al., 1999). Coordination networks provide a way for understanding how negotiated agreements can be implemented and how they influence performance.

The coordination network also represents the structure of communication among team members. One popular view in organizational settings is that information is power. Thus, in the power dynamics of interacting teams, information may not be shared by some team members because of the power that it imparts and as a strategic way of controlling team operations (Wittenbaum, Hollingshead and Botero, 2004). If there is value to be gained for holding and not sharing information, the strategic information sharing literature suggests that some members will act strategically. As a consequence of withholding critical information from the team, some members may not be able to attain their objectives for the team performance. What may be strategic for one team member may interfere with the team reaching its objective. In situations where critical information is necessary for a team to respond accurately and quickly to the task environment, it is easy to see how inefficient lines in the communication structure will lead to failures on the part of teams trying to achieve their objectives when performing dynamic tasks.

The coordination network reflects the communication of information among team members. The coordination network also indicates how the constructs associated with one team member (e.g. feedback, decision mechanism, actions) might influence constructs associated with another team member (e.g. the acquisition and processing of information). The coordination network also highlights how the actions and interactions among the team members are linked. Interpersonal and cross-level effects are implicit within the operations of the coordination network. Conceptually, the coordination network may serve as one of the more compelling directions for potential research that explores team performance of dynamic tasks. If the ways by which cross-level effects of member interactions influence team action is interesting, then by logical extension up the hierarchy, the ways by which multiple teams influence larger systems or organizations also deserve attention.

Multiple Teams Acting in Concert

The members of many teams do not act alone, but often act in concert with other teams. For example, the operations of UAVs are becoming increasingly complex, with a number of UAVs working in unison on a set of similar missions in a region. Consequently, it is possible to go beyond the consideration of a single team (i.e. Figure 6.4) to consider a collection of teams (Figure 6.5). Figure 6.5 indicates that a team-of-teams could be given similar missions and would act in concert. These teams would be linked with interdependence in their missions and would have to coordinate their actions. Such a team-of-teams may report to the same supervisor and may have to spell out specific plans so that their activities do not conflict. With a greater emphasis on teams for confronting complex and dynamic task environments in the future, this coordination and collaboration of teams in dynamic environments will become more common. These teams-of-teams also reflect what is going to be a critical question in research on teams: How do teams interact effectively with other teams? By extending these notions, we can also consider how some teams might control and direct the actions of other teams.

The notion of a team-of-teams, which involves coordinated teams with similar functions, can be extended to consider how teams with different functions collaborate with each other to achieve overarching objectives. The notion of interactions among multiple teams having different functions has been described as a multiteam system (Mathieu, Marks and Zacarro, 2001). In this regard, Figure 6.5 can also be considered to demonstrate a multiteam system in which team performance occurs at another level with interactions and interdependencies between and among a set of teams (Marks et al., 2005). Although it is not illustrated in Figure 6.5, a multiteam system would also include a network of associations among the members of the teams, which is implied in this conceptualization. It is this network of associations that is likely to identify how the teams interact with each other and how effective and ineffective interactions arise (Marks et al., 2005).

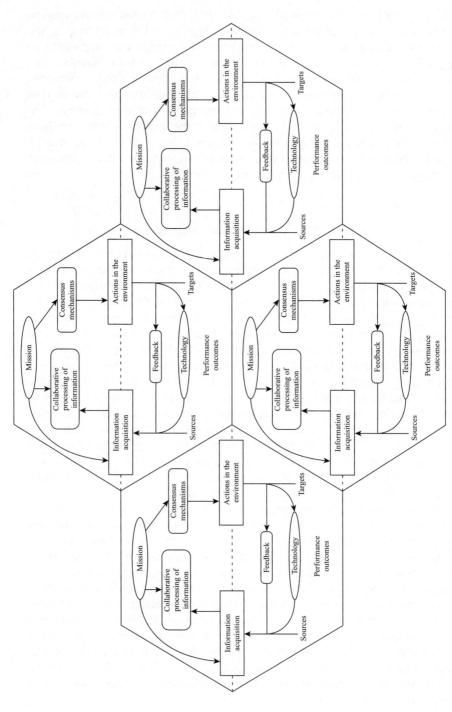

Figure 6.5 A configuration for a set of team-level action-control models illustrating multiple teams acting in concert.

Although research on multiple team interactions is likely to increase, some research already addresses the topic. Marks, Mathieu and Zaccaro (2004) propose that a multisystem is a network of coupled teams that are characterized by goal hierarchies, interteam interdependencies, and dynamic task environments. Marks, Mathieu and Zaccaro (2004) provide a good description of a military strike package as a multiteam system. Mathieu, Marks and Zacarro (2001) illustrate a multiteam system with emergency response teams treating individuals involved in an accident. Marks *et al.* (2005) examined how networks of teams can align their efforts to enhance performance. They argued that cross-level effects (cross-team) were more important for predicting performance than within team processes, which again suggests an asymmetry in the impact of cross-level effects. Marks *et al.* (2005) also note that the nature of the interdependencies among teams had a direct impact on the factors that influenced system effectiveness.

Multiteam systems involve teams having to anticipate and react to changes in the environment resulting from the actions of other teams, which are dynamic entities themselves. Consequently, team members working in a multiteam system have to incorporate an additional level of cognitive processing about the ways other teams will function and operate (i.e. metacognition; Hinsz, 2004). This metacognition about teams can provide team members with a better situational awareness about what the other teams are doing and what they are likely to do next. Therefore, with the greater effort that the additional level of interdependence and coordination that occurs with multiteam systems, they will also place additional cognitive demands on team members and teams for responding appropriately to achieve effective performance.

Additional topics for investigation arise from considering multiple teams acting in concert. In such situations, intergroup relations become important (Worchel and Austin, 1986). One aspect of settings in which teams interact is that members of different teams come to have separate group identities (Abrams and Hogg, 1990). These different group identities can influence reactions to members of one's own team and members of other teams as well (e.g. ingroup favoritism and outgroup hostility; Turner, 1991). Consequently, although the goal of the organization may be for various teams to work in concert and harmony to achieve a mission, rivalry and antagonism between teams may be a likely result.

Intergroup relations often involve conflict (Tajfel and Turner, 1979). Conflict among teams that are expected to be cooperating to reach common goals would be a problem contributing to large deficiencies in team performance. Although intergroup relations are often associated with conflict and competition, cooperation can also arise in properly controlled settings (Worchel, 1986). Research shows that specific conditions enhance the propensity for cooperation to arise among potentially conflicting groups (Worchel and Austin, 1986). One way to induce cooperation and reduce conflict is to make superordinate goals, such as a larger organizational mission, salient to the members of the teams

(Sherif, 1958). In this fashion, all teams working toward a global mission will enhance organizational effectiveness as well as encourage cooperation among teams. It is important to recognize and account for these aspects of intergroup relations in efforts to enhance the effectiveness of each of the teams in multiple team structures.

The interactions between multiple teams can also illustrate important cross-level effects that may not be anticipated. Research on the interindividual–intergroup discontinuity shows that patterns of responses observed between groups cannot be predicted based on similar observations of responses between individuals (see Wildschut et al., 2003, for an excellent review). In particular, interactions between teams are highly likely to be competitive while interactions between individuals facing the same situation are very likely to be cooperative. Additionally, if teams are in a situation in which aggression between teams is possible, they are likely to be more aggressive than a similar situation with the potential for aggression between individuals (Meier and Hinsz, 2004). This research suggests multiple team interactions provide opportunities for powerful cross-level effects. There is a potential for interactions between teams to be qualitatively different from those of interactions among team members. With continued research on teams-of-teams and multiteam systems, it will be important to investigate the unique ways in which interactions among teams differ from those expected based on our conceptualizations of interactions among individuals and team members.

CONCLUDING COMMENTS

The preceding discussion does not include all the potential topics and issues concerning team interaction and performance. Rather, the topics discussed highlight relevant research that relates to team performance on dynamic tasks. Moreover, the conceptual framework and hierarchy of embedded action-control models helps identify topics that contribute to a better understanding of team performance in dynamic task environments. Additional advances to our understanding will come from integrating ideas, notions, and theories across the different topics. Research such as the consideration of motivation in teams (Chen and Kanfer, 2006), goal setting and self-regulation in teams (DeShon et al., 2004), and multiteam systems and leadership (DeChurch and Marks, 2006) reflect just a sampling of the advances that can arise if broader, integrative, and multiple perspective approaches are taken to the conceptualization of team performance in dynamic task environments.

The conceptual framework we offer reflects a number of current perspectives about the nature of team effectiveness. The conceptualization evolves from models of individual performance on dynamic tasks focusing on goal-directed behavior. The conceptualization also builds upon to theoretical developments related to team performance such as control-systems theory, groups as dynamic systems, multilevel modeling, adaptive teams, and self-regulation approaches of teams. A series of embedded models are presented that represent (1) the processes of team members performing their tasks, (2) the processes of interaction among the team members, (3) the processes of the team as a functioning unit, and (4) the relationships among multiple teams performing tasks in concert. These models form a hierarchy of embedded systems for the processes in a dynamic team task environment. The action-control models highlight a number of central topics derived from this conceptualization which can contribute to our understanding of team performance in dynamic task environments.

Based on the conceptualization provided, our understanding of the processes involved in teams performing dynamic task environments is expanded. There are many team-based structures for which this conceptual framework may provide important implications (e.g. UAVs, space shuttle support teams, medical teams, firefighting teams). Models and theoretical formulations of team interaction and performance in dynamic environments have begun to receive attention. We hope that our discussion of the topics and research related to team performance in dynamic task environments as well as the conceptual framework we present will contribute to this emerging view of team performance.

ACKNOWLEDGMENTS

Preparation of this manuscript was supported by grants from the Air Force Office of Scientific Research (F49620-02-1-0234 & F49620-03-1-0353) and the National Science Foundation (BCS 0721796). The views and conclusions contained herein are those of the authors and should not be interpreted as necessarily representing the official policies or endorsements, either expressed or implied, of the U.S. Government. We appreciate the comments of Mike McNeese, Kevin Betts, and Renee Magnan on earlier drafts of this paper.

REFERENCES

Abrams, D. & Hogg, M. A. (1990). *Social Identity Theory: Constructive and Critical Advances*, London and New York: Harvester, Wheatsheaf & Springer.

Araujo, D., Davids, K. & Serpa, S. (2005). An ecological approach to expertise effects in decision-making in a simulated sailing regatta. *Psychology of Sport and Exercise*, **6**, 671–92.

Arrow, H., McGrath, J. E. & Berdahl, J. L. (2000). *Small Groups as Complex Systems*, Newbury Park, CA: Sage.

Artman, H. (2000). Team situation assessment and information distribution. *Ergonomics*, **43**, 1111–28.

Barry, J. (2001). A new breed of soldier. *Newsweek* (December 10), 24–31.

Brehmer, B. (1992). Dynamic decision making: human control of complex systems. *Acta Psychologica*, **81**, 211–41.

Brodbeck, F. C. (1996). Criteria for the study of work group functioning. In M. A. West (Ed.), *Handbook of Work Group Psychology* (pp. 285–315). Chichester: John Wiley & Sons, Ltd.

Burke, C. S., Stagl, K. C., Salas, E. *et al.* (2006). Understanding team adaptation: a conceptual analysis and model. *Journal of Applied Psychology*, **91**, 1189–1207.

Cannon-Bowers, J. A. & Salas, E. (2001). Reflections on shared cognition. *Journal of Organizational Behavior*, **22**, 195–202.

Cannon-Bowers, J. A., Salas, E. & Converse, S. A. (1993). Shared mental models in team decision making. In N. J. Castellan, Jr. (Ed.), *Individual and Group Decision Making* (pp. 221–46). Hillsdale, NJ: Erlbaum.

Carver, C. S. & Scheier, M. F. (1981). *Attention and Self-Regulation: A Control Theory Approach to Human Behavior*, New York: Springer.

Carver, C. S. & Scheier, M. F. (1998). *On the Self-Regulation of Behavior*. New York: Cambridge.

Chan, D. (1998). Functional relations among constructs in the same content domain at different levels of analysis: a typology of composition models. *Journal of Applied Psychology*, **83**, 234–46.

Chen, G., Bliese, P. D. & Mathieu, J. E. (2005). Conceptual framework and statistical procedures for delineating and testing multilevel theories of homology. *Organizational Research Methods*, **8**, 375–409.

Chen, G. & Kanfer, R. (2006). Toward a systems theory of motivated behavior in work teams. *Research in Organizational Behavior*, **27**, 223–67.

Clancy, J. M., Elliott, G. C., Ley, T. *et al.* (2003). Command style and team performance in a dynamic decision making task. In S. Schneider & J. Shanteau (Eds), *Emerging Perspectives in Decision Research* (pp. 586–619). Cambridge: Cambridge University Press.

Cohen, S. G. & Bailey, D. E. (1997). What makes teams work: group effectiveness research from the shop floor to the executive suite. *Journal of Management*, **23**, 239–90.

Cooke, N. J., Gorman, J. C., Duran, J. L. *et al.* (2007). Team cognition in experienced command-and-control teams. *Journal of Experimental Psychology: Applied*, **13**, 146–57.

Cooke, N. J., Gorman, J. C. & Kiekel, P. A. (2008). Communication as team-level cognitive processing. In M. P. Letsky, N. W. Warner, S. M. Fiore & C. A. P. Smith (Eds), *Macrocognition in Teams: Theories and Methodologies* (pp. 51–64). Hampshire: Ashgate.

Cooke, N. J., Kiekel, P. A., Salas, E. *et al.* (2003). Measuring team knowledge: a window to the cognitive underpinnings of team performance. *Group Dynamics*, **7**, 179–99.

Cooke, N. J., Pedersen, H. K., Gorman, J. C. *et al.* (2006). Acquiring team-level command and control skill for UAV operation. In N. J. Cooke, H. Pringle, H. Pedersen & O. Connor (Eds), *Human Factors of Remotely Operated Vehicles* (pp. 287–300). Amsterdam: Elsevier.

Crown, D. F. & Rosse, J. G. (1995). Yours, mine, and ours: facilitating group productivity through the integration of individual and group goals. *Organizational Behavior and Human Decision Processes*, **64**, 138–50.

DeChurch, L. A. & Marks, M. A. (2006). Leadership in multiteam systems. *Journal of Applied Psychology*, **91**, 311–29.

DeShon, R. P., Kozlowski, S. W. J., Schmidt, A. M. *et al.* (2004). A multi-goal, multi-level model of feedback effects on the regulation of individual and team performance. *Journal of Applied Psychology*, **89**, 1035–56.

Devine, D. J., Clayton, L. D., Philips, J. L. *et al.* (1999). Teams in organizations: prevalence, characteristics, and effectiveness. *Small Group Research*, **30**, 678–711.

Diehl, E. & Sterman, J. D. (1995). Effects of feedback complexity on dynamic decision making. *Organizational Behavior and Human Decision Processes*, **62**, 198–215.

Edmondson, A. C., Roberto, M. A. & Watkins, M. D. (2003). A dynamic model of top management team effectiveness: managing unstructured task streams. *Leadership Quarterly*, **14**, 297–325.

Edwards, W. (1962). Dynamic decision theory and probabilistic information processing. *Human Factors*, **4**, 59–73.

Endsley, M. R. (1995). Measurement of situation awareness in dynamic systems. *Human Factors*, **37**, 65–84.

Endsley, M. R. & Jones, W. M. (2001). A model of inter- and intrateam situation awareness: implications for design, training and measurement. In M. McNeese, E. Salas & M. Endsley (Eds), *New Trends in Cooperative Activities: Understanding System Dynamics in Complex Environments* (pp. 46–67). Santa Monica, CA: Human Factors and Ergonomics Society.

Fahey, R. P., Rowe, A. L., Dunlap, K. L. *et al.* (1997). Synthetic Task Design I: Preliminary Cognitive Task Analysis of AWACS Weapons Director Teams. *Report for the Air Force Research Laboratory (HEJC), Brooks AFB, Texas.*

Feltz, D. L. & Lirgg, C. D. (1998). Perceived team and player efficacy in hockey. *Journal of Applied Psychology*, **83**, 557–64.

Feltz, D. L. & Lirgg, C. D. (2001). Self-efficacy beliefs of athletes, teams, and coaches. In R. N. Singer, H. A. Hausenblas & C. M. Janelle (Eds), *Handbook of Sport Psychology*, 2nd edn (pp. 340–61). New York: John Wiley & Sons, Inc.

Gonzalez, C. (2005). Decision support for real-time, dynamic decision-making tasks. *Organizational Behavior and Human Decision Processes*, **96**, 142–54.

Gonzalez, C., Thomas, R. P. & Vanyukov, P. (2005). The relationships between cognitive ability and dynamic decision making. *Intelligence*, **33**, 169–86.

Hackman, J. R. (1987). The design of work teams. In J. W. Lorsch (Ed.), *Handbook of Organizational Behavior* (pp. 315–42). Englewood Cliffs: Prentice-Hall.

Hall, E. & Gugerty, L. (1997). *Predator Operations Cognitive Task Analysis Results*, Briefing prepared by theTexas: Air Force Research Laboratory, Brooks AFB.

Harris, T. D. & Barnes-Farrell, J. L. (1997). Components of teamwork: impact on evaluation of contributions to work team effectiveness. *Journal of Applied Social Psychology*, **27**, 1694–1715.

Hedlund, J., Ilgen, D. R. & Hollenbeck, J. R. (1998). The effect of computer-mediated versus face-to-face communication on decision making in hierarchical teams. *Organizational Behavior and Human Decision Processes*, **76**, 30–47.

Helmreich R. L. & Schaefer, H. G. (1994). Team performance in the operating room. In M. S. Bogner (Ed.), *Human Error in Medicine* (pp. 225–53). Hillside: Erlbaum.

Hinsz, V. B. (1995a). Group and individual decision making for task performance goals: processes in the establishment of goals in groups. *Journal of Applied Social Psychology*, **25**, 353–70.

Hinsz, V. B. (1995b). Mental models of groups as social systems: considerations of specification and assessment. *Small Group Research*, **26**, 200–233.

Hinsz, V. B. (1999). Group decision making with responses of a quantitative nature: the theory of social decision schemes for quantities. *Organizational Behavior and Human Decision Processes*, **80**, 28–49.

Hinsz, V. B. (2001). A groups-as-information-processors perspective for technological support of intellectual teamwork. In M. D. McNeese, E. Salas & M. R. Endsley (Eds), *New Trends in Collaborative Activities: Understanding System Dynamics in Complex Settings* (pp. 22–45). Santa Monica: Human Factors & Ergonomics Society.

Hinsz, V. B. (2004). Metacognition and mental models in groups: an illustration with metamemory of group recognition memory. In E. Salas & S. M. Fiore (Eds), *Team Cognition: Understanding the Factors That Drive Process and Performance* (pp. 33–58). Washington, DC: American Psychological Association.

Hinsz, V. B., Ladbury, J. L. & Park, E. S. (2008). *Team Performance in a Simulated UAV: Combinations-of-Contributions Theory*. Presented at the 23rd annual meeting of the Society for Industrial and Organizational Psychology, San Francisco.

Hinsz, V. B. & Magnan, R. E. (2006). *Metacognition Contributes to Superior Group Performance on Cognitive Tasks*. In T. Reimer & V. B. Hinsz (Chairs). Symposium Metacognition in Groups: How Metacognitive Beliefs Facilitate Group Interaction and Performance at the Annual Meeting of the Society for Personality and Social Psychology, Palm Springs, CA.

Hinsz, V. B., Tindale, R. S. & Nagao, D. H. (2008). The accentuation of information processes and biases in group judgments integrating base-rate and case-specific information. *Journal of Experimental Social Psychology*, **44**, 116–26.

Hinsz, V. B., Tindale, R. S. & Vollrath, D. A. (1997). The emerging conceptualization of groups as information processors. *Psychological Bulletin*, **121**, 43–64.

Hinsz, V. B. & Wallace, D. M. (in press). Comparing individual and team judgment accuracy for target identification under heavy cognitive demand. In D. H. Andrews & T. Hull (Eds), *Human Factors Issues in Combat Identification*. Hampshire: Ashgate.

Hirokowa, R. Y., DeGroyer, D. & Vaide, K. (2007). Characteristics of effective health care teams. In R. Y. Hirokowa, R. S. Cathcart, L. A. Samovar & L. D. Henman (Eds), *Small Group Communication: Theory and Practice*, 8th edn (pp. 148–57). New York: Oxford University Press.

Hitt, M. A., Beamish, P. W., Jackson, S. E. *et al.* (2007). Building theoretical and empirical bridges across levels: multilevel research in management. *Academy of Management Journal*, **50**, 1385–99.

Hollenbeck, J. R., Ilgen, D. R., Sego, D. J. *et al.* (1995). Multilevel theory of team decision-making: decision performance in teams incorporating distributed expertise. *Journal of Applied Psychology*, **80**, 292–316.

Hollenbeck, J. R., Moon, H., Illis, A. P. J. *et al.* (2002). Structural contingency theory and individual differences: examination of external and internal person-fit. *Journal of Applied Psychology*, **87**, 599–606.

Humphrey, S. E., Hollenbeck, J. R., Ilgen, D. R. *et al.* (2004). The changing shape of large-scale programs of research: the MSU-DDD as an illustrative example. In S. G. Schiflett, L. R. Elliott, E. Salas & M. D. Coovert (Eds), *Scaled Worlds: Development, Validation, and Applications* (pp. 220–39). Hampshire: Ashgate.

Ilgen, D. R., Major, D. A., Hollenbeck, J. R. *et al.* (1995). Decision making in teams: raising an individual decision making model to the team level. In R. Guzzo & E. Salas (Eds), *Team Decision Making in Organizations* (pp. 113–48). San Francisco: Jossey-Bass.

Ilgen, D. R., Hollenbeck, J. R., Johnson, M. *et al.* (2005). Teams in organizations: from input-process-output models to IMOI models. *Annual Review of Psychology*, **56**, 517–43.

Judge, W. Q. & Miller, A. (1991). Antecedents and outcomes of decision speed in different environmental contexts. *Academy of Management Journal*, **34**, 449–63.

Kanfer, R. (1992). Work motivation: new directions in theory and research. In C. L. Cooper & I. T. Robertson (Eds), *International Review of Industrial and Organizational Psychology*, Vol. 7 (pp. 1–53). London: John Wiley & Sons, Ltd.

Karau, S. J. & Kelly, J. R. (1992). The effects of time scarcity and time abundance on group performance quality and interaction process. *Journal of Experimental Social Psychology*, **28**, 542–71.

Karoly, P. (1993). Mechanisms of self-regulation: a systems view. *Annual Review of Psychology*, **44**, 23–52.

Kelly, J. R. & Karau, S. J. (1999). Group decision making: the effects of initial preferences and time pressure. *Personality and Social Psychology Bulletin*, 25, 1342–54.

Kelly, J. R. & Loving, T. J. (2004). Time pressure and group performance: exploring underlying processes in the attentional focus model. *Journal of Experimental Social Psychology*, 40, 185–98.

Kerr, N. & Tindale, R. S. (2004). Group performance and decision making. *Annual Review of Psychology*, 55, 623–55.

Klein, H. J. (1989). An integrated control theory model of work motivation. *Academy of Management Review*, 14, 150–72.

Klein, K. J. & Kozlowski, S. W. J. (2000). *Multilevel Theory, Research, and Methods in Organizations: Foundations, Extensions, and New Directions*, San Francisco: Jossey-Bass.

Klimoski, R. & Mohammed, S. (1994). Team mental model: construct or metaphor? *Journal of Management*, 20, 403–37.

Kozlowski, S. W. J. & Bell, B. S. (2003). Work groups and teams in organizations. In W. C. Borman, D. R. Ilgen & R. J. Klimoski (Eds), *Handbook of Psychology: Industrial and Organizational Psychology*, Vol. 12 (pp. 333–75). London: John Wiley & Sons, Ltd.

Kozlowski, S. W. J., Gully, S. M., Nason, E. R. *et al.* (1999). Developing adaptive teams: a theory of compilation and performance across levels and time. In D. R. Ilgen & E. D. Pulakos (Eds), *The Changing Nature of Performance: Implications for Staffing, Motivation, and Development* (pp. 240–92). San Francisco: Jossey-Bass.

Kozlowski, S. W. J. & Ilgen, D. R. (2006). Enhancing the effectiveness of work groups and teams. *Psychological Science in the Public Interest*, 7, 77–124.

Kozlowski, S. W. J., Toney, R. J., Mullins, M. E. *et al.* (2001). Developing adaptability: a theory for the design of integrated-embedded training systems. *Advances in Human Performance and Cognitive Engineering Research*, 1, 59–122.

Ladbury, J. L., Hinsz, V. B. & Park, E. S. (2007). *Combining Individual Efforts into Team Execution: The Effect of Multiple Team Members' Spatial Ability on Performance in an Interdependent Task*. Presented at the meeting of the Society for Personality and Social Psychology, Memphis, TN.

Langan-Fox, J., Code, S. & Langfield-Smith, K. (2000). Team mental models: techniques, methods, and analytic approaches. *Human Factors*, 42, 242–71.

Laughlin, P. R. & Hollingshead, A. B. (1995). A theory of collective induction. *Organizational Behavior and Human Decision Processes*, 61, 94–107.

Letsky M. P., Warner N. W., Fiore S. M. *et al.* (2008). *Macrocognition in Teams: Theories and Methodologies*, Hampshire: Ashgate.

Levine, S. (1998). *Getting to Resolution: Turning Conflict into Collaboration*, San Francisco: Berret-Koehler.

Levine, J. M. & Choi, H. S. (2004). Impact of personnel turnover on team performance and cognition. In E. Salas & S. M. Fiore (Eds), *Team Cognition: Understanding the Factors That Drive Process and Performance* (pp. 153–177). Washington, DC: American Psychological Association.

Locke, E. A. & Latham, G. P. (2002). Building a practically useful theory of goal setting and task motivation. *American Psychologist*, 57, 705–17.

Lord, R. G. & Kernan, M. C. (1989). Application of control theory to work settings. In W. A. Herschberger (Ed.), *Volitional Action* (pp. 493–514). Amsterdam: Elsevier.

Majchrzak, A., Jarvenpaa, S. L. & Hollingshead, A. B. (2007). Coordinating expertise among emergent groups responding to disasters. *Organization Science*, 18, 147–61.

Marks, M. A., DeChurch, L. A., Mathieu, J. E. *et al.* (2005). Teamwork in multiteam systems. *Journal of Applied Psychology*, 90, 964–71.

Marks, M. A., Mathieu, J. E. & Zaccaro, S. J. (2001). A temporally based framework and taxonomy of team processes. *Academy of Management Review*, 26, 356–76.

Marks, M. A., Mathieu, J. E. & Zaccaro, S. J. (2004). Using scaled worlds to study multi-team systems. In S. G. Schiflett, L. R., Elliott, E. Salas & M. D. Coovert (Eds), *Scaled Worlds: Development, Validation, and Applications* (pp. 279–96). Hampshire: Ashgate.

Marks, M. A., Sabella, M. J., Burke, C. S. *et al.* (2002). The impact of cross-training on team effectiveness. *Journal of Applied Psychology*, 87, 3–13.

Mathieu, J. E., Heffner, T. S., Goodwin, G. F. *et al.* (2000). The influence of shared mental models on team process and performance. *Journal of Applied Psychology*, 85, 273–83.

Mathieu, J. E., Marks, M. A. & Zaccaro, S. J. (2001). Multiteam systems. In N. Anderson, D. S. Ones, H. K. Sinagil & C. Viswesvaran (Eds), *Handbook of Industrial, Work, and Organizational Psychology – Volume 2: Organizational Psychology* (pp. 289–313). Thousand Oaks, CA: Sage.

McGrath, J. E. & Argote, L. (2001). Group processes in organizational contexts. In M. Hogg & R. S. Tindale (Eds), *Blackwell's Handbook of Social Psychology, Vol. 3 Group Processes* (pp. 603–27). London: Blackwell.

McNeese, M. D., Salas, E. & Endsley M. R. (2001). *New Trends in Collaborative Activities: Understanding System Dynamics in Complex Settings*, Santa Monica, CA: Human Factors & Ergonomics Society.

Meier, B. P. & Hinsz, V. B. (2004). A comparison of human aggression committed by groups and individuals: an interindividual-intergroup discontinuity. *Journal of Experimental Social Psychology*, 40, 551–59.

Mitchell, T. R. & Silver, W. S. (1990). Individual and group goals when workers are interdependent: effects on task strategies and performance. *Journal of Applied Psychology*, 75, 185–93.

Moon, H., Hollenbeck, J., Humphrey, S. *et al.* (2004). Asymmetric adaptability: dynamic team structures as one-way streets. *Academy of Management Journal*, 47 (5), 681–95.

Mullen, B. (1987). Self-attention theory: the effects of group composition on the individual. In B. Mullen & G. Goethals (Eds), *Theories of Group Behavior* (pp. 125–46). New York: Springer.

Myers, N. D., Feltz, D. L. & Short, S. E. (2004). Collective efficacy and team performance: a longitudinal study of collegiate football teams. *Group Dynamics*, 8, 126–38.

O'Leary-Kelly, A. M., Martocchio, J. J. & Frink, D. D. (1994). A review of the influence of group goals on group performance. *Academy of Management Journal*, 37, 1285–1301.

Omodei, M., Taranto, P. & Wearing, A. (1999). *Networked Fire Chief* (Version 1.4) [Computer Program]: LaTrobe University.

Paich, M. & Sterman, J. D. (1993). Boom, bust, and failures to learn in experimental markets. *Management Science*, 39, 1439–58.

Park, E. S., Hinsz, V. B. & Ladbury, J. L. (2006). Enhancing coordination and collaboration in remotely operated vehicle (ROV) teams. In N. J. Cooke, H. Pringle, H. Pederson & O. Connor (Eds), *Human Factors of Remotely Operated Vehicles* (pp. 301–12). Amsterdam: Elsevier.

Porter, C. O., Hollenbeck, J. R., Ilgen, D. R. *et al.* (2003). Backing up behaviors in teams: the role of personality and legitimacy of need. *Journal of Applied Psychology*, 88, 391–403.

Powers, W. T. (1973). Feedback: beyond behaviorism. *Science*, 179, 351–56.

Qudrat-Ullah, H. (2007). Debriefing can reduce misperceptions of feedback: the case of renewable resource management. *Simulation & Gaming*, 38, 382–97.

Rasmussen, J., Pejtersen, A. M. & Goodstein, L. P. (1994). *Cognitive Systems Engineering*, New York: John Wiley & Sons, Inc.

Reimer, T., Park, E. S. & Hinsz, V. B. (2006). Shared and coordinated cognition in competitive and dynamic task environments: an information-processing perspective for team sports. *International Journal of Sport and Exercise Psychology*, 4, 376–400.

Rentsch, J. R. & Hall, R. J. (1994). Members of great teams think alike: a model of team effectiveness and schema similarity among team members. *Advances in Interdisciplinary Studies of Work Teams*, 1, 223–61.

Rico, R., Sanchez-Manzanares, M., Gil, F. *et al.* (2008). Team implicit coordination processes: a team knowledge-based approach. *Academy of Management Review*, 33, 163–84.

Robinson, S. & Weldon, E. (1993). Feedback seeking in groups: a theoretical perspective. *British Journal of Social Psychology*, 32, 71–86.

Saavedra, R., Earley, P. C. & Van Dyne, L. (1993). Complex interdependence in task-performing groups. *Journal of Applied Psychology*, 78, 61–72.

Salas, E. & Fiore, S. M. (2004). *Team Cognition: Understanding the Factors That Drive Process and Performance*, Washington, DC: American Psychological Association.

Schiflett, S. G., Elliott, L. R., Salas, E. *et al.* (2004). *Scaled Worlds: Development, Validation, and Applications*, Hampshire: Ashgate.

Shebilske, W. L., Jordan, J. A., Goettl, B. P. *et al.* (1999). Cognitive and social influences in training teams for complex skills. *Journal of Experimental Psychology: Applied*, 5, 227–49.

Shebilske, W. L., Levchuk, G. & Freeman, F. (in press). Team training paradigm for better combat identification. In D. H. Andrews & T. Hull (Eds), *Human Factors Issues in Combat Identification* Hampshire: Ashgate.

Shepperd, J. A. (1993). Productivity loss in performance groups: a motivation analysis. *Psychological Bulletin*, 113, 67–81.

Sherif, M. (1958). Superordinate goals in the reduction of intergroup conflict. *American Journal of Sociology*, 43, 349–56.

Steiner, I. D. (1972). *Group process and Productivity*, New York: Academic Press.

Stout, R. J., Cannon-Bowers, J. A. & Salas, E. (1996). The role of shared mental models in developing team situation awareness: implications for training. *Training Research Journal*, 2, 85–116.

Stout, R. J., Cannon-Bowers, J. A., Salas, E. *et al.* (1999). Planning, shared mental models, and coordinated performance: an empirical link is established. *Human Factors*, 41, 61–71.

Tajfel, H. & Turner, J. C. (1979). An integrative theory of intergroup conflict. In W. G. Austin & S. Worchel (Eds), *The Social Psychology of Intergroup Relations* (pp. 33–47). Monterey, CA: Brooks Cole.

Tindale, R. S., Kameda, T. & Hinsz, V. B. (2003). Group decision making. In M. A. Hogg & J. Cooper (Eds), *Sage Handbook of Social Psychology* (pp. 381–403). London: Sage.

Tschan, F., Semmer, N. K., Gautschi, D. *et al.* (2006). Leading to recovery: group performance and coordinating activities in Medical Emergency Driven Groups. *Human Performance*, 19, 277–304.

Tschan, F., Semmer, N., Bizzari, L. *et al.* (2008). Diagnostic Errors in Medical Emergency Driven Teams. Paper presented at the 3rd annual meeting of the Interdisciplinary Network for Group Research (INGRoup), Kansas City, MO.

Turner, J. C. (1991). *Social Influence*, Belmont, CA: Brooks/Cole.

Unmanned Aircraft Systems Roadmap (2005). *Unmanned Aircraft Systems (UAS) Roadmap 2005–2030*. Downloaded from http://www.uavforum.com/library/uav_roadmap_2005.pdf on 25August 2006.

Useem, M., Cook, J. & Sutton, L. (2005). Developing leaders for decision making under stress: Wildland firefighters in the South Canyon Fire and its aftermath. *Academy of Management Learning & Education*, 4, 461–85.

Vroom, V. H. (1969). Industrial social psychology. In G. Lindzey & E. Aronson (Eds), *Handbook of Social Psychology*, 2nd edn, Vol. 5 (pp. 227–40). Reading, MA: Addison-Wesley.

Wallace, D. M. & Hinsz, V. B. (in press). Teams as technology: applying theory and research to model macrocognition processes in teams. *Theoretical Issues in Ergonomic Science*.

Walsh, J. P. (1995). Managerial and organizational cognition: notes from a trip down memory lane. *Organization Science*, 6, 280–321.

Weldon, E. & Weingart, L. R. (1993). Group goals and group performance. *British Journal of Social Psychology*, 32, 307–34.

Wickens, C. D. (1992). *Engineering Psychology and Human Performance*, 2nd edn, New York: HarperCollins.

Wildschut, T., Pinter, B., Vevea, J. L. *et al.* (2003). Beyond the group mind: a quantitative review of the interindividual-intergroup discontinuity effect. *Psychological Bulletin*, 129, 698–722.

Wittenbaum, G. M., Hollingshead, A. B. & Botero, I. C. (2004). From cooperative to motivated information sharing in groups: moving beyond the hidden profile paradigm. *Communication Monographs*, 71, 286–310.

Wittenbaum, G. M., Merry, C. J. & Stasser, G. (1996). Tacit coordination in anticipation of small group task completion. *Journal of Experimental Social Psychology*, 32, 129–52.

Worchel, S. (1986). The role of cooperation in reducing intergroup conflict. In S. Worchel & W. G. Austin (Eds), *Psychology of Intergroup Relations* (pp. 288–304). Chicago: Nelson-Hall.

Worchel, S. & Austin, W. G. (1986). *Psychology of Intergroup Relations*, Chicago: Nelson-Hall.

Zander, A. (1971). *Motives and Goals in Groups*, New York: Academic Press.

Zsambok, C. E. & Klein, G. A. (1997). *Naturalistic Decision Making*, Mahwah: Erlbaum.

Chapter 7

CLARIFYING THE NOTION OF SELF-REGULATION IN ORGANIZATIONAL BEHAVIOR

Richard P. DeShon and Tara A. Rench

Department of Psychology, Michigan State University, E. Lansing, MI, USA

An individual's behavior in an organizational setting is a highly complex, dynamic phenomenon. Performing a single task typically requires a large set of skilled actions that must be appropriately sequenced to yield the desired results. Organization members invariably have multiple, often conflicting, task responsibilities that must be prioritized, acted upon in appropriate sequences, and monitored. Task interruptions are common in organizational settings and so the prioritization of responsibilities and the sequencing of actions to meet the task demands must be robust. Timely, unambiguous feedback that may be used to evaluate the effectiveness of the undertaken actions is difficult, if not impossible, to acquire. If novel tasks or obstacles to task performance are encountered then creative problem solving may be required to develop new action sequences. This process is made even more challenging by the need to coordinate one's own actions with the actions of other organizational members on tasks that are optimally performed through role specialization and teamwork. Finally, the organizational environment in which the sequenced, coordinated actions occur is often in a state of flux requiring constant monitoring and rapid adaptation of priorities and actions. The deceptively simple sounding term 'job' that is used to describe this phenomenon obscures layers upon layers of behavioral complexity.

Self-regulatory models are an increasingly common approach used to study the complexities of organizational behavior. Although the self-regulatory perspective is relatively new to organizational psychology, Kanfer (1992, 2005) highlights that self-regulation theories and models have rapidly become a central focus of the organizational motivation literature. Despite its newcomer

International Review of Industrial and Organizational Psychology, 2009, Volume 24.
Edited by G. P. Hodgkinson and J. K. Ford. Copyright © 2009 John Wiley & Sons, Ltd

status in organizational explanations of behavior, the notion of self-regulation has a long and rich history in both philosophical and psychological investigations of willpower and volition (Ach, 1910; Lewin et al., 1944), goal-oriented behavior (James, 1890, 1899), and Freud's (1920; beyond the pleasure principle) concept of the Ego. Self-regulation concepts have been studied under many different names (e.g. self-regulation, self-control, self-direction, self-discipline, volition, agency, self-determination, purposiveness, autonomy, independence, self-management, and willpower) and from many different theoretical perspectives. At their core, however, self-regulation models associate the cause of behavior with factors that are internal to the individual and, as such, they are the antithesis of the behaviorist approach that was common in the 1950s and 1960s.

Vancouver (2000) provided an excellent review of self-regulatory models and their relevance to theories of behavior in organizational settings. We use Vancouver's review as a starting point for our review and assume that the reader is either familiar with Vancouver's review or at least has a passing familiarity with a variety of self-regulatory models. The developmental history of the construct is also well reviewed by Vancouver and so we limit our treatment of this important topic. We use the freedom provided by prior work to focus instead on issues that have not yet received adequate treatment. Specifically, we focus on how self-regulatory models function when the individual has multiple, potentially conflicting, goals that are pursued in dynamic environments that require flexibility and robustness.

Our purpose here is to review the varied conceptualizations of self-regulation that exist in the general and organizational psychology literatures, to identify the core features of the various conceptualizations, to highlight similarities and differences between the conceptualizations of self-regulation with a focus on multiple goals and dynamics, and finally to provide a road map for possible theoretical and empirical directions that may be taken to improve the usefulness of the self-regulation construct. The organization of the chapter is as follows. We first provide a review of a representative sample of self-regulatory definitions. We use the commonalities and idiosyncrasies identified in this review to then provide a structure for further evaluating models of the self-regulatory process. Next, we present the results of an empirical study on the dynamics of multiple goal regulation. We use the results of the study to provide a concrete base from which to evaluate the self-regulatory models with respect to multiple goals, dynamics, and flexibility. Finally, we summarize the results of our investigation and attempt to provide a road map for improving the modeling of self-regulatory processes.

SELF-REGULATORY DEFINITIONS

We begin by reviewing a representative set of self-regulation definitions provided by various self-regulatory researchers and theoreticians. Taken together, the definitions represent how the self-regulatory process is conceived and provide structure for our subsequent investigations. Table 7.1 presents a chronologically organized sample of representative self-regulation definitions. As can be quickly seen, self-regulation has been discussed from several perspectives, with Vancouver (2000) suggesting that 'researchers each tend to take their own approach and the number of definitions cumulate as a function of the number of researchers' (p. 304). While there is truth to Vancouver's view on the proliferation of self-regulatory perspectives and definitions, this apparent chaos may reflect a healthy developmental process as various perspectives are proposed, evaluated, and modified or discarded.

From a macro perspective, three approaches to self-regulation appear to underlie the variety of self-regulatory definitions in Table 7.1. First, a set of definitions identify self-regulation as the portion of the motivational system that is responsible for translating goals into actions (e.g. Binswanger, 1991; Heatherton and Baumeister, 1996; Kanfer, 1992). A second set of definitions view self-regulation as a heuristic or umbrella term used to describe a conglomeration of motivational processes involved in goal-directed action (e.g. Cervone et al., 2006; Matthews et al., 2000). Finally, at the far end of the spectrum, the perspectives espoused by authors such as Karoly (1993) and Zeidner, Boekaerts and Pintrich (2000) appear to fully encompass the motivational process within the bounds of self-regulation. From this perspective, self-regulation is not simply a process model of motivation, but rather a meta-theory or paradigm for thinking about motivation. Contrasting this last approach to the two other approaches highlights that some authors view self-regulation as a component of the motivational process whereas others appear to view self-regulation as a particular paradigm or research perspective on the concept of motivation itself. Although we find the first approach to be more intellectually satisfying due to its restricted focus, the third perspective emphasizes a dynamic approach to the study of motivation and, as such, has value.

The various conceptualizations represented in Table 7.1, each share the two core concepts of goals and actions. Individuals are thought to possess goals and use actions or behaviors to achieve or maintain the goal states. The plurality of goals is critically important and yet is ill-specified in the majority of perspectives. What are the structure of the goals and the nature of goal pursuits? Are all goals equally important, valenced, or motivating? Can the individual satisfy all goals simultaneously through action or must there be a sequencing or prioritization mechanism? Only a select few approaches refer to a process for prioritizing or selecting a goal or subset of goals for action from the available set of goals that compete for attention and action (e.g. Gollwitzer and Bayer, 1999; Karoly, 1993). Once a goal is selected for pursuit, how are actions selected to achieve or maintain the selected goal? How rigid is the goal pursuit? For instance, Kuhl (1985) viewed self-regulation as the process of protecting current intentions should some other action tendency become salient before the current action is completed. Similarly, it is surprising to find that, unlike the goal construct (e.g. Austin and Vancouver, 1996), the notion of

Table 7.1   Definitions of self-regulation

Source	Definition
Brief and Hollenbeck (1985)	Self-regulation defined in terms of three activities: goal setting, self-monitoring, and self-rewarding/self-punishing contingent upon the magnitude of the discrepancy between the person's behavior and the goal
Kuhl (1985)	Processes which protect a current intention from being replaced should one of the competing tendencies increase in strength before the intended action is completed
Kanfer (1990)	Once a goal is chosen [self-regulatory] processes guide the allocation of time and effort across covert and overt activities directed toward attaining the goal
Bandura (1991)	In social cognitive theory human behavior is extensively motivated and regulated by the ongoing exercise of self-influence. The major self-regulative mechanism operates through three principal subfunctions. These include self-monitoring of one's behavior, its determinants, and its effects; judgment of one's behavior in relation to personal standards and environmental circumstances; and affective self-reaction
Binswanger (1991)	Self-regulation, regulation by the entity itself, means that something within the entity controls its action in a manner appropriate to goal attainment
Kanfer (1992)	Self-regulation and volitional activities pertain to the portion of the motivational system through which persons translate goals into action
Karoly (1993)	Self-regulation as voluntary action management; refers to those processes, internal and/or transactional, that enable an individual to guide his/her goal-directed activities over time and across changing circumstances (contexts). Regulation implies modulation of thought, affect, behavior, or attention via deliberate or automated use of specific mechanisms and supportive metaskills. The processes of self-regulation are initiated when routinized activity is impeded or when goal directedness is otherwise made salient (e.g. the appearance of a challenge, the failure of habitual action patterns and so on). Self-regulation may be said to encompass up to five interrelated and iterative component phases: (1) goal selection, (2) goal cognition, (3) directional maintenance, (4) directional change or reprioritization, and (5) goal termination
Heatherton and Baumeister (1996)	Self-regulation refers to the process by which people initiate, adjust, interrupt, terminate, or otherwise alter actions to promote attainment of personal goals, plans, or standards
Gollwitzer and Bayer (1999)	Self-regulatory processes consist of four phases: predecisional (choice between alternatives), preactional (implementation intentions), actional (bringing goal direct actions to a successful end), and postactional (evaluation as to whether further action is necessary)
Matthews et al. (2000)	Self-regulation is a 'generic umbrella term for the set of processes and behaviors that support the pursuit of personal goals within a changing external environment'

Table 7.1   (*Continued*)

Source	Definition
Vancouver (2000)	In general, regulation refers to keeping something regular; to maintaining a variable at some value despite disturbances to the variable. . . . To achieve or maintain a goal, the system must be able to act to affect its environment (i.e., goal-direction behavior)
Zeidner, Boekaerts and Pintrich (2000)	Self-regulation is currently seen as involving a number of integrated microprocesses, including goal setting, strategic planning, use of effective strategies to organize, code and store information, monitoring and metacognition, action and volitional control, managing time effectively, self-motivational beliefs (self-efficacy, outcome expectations, intrinsic interest and goal orientation, and so on), evaluation and self-reflection, experiencing pride and satisfaction with one's efforts, and establishing a congenial environment
Peterson and Seligman (2004)	Self-regulation refers to how a person exerts control over his or her own responses so as to pursue goals and live up to standards. These responses include thoughts, emotions, impulses, performances, and other behaviors. The standards include ideals, moral injunctions, norms, performance targets, and the expectations of other people
Karoly, Boekaerts and Maes (2005)	A goal-guided process, occurring in iterative phases, that requires the self-reflective implementation of various change and maintenance mechanisms that are aimed at task- and time-specific outcomes
Vancouver and Day (2005)	Self-regulation refers to the processes involved in attaining and maintaining (i.e. keeping regular) goals, where goals are internally represented (i.e. within the self) desired states. The key self-regulation processes . . . include goal establishment (i.e. processes involved in adopting, adapting, or rejecting a goal), planning (i.e. processes involved in preparing to pursue a goal), striving (i.e. processes involved in moving toward or maintaining a goal), and revision (processes involved in the possible change or disengagement from a goal)
Porath and Bateman (2006)	Processes that enable an individual to guide his or her goal-directed activities over time and across changing circumstances, including the modulation of thought, affect and behavior

action has received little theoretical attention in self-regulatory theories. What is an action? How can one tell when a given action ends and another begins? At what level of analysis are actions selected to achieve goals? Can the individual simply chop vegetables to make dinner or does every motion in the chopping process need to be selected, monitored, and controlled?

Another difference among the self-regulatory definitions concerns the distinction between goal setting and goal-striving processes. Lewin (e.g. Lewin *et al.*, 1944) was among the first to recognize the qualitative differences between goal setting and goal striving in the motivational process. More recently,

Gollwitzer (1990) and Austin and Vancouver (1996) have provided useful descriptive stage models of the motivational process. According to Gollwitzer, different 'mind-sets' are required to support deliberative, implemental, actional, and evaluative phases of goal pursuits. For our purposes, the key distinction is between the deliberative stage, where various goals are weighted and compared and a choice is made about what goal to pursue in a given context at a given time point, versus the implemental and actional stages, where actions are selected and implemented to strive toward the chosen goal. Similarly, Karoly (1993) highlighted that self-regulatory models can be characterized in terms of those that address off-line preparation for action through goal selection processes and those that address on-line goal pursuit through goal-striving mechanisms. With respect to the self-regulatory definitions, the majority of self-regulatory perspectives we identified emphasize the implemental and actional aspects (i.e. goal-striving stages) of motivation and pay less attention to the deliberative or goal choice stage. As we highlight later, this distinction is critical to understanding the notion of self-regulation and how self-regulation fits within the broader construct of motivation.

Implicit in the majority of the self-regulation definitions is the notion of the individual's knowledge of internal states, goal levels associated with the internal states, and presumably discrepancies between the internal states and the respective goal levels. This notion is made most explicit by those definitions that explicitly incorporate the notion of monitoring (e.g. Bandura, 1991; Brief and Hollenbeck, 1985; Zeidner, Boekaerts and Pintrich, 2000). Interestingly, not as much attention is given to the ability to perceive the environment or obtain knowledge of the environment that is relevant to the internal states. This issue is highly related to the notion of feedback or knowledge of results described next.

There is a conspicuous absence of the feedback construct in these definitions. Perhaps due to the influence of control theory, the notion of feedback has become strongly associated with self-regulation and Vancouver and Day (2005) list feedback as a core construct in the self-regulatory process. However, our review of the feedback definitions does not highlight a central position for feedback in the construct of self-regulation. In fact, a feedback process is unnecessary if the individual has knowledge of internal states, the ability to perceive goal-relevant aspects of the environment, and the ability to learn associations between actions and changes in the environment. To function in an environment, the individual must be able to perceive goal-relevant objects or aspects of the environment. If an individual can perceive the environment then the individual can perceive change in the environment (assuming a memory system). If changes in the environment can be associated with the undertaken actions then a formal feedback process is not needed. This distinction may be simply a case of semantics or it may turn out to be more profound.

The idiosyncrasies represented in the presented definitions are as interesting and potentially as informative as the commonalities. One interesting source of disagreement occurs with respect to what is regulated. According to authors such as Binswanger (1991), Baumeister and Heatherton (1996) and Peterson and Seligman (2004), actions are regulated or controlled to yield desired states. Karoly (1993) takes a more general approach and views 'thought, affect, behavior, or attention' as being regulated. Vancouver and Day (2005) emphasize the importance of maintaining or regulating goals. Vancouver (2000) and Vohs and Baumeister (2004) view the self as the target of self-regulation such that self-regulation refers to control over oneself. A different source of implicit disagreement deals with the role of the environment in the regulatory process. Karoly (1993), Vancouver (2000) and Matthews *et al.* (2000) each highlight the importance of adapting to environmental dynamics whereas other authors focus much more on the internally driven process of achieving self-set goals with little attention paid to the impact of environmental dynamics on behavior. Kuhl (1985) goes even further and focuses on maintaining the current action despite potentially important changes in the environment. Finally, Karoly, Boekaerts and Maes (2005) are unique in recognizing the time component of goal pursuits with deadlines.

SELF-REGULATORY MODEL EVALUATION

Based on our review of the self-regulatory definitions a number of themes, relevant to our purpose, are clear. The perspectives all include the notion of multiple goals but few attend to the complexity of prioritizing goals. Much less attention is paid to the flexible adaptation of behavior to both environmental and internal dynamics. We next shift our attention to existing models of the self-regulatory process and how these models incorporate the pursuit of multiple goals in dynamic environments. Numerous models of the self-regulation process now exist. To structure our review we provide two thought frameworks. First, we highlight four questions that we feel must be addressed in any model of self-regulation and we structure our review in terms of these questions. Second, we present the results of a small data collection where human participants engaged in multiple goal, self-regulation on a simple task. The concrete nature of the regulatory task and the resulting behavioral data provide a conceptual anvil upon which the details of the various models may be hammered out. Finally, we attempt to address the questions using the information gleaned from the review, our data collection, and our own beliefs about the self-regulatory process.

Self-Regulatory Questions

Scholarly work on the process of theorizing and theory development highlights that a critical step in the process is posing questions and using theory and models to perform thought experiments to explore possible answers to the questions (e.g. Dubin, 1978; Weick, 1989). Poole and Van de Ven (1989) further point out that the inconsistencies and contradictions between theories provide opportunities to develop better theoretical representations of the focal process. Posing critical questions and exploring the answers provided by different explanations of the self-regulatory process is a useful way to highlight differences and tensions between the various explanations. To this end, we next present a set of questions that we believe, if answered, would help structure both self-regulatory thinking and research.

Question 1: What is Regulated?

As we highlighted above, there is ambiguity concerning the target or focus of self-regulatory actions. Possible candidates are action, behavior, emotion, cognition, discrepancies, goals, and the self. Additional foci will become apparent when we review the self-regulatory models. At this stage of theoretical development it is not surprising to see such disagreement or at least ambiguity concerning the focus of self-regulatory efforts. However, this issue is fundamental to models of self-regulation and it is our hope that highlighting the variety of perspectives will lead to theoretical developments that converge to a common perspective over time.

Question 2: How does the Model Incorporate the Existence of Multiple Goals?

This question addresses the cognitive representation of the goals (e.g. fuzzy vs. numeric), the structure of the goals (e.g. queue vs. hierarchical), and the goal prioritization mechanisms (e.g. choice, salience, activation, and so on). It is commonly assumed that an individual has limited capacity to pursue multiple goals simultaneously while maintaining behavioral coherence (cf. DeShon and Gillespie, 2005). If so, there must be some mechanism for prioritizing goals, resolving goal conflicts, or selecting which among the multitude of goals to strive for at any given time point.

Question 3: How does the Regulation Occur?

In other words, what does the individual do to accomplish the regulation? Given the common focus on action highlighted in the definitions above it is clear that the simple answer to this question might be that appropriate actions are undertaken. A more promising response would focus on the dynamics of action selection mechanisms and address the fundamental question of action selection dealing with what to do next to best accomplish the individual's multiplicity of goals. The critical issues for this question deal with the association between goals and actions, the action selection mechanism, and the level of abstraction at which actions are selected.

Question 4: How does the Individual Flexibly Respond to both Internal and External Dynamics?

Here, the focus is on finding a balance between (1) protecting or shielding current goal pursuits so that behavioral dithering between competing goals does not occur, with (2) flexibly responding to changes in internal states or goal-relevant changes in the environment so that opportunities are not missed or that the individual pursues a given goal at the expense of other goals. Imagine the behavioral chaos that would ensue if small changes in environmental stimuli or internal states resulted in substantial alterations in the course of an individual's actions. Unless a mechanism or process prevents behavioral dithering an individual would rapidly oscillate between actions targeted at several goals and, in the end, fail to satisfy any of them.

Self-Regulatory Data Collection

As highlighted above in the review of definitions, there are key components that are shared by virtually all self-regulatory perspectives including multiple goals, perceptions of current states, and actions that may be taken to obtain or maintain current states relative to the goal states. To aid the review and evaluation of the various self-regulatory models, we developed a simple multiple goal task that could be used to collect data from actual individuals engaged in multiple goal regulation. This is a simpler variant of the scheduling task used in Schmidt and DeShon (2007). The individuals were provided with two states of being represented by status bars. In this data collection the two internal states were presented as thirst and hunger. Cross lines on the status bars represented the goal level or threshold for the internal states and were set at 75% for both states. The color of the status bar was green if the current state was above the hunger or thirst threshold and red if it was below. Both states decreased at the same constant rate over time representing internal dynamics. In other words, in the absence of food and water the individual becomes increasingly hungry and thirsty over time. Similar arguments could be made for organizationally relevant psychological variables such as recognition, pay, or trust and task-relevant variables such as production rates, inventory, and delivery logistics. For each trial, two objects representing food and water resources appeared in a random distribution in the environment pane. A cursor (crosshatch) represented the individual's position in the environment and each trial began with the cursor located in the center of the screen. Individuals could perform three actions based on their perceptions of the internal state dynamics and their perception of the environmental dynamics (i.e., relative position of food and water objects over trials). On any given trial, the individual could move the cursor using the keyboard arrow keys to acquire the object representing either food or water (two actions). Alternatively, if both states were above their respective thresholds, the individual could press the space bar to do nothing thus mimicking inactivity or resting. The hunger and thirst states continued to decline at the same rate over the simulated resting period of 10 s. Participants were informed about the nature of the task (e.g. decay of states over time and hunger and thirst thresholds) and instructed on the three possible actions that could be undertaken but no further descriptions were provided on how participants should direct their actions.

Nine participants completed 200 trials of the task and the results of their dynamic action selection decisions are presented next. A standard model, such as a multinomial logistic regression or a discrete choice model, could be fit to the participants' data in either pooled or unpooled forms. As Schmidt and DeShon (2007) found, the model would certainly show that the respective magnitude of the discrepancies between the current states and the goal states was related to goal choice. This is informative but we believe that even more informative results are obtained by focusing on the pattern of action choices over time within and across participants. Figure 7.1 presents the thirst and hunger state discrepancies, with respect to the goal thresholds, maintained by each of the nine participants over the 200 trials of the task. The solid red line in each graph represents the zero discrepancy baseline. A number of important self-regulatory issues become immediately apparent upon viewing these performance graphs. First, there are substantial between-participant differences in the pattern of self-regulatory activity. Second, and equally important, there is substantial within-participant consistency in the self-regulatory efforts over time and goals. For instance, comparing participants 1 and 8 suggests that both participants were consistently different in their self-regulatory efforts. Participant 8 maintained high levels of satiation that were consistently above the goal levels on both states and did so with very little variance in this process over time. Participant 1, on the other hand, also maintained the goal satiation levels consistently above the goal levels but did so with a much higher variance. In other words, participant 8 applied much stricter control to the maintenance of the hunger and thirst states than did participant 1. Neither participant regulated the hunger and thirst states around the goal level but, instead, maintained the states well above the goal levels after the initial phase of task learning occurred. Conversely, participant 7 strove to maintain the hunger and thirst states around the goal levels. As discussed in the following sections, this is behavior that would be predicted from a control theory approach to self-regulation.

Table 7.2 presents detailed descriptive information about the actions taken by each participant over the course of the 200 task trials. Columns 2 through 5 in Table 7.2 represent the information presented graphically in Figure 7.1. Participants differ greatly on the discrepancies that they maintained but they were consistent in their regulation of the states for both goals. Most individuals maintained positive discrepancies and a few (e.g. participants 3, 6, and 8) maintained their states near the maximum possible levels. Only participants 4 and 7 had negative discrepancies on average and, of these two, only participant 7 would likely be considered as engaging in functional regulation. Many participants maintained fairly tight control of their states represented by small standard deviations around 10 points whereas others (e.g. participant 4) had much greater fluctuations in states over time. Columns 6 through 8 provide descriptive information on the action decisions. Clearly, participants distributed their efforts equally between obtaining food and water to meet their state needs. The 'rest' decisions are of primary interest here. All participants

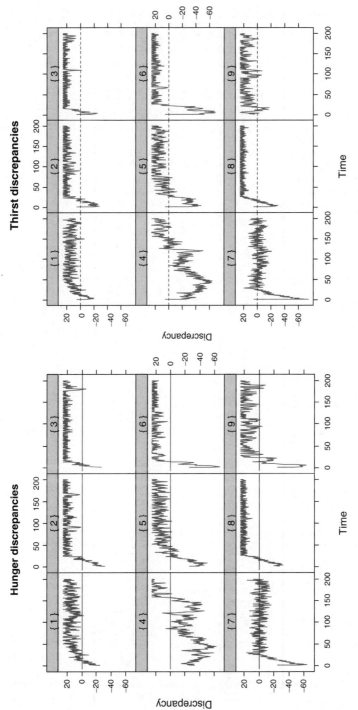

Figure 7.1 Thirst and hunger discrepancies over time.

Table 7.2 Descriptive statistics for dynamic action decisions

ID	Average hunger discrepancy	Standard deviation hunger discrepancy	Average thirst discrepancy	Standard deviation thirst discrepancy	# of rest decisions	# of hunger decisions	# of thirst decisions	Opportunistic decisions	Median decision time (ms)	Median move time (ms)
1	12.24	9.87	12.26	9.08	25	88	87	2	804.0	2820.0
2	16.84	11.52	16.86	11.12	3	101	96	6	639.5	2709.0
3	19.77	7.99	19.45	8.39	4	100	96	3	467.0	2580.0
4	−17.86	23.70	−17.21	23.37	1	105	94	11	829.0	3321.5
5	8.48	16.37	8.03	16.76	23	89	88	7	750.5	2784.0
6	17.33	15.09	13.65	20.97	1	104	95	14	479.5	2404.0
7	−4.15	12.91	−4.87	13.05	29	85	86	0	827.0	2698.0
8	17.68	11.93	18.54	10.56	1	99	100	4	647.5	2641.0
9	12.02	16.76	15.25	9.26	4	100	96	20	382.5	3150.0

chose to rest at least one time over the course of the 200 trials. However, participants 1, 5 and 7 chose to rest or remain inactive on more than 10% of the trials. Perhaps, what appears to be loose regulation of their states is, in reality, functional allocation of effort.

Why invest effort to maintain a state that is well satiated? Anderson's (2003) review of decision avoidance, the choice to engage in no action or to delay action, speaks to this question. One of the principles of decision avoidance is proposed to be 'conservation of energy', or in self-regulatory terms, conservation of resources. Anderson suggests that there are two reasons individuals may engage in decision avoidance. Both intertwine with self-regulatory concepts and thus are interesting explanations for the behavior of participants 1, 5 and 7. First, it may be that once a goal level is reached, some individuals use decision avoidance as a strategy for conserving resources until their current state begins to drop below goal level, as opposed to investing additional resources to surpass the desired goal level. From a self-regulatory perspective, this would still be considered functional regulation. Indeed, it may be even more important to use decision avoidance at times in more volatile environments in order to avoid unnecessary dithering in behaviors to environmental changes. The second possible explanation for decision avoidance is not as applicable to the current task, but may be more relevant to more complex task environments. Rather than choosing no action as a deliberate means to conserve resources, individuals may engage in decision avoidance because they are not aware of the other opportunities to act in the environment. This would suggest poor self-regulation, as individuals who do not notice opportunities may not be adequately monitoring input or feedback from their environment, which is part of the self-regulatory process. The current task is set up such that lack of awareness of opportunities is unlikely. However, when considering inaction in more complex environments, distinguishing between the reasons for inaction (i.e. deliberate conservation vs. missed opportunities) may be important in determining how functional it is.

Column 9 in Table 7.2 presents information that addresses the flexibility of state regulation actions across participants. In this task, a number of trials present the individual with a dilemma. The environmental object (e.g. food or water) associated with the state with the largest discrepancy is further away than an object associated with the state having a smaller discrepancy. This dilemma puts the individual in a situation where they must consider the relative effort required to obtain the objects compared with the relative state discrepancies. The individual may either rigidly adhere to a decision rule associated with satiating states with the largest discrepancies or they may act flexibly and opportunistically engage in action when objects associated with less satiated states are easier to obtain. There are important differences between participants in their likelihood to engage in opportunistic resource allocation decisions. For instance, participant 7 never chose to pursue a closer object with a smaller discrepancy whereas participant 9 made this choice nearly 10% of the time.

The variance across participants in this behavior is striking and successful self-regulatory models must be able to reflect both the opportunistic decisions and the individual differences in this process.

The final two columns in Table 7.2 present the median time required by the participants to make the initial decision of whether to rest, pursue the food object, or pursue the water object and then the time required to obtain the food or water object if they decided not to rest. Again, clear differences emerge in this response time data. Some participants make rapid action selection decisions. If one considers that simple reaction time tasks typically observe reaction times close to 250 ms then the 380 ms decision process exhibited by participant 9 is extremely fast, especially compared to the response times of participants 1, 4, and 7 who took nearly a second to make the action selection decision. Once the initial action decision was made, it took participants between 2.5 and 3 s to acquire the selected object. It is unclear if this variation is meaningful or not at our current stage of model development. Finally, a more subtle but important finding is that the larger the discrepancy the more rapidly or intensely participants moved to acquire the goal. In terms of the hunger state, a regression of the time taken to acquire the hunger object once a decision was made onto the hunger discrepancy was significant ($b = -17.20$; $p < 0.01$; $R^2 = 0.06$). Similarly, for thirst, the regression of move time onto the thirst discrepancy was significant ($b = -9.45$; $p < 0.01$; $R^2 = 0.02$). This finding implies that reasonable models of the self-regulatory process must account for the goal prioritization, the action decision, and the intensity of subsequent effort investments.

Self-Regulatory Models

Armed with a set of questions and empirical data describing actual multiple goal regulatory behavior we are prepared to begin evaluating existing models of the self-regulatory process. We distinguish between models that describe the variables and processes of self-regulation (descriptive models) and models that proscribe how an individual should self-regulate given a set of internal factors and a set of external factors (proscriptive models). To be considered a proscriptive model, the model must be specified in enough detail that a computational model could be constructed to compare model behavior with actual human behavior. Based on these criteria, we identified seven models, presented in the following section, to review.

Descriptive Models

Rubicon model of action phases. The Rubicon model of action phases was first developed by Heckhausen (Heckhausen, Gollwitzer and Weinert, 1987) and elaborated by Gollwitzer (1990). The model maintains Lewin's distinction between goal setting and goal-striving processes but breaks the motivational process into four temporally ordered phases: the predecisional phase, the postdecisional phase, the actional phase, and the postactional phase. The transition points between the phases are marked by goal choice, action initiation, and action conclusion. The first and last phases are considered to be characterized by motivational mind-sets and the two middle phases represent volitional mind-sets.

In the predecisional action phase, individuals weigh competing motives or goals using feasibility and desirability criteria to make the best possible choice between competing goals. The result of this process is that a single goal achieves the highest preference and thus wins the competition among the competing goals. At this point, the wish to achieve a goal is transformed into an intention to achieve the goal to which the individual experiences a sense of commitment or obligation. However, goal intentions differ in 'volitional strength' and this has implications for subsequent phases in the process. Moving from the evaluation of goals to the formation of an intention to act on a specific goal is thought to be analogous to Caesar's crossing of the Rubicon River in 49 BC, an action that marked the beginning of a Roman civil war. Once the goal intention is formed there is no going back and all attention is focused on achieving the goal. The model does not specify the representation or structure of the goals but based on the numerous presentations of the model it appears that the motives or goals are best thought of as residing in an undifferentiated pool. In addition, the model does not specify how the feasibility and desirability evaluations are combined to result in goal preferences.

After the intention is formed, the individual moves into the preactional phase where the individual focuses attention on planning when and where to start acting, what actions to use, and how long to engage in the action. The person's primary task in this phase is to promote the initiation of actions that will best move the individual toward the chosen goal. This planning process results in a behavioral intention – distinct from the original goal intention – that is thought to promote the initiation, execution, and cessation of action in the pursuit of the individual's goal intention. Again, the process by which behavioral intentions are formed for a given goal intention is unspecified in the model.

The connection between goal intentions, behavioral intentions, and actual action is a bit ambiguous. Whether a particular goal intention results in actual action depends upon the relative volitional strength of the goal intention compared with other competing intentions and the situational favorability for the particular goal intention. The notion of situational favorability brings in an explicit recognition of the importance of considering the environment and presumably environmental dynamics. However, the mechanism by which situational favorability is evaluated and associated with the various goal intentions that have been formed is unspecified. Irrespective, action initiation is the transition to the actional phase.

In the actional phase, the individual engages in the goal pursuit by implementing the behavior intention formed in the prior phase. The individual's primary task in this phase is to efficiently execute the actions specified in the prior phase. The intensity of effort devoted to the action is an unspecified function of the volitional strength of the goal intention. This is at least consistent with the observed pattern in our data collection that individuals work more intensely to achieve goals with larger discrepancies. The allocated effort given to the action may be dynamically increased if obstacles to goal pursuit are encountered. The process by which this happens is unspecified. An additional feature of the Rubicon model, relevant to the purpose of our review, is the notion of an actional mind-set. In the actional phase, the individual is thought to adopt an actional mind-set that focuses attention and efforts on achieving the goal and suppressing potential distractions that might inhibit goal achievement such that the individual is 'completely caught up in the actions currently being executed' (Gollwitzer, 1990, p. 66). This implies that goal pursuits are rigidly enacted once the action phase is initiated.

In the final postactional phase, the individual evaluates whether the goal striving has been successful or not. The individual must determine whether the intended outcome and the desired consequences were acquired or not. The evaluation is based on the extent to which the intended outcome has been achieved and whether the value or level associated with the goal striving matches the expected value. If the consequences associated with the goal striving are not what was expected the individual learns how to better calibrate expectations with reality so that more accurate decisions can be made in the future.

Evaluation. With respect to our self-regulatory questions and data, the Rubicon model possesses many positive features. First, it is a temporally organized model that incorporates a limited set of dynamics. The model also explicitly recognizes that there are multiple, conflicting goals and that a choice among the goals must be made before actions can be initiated. The model maintains a valuable distinction between goal choice processes and goal-striving processes. Once action is initiated, the model incorporates an actional mind-set that is used to protect the course of action from distractions and, as a byproduct, will prevent behavioral dithering. However, the approach appears to be overly rigid once actions are initiated. The theory is also somewhat unclear about what quality of the self is regulated. Goals are selected for action based on desirability and feasibility estimates and so it appears that goals are regulated. However, once the goal is chosen, the model focuses intensely upon the regulation of actions to achieve the goal. So, it appears that both goals and actions are the target of regulation in the model. With respect to our multiple goal behavioral data, the model incorporates the notion of volition strength and uses this concept to explain variation in the intensity of effort invested to pursue goals. As with all the descriptive approaches, the Achilles heel of the theory lies in the unspecified connections between the various processes. Without specifying the conceived functions of each process and the linkages between them the model is limited to providing only a heuristic representation of behavior.

Control theory. Control theory has become an umbrella term used to represent a wide variety of self-regulatory models some of which are primarily descriptive and some of which are proscriptive. As such, control theory variants that are descriptive in nature will be discussed here and proscriptive approaches will be discussed in the following section. Descriptive control theory approaches are primarily used as a meta-theory or heuristic to better understand and integrate existing models of motivation (e.g. Hyland, 1988). Control theory approaches applied to human behavior are derivatives of Wiener's (1948) original cybernetic model of machine and animal behavior viewed through the filter of Miller, Galanter and Pribham's (1960) Test-Operate-Test-Exit cycle. Numerous social scientists have invested substantial effort to adapt the model to human behavior and human behavior in organizational settings (Campion and Lord, 1982; Carver and Scheier, 1981, 1982; Hyland, 1988; Klein, 1989; Lord and Hanges, 1987; Lord and Levy, 1994; Powers, 1973). Throughout its development there has been intense debate over the applicability of the model to human self-regulation (e.g. Locke and Latham, 1994).

In all variants of control theory, the negative feedback loop is the basic unit of analysis in a cybernetic control model consisting of four dynamically linked components: an input function, a reference value, a comparator, and an output function. In a human, the input function is typically input from some perceptual system, the reference value is a goal, the comparator is either a conscious or unconscious comparison of the input to goal, and the output is an action or behavior. The output of the system (action) is changed in such a way to reduce the discrepancy between the input signal (perception) and the reference value (goal). Feedback loops are organized hierarchically such that the output of a higher order feedback loop is an operation on a lower order feedback loop. The level at which a feedback loop results in observable actions instead of internal operations on other feedback loops is not currently specified.

Virtually all versions of control theory explicitly recognize that individuals possess multiple goals and that actions taken to reduce discrepancies with respect to one goal will likely increase discrepancies on other goals. However, the majority of control theory incarnations do not provide a mechanism to resolve goal conflict or to select actions. Rather than focusing on goal prioritization and action selection mechanisms required to pursue multiple goals, control theorists have focused almost exclusively on the hierarchical structure of goals that result in a given behavior targeted at reducing a single discrepancy absent conflict with other goals. Vancouver (2000) highlights this as the serial description of feedback loop functioning.

Evaluation. With respect to descriptive variants of control theory, the focus of self-regulatory effort is on minimizing discrepancies between current states and goal states. Presumably the discrepancy minimization process applies equally to both positive and negative discrepancies. The models have not generally been applied to multiple goal pursuits and, as such, do not contain a goal choice or prioritization mechanism to resolve potential conflicts between multiple goals.

The models also provide no mechanism for selecting an action to reduce discrepancies between current states and goal states. The models do allow for internal dynamics and often incorporate the possibility of external dynamics by adding a disturbance term to the standard feedback loop. The disturbance term is used to represent shocks to the system that result in discrepancies that require action to bring the current state back into congruence with the goal state. Because the models do not explicitly incorporate the ability to regulate multiple discrepancies at the same level in the control hierarchy, there can be no cross goal flexibility. Further, because the models do not provide a mechanism for regulating multiple, simultaneous discrepancies the models can make no meaningful predictions about behavior in our multiple goal data collection.

Social cognitive theories.   The social cognitive approach to self-regulation, according to Bandura (1986), is based on the operation of four interrelated processes: goal establishment, self-observation, self-evaluation, and self-reaction. Bandura (1991) later reorganized these four processes into three subfunctions but the essential content remained the same and so we use his original depiction of the theory. Goal establishment refers to the process of setting goals that represent desired behavioral states. The specific goal level selected by the individual is thought to be an unspecified function of the individual's past experiences and level of self-efficacy. Once a goal level is chosen, the individual implements an action or set of actions targeted at achieving the goal and then engages in self-observation to monitor the effectiveness of the actions on the specific task. The monitoring and interpretation of the acquired information is not a veridical record of events, but rather, thought to be biased by variables such as mood, affect, and self-beliefs. The nature and extent of the bias is not specified. After observing behavior for some unspecified period, the individual engages in the self-evaluation process where the information gleaned by the self-observation process is used to compare the current state with the desired goal state. The outcome of this comparison process is a set of self-reactions.

Self-reactions are thought to be the mechanism by which hierarchically structured goals (proximal to distal) regulate motivation and actions through internal rewards and punishments. If the current state meets or exceeds the selected goal state, then the individual is thought to experience satisfaction and increased self-efficacy. A result of the positive affect and increased self-efficacy is that subsequent efforts will be targeted at goals set at higher levels. This discrepancy producing mechanism is argued to be a major distinction between the social cognitive approach and the control theory approach. According to Bandura (1991), self-regulation requires both proactive and reactive control of motivation and action. If the current state is less than the goal state then the individual experiences dissatisfaction and decreased self-efficacy. The dissatisfaction experienced when a negative discrepancy is encountered results in the motivation to engage in cognitive or behavioral actions to decrease the discrepancy. The quality of these cognitive and behavioral actions in response to negative feedback (e.g. increase effort, lower goal, abandon the task) is thought to be heavily influenced by one's level of self-efficacy.

Evaluation. The description of social cognitive theory provided here only provides a rough sketch of the proposed systems and functions. Bandura's writings on the topic provide a more fine-grained treatment of the approach. In terms of our purpose, social cognitive theory provides a rich landscape of variables and potential moderating processes that are relevant to the self-regulatory process. It does not, however, provide details on how these variables interact dynamically in response to internal and external dynamics as the individual uses limited resources to pursue a large number of goals. The theory is variable rich and function poor. Social cognitive theory identifies both motivation and action as the target of regulation (e.g. Bandura, 1988, 1991). It maintains that the individual possesses multiple goals structured in a goal hierarchy and that goal pursuits are focused on both discrepancy reduction and discrepancy production. The conditions under which regulatory efforts are focused on discrepancy reduction versus discrepancy production are not well specified. The theory focuses primary attention on setting goal levels for specific states (e.g. academic achievement) but provides no mechanism for prioritizing goals or selecting actions to meet goals. It acknowledges that both internal and external dynamics occur but does not provide a mechanism for responding to the dynamics. Since there are no goal prioritization or action selection mechanisms, it is unclear how the approach would cope with the need to pursue goals flexibly over time. Social cognitive theory provides a heuristic representation of behavior with a large set of variables and processes that support thinking about human self-regulation but not the modeling of human self-regulation. As such, it does not support the formation of behavioral predictions in multiple goal environments that can be compared to our actual multiple goal regulation data.

Goal-setting theory. According to the individuals primarily responsible for developing goal-setting theory, it is an open theory built by induction through the accumulation of new empirical results. This theoretical malleability is desirable in many ways but it does make it challenging to accurately represent the most current form of the theory. The core finding in goal-setting research and theory is that setting a difficult, specific goal typically results in superior task performance than setting a 'do your best' goal (Locke and Latham, 2002). Difficult, specific goals are thought to have this positive effect through the following four mechanisms: (1) difficult, specific goals direct attention toward goal-relevant activities and away from distracting activities, (2) difficult, specific goals increase the effort devoted to task performance, (3) difficult, specific goals increase the persistence of task-relevant efforts, and (4) difficult, specific goals promote the discovery or use of task-relevant knowledge and strategies. Much of the recent efforts with respect to the theory have been devoted to exploring boundary conditions such as goal commitment and task complexity.

Goal-setting theory has focused its attention on the importance of selecting a *difficult and specific goal level* for a particular goal rather than determining which of the many competing goals an individual may possess will result in manifested goal pursuits. It does not attempt to explain the process by which individuals select goals for action or move from a difficult, specific goal to actions. As such, it is a stretch to refer to goal-setting theory as a model of the self-regulatory process. On the other hand, goal-setting theory does incorporate the two core self-regulatory constructs of goals and action, it addresses effort allocation, effort persistence, the protection of a current intention from interruptions, and recent attempts at integration have led goal-setting researchers to incorporate aspects of other self-regulatory theories, such as self-efficacy and learning goal orientation (e.g. Latham and Locke, 1991, 2007). For these reasons, we include goal-setting theory in our review but recognize that our evaluation of the theory with respect to self-regulation models may be unfair if goal setting is not viewed as a self-regulatory model.

Evaluation. At its core, goal-setting theory addresses goal-level choices on a single goal. The primary goal pursuit mechanism in goal-setting theory is to impact the effort allocated to whatever action is selected by the individual to pursue the goal. Given this, if a quantity is regulated in goal-setting theory, it must surely be effort. Goal-setting theory does not provide a mechanism by which individuals select an action to pursue a given difficult, specific goal. Neither does goal setting incorporate any internal or environmental dynamics nor does it address behavioral flexibility in the pursuit of multiple goals.

With respect to our multiple goal behavioral data, the goal levels associated with each state in the multiple goal task were equally difficult and specific. The two tasks of acquiring food and water were equally difficult. There is no reason to believe that an individual would be more committed to one of the goals over the other and the behavioral data support this belief. As such, goal-setting theory provides no meaningful statements about expected behavior on this task. Clearly, goal-setting theory has made important contributions to the toolbox of motivation interventions but it is not as clear that it contributes to our understanding of the multiple goal self-regulatory process.

Proscriptive Models

Control theory. Powers (1973) version of control theory, termed perceptual control theory (PCT), is a theoretical outsider when it comes to models of self-regulation. Powers (1973) views human behavior as the output of a perceptually driven, goal-referenced feedback system. Unlike other control theory models that view behavior as a result of controlling discrepancies, PCT views an individual's behavior as a means of controlling the *perception* of discrepancies. In PCT, the individual perceives an aspect of the environment in terms of a signal (e.g. position in a lane while driving). The magnitude of the signal is compared to a reference level (e.g. stay in the middle of the lane) and any difference between the reference level and the perception generates an error signal. The error signal drives an action that attempts to bring the perception back in line with the reference level. The central difference between Powers' version of control theory and the other variants is that Powers emphasizes that PCT controls discrepancy perceptions and not actual discrepancies. Clearly, what is regulated in PCT is a perception of a discrepancy between the current state and the desired state. Behavior is a means to achieve the regulation of perceived discrepancies.

Unfortunately, successful demonstrations of PCT focus exclusively on the regulation of a single discrepancy – although the discrepancy may be multidimensional. For instance, tracking a moving object on a computer monitor using a mouse pointer is a single discrepancy that occurs in two dimensions (x and y coordinates). PCT appears to be more relevant to the changes in the magnitude or intensity of an action (e.g. tracking) rather than selection of actions. PCT clearly acknowledges the existence of multiple goals and multiple levels of goals in a control hierarchy (e.g. Powers, 2003). However, it is not clear in the theory how a person would tradeoff perceptions of multiple discrepancies that occur across multiple referent levels or goals. In fact, Powers (1973, p. 253) views goal conflict as a result of an individual wanting to simultaneously act upon two or more incompatible goals. However, he views conflict not as a normal state but rather as 'the most serious kind of malfunction of the brain short of physical damage...'. As such, there is little attempt to provide a prioritization or action selection mechanisms to resolve the conflict between discrepancies on multiple goals. The model clearly allows for both internal and external dynamics but the dynamics are restricted to taking place through the filter of the perceived discrepancies. For a given action used to regulate a particular perceived discrepancy, the model is highly flexible. With respect to multiple goals or multiple discrepancies it provides no mechanism for shifting gears toward regulating a different discrepancy in response to internal or external dynamics. As such, it is highly inflexible in regulating perceptions across goals.

There are, however, variants of control theory that do incorporate resource allocation among multiple goals. Kernan and Lord (1990) provided the first example of this process when they suggested that, all things being equal, states representing larger discrepancies relative to the respective goals should result in higher priority and actions would be targeted at the goal with the highest priority. DeShon et al. (2004) explicitly incorporated this notion into a control theory model that explicitly incorporated multiple goals at the same level of abstraction and incorporated a goal prioritization mechanism based on the comparison of goal discrepancies, goal importance, and relative error sensitivities. Schmidt and DeShon (2007) generalized the goal prioritization and action selection mechanism to include the incentive value or valence of possible outcomes in the current environment. Unlike DeShon et al. (2004), Schmidt and DeShon provided an explicit test of the model predictions and the goal prioritization and action selection were substantially supported in their research.

Evaluation. With respect to our evaluation questions and our multiple goal data, Powers' version of control theory focuses on the control of perceived discrepancies but it does not incorporate multiple goals at the same level of abstraction and provides no real-time mechanism for resolving conflicts between goals. The model also provides no action selection mechanism. As with the descriptive version of control theory, Powers' version is highly flexible with respect to environmental disturbances on the single quantity being controlled but this does not generalize to flexibility in regulating discrepancies across goals. The multiple goal variants of control theory provide an explicit mechanism for prioritizing goals for action based on the discrepancy between the current state and the goal state, possibly influenced by incentive values associated with the respective goals. The target of regulation in these models is clearly the reduction of the largest discrepancy in the goal system. None of the multiple goal models provided an action selection mechanism. As a result, the multiple goal models will sequentially and rigidly focus on reducing the largest discrepancies in the system. Further, if there are two large and roughly equal discrepancies in the goal system the models would surely demonstrate behavioral dithering and would not behave opportunistically or flexibly.

With respect to our behavioral data, the multiple goal variants of control theory would predict that the individual would select the action that reduces the magnitude of the largest discrepancy in the goal system. It would further predict that actions would not be directed at goal states that either do not have discrepancies or have small discrepancies within some tolerable range. Finally, due to the focus on reducing the largest discrepancies in the system of goals, the multiple goal models would not predict behavioral flexibility or opportunistic goal striving. Interestingly, one of the individuals in our multiple goal data (participant 7) provides a behavior stream that is remarkably close to how the multiple goal control systems behave. This individual pursued the goal with the largest discrepancy without fail, rested when the current states were above the respective goal states, and did not demonstrate any opportunistic behavior. On the other hand, the remaining eight participants provided behavior streams that were substantially inconsistent with the multiple goal control theory models. The majority of individuals undertook actions to maintain the states (hunger and thirst) above the goal level and continued to take these actions even when the actions resulted in larger positive discrepancies. No model of control theory in current existence would predict this pattern of behavior and discrepancy control. In addition, most of the participants demonstrated opportunistic behavior by targeting actions to acquire easily obtained objects for goals with smaller overall discrepancies. With the exception of a single participant (participant 7), control theory models do not provide adequate predictions about human behavior in our simple multiple goal environment.

Simon's simple rules model. In the process of developing his notion of satisficing, Simon (1956) developed a functional model of multiple goal self-regulation. While the notion of satisficing is now well established, his model of self-regulation, based on simple decision rules, languished. In fact, none of the other model developers refer to Simon's work in this area. In developing the model, Simon wanted to investigate the simplest set of choice mechanisms or rules that could yield adaptive behavior. For this reason, we term his approach the simple rules model. In Simon's model, the individual is located in an environment that contains spatially distributed goal-relevant objects such as sources of food and water. The individual has multiple needs such as hunger and thirst and a limited set of possible actions that can be used to obtain objects that meet the needs (resting, exploration, and goal-specific striving). The needs are satiable and so, if all needs are currently above threshold, the individual becomes inactive and rests. In Simon's model, the goal strivings are mutually exclusive and so the time spent and resources expended to meet one goal reflect time and resources that cannot be spent to meet a different goal. In other words, goal striving is sequential instead of simultaneous. The concept of storage is a unique feature of Simon's model. Because goal-relevant objects are not colocated, the individual must store enough energy from food to allow the search for water to occur without starving and vice versa. The storage requirements for a particular need or goal are determined by the availability of the needed resources in the environment. So, for instance, water is easier to come by than food and so food storage requirements are greater. Similarly, breathable air is easier to obtain than water and so its storage requirements are less than both food and water. Internal dynamics result in decay of the need states over time. For instance, maintaining body temperature requires energy expenditures and so hunger (i.e. need for energy) increases over time.

Actions are selected using very simple rules. When the state of a need dips below a threshold or goal level, then exploration is initiated. During the process exploration, the individual will run across goal-relevant objects. If a single object, relevant to any of the individual's needs, is perceived in the environment, the individual will enact whatever action is needed to obtain the object irrespective of the need states. If two or more objects are perceived in the environment via exploration that are relevant to different needs then the ratio of the energy required to meet the need (M) to the storage capacity with respect to the need (S) will be compared. The action selection mechanism is simply to pursue the object for the need with the greatest energy to storage ratio. Note that this results in a 1:1 mapping between goals and actions. There is only one action associated with a goal and so once a goal receives priority there is no need to engage in action selection or planning. The model highlights a common theme running through Simon's many published works on human behavior that to understand an individual's behavior you must understand the distribution of goal-relevant objects in the environment. Clearly, this is an interactionist perspective where the individual's behavior is partly a function of internal need states and the distribution of goal-relevant objects in the environment.

Evaluation. The simple rules model provides clear answers to many of our questions and provides a surprisingly good representation of our behavioral data. With respect to our questions, it is clear that internal states of being are regulated and the regulation is accomplished through actions. The model provides a goal prioritization mechanism based on comparing goals with respect to the internal states and the effort required to improve the internal states. Unlike control theory, there is no negative feedback loop required to direct action. The model includes internal dynamics because internal states change and decay over time. The model also incorporates a limited set of environmental dynamics because, as the individual moves through the environment, the position of goal-relevant objects in the environment changes and new goal-relevant objects appear. The model is built to be as simple as possible and, in its current form, it does not incorporate behavioral flexibility. This limitation could be easily overcome by modifying existing rules or adding an additional rule.

With respect to our multiple goal behavioral data, the simple rules model is the only model we have encountered that would predict the behavior of consistently maintaining the internal state well above the goal level. From Simon's perspective, this is due to the storage requirements imposed by the environment and thus is highly adaptive. Control theory models, on the other hand, do not account for storage requirements. The model is not able to predict all aspects of behavior in our multiple goal data. As highlighted above, the model does not incorporate behavioral flexibility and the opportunistic actions taken by many participants are inconsistent with the model predictions. Although Simon mentions that the drive to pursue a course of action should be proportional to the need state, the model does not incorporate an intensity of action component. As a result, the model is unable to explain the relationship between goal discrepancies and the intensity of efforts used to obtain a goal-relevant object in our task. Finally, the model is specified in enough detail that it yields clear, testable behavioral predictions that can be used to revise the model as deviations from behavioral data are found such as the ones we present here.

Dynamics of action.   Atkinson and Birch (1970) developed a dynamic model of action control that focuses on the factors resulting in a change in the activity exhibited by an individual. According to the model, many actions are incompatible with each other and so, to maintain behavioral coherence, the individual can only do one thing at a time. In other words, goal pursuits are sequential rather than simultaneous. The model further assumes that an individual has a wide variety of action tendencies and that the dominant or most active action tendency is expressed in actual behavior. Whatever behavior is currently underway represents the dominant action tendency within the individual at the current time point. The action tendency persists in its present form until either its strength decreases or the strength of a competing action tendency increases beyond the level of the current action tendency. The strength of action tendencies is increased by instigating forces and decreased by consummatory forces. Internal goals, expectancies, valences, and environmental stimuli serve as instigating forces that increase the strength of the action tendency. Engaging in an activity results in a consummatory force that decreases the strength of the action tendency to some fixed extent over time. Activities are thought to differ in their consummatory values such that different activities decrease the tendency at greater, but unspecified, rates. A change in activity occurs when the joint impact of the consummatory and instigating forces impacting action tendencies results in one action tendency becoming stronger than the action tendency currently being manifested in the current activity.

Evaluation. There are many positive features in the Atkinson and Birch approach to modeling human behavior. The model clearly specifies, in mathematical form, the key factors that lead to the cessation of one action and the implementation of a new action. It provides a clear prioritization mechanism for determining the action tendency that will be manifested through an activity at any given time. Further, the dominance relation for action tendencies provides a clear mechanism for resolving conflicts between competing action tendencies. The model includes both internal and external dynamics as causal factors in the strength of the various action tendencies. In principle, these processes are capable of yielding highly flexible behavior across multiple action tendencies.

On the other hand, the representation and structure of the action tendencies is unspecified in the model. There is no mechanism specified for selecting the activity that will be expressed in response to the dominant action tendency. The consummatory force associated with the various actions is unspecified and it is not clear how this quantity would be estimated that would not lead to circular logic. The action selection mechanism used in the model would almost certainly result in too much flexibility and behavioral dithering. It is interesting to note that this model also provides a proscriptive approach to behavior that does not incorporate discrepancies or negative feedback loops.

With respect to our data, we tried to apply the model but were unable to determine how to estimate the key components of the model such as the consummatory force of activities, the valence and expectancy of outcomes, and the strength of action tendencies. In the end, we feel that the dynamics of action model is probably best thought of as an ambitious and engaging intellectual achievement. It certainly provides a useful framework for thinking about behavior but its applicability to actually modeling human behavior is substantially limited.

SUMMARY AND CONCLUSIONS

It is becoming increasingly clear that understanding human behavior requires the dynamic modeling of action as individuals strive to achieve multiple, contextually relevant goals. The relatively recent explosion of interest in self-regulatory approaches to behavior is likely due, in part, to the inclusion of multiple goals and system dynamics in the existing self-regulatory models. It should not be surprising to find that this approach now dominates the study of human motivational processes.

Considered together, our review highlighted a number of interesting discrepancies and gaps in the self-regulatory literature. Based on our review of definitions and models, it is clear that the core constituents of self-regulation are goals and actions and all definitions and models of the regulatory process share these components. However, after this common ground, the agreement breaks down rapidly. There are at least implicit disagreements about what is regulated, the components of the regulatory process, the role of feedback, the structure of goals, and many other less central issues. It is clear that the majority of regulatory models discuss the issue of multiple goals with respect to their vertical order. For a given task, there are many goals at higher and lower levels of analysis that are relevant to goal pursuit (e.g. Vallacher and Wegner, 1987). Far less attention has been paid to goal prioritization decisions or processes at the same level of abstraction. This is a key issue that must be dealt with in the near future to improve our ability to understand and predict human behavior. A similar case can be made for action selection decisions once a goal has been identified for pursuit.

One of the most surprising outcomes of our review is that Simon's simple rules approach fares so well with respect to both the questions we posed and the multiple goal data we collected. At the current stage of development in regulatory theory, we view a model developed in 1956 as the most comprehensive and clearly specified model of the self-regulation process that is best aligned with actual human behavior in multiple goal pursuits. Although this finding is a bit disheartening it does provide an excellent base from which to begin improving models of the self-regulatory process. In contrast, the majority of current self-regulatory perspectives function at a high level of description. They are useful heuristics for thinking about behavior but are substantially limited in their ability to predict and explain behavior. The next step in the development of self-regulatory models is to move beyond the heuristic or descriptive stage of theory development to a point where self-regulation may be used to predict and model actual human behavior in organizations and other contexts. To accomplish this goal, it will likely be necessary to mathematically identify the dynamic relations between the various components of the self-regulation process. The resulting system will likely turn out to be highly complex and computational models of the self-regulation process will likely be required to develop an understanding of the self-regulation dynamics.

We proposed a set of questions to evaluate the existing self-regulatory definitions and models. It seems only fair to provide our own responses to the questions and a definition of the self-regulatory process. Our responses take the following form. Multiple dimensions of being are regulated to obtain or maintain consistency between the current states of being and goal states. The dimensions of being cross common boundaries and include affective states, cognitions, and motives (e.g. achievement, affiliation, agency). In other words, an individual might undertake either an overt or covert sequence of actions to improve his or her mood and stop ruminative thought about a negative event by playing soccer with friends. This example fits nicely in the self-regulatory literature and crosses traditional research boundaries of affect, cognition, and action. Sometimes multiple internal states can be improved, with respect to their goal states, simultaneously. However, it is frequently the case that pursuing one dimension of being (e.g. recognition at work) has a negative impact on another valued dimension of being (e.g. family life). In this case, there must be some mechanism or procedure for prioritizing goal pursuits. Adults have learned a large repertoire of overt and covert behaviors that can be selected to attain or maintain congruence between the current state and the goal state on the multiple dimensions of being. Some mechanism must be responsible for protecting or shielding the current goal pursuit from distracting environmental stimuli or dimensions of being that vie for access to behavior to prevent behavioral dithering. On the other hand, the protection cannot be so complete that the individual misses opportunities or fails to respond to threats that evolve in dynamic environments. Based on these principles we define self-regulation in the following manner:

Self-regulation is that part of the motivational system responsible for dynamically selecting actions or action sequences to regulate internal states (e.g., affect, cognition, biological needs, and learned motives) to attain or maintain congruence between the current state and the goal state in response to both internal and environmental dynamics.

From the perspective of an observer, an individual produces a constant stream of hierarchically organized behavior shifting from doing one thing to doing another. The vast majority of the time the transitions between actions appear to be smooth and effortless (Barker, 1963). From the actor's perspective, behavior must surely be a never ending series of responses to the basic problem of what to do next. Based on the existing self-regulatory and action selection literatures, the basic action selection problem may be represented as: Given knowledge of an individual's internal state (i.e. discrepancy) on each goal in a set of goals, knowledge of goal-relevant objects in the environment, and a repertoire of possible actions, what action or action sequence should be enacted next to optimally improve the internal states with respect to the goal levels? Given this representation, the individual should select an action or action sequence that minimizes the joint goal discrepancies while remaining attentive to changes in the environmental demands or affordances and without neglecting the long-term potential for discrepancies on other goals.

Our conceptualization of this dynamic process is represented in Figure 7.2. The critical notion reflected in this graphic depiction of the process is that objects in the environment impact the salience or activation of the individual's internal states in a bottom up fashion. At the same time, the manner in which environmental stimuli are perceived is impacted by the profile of currently activated internal states. This dynamic process results in environmental perceptions which, in turn, impact the salience or activation of internal states. The profile of internal state activation results in an action being selected and enacted. The individual's actions then impact both the individual's states and the

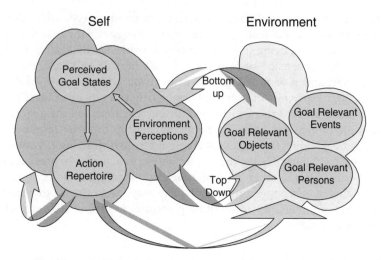

Figure 7.2 The dynamic action selection problem of self-regulation.

environment and the cycle repeats itself. Lord and Levy (1994) provide a more thoroughly developed model of this dynamic, reciprocal activation process.

Finally, the vast majority of thought and research by organizational scholars on the topic of self-regulatory mechanisms represents either an application of general self-regulatory models to understand the behavior in organizations or the development of general self-regulatory models without respect to the unique characteristics present in organizational settings. This raises the question of what is special about self-regulation in an organizational context? We feel that organizational researchers could take far better advantage of the contextual constraints and behavioral norms present in organizational settings to advance both the understanding of organizational behavior and self-regulatory processes in general. Naylor, Pritchard and Ilgen's (1980) treatment of expectancy theory and general motivation in organizational contexts provide an example of how this might be accomplished. The goals pursued, the acceptable actions used to pursue the goals, and the environmental stimuli found in organizations represent highly restricted subsets of goals, actions, and stimuli in the individual's life. Great strides forward are possible if organizational researchers incorporate organizational variables such as climate, norms, roles, teamwork, and leadership into the modeling of self-regulatory processes.

REFERENCES

Ach, N. (2006). On volition (T. Herz, Trans.). (Original work published 1910) from University of Konstanz, Cognitive Psychology, http://www.uni-konstanz. de/kogpsych/ach.htm (accessed 7 July 2008).

Anderson, C. J. (2003). The psychology of doing nothing: forms of decision avoidance result from reason and emotion. *Psychological Bulletin*, **129**, 139–67.

Atkinson, J. W. & Birch, D. (1970). *The Dynamics of Action*, New York: John Wiley & Sons, Inc.

Austin, J. T. & Vancouver, J. B. (1996). Goal constructs in psychology: structure, process, and content. *Psychological Bulletin*, 120, 338–75.

Bandura, A. (1986). *Social Foundations of Thought and Action: A Social Cognitive Theory*, Englewood Cliffs, NJ: Prentice-Hall.

Bandura, A. (1988). Self-regulation of motivation and action through goal systems. In V. Hamilton, G. H. Bower & N. H. Fryda (Eds), *Cognition, Motivation, and Affect: A Cognitive Science View* (pp. 37–61). Dordrecht, Holland: Martinus Nijholl.

Bandura, A. (1991). Social cognitive theory of self-regulation. *Organizational Behavior and Human Decision Processes*, 50, 248–87.

Barker, R. G. (1963). The stream of behavior as an empirical problem. In R. G. Barker (Ed.), *The Stream of Behavior* (pp. 1–22). New York: Appleton-Century-Crofts.

Baumeister, R. F. & Heatherton, T. F. (1996). Self-regulation failure: an overview. *Psychological Inquiry*, 7, 1–15.

Binswanger, H. (1991). Volition as cognitive self-regulation. *Organizational Behavior and Human Decision Processes*, 50, 154–78.

Brief, A. P. & Hollenbeck, J. R. (1985). An exploratory study of self-regulating activities and their effects on job performance. *Journal of Occupational Behavior*, 6, 197–208.

Campion, M. A. & Lord, R. G. (1982). A control systems conceptualization of the goal-setting and changing process. *Organizational Behavior and Human Performance*, 30, 265–87.

Carver, C. S. & Scheier, M. F. (1981). *Attention and Self-Regulation: A Control-Theory Approach to Human Behavior*. New York: Springer.

Carver, C. S. & Scheier, M. F. (1982). Control theory: a useful conceptual framework for personality-social, clinical, and health psychology. *Psychological Bulletin*, 92, 111–35.

Cervone, D., Shadel, W. G., Smith, R. E. & Fiori, M. (2006). Self-regulation: reminders and suggestions from personality science. *Applied Psychology: An International Review*, 55, 333–85.

DeShon, R. P. & Gillespie, J. Z. (2005). A motivated action theory account of goal orientation. *Journal of Applied Psychology*, 90, 1096–1127.

DeShon, R. P., Kozlowski, S. W. J., Schmidt, A. M. *et al.* (2004). Multiple goal feedback effects on the regulation of individual and team performance in training. *Journal of Applied Psychology*, 89, 1035–56.

Dubin, R. (1978). *Theory Building* (Rev. Ed), New York: Free Press, Macmillian.

Freud, S. (1920). *Beyond the Pleasure Principle*, London: Hogarth Press.

Gollwitzer, P. M. (1990). Action phases and mind-sets. In R. M. Sorrentino & E. T. Higgins (Eds), *Handbook of Motivation and Cognition: Foundations of Social Behavior* (pp. 53–92). Guilford Press.

Gollwitzer, P. M. & Bayer, U. (1999). Deliberative versus implementational mindsets in the control of action. In S. Chaiken & Y. Trope (Eds), *Dual-Process Theories in Social Psychology* (pp. 403–22). New York: Guilford.

Heatherton, T. F. & Baumeister, R. F. (1996). Self-regulation failure: past, present, and future. *Psychological Inquiry*, 7, 90–98.

Heckhausen, H., Gollwitzer, P. M. & Weinert, F. E. (1987). *Jenseits des Rubikon: Der Wille in den Humanwissen*, Heidelberg: Springer.

Hyland, M. E. (1988). Motivational control theory: an integrative framework. *Journal of Personality and Social Psychology*, 55, 642–51.

James, W. (1890). *The Principles of Psychology*, Vol. 2, New York: Holt.

James, W. (1899). *Talks to Teachers on Psychology: And to Students on Some of Life's Ideals*, New York: Holt.

Kanfer, R. (1990). Motivation theory and industrial and organizational psychology. In M. D. Dunnette & L. M. Hough (Eds), *Handbook of Industrial and Organizational*

Psychology, 2nd edn, Vol. 1 (pp. 75–170). Palo Alto, CA: Consulting Psychologists Press, Inc.

Kanfer, R. (1992). Work motivation: new directions in theory and research. In C. L. Cooper & I. T. Robertson (Eds), *International Review of Industrial and Organizational Psychology*, Vol. 7 (pp. 1–53). London: John Wiley & Sons, Ltd.

Kanfer, R. (2005). Self-regulation research in work and I/O psychology. *Applied Psychology: An International Review*, **54**, 186–91.

Karoly, P. (1993). Mechanisms of self-regulation: a systems view. *Annual Review of Psychology*, **44**, 23–52.

Karoly, P., Boekaerts, M. & Maes, S. (2005). Toward consensus in the psychology of self-regulation: how far have we come? How far do we have yet to travel? *Applied Psychology: An International Review*, **54**, 300–11.

Kernan, M. C. & Lord, R. G. (1990). The effects of valence, expectancies and goal-performance discrepancies in single and multiple goal environments. *Journal of Applied Psychology*, **75**, 194–203.

Klein, H. J. (1989). An integrated control theory model of work motivation. *Academy of Management Review*, **14**, 150–72.

Kuhl, J. (1985). Volitional mediators of cognition-behavior consistency: self-regulatory processes and action vs. state orientation. In J. Kuhl & J. Beckmann (Eds), *Action Control: From Cognition to Behavior* (pp. 101–28). New York: Springer.

Latham, G. P. & Locke, E. A. (1991). Self-regulation through goal setting. *Organizational Behavior and Human Decision Processes*, **50**, 212–47.

Latham, G. P. & Locke, E. A. (2007). New developments in and directions for goal setting research. *European Psychologist*, **12**, 290–300.

Lewin, K., Dembo, T., Festinger, L. A. & Sears, P. S. (1944). Level of aspiration. In J. M. Hunt (Ed.), *Personality and Behavior Disorders* (pp. 333–78). New York: Ronald Press.

Locke, E. A. & Latham, G. P. (1994). Goal setting theory. In H. F. O'Neil & M. Drillings (Eds), *Motivation Theory and Research* (pp. 13–30). Lawrence Erlbaum Associates.

Locke, E. A. & Latham, G. P. (2002). Building a practically useful theory of goal-setting and task motivation: a 35-year odyssey. *American Psychologist*, **57**, 705–17.

Lord, R. G. & Hanges, P. J. (1987). A control system model of organizational motivation: Theoretical development and applied implications. *Behavioral Science*, **32**, 161–77.

Lord, R. G. & Levy, P. E. (1994). Moving from cognition to action: a control theory perspective. *Applied Psychology: International Review*, **43**, 335–67.

Matthews, G., Schwean, S. E., Campbell, D. H. *et al.* (2000). Personality, self-regulation, and adaptation: a cognitive-social framework. Generic umbrella term. In M. Boekaerts, P. R. Pintrich & M. H. Zeidner (Eds), *Handbook of Self-Regulation*. San Diego, CA: Academic Press.

Miller, G. A., Galanter, E. & Pribham, K. H. (1960). *Plans and the Structure of Behavior*, London: Holt.

Naylor, J. N., Pritchard, R. D. & Ilgen, D. R. (1980). *A Theory of Behavior in Organizations*, New York: Academic Press.

Peterson, C. & Seligman, M. E. P. (2004). Character strengths and virtues: a handbook and classification, Oxford University Press.

Poole, M. S. & Van de Ven, A. H. (1989). Using paradox to build management and organization theories. *Academy of Management Review*, **14**, 562–78.

Porath, C. L. & Bateman, T. S. (2006). Self-regulation: from goal orientation to job performance. *Journal of Applied Psychology*, **91**, 185–92.

Powers, W. T. (1973). *Behavior: The Control of Perception*, Chicago, IL: Aldine Publishing Company.

Powers, W. T. (2003). *PCT and Engineering Control Theory.* Paper presented at the 19th annual meeting of the systems group, Los Angles, CA.

Schmidt, A. M. & DeShon, R. P. (2007). What to do? The effects of goal-performance discrepancies, superordinate goals, and time on dynamic goal prioritization. *Journal of Applied Psychology*, **92**, 928–41.

Simon, H. A. (1956). Rational choice and the structure of the environment. *Psychological Review*, **63**, 129–38.

Vallacher, R. R. & Wegner, D. M. (1987). What do people think they're doing? Action identification and human behavior. *Psychological Review*, **94**, 3–15.

Vancouver, J. B. (2000). Self-regulation in organizational settings: a tale of two paradigms. In M. Boekaerts, P. R. Pintrich & M. H. Zeidner (Eds), *Handbook of Self-Regulation*. San Diego, CA: Academic Press.

Vancouver, J. B. & Day, D. V. (2005). Industrial and organization research on self-regulation: from constructs to applications. *Applied Psychology: An International Review*, **54**, 155–85.

Vohs, K. D. & Baumeister, R. F. (2004). Understanding self-regulation. In R. F. Baumeister & K. D. Vohs (Eds), *Handbook of Self-Regulation* (pp. 1–9). New York: Guilford Press.

Weick, K. E. (1989). Theory construction as disciplined imagination. *Academy of Management Review*, **14**, 516–31.

Wiener, N. (1948). *Cybernetics: Control and Communication in the Animal and the Machine*, Cambridge, MA: M.I.T. Press.

Zeidner, M., Boekaerts, M. & Pintrich, P. R. (2000). Self-regulation: directions and challenges for future research. In M. Boekaerts, P. R. Pintrich & M. H. Zeidner (Eds), *Handbook of Self-Regulation* San Diego, CA: Academic Press.

Chapter 8

INDIVIDUAL DIFFERENCES AND DECISION MAKING: WHAT WE KNOW AND WHERE WE GO FROM HERE

Susan Mohammed and Alexander Schwall

Department of Psychology, Pennsylvania State University, University Park, PA, USA

It was a fruitful methodological advance when psychology rescued individual differences from the scrap heap of scientific anomalies and began to study them.... Treating each individual as a special combination of capacities, accomplishments, and tendencies has been far more productive than treating individuals as though they were all alike or as though they belonged to mutually exclusive types. (Dodge, 1931, p. 6.)

Anecdotal accounts reveal that individuals differ in the way that they make decisions. Some people enjoy thinking through the alternatives, whereas others are less inclined to engage in systematic information processing. Some individuals tend to be bold and risky, whereas others are cautious and risk averse. Some perceive issue ambiguity to be desirable, whereas others are threatened by uncertainty. Some individuals cognitively deliberate for long periods of time, whereas others spontaneously rely on a 'gut' feeling. Indeed, it seems almost commonsensical that individual differences would affect decision-making processes and outcomes. Surprisingly, however, there has been a longstanding reluctance to incorporate individual differences into the study of decision making. For example, a recent review of the decision-making research stated that 'attention to the use of individual differences to predict decision behavior is almost nil in the JDM [judgment and decision making] literature...' (Highhouse, 2001, p. 326). In addition, Irwin Levin devoted his 1999 presidential address to the Society for Judgment and Decision Making to a call for individual differences research in decision making.

Conceptually, it is acknowledged that decision making depends on three categories of factors: task characteristics (e.g. complexity, novelty), environmental

International Review of Industrial and Organizational Psychology, 2009, Volume 24.
Edited by G. P. Hodgkinson and J. K. Ford. Copyright © 2009 John Wiley & Sons, Ltd

conditions (e.g. time pressure, constraints), and person characteristics (e.g. personality, prior knowledge) (Einhorn, 1970; Hunt et al., 1989; Verplanken, 1993). However, although task and environmental factors have dominated the literature and been found to have a strong influence on decision making, the role of traits has received considerably less attention (e.g. Ford et al., 1989; McDougal, 1995; Stanovich and West, 1998a; Verplanken, 1993). Many research areas have recently experienced a 'renaissance' of personality research (e.g. Hogan, 2004, p. 4), including motivation (e.g. Kanfer and Ackerman, 2000; Kanfer and Heggestad, 1999), job satisfaction (e.g. Judge et al., 1999; Staw, Bell and Clausen, 1986), leadership (e.g. Judge et al., 2002a; Lord, de Vader and Alliger, 1986), team performance (e.g. Barrick et al., 1998; Mohammed, Mathieu and Bartlett, 2002), organizational change (e.g. Oreg, 2003; Wanberg and Banas, 2000), career counseling (e.g. Holland, 1997), and training (Colquitt, LePine and Noe, 2000). Despite the interdisciplinary expansion of the study of personality, however, research on individual differences in decision making has not kept up with the general shift toward dispositional research in other areas.

Although the importance of task and situational variables is clearly acknowledged, this chapter seeks to highlight the role that individual differences play in multiple aspects of the decision-making process. It is argued that such attention is long overdue, given the difficulty of disputing the influence of personality on the process of choice, the strong claims by many decision-making scholars concerning the importance of person-related factors, and the resurgence of interest in dispositional effects in many fields. Because of the importance of decision making as a fundamental, ubiquitous process that many fields are actively seeking to improve (e.g. military, medicine, education, government), the lack of systematic attention given to one of the major categories of factors conceptualized to affect the process is surprising. Therefore, the current work is a unifying attempt to both review past research as well as guide future research on individual differences in the decision-making context. The motivating question for this research was, 'What do we now know about personality traits and decision making, and what should we be exploring next?' Specifically, the goals of this chapter are to: (a) review the theoretical and empirical research on individual differences and decision making, (b) explain why there has been a lack of systematic research attention devoted to this area, and (c) offer guidelines to stimulate future research on cognition-based, personality-based, and motivation-based traits in decision making.

We proceed first by providing a review of the treatment of individual differences by theories of decision making and empirical studies. After discussing reasons for the lack of systematic research attention given to individual differences in decision making, we offer guidelines for the study of this topic and conclude with a recapitulation of the insights gleaned from this review.

THE TREATMENT OF INDIVIDUAL DIFFERENCES BY THEORIES OF DECISION MAKING: A REVIEW

While it is beyond the scope of this chapter to elaborate on each specific theory that has emerged through the history of decision-making research (see Goldstein and Hogarth, 1997 for a review), we examine major theoretical perspectives in reference to their treatment of individual differences.

Classical Utility Theories: Preferential Choice

The preferential choice research program has been dominated by the expected utility framework and assumes that a person's choice can be modeled as a consistent preference for the alternative with the highest expected utility. An individual is assumed to make a rational decision if s/he adheres to the expected utility model, but that 'does not mean that different people faced with the same skills will or should make the same decision' (Neumann and Politser, 1992, p. 32). Rather, people's decisions are based on the uncertainties involved in the decision as well as the values that individuals assign to the outcomes. Although both the perception of the situation and the subjective value of an alternative could be affected by characteristics of the person, individual differences have not been actively investigated in this model. In fact, the utility function as the connection between subjective utility and objective value is assumed to be the same basic psychological mechanism for all humans (Larrick, 1993). It is also worth noting that although the shape of the utility function is regarded by the theory as representing the risk averseness of the decision maker (Lopes, 1995), risk averseness is often treated as more situational than dispositional in that it is not measured independently of the decision-making task (e.g. Curley, Yates and Abrams, 1986).

Savage (1954) challenged the objectivity of the probability component of expected utility theory. The resulting subjective expected utility theory had strong appeal among psychologists who recognized that 'probabilities are intrinsically personal and subjective' (Lopes, 1995, p. 181). Again, 'within the model of preferential choice, there was space to represent a person's state of mind about uncertain events' (Goldstein and Hogarth, 1997, p. 9), but research failed to incorporate individual differences. The normative orientation of decision-making research in the 1950s and 1960s caused the focus to be on an ideal standard of cognitive activity, but research indicated that people often deviated from theory predictions (Beach and Lipshitz, 1993; Goldstein and Hogarth, 1997). Yet again, individual differences could have been incorporated to help account for this normative–descriptive gap. Instead, deviations from the ideal were viewed as a flaw of the decision maker, not a flaw of the theory (Lopes, 1995).

The normative–descriptive gap generated intensive research, including Kahneman and Tversky's (1979) prospect theory, which explained preferences between pairs of risky decision alternatives. Because the utility function resembled a psychophysical function and was even referred to as the 'psychophysics of chances' by Kahneman and Tversky (1984), the emphasis was on identifying mechanisms and principles common to all humans. In the attempt to delineate a general pattern of choice behavior of the average person, variance caused by individual differences was considered error. Therefore, although the influence of individual difference variables on decision making was acknowledged by Kahneman and Tversky (1979), prospect theory was nomothetic in scope and did not focus on atypical behavior.

Motivational Theories

In reaction to prospect theory, regret theory proposed that decision making involves the anticipation of regret and not just the combination of probabilities and values (Loomes and Sugden, 1982). The theory assumes that if a chosen alternative has a worse outcome than the foregone choice, individuals will experience regret. Although regret theory links affect to decision making, dispositional variables were not explicitly incorporated.

Whereas judgment and decision-making research under classical theories emphasized a psychophysical vantage point, two more recent models included psychological mechanisms in the decision-making process, while still remaining in the tradition of preferential choice. First, Lopes (1984, 1987) introduced a two-factor model of risky choice, including both a personality factor (need for security) as well as a situational factor (level of aspiration). Similar to risk-seeking propensity, security-minded individuals seek safety, while potential-minded individuals seek opportunity and risk. Level of aspiration is defined as the magnitude of outcome for which the individual is striving and is set by internal standards (e.g. what the individual regards as valuable) and external standards (e.g. the necessity to obtain a minimum outcome).

The core assumption of a second motivational model proposed by Atkinson (1957, 1983) is that people undertake an action that maximizes their feeling of achievement. The tendencies to achieve success and avoid failure represent an approach–avoidance conflict, causing a person to act or not act, depending on which tendency is stronger. Therefore, whereas all other models discussed so far focused on risky choices in lotteries, Atkinson's model describes how individuals decide whether to engage or not engage in an activity. Built on McClelland's (1951) concept of need for achievement, the motive to achieve success and the motive to avoid failure are conceptualized as general and stable dispositions of personality (Atkinson, 1983).

Judgment Models

Most of the judgment literature focuses on how the decision maker derives a judgment from ambiguous and fallible information as well as how multiple, probabilistic and potentially conflicting information sources are integrated (e.g. Goldstein and Hogarth, 1997). Although Brunswick (1952, 1956) and Hammond's (1993; Hammond and Brehmer, 1973) approaches successfully included the situation as a critical factor in decision making, they did not include individual differences. Even though the preferential choice and judgment research streams differ with regard to theory and methodology, they converge in emphasizing the commonalities among individuals as opposed to the idiosyncrasies.

Naturalistic Decision Making

Emerging in 1989 as a reaction against classical decision-making research and laboratory-based approaches, naturalistic decision making (NDM) 'asks how experienced people, working as individuals or groups in dynamic, uncertain, and often fast-paced environments, identify and assess their situation, make decisions and take actions whose consequences are meaningful to them and to the larger organization in which they operate' (Zsambok, 1997, p.5). In recognizing the existence of ill-structured problems, uncertain environments, competing goals, action/feedback loops, time stress, and high stakes, NDM offers a richer and more complex understanding of the situation than previous decision-making theories (Orasunu and Connolly, 1993). In addition, NDM conceptually acknowledges person-oriented factors such as the expertise of the decision maker (Rosen *et al.*, 2008). However, researchers have called for more studies to investigate who is most effective in making decisions in natural contexts (e.g. Howell, 1997; Schmitt, 1997). Motivation to excel, risk taking, creativity, self-reliance, and tolerance for ambiguity have been suggested as promising possibilities, but have not been empirically examined (Schmitt, 1997).

Image theory, one of the most prominent and well-developed NDM theories, divides decision making into two major steps (e.g. Beach and Mitchell, 1987, 1998). The decision maker first screens out unsuitable actions and then characteristics of the choice, environment, and decision maker influence the strategy for choosing the best option. Although strategy selection is seen as a product of mainly situational and task characteristics, the knowledge, abilities, and motivation of the decision maker are acknowledged (Beach and Mitchell, 1998). However, Beach and Mitchell (1998) stated, 'Note, that we have omitted most of the "personality" variables that might be expected to be included (e.g. risk taking and risk aversion). This is because few solid data exist that reliably relate personality characteristics to specific decision strategies' (p. 152). The omission of personality traits appears to be a chicken versus egg problem. Individual differences are not included in current research agendas because they have not shown strong empirical relationships. Yet, the absence of empirical support may be caused by research that has not been guided by a theoretical framework open to individual differences.

Summary of Theoretical Models

The review of decision-making theories presented above reveals a longstanding reluctance to incorporate individual differences into the study of decision making. The normative orientation of classic utility theories and judgment models led to a focus more on commonality than on differences. Nevertheless, there is conceptual room in these models to include person characteristics that could influence decision making. The work of Lopes (1984; Schneider and Lopes, 1986) and Atkinson (1983) began to integrate individual differences into models of decision making. However, this integration was rather minimal (a single individual difference per theory), considering the range of person characteristics that might have an impact. Furthermore, the constructs chosen were very specific to the decision-making context, making the predictions somewhat obvious. For example, security-minded (risk averse) individuals were expected to make fewer risky decisions, and individuals with the motive to achieve success were expected to succeed in their choices (provided that expectancy for success and the incentive value of the task are also high). The complex and value laden environments investigated in NDM allow for individual differences to play a greater role than in the traditional laboratory paradigm. However, despite its promise, the incorporation of individual differences into NDM models has been far from realized. Whereas decision-making theories have progressed from the exclusive focus on the choice event to the inclusion of situational variables, we would argue that the next major step should be widespread conceptual integration of individual differences. Indeed, it has been suggested that the gap between normative and descriptive theories of decision making might be best explained through person-related characteristics (e.g. Stanovich, 1999; Stanovich and West, 2002).

EMPIRICAL RESEARCH ON PERSONALITY TRAITS AND DECISION MAKING: A REVIEW

Consistent with decision-making theories, empirical work has often attempted to focus on common response patterns, only to uncover significant individual differences in the findings. Indeed, 'over the last two decades, vast numbers of reports in the literature have indicated that people often deviate from responses considered as being normative in many judgmental and decision-making tasks' (Shiloh, Salton and Sharabi, 2002). Specifically, strong, reliable individual differences have been evidenced in studies addressing variables such as omission bias (e.g. Baron and Ritov, 2004), overconfidence (e.g. Klayman, Soll and Gonzalez-Vallejo, 1999), and the use of simplification strategies (e.g. Onken,

Hastie and Revelle, 1985). However, these authors did not attempt to identify what differences accounted for participants diverging from overall patterns. In contrast, a body of empirical work has begun to emerge that directly assesses the role of person-related factors in decision making, which is summarized in Table 8.1.

In reviewing the theories of decision making, we utilized the term 'individual differences' quite broadly. For the empirical review, however, we chose to focus on relatively stable traits, including those that are cognition based (e.g. need for cognition, decision-making style), personality based (e.g. Big Five, impulsiveness), and motivation based (action-state orientation, traitlike anxiety). As such, statelike constructs (e.g. affect, self-efficacy), cognitive ability, and demographic variables were excluded, but reviewed in Soane and Nicholson (2008). Clearly, the relationship between decision making and affect (e.g. Elsbach and Barr, 1999; Mittal and Ross, 1998), cognitive ability (e.g. Capon and Davis, 1984; Stanovich and West, 1998a, 1998b), gender (e.g. Brynes, Miller and Schafer, 1999), and age (e.g. Finucane et al., 2002) has been researched in recent years. While we acknowledge the importance of these variables, we chose to focus on personality traits that have received less systematic attention in the decision-making literature toward the goal of stimulating future empirical research.

The range of person-related factors are organized in Table 8.1 as cognition based, personality based, and motivation based. In the case where multiple individual differences were measured across categories, the study was repeated in different categories and only the relevant person-related factor was discussed. In order to be included in Table 8.1, articles had to be empirical studies that examined personality traits as related to decision making, which was conceived broadly to include predecisional stages (e.g. framing, alternative generation), choice/selection, postdecisional stages (e.g. attitudes toward the decision made), and decisional biases. In addition, we focused on individual as opposed to dyadic or group decision making. Therefore, we exclude negotiation studies from our review because they represent interdependent decision making, and the role of individual differences in this literature has been addressed separately (e.g. Thompson, 1990). Because the table highlights the individual difference investigated, the methodology used, and pertinent results, the section below only briefly reviews this extant work.

Cognition-Based Traits

Need for Cognition

Need for cognition (NfC) is a relatively stable individual difference describing the tendency to be engaged in and to enjoy effortful cognitive endeavors (Cacioppo and Petty, 1982). As a key concept in the Elaboration Likelihood

Table 8.1 Summary of empirical research examining the relationship between individual differences and decision-making behaviors

Reference	Individual difference variables	Methodology/measures	Summary of individual difference results[a]
Cognition-based individual differences			
Need for cognition (NfC)			
Chatterjee et al., 2000	Need for cognition	Study 1: $N = 218$ undergraduates Task: Various price discount or increase situations in buying a couch or chair Manipulated: Mixed-gain versus mixed-loss frames, dollar-based versus percentage-based frames, equivalent versus discrepant financial outcomes Measured: Happiness of imaginary person Study 2: $N = 78$ undergraduates Similar method to Study 1, but with the students themselves as decision maker instead of an imaginary person	Study 1: Individuals low in NfC were unable to transfer percentages into absolute values and used nominal percentages to make decisions Study 2: Framing effects only occurred for those lower in NfC and only when gains were evaluated. Low NfC individuals were more careful in the calculation of losses than in the calculation of gains. Those high in NfC responded appropriately to differences in financial value, regardless of frame
Granziano, Panter, and Tanaka, 1990	Need for cognition (split into cognitive complexity and cognitive persistence sub constructs)	$N = 100$ undergraduates Task: Watched videotaped mock court trial Measured: Verdict, reason for verdict, sentence time, verdict confidence	Students higher on cognitive complexity provided more reasons for their verdict, tended to assign longer sentence times for their guilty verdicts, and focused less on factual material in their listed reasons for arriving at a verdict Higher cognitive persistence was associated with lower verdict confidence

Kobbeltvedt, Brun and Laberg, 2005	Need for cognition	Study 4: $N = 63$ cadets Task: Rescue operation Manipulations: Sleep deprivation and time pressure Measured: Time spent on task completion, probability of success, quality	Independently of time pressure, plans made by high NfC cadets were judged better than plans made by low NfC cadets. There was no significant interaction between NfC and time pressure
Kuvaas and Kaufmann, 2004	Need for cognition	$N = 125$ Norwegian students Task: Funding allocation scenario Manipulated: Positive and negative mood, positive and negative framing Measured: Overconfidence, recall	There was a significant interaction between mood, framing, and need for cognition such that the positive effect of mood–framing congruity (positive mood/positive framing and negative mood/negative framing) over mood–framing incongruity on amount of recall and level of overconfidence was stronger for low need for cognition students than high need for cognition students
LeBoeuf and Shafir, 2003	Need for cognition	Study 1: $N = 365$ undergraduates Task: 7 framing problems (positive/negative) Manipulated: Justification (provide reasons behind choice) Measured: Framing effects Study 2: $N = 292$ undergraduates Task: 2 framing problems (received both frames of each problem)	Study 1: Effortful thinking (as measured by NfC) did not reduce framing effects Study 2: Replicated Study 1 in that NfC did not diminish the proclivity to respond in line with the initially available frame Within-subjects analyses suggest that those higher in NfC are more likely to make choices consistent with their earlier responses than those with lower NfC
Levin et al., 2002	Need for cognition	$N = 102$ undergraduates Task: Positively and negatively framed stimuli (attribute, goal, and risky choice framing)	NfC had no significant effect on framing

(Cont'd)

Table 8.1 Summary of empirical research examining the relationship between individual differences and decision-making behaviors (*Continued*)

Reference	Individual difference variables	Methodology/measures	Summary of individual difference results[a]
Levin, Huneke and Jasper, 2000	Need for cognition	$N = 60$ undergraduates Task: Select a notebook computer on ComputerShop Program with pull down menus concerning products, features, and price ranges Manipulated: Instructions regarding whether to include or exclude options Measured: Effort, search orientation, depth of search, breadth of search, information probe, attribute impact	High NfC students expended more effort, exhibited more breadth of search, and probed more information than low NfC students, but differences were primarily revealed in the condition requiring the most effortful thought (inclusion, not exclusion condition) As compared to low NfC students, high NfC students exhibited more attribute-oriented search, but then shifted more to alternative-based search during the final choice stage than they had used in the set formative stage
Ordonez and Benson, 1997	Need for cognition	$N = 157$ undergraduates over three studies Task: Rating the attractiveness and maximum buying price of gambles Manipulated: Time constraint	Low NfC students performing an attractiveness rating task under time constraint tended to use the same multiplicative strategy used in the previous buying price task. When time constraint was removed, these students switched back to an additive strategy
Simon, Fagley and Halleran, 2004	Need for cognition Math ability	Study 1: $N = 233$ undergraduates Manipulated: Request for explicit reasoning and type of frame Task: Positively and negatively framed decision problems were presented. Measured: Number of risky choices Study 2: $N = 301$ undergraduates Manipulated: Depth of processing	Study 1: NfC and math ability both moderated framing effects on risky choices such that no framing effect was observed for those high in both NC and math skill Study 2: Participants high in NfC and in the deep processing condition were not vulnerable to framing effects

Smith and Levin, 1996	Need for cognition	Study 1: $N = 108$ undergraduates Manipulated: Ticket frame (lost ticket) versus money frame (lost $10) Measured: Would you spend $10 for ticket? Study 2: $N = 73$ undergraduates Manipulated: Mortality frame versus survival frame (surgery versus radiation therapy) Measured: Choice	Low NfC participants were clearly influenced by the framing of the problem. High NfC participants were less vulnerable to attempts to bias their decisions by altering frames of reference
Verplanken, 1993	Need for cognition	$N = 90$ Dutch citizens Task: Choice of refrigerator on information display board Measured: Variability of search (equal amount of information for each alternative (compensatory/noncompensatory), pattern of search (dimensionwise vs. alternativewise)	Those high in NfC expended more cognitive effort than those low in NfC, but did not search for more information Under time pressure, low NfC individuals showed more variability in the amount of information acquired across alternatives than did low NfC individuals who worked unpressured (indicating the use of more heuristic strategies) High NfC students did not behave differently in the pressured versus unpressured condition
Verplanken, Hazenberg and Palenewen, 1992	Need for cognition (divided into low and high NfC by a median split)	$N = 53$ paid undergraduates Task: Information display board Measured: Students' desire for external information, but actual information search not investigated	High NfC students requested more information and expended more task-relevant thoughts on the search than low NfC students

(Cont'd)

Table 8.1 Summary of empirical research examining the relationship between individual differences and decision-making behaviors (*Continued*)

Reference	Individual difference variables	Methodology/measures	Summary of individual difference results[a]
Verplanken and Pieters, 1988	Need for cognition	$N = 2439$ Dutch citizens Task: Mail survey on risks and benefits of nuclear energy and coal Two months after the first survey, malfunction in the nuclear power plant in Chernobyl occurred Five months after Chernobyl, face-to-face survey on electricity generation for 212 citizens of Leiden who were randomly chosen from the sample of participants in the first survey	NfC interacted with hindsight bias such that hindsight bias was found for individuals medium and low in NfC, but no systematic bias was found in the high NfC individuals High NfC individuals were better able to remember their first foresight estimate than other individuals, and were more confident that their hindsight estimate was consistent with their foresight estimate than low NfC individuals
Decision/cognitive styles			
Arroba, 1978	No thought style Compliant style Logical style Emotional style Intuitive style Hesitant style	$N = 35$ managers and 29 manual workers Task: Recall 16 decisions from various temporal periods (last day, last week, last year, previous 10 years) Interviews coded to elicit six decision-making styles	Managers used the logical style more, and manual workers used the 'no thought' style more frequently Work-related decisions were more frequently made with a logical style and personal decisions were more frequently made emotionally When a decision is unimportant, the no thought style is used more often and the logical style used less often
Ferrari and Dovidio, 2000	Indecisiveness/decisional procrastination	$N = 130$ undergraduates Task: Searched information about college courses on a board Manipulated: Number of dimensions and number of alternatives Measured: Depth and sequence of search processes	People higher in decisional procrastination took longer to make a decision, searched a higher percentage of information, and made more intradimensional shifts

Ferrari and Dovidio, 2001	Indecisiveness/decisional procrastination (categorized into decisives and indecisives based on median split)	Study 1: $N = 58$ undergraduates Study 2: $N = 100$ undergraduates Participants categorized into decisives and indecisives based on median split Task: Searched information about college courses on a board Manipulated: Cognitive effort (distracter tasks of recalling digits) Measured: Search behavior (depth of search, search sequence, interdimensional transitions, intradimensional transitions), time to complete search, ranking of top three dimensions	When demands increased under the high cognitive load distracter conditions, indecisive-prone persons were more likely to restrict their search within dimensions (Study 2) and searched less overall information (Study 1) than persons more prone toward decisive decision making. Indecisives searched for less information than decisives when the number of alternatives and dimensions increased Under conditions of high cognitive load, indecisives compared to decisives reported less confidence in their choice and made a stronger external attribute to task difficulty as a way to discount themselves for any poor performance (Study 2) Indecisives did not take longer than decisives to complete search
Frost and Shows, 1993	Indecisiveness (above 75th and below 25th percentiles asked to participate)	Study 3: $N = 29$ undergraduates Task: Decide which clothing items they would buy and which college courses they would take Measured: Latency for each choice	Participants scoring high on indecisiveness took longer to make decisions in the experiment and reported more problems with these types of decisions in real life compared to those scoring low on indecisiveness
Hough and Ogilvie, 2005	Cognitive style measured by the Myers–Briggs Intuiting/thinking Intuiting/feeling Sensing/thinking Sensing/feeling	$N = 749$ managers participating in the Looking Glass behavioral simulation involving strategic decision making	Intuiting/thinking managers were more decisive and made higher quality decisions than intuiting/feeling, sensing/feeling, or sensing/thinking managers Sensing/feeling managers made the fewest decisions and had the lowest perceived effectiveness

(Cont'd)

Table 8.1 Summary of empirical research examining the relationship between individual differences and decision-making behaviors (*Continued*)

Reference	Individual difference variables	Methodology/measures	Summary of individual difference results[a]
Hunt *et al.* (1989)	Cognitive styles based on Myers–Briggs Intuitives (intuition and feeling) Analytics (sensing and thinking) Mixed (other combinations)	*N* = 210 undergraduates Task: Business scenario in which advisors represented three cognitive styles (analytical, intuitive, mixed) Measured: Participants indicated the advisor they agreed with	Decision strategy varied as a function of cognitive style, such that cognitive style dictates how one will collect, process, and implement information in decision making Intuitive people preferred an advisor with more of an intuitive style and analytical people preferred an advisor with more of an analytical style
Parker, de Bruin and Fischhoff, 2007	Maximizers Satisficers	*N* = 360 people from social service organizations and community groups filled out a survey	Self-reported maximizing was related to greater dependence on others for information, a stronger tendency to avoid decisions, more spontaneous decision making, greater regret, less decision-making competence, and worse decision outcomes
Phillips, Pazienza and Ferrin, 1984	Rational style Intuitive style Dependent style	*N* = 243 undergraduates Task: Problem-solving appraisal Measured: Problem-solving confidence, approach–avoidance, personal control	Rational and dependent decision makers were more likely to approach rather than avoid problem situations, but dependent decision makers lacked confidence in their decision-making abilities Both rational and intuitive decision makers reported greater confidence and reduced personal control
Schwartz *et al.*, 2002	Maximizers Satisficers	*N* = thousands of undergraduates across four studies Tasks: Recall recent consumer purchase, ultimatum bargaining game Measured: Decision-making behaviors (recalled and actual)	Maximizers considered more products, took longer to decide, reported heightened regret, and engaged in more comparisons regarding recalled consumer decisions Maximizers were more sensitive to regret and less satisfied in an ultimatum bargaining game

Source	Decision style/construct	Method	Findings
Shiloh, Koren and Zaykay, 2001	Compensatory decision-making style (rational) versus noncompensatory decision-making style (less rational)	$N = 120$ 10th graders in Israel Task: Choosing a major Measured: Need for closure; subjective complexity of decision task (number of alternatives and number of dimensions); perceived difficulty	Tendency to use a compensatory decision style increases complexity of decision representations only by increasing the number of dimensions considered Compensatory style affects perceived decision difficulty only through its effects on the complexity of subjective representations of the decision
Shiloh, Salton and Sharabi, 2002	Rational–analytic (need for cognition) versus experiential–intuitive (faith in intuition) thinking styles	Study 1: $N = 128$ undergraduates in Israel Task: Questionnaire measuring heuristic versus normative judgment Study 2: $N = 104$ undergraduates in Israel Task: Choice questionnaire Manipulated: High/low rational, high/low intuitive, positive/negative frame Measured: Risky choices	Study 1: Normative judgments were positively related to rational thinking style and negatively to intuitive thinking style Study 2. High intuitive/high rational and low intuitive/low rational were most vulnerable to framing effects
Sjoberg, 2003	Intuitive style Analytical style	$N = 143$ participants from Stockholm Task: Rated 28 decision situations Measured: Intuitive/analytical mode, risk of negative outcome of decision, chance of positive outcome, extent to which the outcome was under the control of the decision maker	Intuitive decision making is preferred when making personal decisions (consumer choice decisions) and was associated with perceiving greater influence over the outcome than in more analytical, nonpersonalized decision situations Neither analytical nor intuitive decisions were preferred in risky situations

Need for structure/tolerance for ambiguity

Source		Method	Findings
Campbell and Tesser, 1983	Intolerance for ambiguity	$N = 68$ undergraduates Task: Answer true or false to 80 assertions Measured: Hindsight bias	The predictability motive (sum of dogmatism and intolerance for ambiguity scales) correlated positively with the magnitude of hindsight bias

(Cont'd)

Table 8.1 Summary of empirical research examining the relationship between individual differences and decision-making behaviors (*Continued*)

Reference	Individual difference variables	Methodology/measures	Summary of individual difference results[a]
Curley, Yates and Abrams, 1986	Ambiguity avoidance	Study 1: $N = 26$ undergraduates Task: Select Lottery 1 or 2 and record reasons for choices Measured: Risk preference	Responses to risk and ambiguity were independent. Ambiguity avoidance was distinct from risk avoidance
Einhorn and Hogarth, 1985	Attitudes toward ambiguity	Study 2: $N = 32$ Task: Make probability judgments for four scenarios Manipulated: Credibility of source and confusability of the signals	Results showed strong and stable individual strategies in the amount that was adjusted, the direction of the adjustments, and the consistency of executing one's strategy
Einhorn and Hogarth, 1986	Attitudes toward ambiguity	$N = 386$ MBA students across two studies $N = 136$ executives (Study 3) Tasks: Drawing balls from an ambiguous or unambiguous urn, buying and selling insurance, warranty pricing	There was ambiguity avoidance at moderate to high gain probabilities and ambiguity preference at low-gain probabilities
Granziano, Panter and Tanaka, 1990	Need for structure or openness	Sample: Undergraduates Task: Watched videotaped mock court trial (could stop when they felt they had sufficient information) Manipulated: Half were given instructions about what information was needed for them to reach a decision Measured: Verdict, reason for verdict, sentence time, verdict confidence	Providing instructions served as contextual information that allowed low need for structure participants to reach judgments faster than when instructions were not provided

Source	Construct	Method	Findings
Lauriola and Levin, 2001	Attitude toward ambiguity (assessed by estimating the subjective crossover point in which ambiguity-avoiding reactions turn into ambiguity-seeking reactions)	$N = 76$ Italians Tasks: Ellsberg-like two color problem involving forced choice between unambiguous and ambiguous urns; expanded risky choice task that required a forced choice between a pair of alternative contracts matched in expected value (either sure gain/loss or potential gain/loss)	The more subjects positively evaluated the ambiguous urn and preferred it to the unambiguous urn, the more they positively evaluated the risky option and preferred it to the sure thing option The overall relationship between attitude toward ambiguity and risk attitude was stronger (a) to avoid a loss rather than to achieve a gain and (b) for higher levels of probability rather than for lower levels
Lauriola, Levin and Hart, 2007	Attitude toward ambiguity (assessed by estimating the subjective crossover point in which ambiguity-avoiding reactions turn into ambiguity-seeking reactions)	Study 1: 1087 undergraduates Study 2: 630 undergraduates for part 1, 56 for part 2 Study 3: 190 undergraduates Tasks: Students first performed an Ellsberg ambiguity–probability tradeoff task and those with extreme scores returned for a risky decision-making task or scenario-based decisions under ambiguity	Responses to the ambiguity task predict responses to the risk-taking task. There is consistency in decision making under risk and ambiguity
Mayseless and Kruglanski, 1987	Need for structure (possess definite knowledge)	Study 2: $N = 70$ undergraduates in Israel Task: Identify digits on a tachistoscope Manipulated: Fear of invalidity, need for structure (instructions emphasizing need for unambiguous opinions) Measured: Confidence in evaluation Study 3: $N = 30$ undergraduates in Israel Task: Write hypotheses based on 10 photographs Manipulated: High need for structure, high fear of invalidity, control group Measured: Confidence in evaluation, number of hypotheses before a judgment	Study 2: Individuals high in need for structure processed less information compared to individuals high in the fear of invalidity Study 3: High need for structure participants generated fewer hypotheses than control group

(Cont'd)

Table 8.1 Summary of empirical research examining the relationship between individual differences and decision-making behaviors (*Continued*)

Reference	Individual difference variables	Methodology/measures	Summary of individual difference results[a]
Schaninger and Sciglimpaglia, 1981	Tolerance for ambiguity, need for cognitive clarity (certainty), rigidity, cognitive style (tendency to react to uncertain or inconsistent information by avoiding incongruous information rather than seeking clarifying information) Need for cognitive clarity	*N* = 120 housewives *Task:* 4 information display board shopping tasks (dryers, instant coffee, coffee creamer, lemonade mix) varying on novelty, complexity, insolubility *Measured:* Depth of search (# of cues drawn, # of attributes, # alternatives examined)	Participants who were more tolerant of ambiguity and those having clarifier cognitive styles examined more cues and alternatives for all four decisions. They examined more attributes only for the highly complex and insoluble dryer task. The number of cues drawn and alternatives examined were negatively related to cognitive style
Shiloh, Koren and Zaykay, 2001	Need for closure (five factors: decisiveness, close-mindedness, preference for order, discomfort with ambiguity, preference for predictability)	*N* = 120 10th graders in Israel *Task:* Choosing a major *Measured:* Compensatory decision style; subjective complexity of decision task (number of alternatives and number of dimensions); perceived difficulty	Specific facets of need for closure (close-mindedness, preference for order, discomfort with ambiguity) affected subjective decision complexity through their effects on compensatory style and number of dimensions. Nonsignificant findings resulted for the total need for closure scale

Personality-based individual differences

Personality inventories

Henderson and Nutt, 1980	Myers–Briggs Type indicators: Sensation–thinking Sensation–feeling Intuition–thinking Intuition–feeling	$N = 62$ executives from firms and hospitals participating in executive MBA and MHA programs Task: Eight scenarios on capital expansion projects that contained objective (return on investment) and subjective (process used to make return on investment and environment in which it is made) information on risk Measured: Likelihood of adoption and perceived risk	SF executives were most likely to adopt and saw the least risk in the decision (risk tolerant) ST executives were the least likely to adopt and viewed the decision to adopt as more risky than the others (risk averse)
Levin et al., 2002	Big Five (extraversion, neuroticism, agreeableness, openness, conscientiousness), faith in intuition	$N = 102$ undergraduates Task: Responsiveness to positively and negatively framed stimuli (attribute, goal, and risky choice framing)	Conscientiousness and faith in intuition were negatively related and agreeableness was positively related to the attribute framing effect Persons scoring high on neuroticism, low on openness, high on conscientiousness, and low on agreeableness were more apt to show the expected preference reversal Those scoring low on extraversion, high on openness, low on conscientiousness, and high on faith in intuition were more likely to prefer the risky option

(Contd)

Table 8.1 Summary of empirical research examining the relationship between individual differences and decision-making behaviors (*Continued*)

Reference	Individual difference variables	Methodology/measures	Summary of individual difference results[a]
Lauriola and Levin, 2001	Big Five (extraversion, neuroticism, agreeableness, openness, conscientiousness)	$N = 76$ Italians Task: 60 decision-making trials that required a forced choice between a pair of alternative contracts matched in expected value (either sure gain/loss or potential gain/loss) Measured: Risk taking for achieving a gain and avoiding a loss	Personality factors were much more important in decision making to achieve a gain than to avoid a loss For risk taking in the domain of gains, high openness to experience was associated with greater risk taking Persons scoring high on neuroticism were both more apt than others to take risks in the domain of losses and less apt to take risks in the domain of gains
Moon, 2001	Overall conscientiousness and two specific facets (duty and achievement striving)	$N = 360$ undergraduates Task: Escalation of commitment scenario Measured: Degree of continued investment on project	Achievement striving was positively related to escalation of commitment, duty was negatively related to escalation of commitment, and the broad measure of conscientiousness was not significantly related to commitment
Pollay, 1970	California Psychological Inventory (e.g. achievement potential, intellectual interest, socialization, ascendancy)	$N = 29$ undergraduates Task: Selecting one alternative from four descriptions of research and development projects Measured: Time to a decision	Achievement potential was positively correlated with the severity of quitting behavior (as measured by the magnitude of the difference between decision times when all of the alternatives were equally attractive and when two of the alternatives were inferior)

Taylor and Dunnette, 1974	California Psychological Inventory (e.g. dogmatism, flexibility)	$N = 79$ male manufacturing managers Task: Simulated managerial promotion decision Measured: Information processing (amount of information viewed, time to decision, information processing rate, and accuracy in rating information) and postdecision processes (decision accuracy, decision confidence, decision flexibility, and information retention)	Dogmatism exerted a large influence on confidence in holding a decision after it was made
Zuckerman and Kuhlman, 2000	Zuckerman–Kuhlman Personality Questionnaire (e.g. neuroticism–anxiety, aggression–hostility, activity, sociability)	$N = 260$ undergraduates Task: Complete questionnaire assessing behavior in six areas of risk (drinking, smoking, gambling, driving, sex, drugs)	Aggression–hostility and sociability were positively related to the composite risk measure
Impulsiveness			
Hinson, Jameson and Whitney, 2003	Impulsiveness	Study 3: $N = 170$ students People with extreme scores on impulsivity chosen to participate Task: Choosing between hypothetical monetary options varying in amount and delay	People who scored high on impulsiveness discounted delayed rewards to a greater extent. Impulsiveness may occur because working memory dysfunction interferes with the cognitive processes needed to establish anticipatory affective reactions
Levin and Hart, 2003	Impulsivity, shyness, fearfulness, thrill seeking (behavioral measures)	Study 1: $N = 30$ (5–6 years old) Study 2: $N = 72$ child–parent pairs Task: Simple gambles (gain and loss conditions) Measured: Number of risky choices to avoid loss or achieve a gain	Study 1: Impulsivity was positively and shyness was negatively related to risky decision making Study 2: The more risk taking the parent, the more risk taking the child
Yechiam et al., 2005	Impulsivity/ venturesomeness; self-control	$N = 162$ men and women Task: Iowa gambling task Manipulated: Drug abusers versus control participants; high versus low payoff; first versus second half of task	No significant results emerged regarding the relationship between impulsivity and performance on the gambling task

(Cont'd)

Table 8.1 Summary of empirical research examining the relationship between individual differences and decision-making behaviors (*Continued*)

Reference	Individual difference variables	Methodology/measures	Summary of individual difference results[a]
Miscellaneous			
Alker and Hermann (1971)	Dogmatism Rational risk taking Integrative complexity	$N = 120$ males Task: Solving Bayesian problems (drawing chips from a bag) Manipulated: Decision importance, complexity Measured: Deviation from normative solution as predicted by Bayesian prediction	No significant relationships were found between individual differences and the conservativeness of the decision
Buehler and Griffin, 2003	Dispositional optimism	$N = 78$ undergraduates in Study 1 $N = 125$ undergraduates in Study 2 Task: Predict the date and time they would complete their Christmas shopping (Study 1) and university class assignments (Study 2) Manipulated: Future focus Measured: Optimistic bias (the difference between predicted and actual completion times)	There was no significant relationship between dispositional optimism and the predicted completion times, the actual completion times, or the degree of prediction bias for Studies 1 and 2
Campbell and Tesser, 1983	Dogmatism	$N = 68$ undergraduates Task: Answer true or false to 80 assertions Measured: Hindsight bias	The predictability motive (sum of dogmatism and intolerance for ambiguity scales) correlated positively with the magnitude of hindsight bias
Carducci and Wong, 1998	Type A Type B	$N = 305$ undergraduates Task: Reading a series of statements and making a number of decisions concerning various everyday financial matters	Type A individuals took greater financial risks than Type B individuals
Fagley and Miller, 1990	Field independence	Study 2: $N = 109$ undergraduates Task: 5 decision problems Manipulated: Positive or negative frame	Study 2: Field independence did not interact with the framing effect

Josephs et al., 1992	Optimism	Study 1: $N = 78$ undergraduates Task: Play gambles for real money Measured: Risk taking	Optimism did not predict risk taking
Parker and Fischhoff, 2005	Self-monitoring Self-consciousness (concern for how others view one)	$N = 110$ male 18–19 year olds Tasks: 7 exercises assessing decision-making competence (e.g. resistance to framing and sunk costs, applying decision rules, under/overconfidence)	Self-monitoring and self-consciousness were positively correlated with an aggregate measure of decision-making competence
Risk-taking propensity/sensation seeking			
Fagley and Miller, 1990	Risk-taking propensity	Study 1: $N = 190$ undergraduates Study 2: $N = 109$ undergraduates Task: 5 decision problems Manipulated: Positive or negative frame	Risk-taking propensity did not interact with the framing effect
Harris, 2001	Risk-taking preference Sensation seeking	$N = 301$ students Task: Two hypothetical scenarios (investment and job decision) Manipulated: Potential for regret (risky choice/regret minimizing or safe choice/regret minimizing) Measured: Risk behavior	Individuals high in risk preference or high in sensation seeking were more likely to make a risky decision than individuals who scored lower on these variables Personality impacted risk taking more consistently than the tendency to minimize regret, and interactions between the two were minimal
Horvath and Zuckerman, 1993	Sensation seeking	$N = 447$ undergraduates Task: Complete questionnaire containing questions about 30 risky activities	Sensation seeking was a strong predictor of risky behavior, especially in the areas of criminal behavior and social violations. Risk appraisal was negatively related to risky behavior

(Cont'd)

Table 8.1 Summary of empirical research examining the relationship between individual differences and decision-making behaviors (*Continued*)

Reference	Individual difference variables	Methodology/measures	Summary of individual difference results[a]
McDougal, 1995	Risk-taking preference (median split to create risk-averse and risk-seeking groups)	$N = 103$ undergraduates Task: Search matrices of monetary gambles on the computer Manipulated: Likelihood of payoff and goal value Measured: Time, frequency, pattern, sequence of search	Differences in risk preference on information search were most pronounced in the no goal condition, where risk-seeking individuals spent more time searching riskier information Both risk-averse and risk-seeking participants searched the safest information more than any other information for all goal levels Risk-seeking participants made riskier choices than risk-averse participants when there was no goal or a low goal
Seta, McElroy and Seta, 2001	Risk seeking and risk avoiding	Experiment 1: $N = 79$ female students Task: Read a scenario describing a businessman making investments Manipulated: Businessman described as risk seeker or risk avoider Measured: Regret, wisdom Experiment 2: $N = 38$ students Task: Only risk-seeking businessman presented in scenario Measured: Consistency, desirability, regret	Study 1: More regret was associated with inaction in the risk seeker condition and more regret was associated with action in the avoider condition Study 2: Judgments of regret were higher in the inaction condition than the action condition for the risk seeker businessman. Consistency and desirability mediated the relationship between action/inaction and regret
Sitkin and Weingart, 1995	Risk-taking propensity	$N = 38$ MBA students Task: Carter Racing decision making case Manipulated: Successful/unsuccessful outcome history Measured: Decision-making behavior, risk perception	When participants reported higher risk propensity, they also reported lower risk perception Risk perception mediated the link between risk propensity and risky decision-making behavior

Slattery and Ganster, 2002	Risk-taking propensity	$N = 292$ undergraduates. Task: Complex financial task Manipulated: Feedback of meeting or not meeting chosen goal Measured: Goal choices	Participants with higher risk propensity made riskier decisions Risk propensity explained an additional 5% of the variance in each goal choice above situational variables and sex
Taylor and Dunnette, 1974	Risk-taking propensity	$N = 79$ male manufacturing managers Task: Simulated managerial promotion decision Measured: Information processing (amount of information viewed, time to decision, information processing rate, and accuracy in rating information diagnosticity) and postdecision processes (decision accuracy, decision confidence, decision flexibility, and information retention)	High risk takers processed information more slowly
Weber, Blais and Betz, 2002	Domain-specific risk attitude (ethical, investment, gambling, health/safety, recreational, social)	Study 2: $N = 121$ undergraduates Task: Self-reports of common risky behaviors in the recent past; card game involving real monetary payoffs	Self-reported frequencies of past risky behaviors correlated significantly with risk attitude subscale scores The card game results correlated most strongly with the financial risk subscale, but also correlated significantly with the health/safety, ethics, and recreational domains
Wong and Carducci, 1991	Sensation seeking (median split used to classify high and low sensation seekers)	$N = 233$ undergraduates Task: 12 everyday financial decisions that differed in their degrees of risk	High sensation seekers tended to take greater risks with everyday money matters
Zuckerman and Kuhlman, 2000	Impulsive sensation seeking	$N = 260$ undergraduates Task: Complete questionnaire assessing behavior in six areas of risk (drinking, smoking, gambling, driving, sex, drugs)	Impulsive sensation seeking was positively related to the composite risk measure

(Cont'd)

Table 8.1 Summary of empirical research examining the relationship between individual differences and decision-making behaviors (*Continued*)

Reference	Individual difference variables	Methodology/measures	Summary of individual difference results[a]
Motivation-based individual differences			
Action-state orientation (ASO)			
Niederberger, Engemann and Radtke, 1987	Action-state orientation	Task: Process tracing method to trace requests for information about different options regarding practical courses and their attributes Manipulated: Memory load (information disappeared when next request made or required information remained on the screen)	Regardless of condition, state-oriented subjects considered more information than action-oriented subjects Under low memory load, action-oriented participants showed a gradual reduction of options, whereas state-oriented participants hardly reduced the number of options
Stiensmeier-Pelster and Schurmann, 1993	Action-state orientation (hesitation subscale)	Study 1: $N = 40$ individuals assigned to groups on the basis of ASO scores Task: Decide which of 36 dice games they wanted to play Manipulated: Time constraint (3 min) versus no time constraint Study 2: $N = 21$ students assigned to groups on the basis of ASO scores Task: Selecting packages of information to estimate expected stock exchange profits	Study 1: Time pressure prompted action-oriented subjects to resort to the simple expectancy-based rule (more parsimonious information processing, filtration or a substantial change in information processing), whereas state-oriented subjects became even more attached to the more complex expectancy-value rule requiring the processing of more information (acceleration of information processing)

	Measure	Task / Manipulation	Findings
		Manipulated: Time pressure by informing students that payment would depend exclusively on the accuracy of their estimations Study 3: $N = 35$ students Task: 6 sets of 4 gambles on computer Manipulated: Time pressure (20 s)	Study 2: Action-oriented individuals coped with time pressure by decreasing the amount of information processed, and state-oriented individuals processed the same amount of information at a faster rate (acceleration of information processing) Study 3: Action-oriented individuals coped with time pressure by filtering available information, whereas state-oriented individuals responded with an acceleration of information processing (do the same thing, but faster)
Stiensmeier-Pelster et al., 1989	Action-state orientation (hesitation subscale)	Task: Indicate the degree to which decision-related statements are endorsed (e.g. quick decisions are good decisions; I am fearful of making a false decision)	Experiment 2 State-oriented as compared to action-oriented individuals reported having a greater fear of making an incorrect decision and were prepared to spend more time to avoid false decisions Action-oriented individuals considered quick decisions to be good decisions and were prepared to accept the risk of making mistakes when they could save decision time
Stiensmeier-Pelster et al., 1991	Action-state orientation (hesitation subscale)	Experiment 2 Task: Estimate the profit to be expected by a stock exchange broker in various hypothetical situations Manipulated: The importance of the decision problem by means of the size of possible renumeration (1.50 or 5.00)	On decision problems of low importance, state-oriented individuals utilized more information for their estimations (choose more complex strategies) and had more confidence in their solution. Action-oriented (as contrasted to state-oriented) individuals reacted more flexibly to different situational demands (processed more information when importance increased). State-oriented individuals chose more complex strategies irrespective of importance

(Cont'd)

Table 8.1 Summary of empirical research examining the relationship between individual differences and decision-making behaviors (*Continued*)

Reference	Individual difference variables	Methodology/measures	Summary of individual difference results[a]
Anxiety			
Butler and Mathews, 1983	Anxiety Depression	Normal, anxious and depressed participants Task: Rate the risk of a range of positive and negative events, in relation both to themselves and others	Both anxious and depressed participants rated negative events as more likely to happen than did normal controls. Ratings of negative events made by both anxious and depressed patients for themselves were higher than ratings made for another person
Butler and Mathews, 1987	State anxiety Trait anxiety	$N = 57$ students Task: Complete subjective probability questionnaire Manipulated: Half of the students were expecting an examination in the near future and half were not Measured: Risk estimates (How likely is it that will do well on exam?)	Increases in anticipatory anxiety as the exam approached were associated with increased subjective risk of examination failure Trait of anxiety was associated with perceived risk of all self-referred negative events whether or not they related to examinations
Dahlback, 1990	Ability to remain calm in conflict situations Anxiety about deficient control Guilt feelings about deficient control	$N = 71$ male students Tasks: 14 choice dilemma problems, 48 hypothetical gambling problems, 14 roulette problems	Students who have a greater ability to remain clam in conflict situations and who do not tend to become anxious and to develop guilt feelings when control is deficient tend to be bolder in risk taking than students who have little ability to remain cool in conflict situations and who tend to become anxious and to develop guilt feelings when control is deficient

Schaninger and Sciglimpaglia, 1981	Trait anxiety	$N = 120$ housewives Task: 4 information display board shopping tasks (dryers, instant coffee, coffee creamer, lemonade mix) varying on novelty, complexity, insolubility Measured: Depth of search (# of cues drawn, # of attributes, # alternatives examined)	The number of cues drawn and alternatives examined were negatively related to trait anxiety
Mayseless and Kruglanski, 1987	Fear of invalidity (avoid judgmental mistakes)	Study 1: $N = 28$ undergraduates in Israel Task: Identify digits on a tachistoscope Manipulated: Fear of invalidity (promised extra credit if successful on task) Measured: Confidence in evaluation, perceptual threshold Study 2: $N = 70$ undergraduates in Israel Task: Identify digits on a tachistoscope Manipulated: Fear of invalidity, need for structure (instructions emphasizing need for unambiguous opinions) Measured: Confidence in evaluation Study 3: $N = 30$ undergraduates in Israel Task: Write hypotheses based on 10 photographs Manipulated: High need for structure, high fear of invalidity, control group Measured: Confidence in evaluation, number of hypotheses before a judgment	Study 1: High fear participants sought more information and reported higher confidence in their final decision than low fear participants Study 2: Results of Study 1 were replicated. Individuals high in need for structure processed less information compared to individuals high in the fear of invalidity. High fear of validity participants sought significantly more information than control group Study 3: High fear of invalidity individuals generated more hypotheses than control group

(*Cont'd*)

Table 8.1 Summary of empirical research examining the relationship between individual differences and decision-making behaviors (*Continued*)[a]

Reference	Individual difference variables	Methodology/measures	Summary of individual difference results[a]
Nichols-Hoppe and Beach, 1990	Test anxiety	$N = 96$ females who scored in the upper and lower quartiles of anxiety Task: Information board of job and apartment decisions Manipulated: Evaluation pressure, decision importance, and task complexity Measured: Compensatory and noncompensatory search strategies, amount of information searched	Participants who scored high on test anxiety inspected and reinspected significantly more information in the course of predecisional searches across all conditions than did participants who scored low on test anxiety
Stober, 1997	State anxiety Trait anxiety	Study 1: $N = 68$ German students Study 2: $N = 60$ German students Task: Participants given texts about possible negative and positive events with omissions for the two risk dimensions and chose the most plausible risk descriptions Manipulation: Musical mood to induce state anxiety Measured: Risk appraisal	In both studies, high trait-anxious individuals showed an elevated risk appraisal for all events. High trait-anxious individuals chose significantly higher degrees of both probability and utility as the most plausible alternatives when the events were negative, whereas they chose significantly lower degrees when the events were positive
Wray and Stone, 2005	Anxiety	Study 1: $N = 233$ undergraduates Study 2: $N = 270$ undergraduates Task: Five relationship-based scenarios Manipulated: Decisions for self versus others Measured for Study 1: Risk taking Measured for Study 2: Probability of successful outcome, feelings about positive, negative, and risk-averse outcomes	In both studies, lower anxiety participants made more risk-seeking decisions than high anxiety participants. Anxiety levels were related to risk taking for the self, but not for others. The self-other decision-making difference was more pronounced for higher anxiety individuals Study 2: Effects of anxiety on personal decision making were partially mediated by success expectations and feelings toward negative outcomes

Self-esteem

Study			
Josephs et al., 1992	Self-esteem (selected upper and lower quartiles)	Study 1: $N = 78$ undergraduates Study 2: $N = 89$ undergraduates Study 3: $N = 101$ undergraduates Task: Play gambles for real money Manipulations: Feedback or no feedback on chosen alternative (Study 2); feedback or no feedback on forgone alternative (Study 3) Measured: Risk taking	Study 1 and 2: When feedback was expected, low self-esteem students were significantly less risk seeking in choices about gains than in choices about losses. High self-esteem students did not shift their risk preference as a function of decision frame Study 3: Low self-esteem subjects were more likely than high self-esteem subjects to choose low risk lotteries if they anticipated feedback on the forgone alternative. Low self-esteem individuals preferred not to learn about the result of the forgone lottery, whereas high self-esteem individuals did
Schaninger and Sciglimpaglia, 1981	Self-esteem	$N = 120$ housewives Task: 4 information display board shopping tasks (dryers, instant coffee, coffee creamer, lemonade mix) varying on novelty, complexity, insolubility Measured: Depth of search (# of cues drawn, # of attributes, # alternatives examined)	Housewives who had higher self-esteem examined more cues and alternatives for all four decisions. They examined more attributes only for the highly complex and insoluble dryer task
Wray and Stone, 2005	Self-esteem	Study 1: $N = 233$ undergraduates Study 2: $N = 270$ undergraduates Task: Five relationship-based scenarios Manipulated: Decisions for self versus others Measured for Study 1: Risk taking Measured for Study 2: Probability of successful outcome, feelings about positive, negative, and risk-averse outcomes	In both studies, high self-esteem participants made more risk-seeking decisions than low self-esteem participants. Self-esteem was related to risk taking for the self, but not for others The self–other decision-making difference was more pronounced for low self-esteem individuals Study 2: Effects of self-esteem on personal decision making were partially mediated by success expectations and feelings toward negative outcomes

[a]Results are limited to findings specifically related to individual differences and decision making.

Model of persuasion and attitude change, information is processed more deeply and systematically by high than low NfC individuals (Cacioppo and Petty, 1982). Of the studies that have examined the influence of NfC on decision making, most have focused on framing effects, with sparser attention being given to information search behaviors, choice, and biases. Framing studies have yielded mixed results, with experiments finding either no significant NfC effects (e.g. LeBoeuf and Shafir, 2003; Levin et al., 2002), direct effects (e.g. Kobbeltvedt, Brun and Laberg, 2005; Smith and Levin, 1996), or qualified effects under certain conditions (e.g. Chatterjee et al., 2000; Kuvaas and Kaufmann, 2004; Simon, Fagley and Halleran, 2004). Stronger findings resulted for information search processes, with those higher in the NfC expending more cognitive effort, requesting more information (e.g. Verplanken, Hazenberg and Palenewen, 1992), and delivering more reasons for their decisions (e.g. Granziano, Panter and Tanaka, 1990). However, situational factors qualified many NfC results, including the amount of effortful thought (e.g. Levin, Huneke and Jasper, 2000) and time constraint and pressure (e.g. Ordonez and Benson, 1997; Verplanken, 1993).

Need for Structure/Tolerance for Ambiguity

Tolerance for ambiguity refers to the tendency to perceive ambiguous, inconsistent situations as desirable as opposed to threatening (Budner, 1962). Novel, complex, and insoluble situations are categorized as ambiguous (Budner, 1962). Closely related, the need for closure or structure represents a desire for definitive knowledge and an aversion for ambiguity (e.g. Mayseless and Kruglanski, 1987; Shiloh, Koren and Zaykay, 2001). Einhorn and Hogarth (1985, 1986) proposed a descriptive model of how people make judgments under different amounts of ambiguity, which includes attitudes toward ambiguity as an individual difference. Comparison across empirical work is made difficult by the variety of ways that tolerance for ambiguity has been assessed, including survey measurement (e.g. Schaninger and Sciglimpaglia, 1981), an ambiguity–probability tradeoff task (involving selections from unambiguous or ambiguous urns; Lauriola and Levin, 2001), and manipulation via instructions stressing the importance of forming unambiguous opinions (Mayseless and Kruglanski, 1987). Individuals high in the need for structure processed less information (Mayseless and Kruglanski, 1987; Schaninger and Sciglimpaglia, 1981), and those low in the need for structure reached judgments faster when instructions were provided (Granziano, Panter and Tanaka, 1990).

Decision Making/Cognitive Styles

Decision style refers to the unique manner by which individuals perceive, approach, and respond to decision-making situations (Arroba, 1978; Harren, 1979). Similarly, cognitive style refers to differences between individuals in thinking, knowing, and processing information (Armstrong and Priola, 2001). Thunholm (2004) considers decision style to be broader than the definition of cognitive styles, although some authors use the terms interchangeably (e.g. Andersen, 2000). Because the distinctions between cognitive and decision styles have not been well established and the constructs appear to share many commonalities, they are categorized together. For the most part, cognitive and decision styles are considered to be relatively stable over time (e.g. Armstrong and Priola, 2001; Scott and Bruce, 1995). Therefore, whereas intuition and analysis/reasoning have been proposed as two fundamental types of cognitive processes in decision making (e.g. Hammond *et al.*, 1997; Kahneman and Frederick, 2002), intuitive and rational decision styles capture dispositional tendencies in the way that individuals respond to decision-making situations (e.g. Scott and Bruce, 1995).

Thus far, the conceptual framework underlying decision styles is not well established. For example, whereas some authors view decision styles as personality based (e.g. Rowe and Boulgarides, 1992), others view them as learned habit-based propensities to make decisions in a certain way (Driver, Brousseau and Hunsaker, 1990). In addition, there is debate regarding whether analysis and intuition represent a unidimensional continuum (e.g. Allinson and Hayes, 1996) or derive from independent cognitive systems that allow individuals to switch back and forth (e.g. Hodgkinson and Clark, 2007; Hodgkinson and Sadler-Smith, 2003; Pacini and Epstein, 1999). As evidenced in Table 8.1, comparisons across studies are difficult because a number of different typologies of decision and cognitive styles have been proposed, and it is not entirely clear whether just the terminology or the actual constructs are distinct (e.g. Is a rational style or compensatory style the same as a maximizing style? Is indecisiveness the same as an avoidant decision style?).

Given the undeveloped nature of existing work, research has sought to test whether individuals with a particular style actually exhibit the expected decision-making behaviors. For example, individuals with more of a rational style were more likely to approach rather than avoid problems (Phillips, Pazienza and Ferrin, 1984), a logical style was used less often when decisions were unimportant (Arroba, 1978), and intuitives preferred other intuitives, whereas analytics preferred other analytics (Hunt *et al.*, 1989).

Pointing to the need for further research, some results were contradictory across studies. For example, as compared to decisive individuals, Ferrari and Dovidio (2000) found that decisional procrastinators searched for more information about chosen alternatives, but a later study by the same authors in 2001 found that decisional procrastinators searched less overall information. In addition, whereas some studies found that indecisives took longer to make decisions than decisives (e.g. Ferrari and Dovidio, 2000; Frost and Shows, 1993), other studies concluded that there were no differences between indecisives and decisives with regard to search completion times (Ferrari and Dovidio, 2001).

Personality-Based Traits

Personality Inventories and Individual Traits

Personality inventories employed in the decision-making context include the Myers–Briggs (e.g. Henderson and Nutt, 1980), the Big Five (e.g. Lauriola and Levin, 2001; Levin et al., 2002), the California Psychological Inventory (Pollay, 1970; Taylor and Dunnette, 1974), and the Zuckerman–Kuhlman Five-Factor Personality questionnaire (Zuckerman and Kuhlman, 2000). In general, Big Five Traits have been found to exert influence on framing (Lauriola and Levin, 2001; Levin et al., 2002) and escalation of commitment (Moon, 2001), whereas Myers–Briggs and Zuckerman–Kuhlman indicators influenced perceived risk (Henderson and Nutt, 1980; Zuckerman and Kuhlman, 2000).

In terms of individual traits, impulsiveness (action taken without regard for all of the consequences) has been associated with discounting delayed rewards (Hinson, Jameson, and Whitney, 2003) and greater risky decision making in children (Levin and Hart, 2003), but not adults (Yechiam et al., 2005). In addition, Type As take greater risks as compared to Type Bs (Carducci and Wong, 1998). Furthermore, self-monitoring and self-consciousness were positively related to an aggregate measure of decision-making competence (Parker and Fischhoff, 2005). In terms of null effects, field dependence, or the extent to which a person relies on the surrounding visual field in perceiving objects, was not significantly related to framing (Fagley and Miller, 1990). Dogmatism (tendency to hold decisions confidently and inflexibly) was not found to impact decision conservativeness (Alker and Hermann, 1971).

Risk-Taking Propensity/Preference and Sensation Seeking

Although classical decision theory has regarded the propensity for risk seeking or risk avoidance as situational (Kahneman and Tversky, 1979), several authors have long acknowledged that an individual's desire to accept or avoid risk is a key part of personality (e.g. Bromiley and Curley, 1992; Dahlback, 1990; Jackson, Hourany and Vidmar, 1972). Risk-seeking individuals desire potential and are motivated to pursue the best outcomes; in contrast, risk-averse individuals desire security and are motivated to avoid the worst outcomes (McDougal, 1995). There is ongoing debate concerning the stability of the construct, with some simultaneously regarding risk propensity as a persistent, dispositional variable that can vary with the situation (e.g. Sitkin and Weingart, 1995; Soane and Chmiel, 2005). Closely related and sometimes categorized as a subdimension to risk-taking preference, sensation seeking is one of the most investigated traits in risk-taking research (e.g. Lauriola and Levin, 2001). The construct refers to the tendency to seek novel, varied, complex, and intense experiences as well as the willingness to take risks for such experiences (Zuckerman, 1994).

In the expected utility framework, risk attitude refers to the curvature of the utility function underlying choice (Weber, Blais and Betz, 2002). In fact, some of the research using gambles has tended to confound the behavior with the trait in that both are assessed simultaneously (e.g. Curley, Yates and Abrams, 1986). Therefore, individuals are deemed to be risk averse or risk seeking when they select the sure thing or the gamble, respectively. In this review, we have attempted to focus on research that has approached the construct as dispositional rather than simply situational and has measured risk preference as defined by the decision maker separately from the decision-making task. The primary finding of this research is that those higher in risk propensity and sensation seeking are more likely to make risky decisions (e.g. Harris, 2001; Horvath and Zuckerman, 1993; Sitkin and Weingart, 1995; Slattery and Ganster, 2002; Wong and Carducci, 1991; Weber, Blais and Betz, 2002; Zuckerman and Kuhlman, 2000). Although the most robust findings have been found for risky choice, a limited number of studies have also investigated the impact of risk preference on information processing (McDougal, 1995; Taylor and Dunnette, 1974).

Motivation-Based Traits

Action-State Orientation

Action-state orientation (ASO) addresses the ability to initiate and maintain intentions, avoid procrastination, handle multiple competing demands, and persist in the face of failure (Kuhl and Beckmann, 1994). Embedded within a broader theory of action-control, ASO emphasizes the role of volitional functioning when people accomplish or fail to accomplish successful action (Kuhl, 1994b). Specifically, individuals who are more action oriented are generally better at initiating action, ignoring distractions, and persisting toward goal-directed activities. In contrast, individuals who are more state oriented tend to miss opportunities to act, ruminate about negative possibilities, and become more easily distracted and discouraged (Kuhl and Beckmann, 1994). State-oriented persons tend to consider more information (Niederberger, Engemann and Radtke, 1987) and report greater fear of making an incorrect decision (Steinsmeier-Pelster et al., 1989). In addition, several studies point to action-oriented individuals being more flexible in response to situational demands (e.g. time pressure, low memory load, decision importance), whereas state-oriented individuals are slower in altering their strategy under different conditions (e.g. Niederberger, Engemann and Radtke, 1987; Steinsmeier-Pelster and Schurmann, 1993; Steinsmeier-Pelster et al., 1989).

Anxiety

Anxiety emerges in response to the perception of threat. Some authors distinguish between state and trait anxiety, with trait anxiety being more stable (e.g.

Butler and Mathews, 1987; Stober, 1997). As the focus of this chapter is on relatively stable dispositions, the research findings regarding trait anxiety will be emphasized. Subjective risk has been the primary dependent variable studied, and those lower in anxiety are more risk seeking (Dahlback, 1990; Wray and Stone, 2005). With regard to information search, contradictory findings have been reported across studies. Specifically, Nichols-Hoppe and Beach (1990) as well as Mayseless and Kruglanski (1987) found that higher anxiety/fear of invalidity was associated with more information seeking, whereas Schaninger and Sciglimpaglia (1981) found that higher trait anxiety was associated with a lower the number of alternatives examined.

Self-Esteem

Negatively correlated with anxiety (e.g. Wray and Stone, 2005), self-esteem refers to the extent to which people like, value, and accept themselves. Higher self-esteem has been associated with higher risk seeking (e.g. Josephs et al., 1992; Wray and Stone, 2005) as well as examining more cues and alternatives (Schaninger and Sciglimpaglia, 1981).

Summary of Empirical Research

As Table 8.1 reveals, when combined together, a sizable number of studies have examined the impact of personality traits on decision-making processes, although the number is still comparatively small when compared to the huge literature describing the impact of situation and task characteristics on how people make decisions. However, several factors have served to mute the impact of this work on the field. First, because of the eclectic and interdisciplinary nature of decision-making research, empirical studies of individual differences are scattered across many disciplines (e.g. consumer behavior, psychology, management) and journals. While some specialty journals focus on individual differences (e.g. *Journal of Research in Personality, Personality and Individual Differences*), others focus on decision making (e.g. *Journal of Behavioral Decision Making*). In addition, top-tier psychology journals are also represented (e.g. *Journal of Personality and Social Psychology, Organizational Behavior and Human Decision Processes*) as well as several management journals (e.g. *Academy of Management Journal, Journal of Management, Management Science*). Second, interest in individual differences in decision making has spanned a large segment of time, with some studies dated as far back as 1970 (Pollay, 1970) and others as recent as 2007 (e.g. Lauriola, Levin and Hart, 2007). Third, although much of the research on person-related factors has focused on risky decision making, criterion variables also include framing, information search, and biases.

On the positive side, this diversity in outlets, time frames, and decision-related dependent variables reflects broad acknowledgment of the importance of individual differences within the decision-making context. On the negative side, the impact of this work has not been fully realized, in part, because it has been scattered across disparate outlets and disciplines, many decades, and multiple dependent variables. Indeed, summarizing the results of this work is difficult, as several studies report insignificant or mixed results (e.g. Alker and Hermann, 1971; Buehler and Griffin, 2003; Fagley and Miller, 1990; LeBoeuf and Shafir, 2003) as well as inconsistencies across studies (e.g. anxiety: Nichols-Hoppe and Beach, 1990; Mayseless and Kruglanski, 1987; Schaninger and Sciglimpaglia, 1981; decision styles: Ferrari and Dovidio, 2000, 2001; Frost and Shows, 1993). The variety of experimental tasks, individual differences, and outcome measures employed makes the use of meta-analysis implausible because statistical combinations may mask important differences in research findings (Cooper, 2003). Thus, this chapter provides a qualitative review of existing research as well as offers guidelines for future research on personality traits and decision making.

INDIVIDUAL DIFFERENCES AND DECISION MAKING: WHY THE LACK OF SYSTEMATIC RESEARCH ATTENTION

Having provided a review of the current state of affairs both theoretically and empirically, we now turn our attention to addressing the question of why there has not been a coherent, compelling case for the role of individual differences in decision making. Initially, it is worth addressing whether the lack of systematic research attention is reflective of the reality that personality traits actually contribute nothing or very little to the study of decision making. We would argue against this explanation for several reasons. First, the relevance of personality variables to key areas such as motivation (e.g. Kanfer and Ackerman, 2000), leadership (e.g. Judge et al., 2002a), training (e.g. Colquitt, LePine and Noe, 2000), and career counseling (e.g. Holland, 1997) makes it highly unlikely that individual differences would play no role in ubiquitous decision making. Indeed, it seems commonsensical that person characteristics affect decision-making processes, and anecdotal decision maker accounts highlight the importance of the individual. Second, person characteristics are commonly regarded as one of the three main categories of factors contributing to decision making, along with environmental conditions and task characteristics (Einhorn, 1970; Verplanken, 1993). Third, despite the search for overall patterns of decision-making behaviors, strong, reliable individual differences have been evidenced in many studies (e.g. Baron and Ritov, 2004; Klayman, Soll and Gonzalez-Vallejo, 1999; Onken, Hastie and Revelle, 1985). Fourth and most persuasively, empirical work is beginning to demonstrate that individual differences predict decision-making behaviors (e.g. Levin, Huneke and Jasper, 2000; Schwartz et al., 2002; Stober, 1997; Verplanken, 1993), despite the significant limitations of a nonsupportive theoretical framework and an experimental paradigm that serves to minimize the influence of personality traits. We propose that a more plausible explanation for the lack of a concentrated, sustained effort in examining the impact of individual differences on decision behaviors involves both theoretical as well as methodological considerations. Each will be discussed sequentially.

Although it is rather easy to find positive evidence for the presence of a particular line of theory, it is more difficult to find evidence for the absence of a theory or to discern reasons for the failure to pursue a line of research. Nevertheless, we conjecture that the normative orientation of many of the classic theories of decision making resulted in a focus on commonality rather than differences, resulting in the treatment of person-related characteristics as error to be minimized rather than variance to be studied in its own right. Despite the emphasis on ideal standards of cognitive activity (Beach and Mitchell, 1998), however, studies have found that individuals strongly diverge from the normative model (e.g. Beach and Lipshitz, 1993). The normative–descriptive gap led to intensive research (e.g. prospect theory), but individual differences were not incorporated. Instead, the approach taken by many classical theorists to deviations from ideal model predictions was to 'damn the behavior' (Beach and Lipshitz, 1993, p. 22) or to declare the decision maker irrational rather than view the theory as flawed (Stanovich, 1999). Given this response, a conducive climate did not exist for investigating decision maker characteristics that may have explained some of the inconsistencies between observed behavior and model predictions.

The lack of a supportive theoretical framework, in turn, has served to substantially reduce the impact of empirical work on individual differences and decision making. Indeed, a recursive cycle may have developed between nonpersuasive empirical findings and the failure to develop a theoretical perspective supporting individual differences, creating a negative feedback loop from one to the other. Whereas the complaint in many areas is that empirical research substantially lags theoretical work (e.g. image theory, NDM), it is more accurate in this case to say that empirical research has proceeded despite nonsupportive theory. However, the lack of a unifying conceptual framework has contributed to the haphazard nature of this work as well as to insignificant results or weak findings (e.g. Alker and Hermann, 1971; Fagley and Miller, 1990; LeBoeuf and Shafir, 2003) regarding the impact of person characteristics on decision-making outcomes. Shown in Table 8.1, empirical results have been mixed, and even contradictory across studies in some cases (e.g. anxiety: Nichols-Hoppe and Beach, 1990; Mayseless and Kruglanski, 1987; Schaninger and Sciglimpaglia, 1981; decision styles: Ferrari and Dovidio, 2000, 2001; Frost and Shows, 1993).

Furthermore, although risk propensity has received the most attention of the personality traits examined in the decision-making literature, the primary result is that those higher in risk taking are more likely to make risky decisions (e.g. Wong and Carducci, 1991; Weber, Blais and Betz, 2002). Rather than a compelling research finding, this appears to be little more than construct validity evidence in that 'it seems tautological to select people who are risk averse and risk seeking to predict risk preference' (Larrick, 1993, p. 444).

A methodological explanation for the lack of systematic attention given to individual differences involves the dominance of the experimental paradigm in decision-making research, which has been largely unsuitable to assess the effects of individual differences. As shown in Table 8.1, the studies listed utilize students in a laboratory context, with few exceptions (e.g. Arroba, 1978; Henderson and Nutt, 1980; Schaninger and Sciglimpaglia, 1981; Verplanken, 1993). The focus, therefore, has been on decision-making tasks that can be affected by short-term manipulations and situational variables. However, strong manipulations tend to attenuate or negate individual difference effects (Mischel, 1968). According to Buss (1989), the novel context, brief time frame, and detailed instructions of most experiments emphasize situational manipulations at the expense of personality traits. In contrast, the role of traits is maximized in familiar situations of a lengthy duration where participants are provided with few instructions and minimal guidelines for behavior (Buss, 1989).

A typical decision-making experiment presents short, novel tasks which simply require undergraduates to select between a provided set of alternatives (e.g. Stevenson, Busemeyer and Naylor, 1990), thereby limiting choice and restricting behavior. Given this highly structured and constrained setting, personality traits have little opportunity to manifest and are easily overwhelmed by the strength of manipulations. It is likely that the popularity of the experimental paradigm in decision-making research has both demotivated the incorporation of individual differences theoretically as well as washed out effects empirically. However, we would argue that there are ways to make decision-making research more conducive to the study of individual differences. Therefore, the remainder of the chapter is devoted to merging frameworks from personality as well as decision making in order to provide direction for future studies.

GUIDELINES FOR THE STUDY OF PERSONALITY TRAITS AND DECISION MAKING

For organizationally based fields, the 1990s were characterized by the rebirth of personality research (Smith and Schneider, 2004). Clearly, the Five-Factor Model as an organizing and descriptive taxonomy has, in large part, been responsible for the significant strides of personality research in recent years. In addition, important gains have been made in resolving key areas of contention in this literature, including the person–situation debate (Is behavior is the result of disposition or the environment?) and the bandwidth-fidelity debate (Are broad or narrow traits most appropriate for personality measurement?). Using current personality research frameworks regarding broad versus narrow traits and persons versus environments, we now identify the general mechanisms by which personality traits can be expected to be linked to decision making.

Broad versus Narrow Traits

The current consensus regarding the bandwidth-fidelity debate is that theory should drive the appropriate level of specificity needed for personality measurement (Smith and Schneider, 2004). Specifically, there should be a close conceptual match between the generality or specificity of independent and dependent variables. For example, broad traits such as conscientiousness and emotional stability have been found to predict overall job performance (Barrick, Mount and Judge, 2001) and have strong predictive capacity over time (Judge *et al.*, 1999; Stewart, 1999). However, there is a growing body of literature promoting more narrow aspects of personality than the Five-Factor Model (FFM) (e.g. Hough, 1992; Mount and Barrick, 1995; Stewart, 1999), especially when the criteria constitute specific behaviors (Buss, 1989). While the popularity and success of the FFM in furthering personality research cannot be disputed, this taxonomy has been criticized for limiting research on other personality constructs and masking details associated with narrower traits (e.g. Hough and Ones, 2001; Smith and Schneider, 2004). In a recent review of personality research, Smith and Schneider (2004) concluded that it was 'time to give the FFM a more circumscribed role in future applied personality research' and 'open our eyes a bit to the broader landscape of personality characteristics' (p. 394).

Consistent with this rationale, we recommend that future research go beyond the Big Five and consider more narrowly defined traits that are likely to be aligned with decision making to a greater extent than broad traits. In contrast to overall job performance, decision making represents a specific behavioral dimension. Given the more restricted nature of decision-making processes and outcomes, the appropriate level of measurement for personality traits would most likely be narrow as opposed to broad. Because each of the Big Five comprises more specific facets that may correlate differently across criteria (Hough, 1992), the composite may be too heterogeneous to serve as a good predictor of decision making. In fact, Moon (2001) demonstrated this empirically with duty and achievement striving as specific facets of conscientiousness in relation to escalation of commitment. Interestingly, conscientiousness as a composite factor was unrelated to the propensity to escalate, whereas duty was negatively related and achievement striving was positively related to escalation of commitment.

Similarly, Shiloh, Koren and Zaykay (2001) reported that the total need for closure scale was not found to affect subjective decision complexity, but significant results were revealed when the overall scale was broken into specific facets (e.g. close-mindedness, preference for order, discomfort with ambiguity). Therefore, focusing on broad personality domains may obscure meaningful relationships in the data. In addition, some personality traits of relevance to decision making such as risk preference (e.g. Ashton *et al.*, 1998; Paunonen and Jackson, 1996) and ASO (Diefendorff *et al.*, 2000) have not been found to be strongly related to the Big Five. Although there has been some research to suggest that self-esteem, anxiety, and impulsivity are lower order factors of neuroticism and core job evaluations (e.g. Costa and McCrae, 1992; Judge *et al.*, 2002b; Watson, Suls and Haig, 2002), we would recommend that decision-making researchers decompose superordinate constructs into more basic units to precisely determine the exact source of the associations that emerge:

Guideline 1: Narrow traits are more likely to predict specific decision making processes as compared to broad traits.

Although we do advocate the use of narrow traits, we would also support the incorporation of individual differences that have 'conceptual distance' to decision-making processes. Clearly, variables such as risk preference and decision styles have little relevance outside of the decision-making context. However, traits such as NfC, optimism, and self-esteem, while narrow in scope, also have broader appeal than just decision making. Unfortunately, existing work on risk preference and decision styles has not gone much beyond, 'risk-seeking individuals make riskier decisions' and 'avoidant decision makers avoid making decisions', respectively. However, we would advocate that future work on traits closely related to decision making extends beyond construct validity checks to more fully incorporate the range of decision-making behaviors. In addition, we would encourage the examination of narrow traits with greater conceptual distance to decision-making processes.

Decision Making as a Process versus an Isolated Choice

Buss (1989) distinguishes between a passive model in which the environment shapes the individual and an active model in which the person and environment interact, thereby allowing the person to alter the environment. Whereas the impact of manipulations is facilitated in a passive environment, the impact of traits is facilitated in an active environment. Much of the empirical work in behavioral decision research has been dominated by tasks in which people evaluate combinations of financial events (e.g. Einhorn and Hogarth, 1986; Kahneman and Tversky, 1984). However, by reducing task demands to a simple choice between two-outcome gambles with explicitly stated probabilities and payoffs, much of the richness of real-life decision making in which issues have to be defined, diagnosed, developed, screened, and evaluated (e.g. Mintzberg, Raisinghani and Theoret, 1976) is stripped away. Whereas alternatives are given (although their consequences are not) for decision making under conditions of uncertainty, almost nothing is given or easily determined for decision making under ambiguity (Mintzberg, Raisinghani and Theoret, 1976). Specifically, the decision-making process is often 'characterized by novelty, complexity, and open-endedness, by the fact that the organization usually begins with little understanding of the decision situation it faces or the route to its solution, and only a vague idea of what the solution might be and how it will be evaluated when it is developed' (Mintzberg, Raisinghani and Theoret, 1976, p. 250). It would be in this type of context that 'the impact of traits is advanced by allowing sufficient latitude for the subject to choose the environment, modify it, or even modify its impact' (Buss, 1989, p. 1382). In contrast, by restricting the repertoire of behaviors to choice in laboratory gambling situations, a passive model is adopted, which minimizes the role of individual differences.

According to Mintzberg, Raisinghani and Theoret (1976), the fact that most of the decision-making literature has focused on choice is 'rather curious since this routine seems to be far less significant in many of the decision processes we studied than diagnosis or design' (p. 257). Similarly, we would argue that individual differences are reflected not only in the decision act itself, but even more so in the broader predecisional processes and postdecisional outcomes involved in making decisions. Decision processes include an array of strategies and behaviors distributed across several stages of decision making (e.g. issue interpretation, generation of alternatives) that culminate in choice (e.g. Fuller and Aldag, 2001). Decision outcomes encompass postdecision performance output as well as evaluation of the output (e.g. Naylor, Pritchard and Illgen, 1980). Allowing participants to define the issues presented, engage in information search behaviors, and/or develop a strategy for implementing decisions reached would allow more latitude for individual differences to assert themselves. Whereas personality measures generally account for little variance in single situations, their predictive power increases with aggregate observations over time and situations (Epstein, 1979). Therefore, in addition to creating more of an active environment for participants, broadening the scope of decision making to include action sequences before and after the decision choice would improve the likelihood of personality traits having a meaningful impact.

As discussed previously, Atkinson's (1983) model expands beyond risky choices in lotteries to examine how individuals decide whether to engage in an activity. Although Larrick (1993) viewed this as a main drawback of this theory, broadening the scope of decision making creates a more conduce environment for individual differences to manifest themselves. In addition, NDM encompasses the entire decision episode, including the stages before and after choice (e.g. Lipshitz, 1993; Orasunu and Connolly, 1993). Furthermore, with its emphasis on studying how expert decision makers solve ill-structured problems in realistic environments, this movement adopts a more active model, permits maximal choice by participants, and thereby overcomes some of the restrictions in classical approaches that may have hindered the expression of individual differences.

Clearly, NDM is a promising venue for examining the role of person characteristics in decision making, and we urge researchers to take advantage of this area's many strengths. We agree that 'it is time to move beyond the tidy experiments and axiomatizations built on the explicit lottery' (Einhorn and Hogarth, 1986, p. S248) in order to better reflect real-life situations as well as create an environment more conducive to the expression of individual differences. However, we also recognize the dominance and value of the experimental tradition in this literature, as much can be gained from studying the strategic decision-making process in a controlled environment where contextual variables can be manipulated (Schwenk, 1995; Taylor, 1992). Therefore, we advocate that laboratory studies be structured less passively by allowing participants more freedom to express their individual preferences through examining a greater spectrum of the decision-making process:

> Guideline 2: Personality traits are more likely to exert significant effects when decision making measurement is expanded to include pre-decisional processes and/or post-decisional outcomes as opposed to choice alone.

Person versus Situation

Whereas trait theory identifies consistencies in behavior and social cognitive theory explains inconsistencies in behavior, the merging of both is viewed as a promising direction for future research in personality psychology (Smith and Schneider, 2004). According to Mischel (2004), individuals are characterized by both stable patterns of behavior as well as variability in actions across situations. Therefore, the need to consider both the person and the situation has been acknowledged, 'making dispositions situationally hedged, conditional, and interactive with the situations in which they were expressed' (Mischel, 2004, p. 5). As decision making has been found to be a highly contingent form of information processing that is affected by both task and context effects (e.g. Payne, 1982), it is likely that the impact of individual differences on decision processes will be situation qualified. Therefore, in general, interactions would be expected to be the rule and main effects the exception.

Consistent with the reasoning presented above, Stewart and Roth (2001) expressed, 'risk propensity appears to lie at the crux of a constellation of constructs that form an interconnected situation-trait rubric of entrepreneurial risk behavior' (p. 151). Indeed, many of the more compelling results from Table 8.1 appear to be from studies that examined moderated results. For example, significant interactions have been found between individual differences and various situational variables such as monetary goal (McDougal, 1995), cognitive load/effortful thought (Ferrari and Dovidio, 2001; Levin, Huneke and Jasper, 2000), and time pressure (Ordonez and Benson, 1997). In some studies, traits have been treated as the moderator (e.g. Kuvaas and Kaufmann, 2004; Ordonez and Benson, 1997; Wray and Stone, 2005), whereas others have treated the situational or task context as the moderator (e.g. Josephs *et al.*, 1992; McDougal, 1995). One notable example of a study finding a person–situation interaction was conducted by Josephs *et al.* (1992), who postulated that risky decisions are inherently self-esteem threatening since the chosen alternative may yield a less desirable outcome than the foregone alternative. By manipulating feedback, results revealed that low self-esteem participants made regret minimizing choices when they expected to know the outcome of their decisions, but individual difference effects disappeared when decision outcomes were unknown.

The content of the decision has emerged as an important situational factor in several studies. For example, Weber, Blais and Betz (2002) found that risk taking was highly domain specific, with reported intentions to take risks lowest for gambling situations and highest for social risks. In addition, emotional or intuitive decision styles were associated more with personal or consumer choice decisions, whereas logical decision styles were associated more with work-related decisions (Arroba, 1978; Sjoberg, 2003).

Situational strength and trait relevance are two concepts from the personality literature that provide more guidance in determining the ways in which individual differences interact with the larger context to affect decision-making processes. Each will be discussed in turn.

Situational Strength

A key lesson from the person–situation debate is that the strength of a situation needs to be taken into account when determining the value of including person characteristics (Stewart and Barrick, 2004). Dispositional effects have the greatest impact in weak situations and the smallest impact in strong situations (Mischel, 1968). Because people tend to respond in a similar manner when salient environmental cues provide clear prescriptions for how they should act, strong situations generally overpower individual differences in determining behavior. In contrast, personality traits have more room to play a significant role when the situation is ambiguous and weak (Mischel, 1968).

As discussed earlier, the demands and requirements of laboratory experiments tend to inhibit or completely negate trait expression in decision making. Nevertheless, weakening the situation to provide fewer normative guidelines and allow for more autonomy would allow individual differences to be more easily expressed (Stewart and Barrick, 2004). For example, McDougal (1995) found that risk-seeking individuals spent more time on information search and made riskier choices as compared to risk-averse individuals only when there was either no monetary goal or a low goal. In contrast, no significant differences in risk preference emerged under the high goal condition. Whereas the high monetary goal condition represented a situation powerful enough to negate individual differences in trait-expressive behavior, 'when there is no goal, individuals are not so constrained – the only thing that they must do is search and decide, and so they are free to follow their inclinations and search as they please' (McDougal, 1995, p. 780). Clearly, ill-structured as opposed to well-structured decision making allows more leeway for personality to assert itself.

Trait Relevance

In addition to situation strength, trait relevance has been proposed as another key concept in the person–situation debate. Tett and Burnett (2003) proposed a person–situation interactionist model of job performance which highlights the importance of trait activation or the process by which people express their traits in response to trait-relevant situational cues. Trait relevance is defined as the 'qualitative feature of situations that makes it reasonable to expect expression of one trait rather than another' (Tett and Burnett, 2003, p. 502). In assessing whether cues for trait expression are supplied by the situation, trait relevance is a more specific and fundamental concept than situational strength. According to Tett and Burnett (2003), trait-expressive behavior will be most pronounced in weak situations where traits are relevant to the context. Although their model is proposed in the context of job performance, several features can be easily adapted to enhance the study of individual differences on decision making.

Obviously, not all individual differences will predict decision-making behaviors in all situations. Yet, due to the lack of a strong theoretical framework, individual differences have often been linked to decision-making processes rather indiscriminately. For example, it is unlikely that a person's extraverted tendencies will be activated in a typical decision-making laboratory study in which the task is completed individually under conditions of high structure, specific directions, and a limited time frame. Therefore, carefully matching traits and situations by relevance is a prerequisite for getting significant results. Demonstrating the concept of relevance, Levin, Huneke and Jasper (2000) found that differences between high and low NfC participants on breadth of search were revealed mainly in the condition requiring the most effortful thought:

> Guideline 3: Personality traits are more likely to interact with task characteristics and/or situational variables to affect decision making than exert strong direct effects. Furthermore, the relationship between personality traits and decision-making processes will increase as situational strength decreases and trait relevance increases.

OPERATIONALIZING THE GUIDELINES IN THE DECISION-MAKING CONTEXT

Although the guidelines presented above are well known in the personality literature, we contend that they are not being systematically applied in the decision-making context and therefore need to be reiterated in this literature. In perusing Table 8.1, several guidelines have been violated to some extent, as many studies have predicted main effects for individual differences on choice alone in strong, trait irrelevant, experimental contexts. Having identified the general mechanisms by which personality traits can be expected to be linked to decision making, we now illustrate how the guidelines can be utilized to stimulate future empirical research.

According to Taylor and Dunnette (1974), the 'systematic mapping of the relationships between decision maker attributes and decision-processes offers many potentially fruitful approaches for research directed toward understanding how decisions are made and, hopefully, how they can be made more effectively' (p. 296). Toward this goal, we feature a few traits in Table 8.2 that we believe hold promise and have relevance for the study of individual differences in decision making. In selecting these constructs, we highlight how a range of cognition-, personality-, and motivation-based traits may exert influence across a range of decision-making processes. Specifically, Table 8.2 depicts a sampling of narrow traits (Guideline 1) arrayed against predecisional and postdecisional decision processes (Guideline 2) and highlights where the individual differences might be expected to have the greatest relevance (Guideline 3).

As stated in Guidelines 3, we suggest that future research regarding individual differences and decision making is likely to make meaningful contributions when situational and task influences are taken into account. Several situational factors have been proposed in the decision-making literature, including time pressure, decision complexity, environmental uncertainty, decision importance, and issue ambiguity (e.g. Payne, 1982). Whereas there is substantial evidence that task characteristics influence decisions (e.g. Payne, Bettman and Johnson, 1993) and initial evidence that individual differences affect various stages of decision making (see Table 8.1), what is not clear is the nature of relations among situational variables, individual differences, and decision-making processes. According to Edwards (1990), decision-making research requires a systematic classification of human characteristics, decision environments, and decision processes. Although by no means answering this call entirely, we discuss how personality traits can be matched with predecisional or postdecisional decision stages and situational characteristics. The following discussion is offered, not as a cumulative, definitive listing of research possibilities, but rather as an initial, suggestive tool to illustrate how the guidelines can be further operationalized.

Which Traits Matter for Which Decision-Making Processes under What Situational Conditions?

Several models of the decision-making process have been proposed (e.g. Aldag and Fuller, 1993; Mintzberg, Raisinghani and Theoret, 1976), but they all tend to include the same basic stages. Rather than linear, the actual decision process

Table 8.2 Sampling of promising individual difference variables and where they may be especially relevant in the decision-making process

	Predecisional			Postdecisional	
Individual difference	Issue interpretation	Information search/generation of alternatives	Choice/selection	Attitudes toward decision made (e.g. satisfaction, regret)	Decision implementation
Cognition based					
Need for cognition		X			
Decision styles		X			
Personality based					
Locus of control	X	X			
Optimism	X		X		
Motivation based					
Action-state orientation				X	X
Self-esteem			X	X	X

is often recursive and discontinuous, consisting of numerous interrupts and delays (Mintzberg, Raisinghani and Theoret, 1976). However, for the sake of organization and clarity, each stage listed in Table 8.2 will be discussed sequentially.

In the predecisional state, a person has not committed to a specific decision, but determines the nature and scope of the issue(s) as well as how many and what type of alternatives to consider. Many strategic decisions do not arrive preformulated (Mintzberg, Raisinghani and Theoret, 1976); therefore, decision makers must engage in the process of sensemaking or interpretation in order to endow issues with meaning (Daft and Weick, 1984). Because how an issue is framed can have important implications for strategies and outcomes, many scholars consider identification to be the first and most crucial stage in the decision-making process (e.g. Cowan, 1986; Thomas, Clark and Gioia, 1993). Ironically, however, it tends to be the least researched (Lyles and Mitroff, 1980), although empirical evidence linking the initial interpretive phase to decision-making outcomes has begun to emerge (e.g. Dutton, Stumpf and Wagoner, 1990; Thomas, Clark and Gioia, 1993).

In much of the decision-making literature, the term 'framing' refers to the wording of formally identical problems in which the problem is defined for the decision maker (e.g. Kahneman and Tversky, 1984). However, in order to weaken situational demands (Guideline 3), we would suggest that issues be presented ambiguously so that decision makers have the autonomy to impose their subjective interpretation. Issue interpretation generally refers to the degree to which an issue represents a threat or an opportunity (e.g. Jackson and Dutton, 1988), although an expanded conceptualization can include other categories (e.g. crisis, problem), content domains (e.g. political, social), or dimensions (e.g. urgency, feasibility) (Mohammed, 2001). Although studies have found that national culture (Schneider and De Meyer, 1991) and state-like traits such as self-efficacy (Mohammed and Billings, 2002) and affect (Mittal and Ross, 1998) influenced the extent to which issues were interpreted as threats or opportunities, future work should examine what personality traits predispose individuals to categorize issues in certain ways.

Locus of control and optimism are two characteristics that are likely to have relevance for how individuals interpret issues. The internal–external locus of control distinction describes the stable, causal belief that outcomes are due to either one's behavior (internal locus of control) or external contingencies such as luck, chance, or fate (external locus of control) (Rotter, 1966). Because opportunity is generally associated with a sense of control, whereas threat is associated with the loss of control (Jackson and Dutton, 1988), it follows that there would be a positive relationship between internal locus of control and framing an issue as more of an opportunity and external locus of control and framing an issue as more of a threat (Hodgkinson, 1992).

The personality dimension of optimism versus pessimism deals with generalized expectancies regarding future outcomes (Carver, Reynolds and Scheier,

1994). Because optimists expect positive events in the future and pessimists expect negative events from life, it would be expected that optimists and pessimists would be more likely to view issues as opportunities and threats, respectively. However, taking the context into account, issues are ambiguous in weak situations and do not clearly connote threat or opportunity, whereas in strong situations, issues possess task characteristics that conclusively indicate threat or opportunity (e.g. Jackson and Dutton, 1988; Mohammed and Billings, 2002). Whereas unambiguous issues would tend to be rated as members of a category, regardless of disposition, optimism/pessimism would have a greater influence on the rating of ambiguous issues since there is more room for interpretation.

In addition to issue interpretation, the predecisional process also includes information search and alternative generation, which are often conducted simultaneously (Mintzberg, Raisinghani and Theoret, 1976). Problem-solving research has placed more emphasis on generating alternatives, whereas decision-making research has traditionally placed more emphasis on selection from a provided set of alternatives (Stevenson, Busemeyer and Naylor, 1990). However, because it consumes most decision-making resources, development of alternatives constitutes the heart of the decision-making process (Mintzberg, Raisinghani and Theoret, 1976). Requests for more information (e.g. Verplanken, Hazenberg and Palenewen, 1992), the number and quality of alternatives generated (e.g. Shiloh, Koren and Zaykay, 2001), and reasons provided for decisions (e.g. Granziano, Panter and Tanaka, 1990) are operationalizations of this decision-making process. Therefore, we expect that cognition-based individual differences such as NfC, tolerance for ambiguity, and decision styles would have relevance at this stage. In addition, with regard to locus of control, internals may be more likely to engage in information search and generation of alternatives than externals because they expect that outcomes depend on their efforts.

The majority of NfC studies in decision making have focused on framing, but have yielded mixed results (e.g. LeBoeuf and Shafir, 2003; Kobbeltvedt, Brun and Laberg, 2005; Simon, Fagley and Halleran, 2004), perhaps because this stage of decision making may be less relevant for this individual difference. It is anticipated that NfC will exert strong effects on alternative generation. Because of their enjoyment of effortful cognitive endeavors, we expect that those higher in the NfC would search for more information and generate more alternatives.

Ironically, decision styles have been investigated more in vocational behavior and career development (e.g. Arroba, 1978; Harren, 1979; Phillips, Pazienza and Ferrin, 1984) than in decision making. Therefore, there are considerable opportunities for conceptual and methodological advancement in future decision-making research. Nevertheless, the current state of affairs regarding decision styles presents a number of challenges because of the lack of an established conceptual framework with respect to the number and type of decision styles.

In general, we would expect differences in decision styles to have particular relevance for the amount of information searched for as well as the number of alternatives identified when reaching decisions. For example, as compared with individuals with spontaneous, intuitive, or avoidant styles, those with a rational style would not only be expected to engage in more thorough alternative generation, but also take longer to search for information. Although seemingly commonsensical, these kinds of predictions testing the construct validity of decision styles have yet to be empirically demonstrated in the literature. Given contradictory empirical results regarding whether decisional procrastinators engage in more or less information search as well as are more or less likely to take longer to make decisions (e.g. Ferrari and Dovidio, 2000, 2001; Frost and Shows, 1993), it would be interesting to investigate whether individuals prone to indecision search for more information as a way to avoid making a choice or whether they tend to short cut all stages of the decision-making process.

The expression as well as the effectiveness of a decision style is likely to be dependent on situational characteristics. For example, even if an individual possessed more of a rational style, extreme time pressure would tend to inhibit trait expression and make the utilization of this decision style dysfunctional. Therefore, high time pressure would constitute a strong situation, minimizing the differences between decision styles, whereas low time pressure would allow more room for decision styles to manifest.

The act of choice occurs when the decision maker selects a course of action. Choice is considered the last step in the decision-making process and involves a multistage, iterative process including screening and evaluation (Mintzberg, Raisinghani and Theoret, 1976). Optimists do not simply agree with general statements about the future being bright, but translate their hopes into specific expectations (Carver, Reynolds and Scheier, 1994). As such, optimism would be predicted to positively influence risky choice. In utilizing the traditional gambling task in which participants had to select among outcomes with different probabilities, Josephs et al. (1992) found that optimism did not predict risk taking. However, relaxing the task constraints by requiring the decision maker to generate their own subjective probability may make the effects of optimism and pessimism more salient. In addition, self-esteem is also relevant to choice in that those higher in self-esteem would be more likely to take risks (e.g. Josephs et al., 1992).

Although the exact point at which judgments end and actions begin is not always clear-cut, the postdecisional stage can be said to start when consequences contingent on actions follow from the decision (Stevenson, Busemeyer and Naylor, 1990). Specifically, the postdecisional state involves an affective evaluation of the decision(s) as well as implementation. The two broad categories that have been used to assess group decision-making effectiveness are decision outcomes and affective outcomes. Decision outcomes include decision accuracy or quality as well as whether the decision stands or is subsequently overturned and acceptance of the decision by those affected by it (e.g.

Fuller and Aldag, 2001). Affective outcomes include satisfaction with the final decision(s) and the fairness of the processes used to arrive at consensus. A comprehensive assessment of decision quality may only be garnered in the long term and outcomes such as decision acceptance often involve others, making the relationship to a single decision maker's characteristics more tenuous. Therefore, because decision outcomes are viewed as more distal, whereas affective outcomes are viewed as more proximal, personality traits are predicted to exert more influence on affective outcomes. On the positive side, attitudes toward decisions include the degree of satisfaction with and confidence in the decision(s) made. On the negative side, regret and disappointment (e.g. Zeelenberg *et al.*, 1998) are examples of affective outcomes.

Implementation causes the choice to be carried out and transformed into action. Although relatively little research has been done on decision implementation (Taylor, 1992) and some decision-making models do not include this stage (e.g. Mintzberg, Raisinghani and Theoret, 1976), Pfeffer (1981) noted that, 'implementation of and commitment to the decision may be as important, if not more so, than the decision itself' (p. 156). Clearly, some individuals may not be authorized to commit a larger collective (e.g. family, department, team) to a course of action or may need to engage others in the implementation process because of the broader considerations involved. However, personality traits would be expected to exert stronger influences when individuals have primary responsibility for implementation. In addition, as there can be different lengths of time between when a decision is made and when it is put into action, individual differences would be more likely to influence more proximal than distal implementation. Although actual implementation may be optimally investigated under a naturalistic decision-making research paradigm, having participants generate plans for implementation or report perceptions regarding the feasibility and anticipated time frame of implementation could be assessed in laboratory settings (e.g. Mohammed and Ringseis, 2001).

Self-esteem and ASO are expected to be relevant to postdecisional processes. Low self-esteem individuals are likely to experience more decision regret and less satisfaction as well as expect greater difficulty with implementation. ASO comprises three dimensions: hesitation versus initiative, volatility versus persistence, and preoccupation versus disengagement (Kuhl, 1994b). Hesitation taps the extent to which there is difficulty initiating intended goals, with action-oriented individuals easily beginning work on tasks and state-oriented individuals procrastinating and failing to act upon opportunities. The volatility–persistence dimension refers to the ability to maintain focus until task completion. The preoccupation/disengagement dimension reflects the degree to which individuals process information when intrusive thoughts occur.

Because it matters more for goal pursuit rather than goal choice (Kuhl, 1994a), it is expected that ASO will be especially relevant for postdecisional processes. Hesitation emphasizes the behavioral capability to mobilize action and volatility reflects the ability to maintain focus until task completion;

therefore, these dimensions are expected to impact decision implementation. Distinct from the other two dimensions in that it emphasizes whether distracting thoughts interfere with initiating action, preoccupation is expected to impact attitudes toward the decision made. Specifically, preoccupation-prone individuals may have a greater tendency to experience regret. In addition, state-oriented individuals may have more difficulty moving from the predecisional, reflective state to the postdecisional, task execution state.

Several situational factors may influence the magnitude of the effect of ASO on postdecisional processes. For example, ASO is expected to have maximum impact when there is a need for individuals to overtly regulate their behavior and when tasks are not heavily constrained or externally controlled (Diefendorff, Richard and Gosserand, 2006). Whereas action- and state-oriented individuals may behave similarly for simple tasks, differences may be seen most clearly for challenging tasks where there is a potential for failure with realistic consequences.

In our view, specific individual differences vary in their importance over time as people progress through the various stages of decision making. In general, we advocate that the cognition-based and personality-based traits depicted in Table 8.2 will be especially relevant in the predecisional stages, whereas the motivation-based traits will be especially relevant in the postdecisional stages of decision making. Indeed, characteristics that are well suited for the contemplative stages of decision making (e.g. NfC, state orientation) may be rather ill suited for decision execution. That is, too much deliberation may impede or delay implementation. Therefore, what constitutes successful decision making across its multiple processes may necessitate a mixture of various individual differences.

CONCLUSION

In response to the strong pleas repeatedly made by decision-making scholars to take full account of individual differences (e.g. Highhouse, 2001; Klayman, Soll and Gonzalez-Vallejo, 1999; Shiloh, Koren and Zaykay, 2001; Steinsmeier-Pelster and Schurmann, 1993; Taylor and Dunnette, 1974), this chapter has reviewed existing research as well as provided guidelines for future research on personality traits and decision making. Although decision making is conceptually understood to depend on three categories of factors (e.g. Einhorn, 1970), research has given primary emphasis to task attributes and environmental conditions, whereas decision-maker characteristics have received considerably less attention (e.g. Ford et al., 1989). Given the renewed emphasis on individual differences that many fields (e.g. motivation, leadership, organizational change) have experienced in recent years, it is worth asking why decision making has not kept up with the general shift toward dispositional research. We contend that the normative orientation of many decision-making theories as well as an experimental paradigm that minimizes the influence of personality traits has contributed to the longstanding reluctance to systematically incorporate individual differences into the study of decision making. Indeed, a recursive cycle may have developed between the failure to develop theoretical perspectives supporting individual differences and nonpersuasive empirical findings, creating a negative loop from one to the other.

Whereas decision-making theories have progressed from the exclusive focus on the choice event to the inclusion of situational variables, we would argue that the next major step should be widespread conceptual integration of decision-maker characteristics. Just as the integration of trait theory and social cognitive theory was advantageous to personality psychology, we view the merging of traditional normative models (identify consistencies in decision making) with an individual difference approach (explains deviations from the expected behavior) as a promising future direction for research. Whereas Stevenson, Busemeyer and Naylor (1990) criticized decision-making research for not making substantive contributions to the understanding of psychological processes in their comprehensive review, adopting an individual differences approach may allow for more of an in-depth understanding of cognition and choice. Indeed, rather than merely being treated as error variance, individual differences may help to account for the gap between normative and descriptive theories of decision making (e.g. Stanovich and West, 2002). In turn, being able to explain some of the inconsistencies between observed behavior and nomothetic models may assist attempts to improve decision making and avoid tragic decision errors. Furthermore, individual differences may help to resolve contradictions in previous empirical research. For example, authors have debated whether decision makers regret action more than inaction (e.g. Gilovich and Medvec, 1995; Kahneman and Tversky, 1982). However, when person characteristics were incorporated, Seta, McElroy and Seta (2001) reported that risk avoiding was associated with more regret for action, but risk taking was associated more with regret for inaction.

This chapter contributes to the decision-making literature in several ways. First, the interdisciplinary empirical work on individual differences, which has been scattered across disparate outlets, disciplines, and decades, was compiled and summarized. Second, major theoretical perspectives were reviewed in reference to their treatment of individual differences, and conceptual and methodological reasons were provided to help explain why the impact of decision maker characteristics has not been fully realized to date. Third, based on current personality research (e.g. Mischel, 2004; Tett and Burnett, 2003), the chapter also added value by providing guidelines to offer direction for how the study of traits in decision making can be more fruitful and to lay the groundwork for specifying the conditions under which personality traits will predict decision-making processes in particular situations.

Because of the many exciting possibilities for future research, we view this chapter as more of a launching point than a final destination. In addition to the decision processes discussed, it would be useful to explore what personality traits underlie decision-making phenomena such as unrealistic optimism, time discounting, anticipated regret, and the ability to cope with time pressure. In addition, although existing research has examined personality constructs in isolation, multiple traits and how they interact in the prediction of decision-making behaviors should be explored. Complicating matters further, individual differences may exert unique effects on various decision-making stages; therefore, examining how events unfold over time from predecisional to postdecisional processes would be advantageous.

As it was necessary to reduce the scope of the chapter, we limited our consideration of individual differences to relatively stable traits. However, more attention should also be given to demographic variables, cognitive ability, and statelike characteristics. Whereas we focused exclusively on individual-level decision making, there is a role for personality traits at the dyadic as well as team levels of analysis, and promising work in this regard is already being conducted (e.g. Gunnthorsdottir, Houser and McCabe, 2007; Gunnthorsdottir, McCabe and Smith, 2002).

Compared with the huge literature describing how people make decisions, research on how individual differences affect the decision-making process is in its infancy. Adapting from the quote by Dodge (1931) at the beginning of the chapter, we would like to be able to say in future years that, 'It was a fruitful advance when the decision making field rescued individual differences from the scrap heap of scientific anomalies and began to study them, treating individuals as special combinations of capacities, accomplishments, and tendencies in the prediction of decision processes and outcomes.'

REFERENCES

Aldag, R. J. & Fuller, S. R. (1993). Beyond fiasco: a reappraisal of the groupthink phenomenon and a new model of group decision processes. *Psychological Bulletin*, 113, 533–52.

Alker, H. & Hermann, M. (1971). Are Bayesian decisions artificially intelligent? The effect of task and personality on conservatism in information processing. *Journal of Personality and Social Psychology*, 19, 31–41.

Allinson, C. W. & Hayes, J. (1996). The cognitive style index: a measure of intuition-analysis for organizational research. *Journal of Management Studies*, 33, 119–35.

Andersen, J. A. (2000). Intuition in managers: are intuitive managers more effective? *Journal of Managerial Psychology*, 15 (1), 46–67.

Armstrong, S. J. & Priola, V. (2001). Individual differences in cognitive style and their effects on task and social orientations of self-managed work teams. *Small Group Research*, 32 (3), 283–312.

Arroba, T. Y. (1978). Decision-making style as a function of occupational group, decision content and perceived importance. *Journal of Occupational Psychology*, 51, 219–26.

Ashton, M., Jackson, D., Helmes, E. & Paunonen, S. (1998). Joint factor analysis of the Personality Research Form and the Jackson Personality Inventory: comparisons with the Big Five. *Journal of Research in Personality*, **32** (2), 243–50.

Atkinson, J. W. (1957). Motivational determinants of risk-taking behavior. *Psychological Review*, **64**, 359–72.

Atkinson, J. W. (1983). Old and new conceptions of how expected consequences influence actions. In N. T. Feather (Ed.), *Expectations and Actions: Expectancy-Value Models in Psychology* (pp. 17–52). Hillsdale, NJ: Erlbaum.

Baron, J. & Ritov, I. (2004). Omission bias, individual differences, and normality. *Organizational Behavior and Human Decision Processes*, **94**, 74–85.

Barrick, M. R., Mount, M. K. & Judge, T. A. (2001). The FFM personality dimensions and job performance: meta-analysis of meta-analysis. *International Journal of Selection and Assessment*, **9**, 9–30.

Barrick, M. R., Stewart, G. L., Neubert, M. J. & Mount, M. K. (1998). Relating member ability and personality to work-team processes and team effectiveness. *Journal of Applied Psychology*, **83** (3), 377–91.

Beach, L. R. & Lipshitz, R. (1993). Why classical decision theory is an inappropriate standard for evaluating and aiding most human decision making. In G. A. Klein, J. Orasanu, R. Calderwood & C. E. Zsambok (Eds), *Decision Making in Action: Models and Methods* (pp. 21–35). Norwood, NJ: Ablex Publishing.

Beach, L. R. & Mitchell, T. R. (1987). Image theory: principles, goals, and plans in decision making. *Acta Psychologica*, **66** (3), 201–20.

Beach, L. R. & Mitchell, T. R. (1998). The basics of image theory. In L. R. Beach (Ed.), *Image Theory: Theoretical and Empirical Foundations* (pp. 3–18). Mahwah, NJ: Lawrence Erlbaum.

Bromiley, P. & Curley, S. (1992). Individual differences in risk taking. In J. F. Yates (Ed.), *Risk Taking Behavior* (pp. 87–132). New York: John Wiley & Sons, Inc.

Brunswick, E. (1952). The conceptual framework of psychology. In O. Neurath (Ed.), *International Encyclopedia of Unified Science*, Vol. 1. Chicago: University of Chicago Press.

Brunswick, E. (1956). *Perception and the Representativeness Design of Psychological Experiments*, 2nd edn, Berkeley: University of California Press.

Brynes, J. P., Miller, D. C. & Schafer, W. D. (1999). Gender differences in risk taking: a meta-analysis. *Psychological Bulletin*, **125**, 367–83.

Budner, J. (1962). Tolerance of ambiguity as a personality variable. *Journal of Personality*, **30**, 29–40.

Buehler, R. & Griffin, D. (2003). Planning, personality, and prediction: the role of future focus in optimistic time predictions. *Organizational Behavior and Human Decision Processes*, **92**, 80–90.

Buss, A. H. (1989). Personality as traits. *American Psychologist*, **44** (11), 1378–88.

Butler, G. & Mathews, A. (1983). Cognitive processes in anxiety. *Advances in Behavior Research and Therapy*, **5**, 51–62.

Butler, G. & Mathews, A. (1987). Anticipatory anxiety and risk perception. *Cognitive Therapy and Research*, **11**, 551–65.

Cacioppo, J. T. & Petty, R. E. (1982). The need for cognition. *Journal of Personality and Social Psychology*, **42**, 116–31.

Campbell, J. D. & Tesser, A. (1983). Motivational interpretations of hindsight bias: an individual difference analysis. *Journal of Personality*, **51** (4), 605–20.

Capon, N. & Davis, R. (1984). Basic cognitive ability measures as predictors of consumer information processing strategies. *Journal of Consumer Research*, **11**, 551–63.

Carducci, B. J. & Wong, A. (1998). Type A and risk-taking in everyday money matters. *Journal of Business and Psychology*, **12**, 355–9.

Carver, C. S., Reynolds, S. L. & Scheier, M. F. (1994). The possible selves of optimists and pessimists. *Journal of Research in Personality*, **28**, 133–41.

Chatterjee, S., Heath, T. B., Milberg, S. J. & France, K. R. (2000). The differential processing of price in gains and losses: the effects of frame and need for cognition. *Journal of Behavioral Decision Making*, **13**, 61–75.

Colquitt, J. A., LePine, J. A. & Noe, R. A. (2000). Toward an integrative theory of training motivation: a meta-analytic path analysis of 20 years of research. *Journal of Applied Psychology*, **85** (5), 678–707.

Cooper, H. (2003). Editorial. *Psychological Bulletin*, **129** (1), 3–9.

Costa, P.T. Jr & McCrae, R. R. (1992). *NEO-PI: Revised NEO Personality Inventory (NEO-PI-R)*, Odessa, FL: Psychological Assessment Resources.

Cowan, D. A. (1986). Developing a process model of problem recognition. *Academy of Management Review*, **11**, 763–76.

Curley, S. P., Yates, J. F. & Abrams, R. A. (1986). Psychological sources of ambiguity avoidance. *Organizational Behavior and Human Decision Processes*, **38**, 230–56.

Daft, R. L. & Weick, K. E. (1984). Toward a model of organizations as interpretive systems. *Academy of Management Review*, **9**, 284–95.

Dahlback, O. (1990). Personality and risk-taking. *Personality and Individual Differences*, **11**, 1235–42.

Diefendorff, J. M., Hall, R. J., Lord, R. G. & Strean, M. L. (2000). Action-state orientation: construct validity of a revised measure and its relationship to work-related variables. *Journal of Applied Psychology*, **85** (2), 250–63.

Diefendorff, J. M., Richard, E. M. & Gosserand, R. H. (2006). Examination of situation and attitudinal moderators of the hesitation and performance relation. *Personnel Psychology*, **59** (2), 365–93.

Dodge, R. (1931). *Conditions and Consequences of Human Variability*, New Haven, CT: Yale University Press.

Driver, M. J., Brousseau, K. E. & Hunsaker, P. L. (1990). *The Dynamic Decision Maker*, New York: Harper and Row.

Dutton, J. E., Stumpf, S. & Wagoner, D. (1990). Diagnosing strategic issues and the investment of resources. In R. Lamb & P. Shrivastava (Eds), *Advances in Strategic Management*, Vol. 6 (pp. 143–67). Greenwich, CT: JAI Press.

Edwards, W. (1990). Unfinished tasks: a research agenda for behavioral decision theory. In R. M. Hogarth (Ed.), *Insights in Decision Making: A Tribute to Hillel J. Einhorn* (pp. 44–65). Chicago: University of Chicago Press.

Einhorn, H. J. (1970). The use of nonlinear noncompensatory models in decision making. *Psychological Bulletin*, **73**, 221–30.

Einhorn, H. J. & Hogarth, R. M. (1985). Ambiguity and uncertainty in probabilistic inference. *Psychological Review*, **92**, 433–61.

Einhorn, H. J. & Hogarth, R. M. (1986). Decision making under ambiguity. *Journal of Business*, **59**, S225–50.

Elsbach, K. D. & Barr, P. S. (1999). The effects of mood on individuals' use of structured decision protocols. *Organization Science*, **10**, 181–98.

Epstein, S. (1979). The stability of behavior: on predicting most of the people most of the time. *Journal of Personality and Social Psychology*, **37**, 1097–1126.

Fagley, N. S. & Miller, P. M. (1990). The effect of framing on choice: interactions with risk-taking propensity, cognitive style, and sex. *Personality and Social Psychology Bulletin*, **16**, 496–510.

Ferrari, J. R. & Dovidio, J. F. (2001). Behavioral information search by indecisives. *Personality and Individual Differences*, **30**, 1113–23.

Ferrari, J. R. & Dovidio, J. F. (2000). Information search processes by indecisives: individual differences in decisional procrastination. *Journal of Research in Personality*, **34**, 127–37.

Finucane, M. L., Slovic, P., Hibbard, J. H. *et al.* (2002). Aging and decision making competence: an analysis of comprehension and consistency in older versus younger adults considering health-plan options. *Journal of Behavioral Decision Making*, 15, 141–64.

Ford, J. K., Schmitt, N., Schechtman, S. L. *et al.* (1989). Process tracing methods: contributions, problems, and neglected research questions. *Organizational Behavior and Human Decision Processes*, 43, 75–117.

Frost, R. O. & Shows, D. L. (1993). The nature and measurement of compulsive indecisiveness. *Behavioral Research Therapy*, 31, 683–92.

Fuller, S. R. & Aldag, R. J. (2001). The GGPS model: broadening the perspective on group problem solving. In M. E. Turner (Ed.), *Groups at Work: Theory and Research* (pp. 3–24). Mahwah, NJ: Lawrence Erlbaum Associates.

Gilovich, T. & Medvec, V. H. (1995). The experience of regret: what, when, and why. *Psychological Review*, 102, 379–95.

Goldstein, W. M. & Hogarth, R. M. (1997). Judgment and decision research: some historical context. In R. M. Hogarth & W. M. Goldstein (Eds), *Research on Judgment and Decision Making: Currents, Connections, and Controversies* (pp. 3–65). New York: Cambridge University Press.

Granziano, S. J., Panter A. T. & Tanaka, J. S. (1990). Individual differences in information processing strategies and their role in juror decision making and selection. *Forensic Reports*, 3, 279–301.

Gunnthorsdottir, A., McCabe, K. & Smith, V. (2002). Using the Machiavellianism instrument to predict trustworthiness in a bargaining game. *Journal of Economic Psychology*, 23, 49–66.

Gunnthorsdottir, A., Houser, D. & McCabe, K. (2007). Disposition, history, and contributions in public goods experiments. *Journal of Economic Behavior and Organization*, 62 (2), 304–315.

Hammond, K. R. (1993). Naturalistic decision making from a Brunswikian viewpoint: its past, present, future. In G. A. Klein, J. Orasanu, R. Calderwood & C. E. Zsambok (Eds), *Decision Making in Action: Models and Methods*. Norwood, NJ: Ablex.

Hammond, K. R. & Brehmer, B. (1973). Quasi-rationality and distrust: implications for international conflict. In L. Rappoport & D. A. Summers (Eds), *Human Judgment and Social Interaction* (pp. 338–91). New York: Holt, Rinehart, and Winston.

Hammond, K. R., Hamm, R. M., Grassia, J. & Pearson, T. (1997). Direct comparison of the efficacy of intuitive and analytical cognition in expert judgment. In W. M. Goldstein & R. M. Hogarth (Eds), *Research on Judgment and Decision Making: Currents, Connections, and Controversies* (pp. 144–80). New York: Cambridge University Press.

Harren, V. A. (1979). A model of career decision making for college students. *Journal of Vocational Behavior*, 14, 119–33.

Harris, R. R. (2001). *Risk preference and sensation seeking as moderators of anticipated regret in risky decisions*. Unpublished Master's Thesis, Pennsylvania State University.

Hogan, R. (2004). Personality psychology for organizational researchers. In B. Schneider & D. B. Smith (Eds), *Personality and Organizations* (pp. 3–23). Mahwah, NJ: Lawrence Erlbaum Associates.

Henderson, J. C. & Nutt, P. C. (1980). The influence of decision style on decision making behavior. *Management Science*, 26, 371–86.

Highhouse, S. (2001). Judgment and decision-making research: relevance to industrial and organizational psychology. In N. Anderson, D. S. Ones, H. K. Sinangil & C. Viswesvaran (Eds), *Handbook of Industrial, Work, and Organizational Psychology*, Vol. 1 (pp. 314–31). Thousand Oaks: Sage.

Hinson, J. M., Jameson, T. L. & Whitney, P. (2003). Impulsive decision making and working memory. *Journal of Experimental Psychology: Learning, Memory, and Cognition*, **29**, 298–306.

Hodgkinson, G. P. (1992). Development and validation of the strategic locus of control scale. *Strategic Management Journal*, **13**, 311–17.

Hodgkinson, G. P. & Clark, I. (2007). Exploring the cognitive significance of organizational strategizing: a dual process framework and research agenda. *Human Relations*, **60** (1), 243–55.

Hodgkinson, G. P. & Sadler-Smith, E. (2003). Complex or unitary? A critique and empirical re-assessment of the Allinson-Hayes cognitive style index. *Journal of Occupational and Organizational Psychology*, **76**, 243–68.

Holland, J. L. (1997). *Making Vocational Choices: A Theory of Vocational Personalities and Work Environments*, 3rd edn, Odessa, FL: Psychological Assessment Resources.

Horvath, P. & Zuckerman, M. (1993). Sensation seeking, risk appraisal, and risky behavior. *Personality and Individual Differences*, **14** (1), 41–52.

Hough, L. M. (1992). The 'Big Five' personality variables – construct confusion: description versus prediction. *Human Performance*, **5**, 139–55.

Hough, J. R. & Ogilvie, D. (2005). An empirical test of cognitive style and strategic decision outcomes. *Journal of Management Studies*, **42** (2), 417–48.

Hough, L. M. & Ones, D. S. (2001). The structure, measurement, validity, and use of personality variables in industrial, work, and organizational psychology. In N. Anderson, D. S. Ones, H. K. Sinangil & C. Viswesvaran (Eds), *Handbook of Industrial, Work, and Organizational Psychology*, Vol. 1 (pp. 233–77). Thousand Oaks: Sage.

Howell, W. C. (1997). Progress, prospects, and problems in NDM: a global view. In C. E. Zsambok & G. Klein (Eds), *Naturalistic Decision Making* (pp. 37–48). Mahwah, NJ: Lawrence Erlbaum Associates.

Hunt, R. G., Krzystofiak, F. J., Meindl, J. R. & Yousry, A. M. (1989). Cognitive style and decision making. *Organizational Behavior and Human Decision Processes*, **44**, 436–53.

Jackson, S. E. & Dutton, J. E. (1988). Discerning threats and opportunities. *Administrative Science Quarterly*, **30**, 370–87.

Jackson, D. N., Hourany, L. & Vidmar, N. J. (1972). A four-dimensional interpretation of risk taking. *Journal of Personality*, **40**, 483–501.

Josephs, R. A., Larrick, R. P., Steele, C. M. & Nisbett, R. E. (1992). Protecting the self from the negative consequences of risky decisions. *Journal of Personality and Social Psychology*, **62** (1), 26–37.

Judge, T. A., Bono, J. E., Ilies, R. & Gerhardt, M. W. (2002a). Personality and leadership: a qualitative and quantitative review. *Journal of Applied Psychology*, **87** (4), 765–80.

Judge, T. A., Erez, A., Bono, J. E. & Thoresen, C. J. (2002b). Are measures of self-esteem, neuroticism, locus of control, and generalized self-efficacy indicators of a common core construct? *Journal of Personality and Social Psychology*, **83**, 693–710.

Judge, T. A., Higgins, C. A., Thoresen, C. J. & Barrick, M. R. (1999). The Big Five personality traits, general mental ability, and career success across the life span. *Personnel Psychology*, **52** (3), 621–52.

Kahneman, D. & Frederick, S. (2002). Representativeness revisited: attribute substitution in intuitive judgment. In T. Gilovich, D. Griffin & D. Kahneman (Eds), *Heuristics and Biases* (pp. 49–81). New York: Cambridge University Press.

Kahneman, D. & Tversky, A. (1979). Prospect theory: an analysis of decision under risk. *Econometrica*, **47**, 263–91.

Kahneman, D. & Tversky, A. (1982). The psychology of preferences. *Scientific American*, **246**, 160–73.

Kahneman, D. & Tversky, A. (1984). Choices, values, and frames. *American Psychologist*, **39**, 341–50.

Kanfer, R. & Ackerman, P. L. (2000). Individual differences in work motivation: further explorations of a trait framework. *Applied Psychology: An International Review*, **49**, 470–82.

Kanfer, R. & Heggestad, E. (1999). Individual differences in motivation: traits and self-regulatory skills. In P. L. Ackerman, P. C. Kyllonen & R. D. Roberts (Eds), *Learning and Individual Differences: Process, Trait, and Content Determinants* (pp. 293–309). Washington, DC: American Psychological Association.

Klayman, J., Soll, J. B. & Gonzalez-Vallejo, C. (1999). Overconfidence: it depends on how, what, and whom you ask. *Organizational Behavior and Human Decision Processes*, **79** (3), 216–47.

Kobbeltvedt, T., Brun, W. & Laberg, J. C. (2005). Cognitive processes in planning and judgments under sleep deprivation and time pressure. *Organizational Behavior and Human Decision Processes*, **98**, 1–14.

Kuhl, J. (1994a). A theory of action and state orientations. In J. Kuhl & J. Beckmann (Eds), *Volition and Personality: Action Versus State Orientation* (pp. 9–46). Seattle, WA: Hogrefe & Huber.

Kuhl, J. (1994b). Action versus state orientation: psychometric properties of the action control scale (ACS-90). In J. Kuhl & J. Beckmann (Eds), *Volition and Personality: Action Versus State Orientation* (pp. 47–59). Seattle, WA: Hogrefe & Huber.

Kuhl, J. and Beckmann, J. (eds) (1994). *Volition and Personality: Action Versus State Orientation*, Seattle, WA: Hogrefe & Huber.

Kuvaas, B. & Kaufmann, G. (2004). Impact of mood, framing, and need for cognition on decision makers' recall and confidence. *Journal of Behavioral Decision Making*, **17**, 59–74.

Larrick, R. P. (1993). Motivational factors in decision theories: the role of self-protection. *Psychological Bulletin*, **113** (3), 440–50.

Lauriola, M. & Levin, I. P. (2001). Relating individual differences in attitude toward ambiguity to risky choices. *Journal of Behavioral Decision Making*, **14**, 107–22.

Lauriola, M., Levin, I. P. & Hart, S. S. (2007). Common and distinct factors in decision making under ambiguity and risk: a psychometric study of individual differences. *Organizational Behavior and Human Decision Processes*, **104**, 130–49.

LeBoeuf, R. A. & Shafir, E. (2003). Deep thoughts and shallow frames: on the susceptibility to framing effects. *Journal of Behavioral Decision Making*, **16**, 77–92.

Levin, I. P. Gaeth, G. J., Schreiber, J. & Lauriola, M. (2002). A new look at framing effects: distribution of effect sized, individual differences, and independence of types of effects. *Organizational Behavior and Human Decision Processes*, **88**, 411–29.

Levin, I. P. & Hart, S. S. (2003). Risk preferences in young children: early evidence of individual differences in reaction to potential gains and losses. *Journal of Behavioral Decision Making*, **16**, 397–413.

Levin, I. P., Huneke, M. E. & Jasper, J. D. (2000). Information processing at successive stages of decision making: need for cognition and inclusion-exclusion effects. *Organizational Behavior and Human Decision Processes*, **82**, 171–93.

Lipshitz, R. (1993). Converging themes in the study of decision making in realistic settings. In G. A. Klein, J. Orasanu, R. Calderwood & C. E. Zsambok (Eds), *Decision Making in Action: Models and Methods* (pp. 103–137). Norwood, NJ: Ablex Publishing.

Loomes, G. & Sugden, R. (1982). Regret theory: an alternative theory of rational choice under uncertainty. *Economic Journal*, **92**, 805–24.

Lopes, L. L. (1984). Risk and distributional inequality. *Journal of Experimental Psychology: Human Perception and Performance*, 10, 465–85.

Lopes, L. L. (1987). Between hope and fear: the psychology of risk. In L. Berkowitz (Ed.), *Advances in Experimental Social Psychology*, Vol. 20 (pp. 255–95). San Diego, CA: Academic Press, Inc.

Lopes, L. L. (1995). Algebra and processes in the modeling of risky choice. *The Psychology of Learning and Motivation*, 32, 177–219.

Lord, R. G., de Vader, C. L. & Alliger, G. M. (1986). A meta-analysis of the relationship between personality traits and leadership perceptions: an application of validity generalization procedures. *Journal of Applied Psychology*, 7 (3), 402–10.

Lyles, M. A. & Mitroff, I. I. (1980). Organizational problem formulation: an empirical study. *Administrative Science Quarterly*, 25, 102–19.

Mayseless, O. & Kruglanski, A. W. (1987). What makes you so sure? Effects of epistemic motivations on judgmental confidence. *Organizational Behavior and Human Decision Processes*, 39, 162–83.

McClelland, D. C. (1951). *Personality*, New York: William Sloane.

McDougal, Y. B. (1995). Decision making under risk: risk preference, monetary goals and information search. *Personality and Individual Differences*, 18, 771–82.

Mintzberg, H., Raisinghani, D. & Theoret, A. (1976). The structure of unstructured decision processes. *Administrative Science Quarterly*, 21, 246–75.

Mischel, W. (1968). *Personality and Assessment*, New York: John Wiley & Sons, Inc.

Mischel, W. (2004). Toward an integrative science. *Annual Review of Psychology*, 55, 1–22.

Mittal, V. & Ross, W. T. J. (1998). The impact of positive and negative affect and issue framing on issue interpretation and risk taking. *Organizational Behavior and Human Decision Processes*, 76, 298–324.

Mohammed, S. (2001). Toward an understanding of cognitive consensus in a group decision making context. *Journal of Applied Behavioral Science*, 37 (4), 408–25.

Mohammed, S. & Billings, R. S. (2002). The effect of self-efficacy and issue characteristics on threat and opportunity categorization. *Journal of Applied Social Psychology*, 32 (6), 1253–75.

Mohammed, S., Mathieu, J. E. & Bartlett, A. L. (2002). Technical-administrative task performance, leadership task performance, and contextual performance: considering the influence of team- and task-related composition variables. *Journal of Organizational Behavior*, 23, 795–814.

Mohammed, S. & Ringseis, E. (2001). Cognitive diversity and consensus in group decision making: the role of inputs, processes, and outcomes. *Organizational Behavior and Human Decision Processes*, 85 (2), 310–35.

Moon, H. (2001). The two faces of conscientiousness: duty and achievement striving in escalation of commitment dilemmas. *Journal of Applied Psychology*, 86 (3), 535–40.

Mount, M. K. & Barrick, M. R. (1995). The Big Five personality dimensions: implications for research and practice in human resource management. *Research in personnel and Human Resources Management*, 13, 153–200.

Naylor, J. C., Pritchard, R. D. & Illgen, D. L. (1980). *A Theory of Behavior in Organizations*, New York: Academic Press.

Neumann, P. J. & Politser, P. E. (1992). Risk and optimality. In J. F. Yates (Ed.), *Risk Taking Behavior* (pp. 27–48). Chichester: John Wiley & Sons, Ltd.

Nichols-Hoppe, K. T. & Beach, L. R. (1990). The effects of test anxiety and task variables on predecisional information search. *Journal of Research in Personality*, 24, 163–72.

Niederberger, U., Engemann, A. & Radtke, M. (1987). Extent of information processing in decision making: the influence of memory load and action orientation/Umfang der Informationsverarbeitung bei Entscheidungen: der Einfluss von Gedaechtnis-belastung und Handlungsorientierung. *Zeitschrift fuer Experimentelle und Angewandte Psychologie*, **34** (1), 80–100.

Onken, J., Hastie, R. & Revelle, W. (1985). Individual differences in the use of simplification strategies in a complex decision-making task. *Journal of Experimental Psychology: Human Perception and Performance*, **11**, 14–27.

Orasunu, J. & Connolly, T. (1993). The reinvention of decision making. In G. A. Klein, J. Orasunu, R. Calderwood & C. E. Zsambok (Eds), *Decision Making in Action: Models and Methods* (pp. 3–20). Norwood, NJ: Ablex Publishing Company.

Ordonez, L. & Benson, L. (1997). Decisions under time pressure: how time constraint affects risky decision making. *Organizational Behavior and Human Decision Processes*, **71** (2), 121–40.

Oreg, S. (2003). Resistance to change: developing an individual differences measure. *Journal of Applied Psychology*, **88** (4), 680–93.

Pacini, R. & Epstein, S. (1999). The relation of rational and experiential information processing styles to personality, basic beliefs, and the ratio-bias phenomenon. *Journal of Personality and Social Psychology*, **76** (6), 972–87.

Parker, A. M., Bruine de Bruin, W. & Fischhoff, B. (2007). Maximizers and satisficers: decision making styles, competence, and outcomes. *Judgment and Decision Making*, **2** (6), 342–50.

Parker, A. M. & Fischhoff, B. (2005). Decision-making competence: external validation through an individual-differences approach. *Journal of Behavioral Decision Making*, **18**, 1–27.

Paunonen, S. & Jackson, D. (1996). The Jackson Personality Inventory and the Five-factor model of personality. *Journal of Research in Personality*, **30**, 42–59.

Payne, J. W. (1982). Contingent decision behavior. *Psychological Bulletin*, **92** (2), 382–402.

Payne, J. W., Bettman, J. R. & Johnson, E. J. (1993). *The Adaptive Decision Maker*, Cambridge: Cambridge University Press.

Pfeffer, J. (1981). *Power in Organizations*, Marshfield, MA: Pitman & Sons.

Phillips, S. D., Pazienza, N. J. & Ferrin, H. H. (1984). Decision making styles and problem-solving appraisal. *Journal of Counseling Psychology*, **31**, 497–502.

Pollay, R. W. (1970). The structure of executive decisions and decision times. *Administrative Science Quarterly*, **15**, 459–71.

Rosen, M. A., Salas, E., Lyons, R. & Fiore, S. M. (2008). Expertise and naturalistic decision making in organizations: mechanisms of effective decision making. In G. P. Hodgkinson & W. H. Starbuck (Eds), *The Oxford Handbook of Organizational Decision Making* (pp. 211–30). Oxford University Press.

Rotter, J. B. (1966). Generalized expectancies for internal versus external control of reinforcement. *Psychological Monographs: General and Applied*, **80** (1), Whole no. 609.

Rowe, A. J. & Boulgarides, J. D. (1992). The decision maker. In A. J. Rowe & J. D. Boulgarides (Eds), *Managerial Decision Making: A Guide to Successful Business Decisions* (pp. 21–43). New York: Macmillan.

Savage, L. J. (1954). *The Foundations of Statistics*, New York: John Wiley & Sons, Inc.

Schaninger, C. M. & Sciglimpaglia, D. (1981). The influence of cognitive personality traits and demographics on consumer information acquisition. *Journal of Consumer Research*, **8**, 208–16.

Schmitt, N. (1997). Naturalistic decision making in business and industrial organizations. In C. E. Zsambok & G. Klein (Eds), *Naturalistic Decision Making* (pp. 91–8). Mahwah, NJ: Lawrence Erlbaum Associates.

Schneider, S. C. & De Meyer, A. (1991). Interpreting and responding to strategic issues: the Impact of national culture. *Strategic Management Journal*, **12**, 307–20.

Schneider, S. L. & Lopes, L. L. (1986). Reflection in preferences under risk: who and when may suggest why. *Journal of Experimental psychology: Human Perception and Performance*, **12**, 535–48.

Schwartz, B., Ward, A., Monterosso, J. *et al.* (2002). Maximizing versus satisficing: happiness is a matter of choice. *Journal of Personality and Social Psychology*, **83**, 1178–97.

Schwenk, C. R. (1995). Strategic decision making. *Journal of Management*, **21** (3), 471–93.

Scott, S. G. & Bruce, R. A. (1995). Decision-making style: the development and assessment of a new measure. *Educational and Psychological Measurement*, **55** (5), 818–31.

Seta, J. J., McElroy, T. & Seta, C. E. (2001). To do or not to do: desirability and consistency mediate judgments of regret. *Journal of Personality and Social Psychology*, **80**, 861–70.

Shiloh, S., Koren, S. & Zaykay, D. (2001). Individual differences in compensatory decision-making style6 and need for closure as correlates of subjective decision complexity and difficulty. *Personality and Individual Differences*, **30**, 699–710.

Shiloh, S., Salton, E. & Sharabi, D. (2002). Individual differences in rational and intuitive thinking styles as predictors of heuristic responses and framing effects. *Personality and Individual Differences*, **32**, 415–29.

Simon, A. F., Fagley N. S. & Halleran, J. G. (2004). Decision framing: moderating effects of individual differences and cognitive processing. *Journal of Behavioral Decision Making*, **17**, 77–93.

Sitkin, S. B. & Weingart, L. R. (1995). Determinants of risky decision making behavior: a test of the mediating role of risk perceptions and risk propensity. *Academy of Management Journal*, **38**, 1573–92.

Sjoberg, L. (2003). Intuitive vs. analytical decision making: which is preferred? *Scandinavian Journal of Management*, **19**, 17–29.

Slattery, J. P. & Ganster, D. C. (2002). Determinants of risk taking in a dynamic uncertain context. *Journal of Management*, **28** (1), 89–106.

Smith, D. B. & Schneider, B. (2004). Where we've been and where we're going: some conclusions regarding personality and organizations. In B. Schneider & D. B. Smith (Eds), *Personality and Organizations* (pp. 387–404). Mahwah, NJ: Lawrence Erlbaum Associates.

Smith, S. M. & Levin, I. P. (1996). Need for cognition and choice framing effects. *Journal of Behavioral Decision Making*, **9**, 283–90.

Soane, E. & Chmiel, N. (2005). Are risk preferences consistent? The influence of decision domain and personality. *Personality and Individual Differences*, **38**, 1781–91.

Soane, E. & Nicholson, N. (2008). Individual differences and decision making. In G. P. Hodgkinson & W. H. Starbuck (Eds), *The Oxford Handbook of Organizational Decision Making* (pp. 342–60). Oxford University Press.

Stanovich, K. E. (1999). *Who Is Rational? Studies of Individual Differences in Reasoning*, Mahwah, NJ: Lawrence Erlbaum Associates.

Stanovich, K. E. & West, R. F. (1998a). Individual differences in framing and conjunction effects. *Thinking and Reasoning*, **4**, 289–317.

Stanovich, K. E. & West, R. F. (1998b). Individual differences in rational thought. *Journal of Experimental Psychology*, **127** (2), 161–88.

Stanovich, K. E. & West, R. F. (2002). Individual differences in reasoning: implications for the rationality debate? In T. Gilovich, D. Griffin & D. Kahneman (Eds), *Heuristics and Biases: The Psychology of Judgment* (pp. 421–40). Cambridge University Press.

Staw, B. M., Bell, N. E. & Clausen, J. A. (1986). The dispositional approach to job attitudes: a lifetime longitudinal test. *Administrative Science Quarterly*, **31** (1), 56–77.

Steinsmeier-Pelster, J., John, M., Stulik, A. & Schurmann, M. (1989). The choice of decision-making strategies: the effects of action vs. state orientation and the role of psychological costs/Die Wahl von Entscheidungsstrategien: der Einfluss von Handlungs- und Lageorientierung und die Bedeutung psychologischer Kosten. *Zeitschrift für Experimentelle und Angewandte Psychologie*, **36** (2), 292–310.

Steinsmeier-Pelster, J. & Schurmann, M. (1993). Information processing in decision making under time pressure: the influence of action versus state orientation. In O. Svenson & A. J. Maule (Eds), *Time Pressure and Stress in Human Judgment and Decision Making* (pp. 241–53). New York: Plenum Press.

Steinsmeier-Pelster, J., Schurmann, M., John, M. & Stulik, A. (1991). Extent of information processing in decision making: the influence of action orientation in decisions of varying degrees of urgency and importance/Umfang der Informationsverarbeitung bei Entscheidungen: der Einfluss von Handlungsorientierung bei unterschiedlich dringlichen und wichtigen Entscheidungen. *Zeitschrift fuer Experimentelle und Angewandte Psychologie*, **38** (1), 94–112.

Stevenson, M. K., Busemeyer, J. R. & Naylor, J. C. (1990). Judgment and decision-making theory. In D. Dunnette & L. M. Hough (Eds), *Handbook of Industrial and Organizational Psychology*, Vol. 1 (pp. 283–374). Palo Alto, CA: Consulting Psychologists Press, Inc.

Stewart, G. L. (1999). Trait bandwidth and stages of job performance: assessing differential effects for conscientiousness and its subtraits. *Journal of Applied Psychology*, **84**, 959–968.

Stewart, G. L. & Barrick, M. P. (2004). Four lessons learned from the person-situation debate: a review and research agenda. In B. Schneider & D. B. Smith (Eds), *Personality and Organizations* (pp. 61–85). Mahwah, New Jersey: Lawrence Erlbaum Associates.

Stewart, W. H. & Roth, P. L. (2001). Risk propensity differences between entrepreneurs and managers : a meta-analytic review. *Journal of Applied Psychology*, **86** (1), 145–53.

Stober, J. (1997). Trait anxiety and pessimistic appraisal of risk and chance. *Personality and Individual Differences*, **22**, 465–76.

Taylor, R. N. (1992). Strategic decision making. In M. D. Dunnette & L. M. Hough (Eds), *Handbook of Industrial and Organizational Psychology*, 2nd edn, Vol. 3 (pp. 961–1007). Palo Alto, CA: Consulting Psychologists, Inc.

Taylor, R. X. & Dunnette, M. D. (1974). Relative contribution of decision-maker attributes to decision processes. *Organizational Behavior and Human Performance*, **12**, 286–98.

Tett, R. P. & Burnett, D. D. (2003). A personality trait-based interactionist model of job performance. *Journal of Applied Psychology*, **88**, 500–17.

Thomas, J. B., Clark, S. M. & Gioia, D. A. (1993). Strategic sensemaking and organizational performance: linkages among scanning, interpretation, action, and outcomes. *Academy of Management Journal*, **36**, 239–70.

Thompson, L. (1990). Negotiation behavior and outcomes: empirical evidence and theoretical issues. *Psychological Bulletin*, **108** (3), 515–32.

Thunholm, P. (2004). Decision-making style: habit, style or both? *Personality and Individual Differences*, **36**, 931–44.

Verplanken, B. (1993). Need for cognition and external information search: responses to time pressure during decision making. *Journal of Research in Personality*, **27**, 238–52.

Verplanken, B. & Pieters, R. G. M. (1988). Individual differences in hindsight bias: I never thought something like Chernobyl would happen. Did I? *Journal of Behavioral Decision Making*, **1**, 131–47.

Verplanken, B., Hazenberg, P. T. & Palenewen, G. R. (1992). Need for cognition and external information search effort. *Journal of Research in Personality*, **26**, 128–36.

Wanberg, C. R. & Banas, J. T. (2000). Predictors and outcomes of openness to changes in a reorganizing workplace. *Journal of Applied Psychology*, **85** (1), 132–42.

Watson, D., Suls, J. & Haig, J. (2002). Global self-esteem in relation to structural models of personality and affectivity. *Journal of Personality and Social Psychology*, **83**, 185–97.

Weber, E. U., Blais, A. & Betz, N. E. (2002). A domain specific risk-attitude scale: measuring risk perceptions and risk behaviors. *Journal of Behavioral Decision Making*, **15**, 263–90.

Wong, A. & Carducci, B. J. (1991). Sensation seeking and financial risk taking in everyday money matters. *Journal of Business and Psychology*, **5**, 525–30.

Wray, L. D. & Stone, E. R. (2005). The role of self-esteem and anxiety in decision making for self versus others in relationships. *Journal of Behavioral Decision Making*, **18**, 124–44.

Yechiam, E., Stout, J. C., Busemeyer, J. R. *et al.* (2005). Individual differences in the response to forgone payoffs: an examination of high functioning drug abusers. *Journal of Behavioral Decision Making*, **18**, 97–110.

Zeelenberg, M., van Dijk, W. W., vander Pligt, J. *et al.* (1998). Emotional reactions to the outcomes of decisions: the role of counterfactual thought in the experience of regret and disappointment. *Organizational Behavior and Human Decision Processes*, **75** (2), 117–41.

Zsambok, C. E. (1997). Naturalistic decision making: where are we now? In C. E. Zsambok & G. Klein (Eds), *Naturalistic Decision Making* (pp. 3–16). Mahwah, NJ: Lawrence Erlbaum Associates.

Zuckerman, M. (1994). *Behavioral Expressions and Biosocial Bases of Sensation Seeking*, New York: Cambridge University Press.

Zuckerman, M. & Kuhlman, D. M. (2000). Personality and risk-taking: common biosocial factors. *Journal of Personality*, **68**, 1000–29.

INDEX

Note: Page numbers in *italics* refer to figures or tables.

action-control models 192–4, 196–9, 205, *206*
action–state orientation (ASO), decision making *269–71*, 283, 289, 295, 299–304
actions
dynamic task environments 202–3
see also action-control models
self-regulatory models 221, 222, 223, 229, 230, 242
dynamic action model 240–1
dynamic action selection process 243–4
perceptual control theory 237, *238*
Rubicon model of action phases 230–2
Simon's simple rules model 239, *240*
adaptive expertise 51
affect
intuitions 3–4, *5*
creative 10, 27
future research 27–8
moral 7, 9, 24, 27
problem-solving 6, 7, 9, 27
psychological contract breach 97, 99
see also emotion
affect priming, intuition measurement *18*, 25–6
aggression 134–5, 138
agreement, psychological contracts 82–3, 93, *109–10*
alternatives generation, decision making 297
ambiguity, tolerance for *263–5*, 280, 297
analytical/rational decision making
individual differences *261*, 262, 263, 281, 298
intuition and 4, 14–16, 30–2
anthropomorphism, psychological contracts 79, 84, *111*, 114–15
antisocial (counterproductive) workplace behaviors 134–5, 136, 137, 140, 142
anxiety, decision making *274–5*, 283–4, 289

attitudes, psychological contract breach 97, 98–9
autonomy *see* self-regulation

behavior change, transfer of training 60–4
behavior modeling training 46, 50
behavioral intentions, self-regulatory models 231
beliefs
psychological contracts 77–8, 80–2, 85, 87–8, 89–91, 93–4, *109*
security climate 141
biases, dynamic team task environments 202
Big Five Traits (Five Factor Model; FFM), decision making *267–8*, 282, 287, 288, 289
brain imaging, intuition measurement 24
breach (violation), psychological contracts 75, 78, 79, 92, 94–106, 117
bullying 132, 134

California Psychological Inventory *268–9*, 282
change *see* organizational change research
choice
decision-making process 289–91, 298
transfer of training 54–6
see also decision making, individual differences
citizenship behaviors, safety 135
climates, organizational 143–4
security 137, 138–41, 142–4
closed skills training 51, 52
closure (structure), need for *263–5*, 280, 288
cognition
dynamic team task environments 301
sensemaking 151, 157–9, 174
social *see* social cognition
see also information processing

International Review of Industrial and Organizational Psychology

CONTENTS OF PREVIOUS VOLUMES

CONTENTS OF PREVIOUS VOLUMES

Schmitt, Clause and Pulakos; **Common Practices in Structural Equation Modeling**, Kelloway; **Contextualism in Context**, Payne; **Employee Involvement**, Cotton; **Part-time Employment**, Barling and Gallagher; **The Interface between Job and Off-job Roles: Enhancement and Conflict**, O'Driscoll

VOLUME 10—1995

The Application of Cognitive Constructs and Principles to the Instructional Systems Model of Training: Implications for Needs Assessment, Design, and Transfer, Ford and Kraiger; **Determinants of Human Performance in Organizational Settings**, Smith; **Personality and Industrial/Organizational Psychology**, Schneider and Hough; **Managing Diversity: New Broom or Old Hat?**, Kandola; **Unemployment: Its Psychological Costs**, Winefield; **VDUs in the Workplace: Psychological Health Implications**, Bramwell and Cooper; **The Organizational Implications of Teleworking**, Chapman, Sheehy, Heywood, Dooley, and Collins; **The Nature and Effects of Method Variance in Organizational Research**, Spector and Brannick; **Developments in Eastern Europe and Work and Organizational Psychology**, Roe

VOLUME 9—1994

Psychosocial Factors and the Physical Environment: Inter-relations in the Workplace, Evans, Johansson, and Carrere; **Computer-based Assessment**, Bartram; **Applications of Meta-Analysis: 1987–1992**, Tett, Meyer, and Roese; **The Psychology of Strikes**, Bluen; **The Psychology of Strategic Management: Emerging Themes of Diversity and Cognition**, Sparrow; **Industrial and Organizational Psychology in Russia: The Concept of Human Functional States and Applied Stress Research**, Leonova; **The Prevention of Violence at Work: Application of a Cognitive Behavioural Theory**, Cox and Leather; **The Psychology of Mergers and Acquisitions**, Hogan and Overmyer-Day; **Recent Developments in Applied Creativity**, Kabanoff and Rossiter

VOLUME 8—1993

Innovation in Organizations, Anderson and King; **Management Development**, Baldwin and Padgett; **The Increasing Importance of Performance Appraisals to Employee Effectiveness in Organizational Settings in North America**, Latham, Skarlicki, Irvine, and Siegel; **Measurement Issues in Industrial and Organizational Psychology**, Hesketh; **Medical and Physiological Aspects of Job Interventions**, Theorell; **Goal Orientation and Action Control Theory**, Farr, Hofmann, and

Cognitive Style and Complexity, Streufert and Nogami; Coaching and Practice Effects in Personnel Selection, Sackett, Burris, and Ryan; Retirement, Talaga and Beehr; Quality Circles, Van Fleet and Griffin; Control in the Workplace, Ganster and Fusilier; Job Analysis, Spector, Brannick, and Coovert; Japanese Management, Smith and Misumi; Casual Modelling in Organizational Research, James and James

VOLUME 3—1988

The Significance of Race and Ethnicity for Understanding Organizational Behavior, Alderfer and Thomas; Training and Development in Work Organizations, Goldstein and Gessner; Leadership Theory and Research, Fiedler and House; Theory Building in Industrial and Organizational Psychology, Webster and Starbuck; The Construction of Climate in Organizational Research, Rousseau; Approaches to Managerial Selection, Robertson and Iles; Psychological Measurement, Murphy; Careers, Driver; Health Promotion at Work, Matteson and Ivancevich; Recent Developments in the Study of Personality and Organizational Behavior, Adler and Weiss

VOLUME 2—1987

Organization Theory, Bedeian; Behavioural Approaches to Organizations, Luthans and Martinko; Job and Work Design, Wall and Martin; Human Interfaces with Advanced Manufacturing Systems, Wilson and Rutherford; Human–Computer Interaction in the Office, Frese; Occupational Stress and Health, Mackay and Cooper; Industrial Accidents, Sheehy and Chapman; Interpersonal Conflicts in Organizations, Greenhalgh; Work and Family, Burke and Greenglass; Applications of Meta-analysis, Hunter and Rothstein Hirsh

VOLUME 1—1986

Work Motivation Theories, Locke and Henne; Personnel Selection Methods, Muchinsky; Personnel Selection and Equal Employment Opportunity, Schmit and Noe; Job Performance and Appraisal, Latham; Job Satisfaction and Organizational Commitment, Griffin and Bateman; Quality of Worklife and Employee Involvement, Mohrman, Ledford, Lawler, and Mohrman; Women at Work, Gutek, Larwood, and Stromberg; Being Unemployed, Fryer and Payne; Organization Analysis and Praxix, Golembiewski; Research Methods in Industrial and Organizational Psychology, Stone